ID0984677

Mathematics Teachers
in Transition

Mathematics Teachers in Transition

Edited by:

Elizabeth Fennema
Wisconsin Center for Education Research
University of Wisconsin–Madison

Barbara Scott Nelson
Education Development Center

IEA LAWRENCE ERLBAUM ASSOCIATES, PUBLISHERS
1997 Mahwah, New Jersey

Lawrence Erlbaum Associates, Inc., Publishers
10 Industrial Avenue
Mahwah, New Jersey 07430

Cover design by Kathryn Houghtaling

Library of Congress Cataloging-in-Publication Data

Mathematics Teachers in Transition / Elizabeth Fen-
nema, Barbara Scott Nelson (editors).
      p. cm.
    ISBN 0-8058-2583-5 (cloth : alk. paper). —
ISBN 0-8058-2688-2 (pbk. : alk. paper)
    1. Mathematics—Study and teaching—United
States. 2. Mathematics teachers—Training
of—United States. I. Fennema, Elizabeth. II.
Nelson, Barbara Scott.
    QA13.M368 1997
    510'.71'073—dc21   96–37791
                                  CIP

Printed in the United States of America
10 9 8 7 6 5 4 3 2 1

Contents

Preface

Recognizing that mathematics learning is directly related to the educational experiences provided by teachers, the National Center for Research in Mathematical Sciences Education (funded by the Office of Educational Research and Improvement) had as one if its major purposes integrating the study of learning and teaching. Directors of the Center recognized that, compared to the study of learning, the study of teaching was in its infancy. In response to this, and in cooperation with the Center for the Development of Teaching at the Education Development Center, a small invisible college of scholars was initiated. The first members were people who were already studying mathematics teachers and their teaching. Members of this group met over several years to discuss and formulate methodologies for studying the transition of teachers as they modified their instruction to meet current recommendations. Participants were encouraged to write short, informal papers that described their approach to studying teacher change. The papers were critiqued and discussed, and many were rewritten as the authors' ideas were clarified and expanded. Some of the papers written for those initial conferences provided the basis of this book. Those chapters have been supplemented with others that reflect the current state of knowledge about teachers and transitions in their knowledge, beliefs, and pedagogy that occur throughout their professional careers.

Three recent integrated developments provided the specific motivation for this book. The first was recommendations for fundamental change in teaching and learning mathematics. These have been seen most visibly in the various *Standards* documents issued by the National Council of Teachers of Mathematics (NCTM, 1989, 1991, 1995). They carefully delineated what mathematics should be taught and learned, the mathematical emphasis of instructional activities, how classrooms should be organized, and how learning should be assessed. Because of the wide acceptance of these recommendations, there is consensus that elemental change is required in what teachers do as they plan for and implement mathematics instruction.

Second, new paradigms of studying teaching have matured and emerged. There has been increased scholarly attention to the study of teaching throughout the educational community as well as specifically within mathematics education. Recent studies of teaching have built on pioneering work by Nathaniel Gage and his students who worked in disciplines other than mathematics, and who argued persuasively that teaching must be studied in the classroom, work done in mathematics education by scholars like Kenneth Henderson in his studies of "teachers' moves," and the School Mathematics Study Group studies, which identified both critical and noncritical variables related to teachers. More recently, many process–product studies, exemplified so well by the work of Douglas Grouws and Thomas Good, indicated clearly that specific actions of teachers do make a difference. Using this work as a foundation, a new generation of scholars is studying teaching in a way that portends a deeper understanding of teaching than we have ever had before.

The third development was the success of several innovative professional development projects. These projects focused on developing classrooms that implement the vision of the reform recommendations, and they have resulted in marked instructional change by some teachers. Although the various projects have approached their tasks quite differently, they share some critical components: a reformulation of the goals of mathematics instruction so that students learn critical kinds of mathematics with understanding, emphasis on research-based knowledge about decision making, and the study of the process of change that takes place in teachers.

The title *Mathematics Teachers in Transition* was chosen to reflect what we believe about teaching and the scholarship concerned with teaching. Transition implies a passage or evolution from one form, stage, or style to another. It is an active never-ending process. The chapters clearly illustrate that the authors do not believe that teachers can, or should, achieve some static perfection. Instead, as teachers continually reflect on their teaching, their instruction changes and grows. As knowledge about teaching and learning changes, and as society places new demands and expectations on its schools, the expectations and goals for teaching change shape and definition. Thus, an ideal teacher is one who is in constant change.

The knowledge of scholars who study teaching is also continually growing. As teachers' understanding grows, it both requires and enables researchers to continually improve their own understanding and the methodologies used to study teachers and their work.

As many chapters in the book illustrate, a particular form of instruction cannot be imposed on the people who are teaching. Only as teachers increase their understanding of and ability to implement instruction does their instruction change. Each of the chapters in this book provides evidence that both practitioners and researchers make substantial contributions to understanding what effective teachers are and what contributes to their professional development.

Throughout the book, the complexity of understanding and studying teaching is emphasized. In a sense, the book represents a transition between traditional and reformed knowledge about teaching and its study. We hope this volume will facilitate new studies of teaching as well as provide an impetus for teachers to evolve, change, and improve.

OVERVIEW

The book is divided into five basic parts. The introduction (Nelson) provides an organizing framework for the major ideas presented in the chapters that follow. Section 2 (chapters by Goldsmith & Schifter; Simon; Cooney & Shealy; and Campbell) presents and discusses diverse methodologies for scholarly work that studies teachers in transition and the issue of gender equity in classrooms. Included in Section 3 (chapters by Jones; Stein & Brown; Secada & Adajian) are arguments that teachers in transition must be studied in the context in which they work and learn. Section 4 (chapters by Lubinski & Jaberg; Franke, Fennema, & Carpenter; Stocks & Schofield; Campbell & White; Romberg; Barnett & Friedman) includes descriptions of innovative professional development programs and presents intense evaluations of their effectiveness. In reprise in the last section, Nelson summarizes and synthesizes the diverse ideas about teachers in transition.

ACKNOWLEDGMENTS

We would like to express our thanks to Drs. Janet Warfield and Laura Brinker for providing professional assistance (and severe reminders) to the editors and authors of this book. Fae Dremock was the technical editor of the book who improved its readability a great deal. Without the expert and cheerful help of these three people, the book would have been less than it is and would never have been published.

The preparation of the book was supported by the National Center for Research in Mathematical Sciences Education through a grant from the Office of Educational Research and Improvement, United States Department of Education (grant No. R117G1002); the Wisconsin Center for Education Research, University of Wisconsin–Madison; and the Center for the Development of Teaching at Education Development Center in Newton, Massachusetts, through a grant from the DeWitt Wallace–Reader's Digest Fund.

I

INTRODUCTION

1

Learning About Teacher Change in the Context of Mathematics Education Reform: Where Have We Come From?

Barbara Scott Nelson
Education Development Center, Inc.

The years since 1989 have been rich and productive ones in the field of mathematics teacher education. The National Council for Teachers of Mathematics' (NCTM) *Curriculum and Evaluation Standards for School Mathematics* (1989) and *Professional Standards for Teaching Mathematics* (1991) set mathematics education on a new track, and the *Standards* documents, together with the epistemological position that undergirds them, have had important implications for thought about the nature of mathematics teaching. Based as they are on a sociocon-structivist view of the nature of mathematical knowledge, in which knowledge is taken to be the product of the intellectual work of communities of creative individuals, the *Standards* documents imply a new role for teachers as facilitators of the development of students' mathematical thought, rather than as deliverers of concepts, facts, and skills. No longer is it adequate for teachers to turn the textbook page to the next day's topic, present students with the new ideas discussed there, and provide opportunities for practice in applying them. The view that each learner comes into the classroom with existing ideas, and uses new experiences and data to expand and extend those ideas, implies a new view of teaching. Such a perspective requires attending to the state of students' mathematical thinking and building an intellectually rich material and social environment through which students' thinking can be both supported and challenged.

Although research on children's learning of mathematics conducted in previous decades provided important foundations for the *Standards* documents, their emergence on the scene in the late 1980s and early 1990s created practical demands for new forms of teacher education, new curricula, and new forms of assessment, on a broad scale. However, in 1989 the intellectual resources available to help teachers transform their practice in the ways indicated by new views of the nature of learning were slim. Much staff development prior to that time had been oriented toward helping teachers assimilate new techniques into an existing system of ideas about pedagogy and subject matter knowledge. Now, however, that system of ideas itself was in question.

Only since the mid-1970s had the mental life of the teacher been a central topic in studies of teaching. Research on teaching shifted from a process–product paradigm, in which the object of study was teachers' behaviors, to a focus on teachers' thinking, which was influenced by then prevalent information-processing and cognitive science paradigms (Thompson, 1992). Early work focused on three basic types of cognitive process research on teaching—studies of the processes involved in teachers' planning; investigation of teaching as problem solving; and the use of the methods of judgment and decision-making research to model teachers' cognitions about students (Shulman, 1986a; Shulman & Elstein, 1975). By the mid-1980s some researchers also were beginning to focus on the *content* of teachers' ideas, tracing the impact of teachers' understanding of subject matter on their teaching (Shulman, 1986a; Zimpher & Howey, 1990). It also was argued that teachers would need to see mathematics not as a fixed system of ideas, but as a way of thinking and constructing meaning (Ernest, 1991; Shulman, 1986b).

In the late 1980s, when the NCTM Standards came on the scene, four basic positions on the process of changing teacher practice were developing, each with somewhat different theoretical roots. Schifter and her colleagues (Schifter, 1996a, 1996b; Schifter & Fosnot, 1993; Schifter & Simon, 1992) took a Piagetian position, arguing that change in teachers' ideas about the nature of learning and mathematics was necessary and required a process of disequilibration of prior ideas and the reconstruction of more powerful ones. In this view, efforts to help teachers reconsider their ideas about the nature of learning and mathematics required creating activities and events that would stimulate cognitive reorganization on the part of participating teachers. Carpenter, Peterson, and Fennema (Carpenter, Fennema, Peterson, & Carey, 1988; Fennema et al., 1996; Peterson et al., 1989), with their roots in cognitive science, suggested that teacher change was a matter of change in the content and organization of teachers' knowledge—specifically, research-based knowledge about the evolution of children's mathematical thought. Carpenter, Fennema, and Peterson suggested that teacher change occurred when teachers acquired such knowledge, organized it into a framework that related it to children's problem-solving strategies, and used the framework to guide their teaching. The third position, taken by Cobb, Wood, and Yackel, (Cobb, Wood, & Yackel, 1990; Wood, Cobb, & Yackel, 1991) started from a psychological constructivist position but soon moved to a socioconstructivist one (Cobb & Yackel, in press). They posited that as teachers and their students renegotiated the norms of the classroom to legitimate students' construction of mathematical concepts and discussion of mathematical ideas, teachers encountered and resolved conflicts between their prior beliefs about learning and what they observed happening in their classrooms. Finally, Shulman and others (Ball, 1988; McDiarmid & Wilson, 1991; Schifter, 1993; Shulman, 1986b) argued that the content of teachers' mathematical knowledge itself was critical and that the character of many teachers' mathematical knowledge needed to change, becoming less algorithmic and more conceptual, if teachers were to understand their students' mathematical thinking, develop representations of mathematical ideas for use with their students, and facilitate mathematical discourse in their classrooms.

Early work included case studies of teacher change (Carpenter, Fennema, Peterson, & Carey, 1988; Fennema, Carpenter, Franke, & Carey, 1993; Lampert, 1987; Schifter & Fosnot, 1993; Thompson, 1991; Wasley, 1990; Wood, Cobb, & Yackel, 1991). These early case studies identified a set of interconnected changes in belief that teachers underwent as they shifted their teaching to a mode based on a constructivist view of learning:

- coming to see one's students as learners who are intellectually generative and have the capacity to pose questions, develop solutions to problems, and construct theories and knowledge, rather than as vessels waiting to be filled;
- coming to see that instruction could be based on the development of students' thinking rather than on the "covering" of the text;
- redefining the locus of intellectual authority from teachers and text, to rigorous argument in the classroom facilitated by both teachers and students;
- coming to see that teachers and students can use the discipline's modes of reasoning to generate and validate mathematical knowledge.

But the kinds of experiences that would help teachers negotiate these shifts in belief, and the relationships between changes in belief and the development of new instructional practices, were as yet unclear, as was the nature of mathematics knowledge that teachers would need in order to be on solid ground in this new form of teaching. Furthermore, each theoretical position implied somewhat different intervention strategies.

Nonetheless, it was clear that the task of transforming teaching to facilitate students' development of mathematical thinking would not be a matter simply of adding a few new techniques to an existing repertoire—"changing your socks" as Cohen and Ball (1990, p. 334) put it—but rather an ongoing process of reconceiving ideas about the nature of learning itself; experiencing, often for the first time, what it might mean to understand a mathematical idea; and constructing a new image of what teaching that supported students in the development of *their* mathematical thought might be.

RESEARCH IN THE 1990S

There is now a growing body of research on the nature of teacher change as it occurs in the context of the mathematics education reform movement—a steady stream of work from research programs of substantial duration, designed on the basis of well-considered theoretical positions. The chapters in this book have grown from and contribute to that stream of work. Reported here are studies of large-scale empirical work, long-term programs of research, and theoretical contributions to our understanding of teacher change, as well as case studies of individual teachers, groups of teachers, and intervention projects. These chapters have been organized according to their general type. Theoretical perspectives on teacher change in the first section are followed in the second section by chapters on context and instructional change, and in the third section by chapters that report on professional development programs in action. This introductory chapter and the chapter that serves as the conclusion to the book take an orthogonal cut through that organization to ask where we have come in the years since 1989 and to sketch out issues that lie ahead. In this chapter I discuss the several forms of work that have emerged—the development of theories of teacher change, empirical work, case studies, and the reconceptualization of teaching—largely as they are illustrated by the chapters in this book. In the concluding chapter, I summarize what we have been learning about teacher change from this body of work and suggest some important questions to be addressed in the future.

Theory

In this volume we see the emergence of theorizing about the nature of teacher change. Some chapters in this volume (Cooney & Shealy, chap. 1; Goldsmith & Schifter, chap. 2; Jones, chap. 6; Simon, chap. 3; Stein & Brown, chap. 7) explicitly offer theoretical positions that provide coherent guides to conceptualization of the process of teacher change and allow for explicit and systematic consideration of alternative conceptualizations. Others (Barnett & Friedman, chap. 14; Franke, Fennema, & Carpenter, chap. 10; Lubinski & Jaberg, chap. 9; Romberg, chap. 13; Stocks & Schofield, chap. 11) report on teacher change projects that were systematically designed according to well-articulated theoretical positions.

Several of the theoretical positions in this volume come from different strands of psychology—cognitive development, ego psychology, and cognitive science. Goldsmith and Schifter (chap. 2) propose a theoretical position based on the perspective of cognitive development, as it has emerged in the field of developmental psychology. In their view, a developmental theory has three characteristics: (a) qualitative reorganizations of understanding (stages of thought); (b) orderly progression from one stage to another; and (c) transition mechanisms. Goldsmith and Schifter also propose a fourth component, the influence of motivational and dispositional factors. Goldsmith and Schifter argue that if the transformation of teaching from a practice based on a transmission view of learning to a practice based on a constructivist view of learning were to be a developmental process, then the changes in knowledge, belief, and practice that occur could be described in terms of these four components. This is essentially the prospectus for a long term research program, and the authors review some of the current research with an eye to identifying its contribution to a developmental theory. They also identify from their own work two strands in a belief/behavior complex that appear to undergo qualitative change in the process of teacher change: teachers' view of the nature of knowledge (epistemology) as it is enacted in classroom practice; and teachers' personal understanding of mathematics as it is enacted in classroom practice. They invite the identification of further strands and description of reorganizations in them.

Using constructs from ego psychology, Cooney and Shealy (chap. 4) argue that the shift in ideas about the nature of mathematics and learning that are embedded in the mathematics education reform movement entails shifts in view on the nature and locus of authority—from being an external source to which one can appeal, to being internally located, conditional, and dependent on argument and evidence. Cooney and Shealy call up psychological theories about the development of individuals' views of the nature of knowledge, in which the source of authority for truth changes (Belenky, Clinchy, Goldberger, & Tarule, 1986; Perry, 1970), and use these theoretical lenses to interpret the nature of beliefs about teaching, learning, and mathematics held by students in a teacher education program. They suggest that structural features of students' beliefs—their centrality, interconnectedness, and permeability—influence the likelihood that these beliefs will change over time toward the relativistic perspective on authority characteristic of the mathematics education reform movement.

The work of Franke, Fennema, and Carpenter (chap. 10) and that of Lubinski and Jaberg (chap. 9), which draws on the Cognitively Guided Instruction (CGI) project, and the work of Barnett and Friedman (chap. 14), have roots in cognitive science. The CGI work is based on the hypothesis that, when teachers have well-structured knowledge about how children's mathematical thinking develops and can use this knowledge as a lens through which to reflect on the thinking of children in their classrooms, their instructional practice will change (Fennema et al., 1996). The CGI authors discovered that most teachers, upon joining the CGI program, had a great deal of intuitive knowledge about how children solve arithmetic problems, but their knowledge had gaps and was not always coherently organized (Carpenter, Fennema, Peterson, & Carey, 1988; Fennema & Franke, 1992). The main effort of the program was to help teachers structure their knowledge of children's learning, make it coherent, and build on it (Hiebert & Carpenter, 1992).

Barnett and Friedman (chap. 14) take teaching to be an ill-structured, rather than well-structured, domain and use the analysis of learning in ill-structured domains done by Rand Spiro and his colleagues (Spiro, Vispoel, Schmitz, Samarapungauvan, & Boerger, 1987; Spiro, Coulson, Feltovich, & Anderson, 1988) as the basis for the design of teacher enhancement based on cases intended to build teachers' pedagogical content knowledge and ability for critical analysis. The cases present opportunities for teachers to examine ideas from different vantage points and in new contexts, thus offering the possibility of establishing multiple connections among experiences that on the surface may seem dissimilar.

Other chapters in this volume take a more sociological view of teacher change. Simon (chap. 3) adopts Cobb's emergent perspective, which coordinates a constructivist psychological perspective on the development of mathematical knowledge with an interactionist social perspective on the development of the social norms of mathematics classrooms (Cobb & Yackel, in press). In Simon's position, as prospective elementary teachers construct their mathematics and pedagogical knowledge in interaction with their instructor and with each other, they are simultaneously constructing the mathematical, cultural, and social norms of the classroom itself. Social norms evolve as students reorganize their knowledge and beliefs, and, conversely, the reorganization of these beliefs is both enabled and constrained by those evolving social norms. This emergent position permits Simon to analyze the students' and teacher educators' roles from both cognitive and social perspectives.

Jones (chap. 6) develops a position that blends psychological and sociological positions in a subtly different way. He argues that the several aspects of context for teaching (state, federal, and local policy; curricula developed elsewhere; classroom norms; the norms and practices of doing mathematics itself) are interactively reconstructed at the interpersonal, local level. This local, interactive construction permits policies and programs to be reinterpreted in such way as to take into account local priorities and practices. Stocks and Schofield (chap. 11), too, adopt both psychological and sociological lenses, looking at both individual change and the role of community supports in teacher change.

Stein and Brown (chap. 7) move further in the direction of sociocultural interpretation as they examine teacher learning or change situated in the complex social and organizational settings of urban middle schools, with the school mathematics program taken as the unit of change. They construe teacher learning as primarily social in nature and offer an analysis that is not psychological but sociocultural, focusing on the way that teachers develop new habits of mind and skills of interpretation through engagement with others in the day-to-day practices of mathematics teaching and program development. Entering a mature mathematics education culture, Stein and Brown argue, provides the opportunity for teachers to acquire not only new techniques and particular skills, but also the deeper values and orientations that undergird the mathematics education reform movement. To illustrate how this plays out, they use Lave and Wenger's (1991) notion of legitimate peripheral participation to analyze one case and Tharp and Gallimore's (1988) view of learning to analyze a second. Also focusing on the effects of professional community, Secada and Adajian (chap. 8) conducted an observation and interview study of how the nature of the professional community present in their school sustained a group of elementary teachers in their efforts to transform their teaching practice.

Empirical Work

In addition to the development of new theoretical perspectives on teacher change, we now have a number of empirical studies of groups of teachers who are transforming their instructional practice. From such studies we have questionnaire and interview instruments for gathering data about teachers' knowledge and beliefs, increasing numbers of classroom observations of teachers' instruction at different points in the change process, and detailed descriptions of the nature of the interventions. In this volume, Campbell and White (chap. 12) report on a multiyear study of over 100 teachers in the Montgomery County, Maryland public schools; Franke et al. (chap. 10) report on 21 teachers in a 4-year longitudinal study; Lubinski and Jaberg (chap. 9) report on all 11 teachers in a rural elementary school; Secada and Adajian (chap. 8) report on several teachers in a midwestern elementary school. Although not reported here, Barnett has worked with many hundreds of teachers in her case discussion classes, and Schifter and her colleagues worked with hundreds of teachers over the years on the project of reconstructing their mathematics. Studies of such projects give us not only the advantage of numbers, but also careful descriptions of the interventions themselves.

Romberg (chap. 13) offers yet another strategy for learning about teacher change, looking at a set of case studies of teachers who were using pilot, prepilot, or field test versions of an innovative middle school curriculum. Romberg analyzes the aspects of traditional mathematics teaching practice that were challenged in the teachers' attempts to use the new curriculum—the pattern of instruction in daily classes, the challenges to teachers' mathematics knowledge and to the way that knowledge was organized, the intellectual division of labor between teacher and students, and the link between what happened in math class and the expectations of the larger society. As did Lampert (1987) in a study of students and teachers learning to use the Geometric Supposer, and Cobb and his colleagues in their work with teachers implementing an experimental curriculum (Cobb et al, 1990), Romberg uses the classroom implementation of an innovative piece of curriculum as a place to look for issues of teacher change.

Case Studies

Case studies such as those in this volume continue to play an important role in deepening our understanding of the nature of teacher change and of the nature of teaching, itself, as reconceived. As evidenced by Barnett and Friedman in chapter 14, the case study (in this instance, the story of Friedman's own growth as a teacher and as the facilitator of case discussions) allows us an up-close view of the process of change and the kind of thinking that teachers learn to engage in as they teach. We see Friedman puzzling about what her students were learning, or not learning, about fractions by using fraction kits, in the end deciding that "the true gauge of the value of any fraction teaching method was what it led students to say and do" (p. 379). The concreteness and specificity of Friedman's descriptions of her thinking about teaching makes the instructional process in her classroom quite clear and gives us a view of the process of change from inside the head of the teacher herself. We see Friedman's puzzlement, her attempt to try something new, her disappointment when it didn't seem to have the desired result, her search for additional methods for a period of several months, and finally the realization that she needed to understand why students weren't engaging with the *ideas* of fractions as she wanted them to. The case studies reported by Romberg, although not in the first person, provide a similarly concrete and detailed view of the issues teachers grappled with as they began to teach a reform curriculum.

At a time when we still have a great deal to learn about the process in which teachers engage as they transform their teaching, the concreteness and detail provided by the case study are still quite helpful. Further, new forms of teaching are still being invented by many teachers and teacher/researchers, and what teaching based on new ideas about learning and mathematics looks like is still emerging. Images of this kind of teaching, and of the kind of reflection that teachers undertake in doing it, are necessary for the development of the practice itself.

Stein and Brown's (chap. 7) use of the case study is at a different level. They provide studies of two school sites in the QUASAR project, with the intent of illustrating what a sociocultural lens on teacher change makes visible. This, too, is a viable use of the case study—a way to probe the nature of a theoretical position. In fact, Stein and Brown's use of cases may be quite analogous to the use of the cases of individual change done in the late 1980s and early 1990s, when pictures of individual teachers undergoing change were seen through a theoretical lens which emphasized radical change in epistemology.

Stocks and Schofield (chap. 11) provide us with a case study of the evolution of a professional development program, with all the course corrections inevitable in such enterprises but all too seldom presented for inspection. In their story, teachers discovered that the program was more intense and time-consuming than they had initially expected; that the original plan, to share research papers with teachers, did not work as well as anticipated and had to be modified; that teachers' early efforts to change their practice were more superficial than project leaders had hoped; and so on. Such problems are quite typical. This view of the inside of the intervention process (present also in Campbell & White, and Lubinski & Jaberg) is invaluable, because without it we are in danger of making professional development programs into "black boxes," about which we know the inputs and outcomes but have little understanding of what happened in-between, and how what happened relates to the results.

The Reconceptualization of Teaching

In addition to using theoretical tools from psychology and sociology, conducting empirical studies of sites rich in the potential for change, and developing case studies of individual and group change, scholars in the area of teacher change—and in some cases teachers them-selves—are doing considerable work to reconceptualize the nature of teaching: They are working out the implications (for the craft of teach-ing) of new ideas about the nature of learning and mathematics and are exploring the enactment of new practice. (See Goldsmith & Schifter, chap. 2; Cooney & Shealy, chap. 4; and Simon, chap. 3 in this volume.) For example, in reporting on the process by which teachers come to have a new kind of ear for their students' mathematical thinking and, further, come to base their instructional decisions on what they hear rather than on what is in the textbook, Goldsmith and Schifter are saying not only that many teachers will need to make such shifts in this time of transition, but also that listening to students' mathematics thinking is an intrinsic part of reconceived teaching. Cooney and Shealy, in reporting on the structural characteristics of those beliefs about authority that seem changeable—as distinct from those that seem relatively immutable—are not only helping us understand which prospective teachers are likely to have an easier time developing the new form of teaching practice, but are simultaneously reconceptualizing the role of authority in the classroom.

Simon contributes to this line of work when he argues that, as a field, we need integrated models of mathematics teaching and learning, in which perspectives on teaching and learning are compatible and interdependent. Such models, he argues, provide the conceptual underpinning for research on teacher change, which would focus on teachers' movement toward the types of teaching described by the models. Simon offers his own model of mathematics teaching, which posits a relationship among the teacher's mathematics knowledge, goals for students, anticipation of student learning, planning, and interaction with students. In this conceptualization of mathematics teaching, the teacher is involved in a continual process of building and modifying models of students' mathematical understanding and making predictions of how students' learning will evolve in the context of the learning activities. Interaction with students in the classroom leads to modifications in the teachers' ideas and knowledge, as he or she makes sense of what is happening and modifies predictions about the student's learning. The nature of the teacher's knowledge of mathematics, knowledge of how students develop mathematical knowledge, ability to anticipate how students' learning might ensue, and ability to construct lessons consistent with his or her model of teaching are constituent elements. Simon argues that such a model, specifying what teachers might be changing toward, is necessary to conceptually ground research on teacher change.

Finally, Secada and Adajian, in arguing that the strength, nature, and focus of teachers' professional community play important roles in teachers' efforts to change their instructional practice, suggest not only that we pay attention to professional community as a mediating factor in teacher change, but also that teaching, reconceived, might be thought of as a less isolated, more collaborative enterprise.

Campbell's chapter on teacher change in relation to gender equity in mathematics does not fit easily into the categories identified above. However, this chapter fills a different niche. It serves to alert readers that some groups of learners have traditionally benefited less from conventional teaching than have other more dominant groups. Further, there is little in the reform movement that specifically addresses these inequities. Most of the reform movement is based on the assumption that one curriculum and one pedagogy is equally suited for all learners. Campbell's chapter points out the need to examine this assumption, because it clearly illustrates that gender inequities still exist.

In summary, we see that studies of teacher change in the context of mathematics education reform have emerged from strong lines of work in the past and use a variety of modes of investigation—theoretically driven studies; empirical work, including case studies; and conceptual work on the nature of teaching itself. The chapters in this volume provide a rich landscape of work, in which we can see the strengths of the strategies that the researchers have chosen and the range of insights about the nature of teacher change that are emerging from the work.

ACKNOWLEDGMENTS

The preparation of this introduction was supported in part by a grant from the DeWitt Wallace–Reader's Digest Fund. I wish to thank Elizabeth Fennema, Lynn Goldsmith, David Hammer, and Deborah Schifter for their comments on earlier versions.

REFERENCES

Ball, D. L. (1988). *Knowledge and reasoning in mathematical pedagogy: Examining what prospective teachers bring to teacher education.* East Lansing: Michigan State University.

Belenky, M. F., Clinchy, B. M., Goldberger, N. R., & Tarule, J. M. (1986). *Women's ways of knowing.* New York: Basic Books.

Carpenter, T. P., Fennema, E., Peterson, P., & Carey, D. (1988). Teachers' pedagogical content knowledge of students' problem-solving in elementary arithmetic. *Journal for Research in Mathematics Education (19)*, 385–401.

Cobb, P., Wood. T., & Yackel, E. (1990) Classrooms as learning environments for teachers and researchers. In R. Davis, C. Maher, & N. Noddings (Eds.), Constructivist views on the teaching and learning of mathematics. *Journal for Research in Mathematics Education, Monograph no. 4*, 125–146. Reston, VA: National Council for Teachers of Mathematics.

Cobb, P., & Yackel, E. (in press). Constructivist, emergent, and sociocultural perspectives in the context of developmental research. *Journal of Educational Psychology.*

Cohen, D., & Ball, D. L. (1990). Relations between policy and practice: A commentary. *Educational Evaluation & Policy Analysis, 12* (3), 331–338.

Ernest, P. (1991). *The philosophy of mathematics education.* London: Falmer Press.

Fennema, E., Carpenter, T.P., Franke, M., & Carey, D. (1993). Learning to use children's mathematical thinking: A case study. In Davis, R. B., and Maher, C. A. (Eds.), *Relating schools to reality.* Boston: Allyn & Bacon.

Fennema, E., Carpenter, T. P., Franke, M. L., Levi, L., Jacobs, V. R., & Empson, S. B. (1996). A longitudinal study of learning to use children's thinking in mathematics instruction. *Journal for Research in Mathematics Education.*

Fennema, E., & Franke, M. L. (1992). Teachers' knowledge and its impact. In Grouws, D. A. (Ed.) *Handbook of research on mathematics teaching and learning: A project of the National Council of Teachers of Mathematics.* New York: Macmillan.

Hiebert, J., & Carpenter, T. P. (1992). Learning and teaching with understanding. In Grouws, D. A. (Ed.) *Handbook of research on mathematics teaching and learning: A project of the National Council of Teachers of Mathematics.* New York: Macmillan.

Lampert, M. (1987). *Teachers' thinking about students' thinking about geometry: The effects of new teaching goals.* Education Technology Center, Harvard Graduate School of Education. Cambridge, MA: Harvard University.

Lave, J., & Wenger, E. (1991). *Situated learning: Legitimate peripheral participation.* Cambridge: Cambridge University Press.

McDiarmid, G. W., & Wilson, S. M. (1991). An exploration of the subject matter knowledge of alternate route teachers: Can we assume they know their subject? *Journal of Teacher Education, 42*(2), 93–103.

National Council of Teachers of Mathematics (1989). *Curriculum and evaluation standards for school mathematics.* Reston, VA: Author.

National Council of Teachers of Mathematics (1991). Professional standards for teaching mathematics. Reston, VA: Author.

Perry, W. G. (1970). *Forms of intellectual and ethical development in the college years.* New York: Holt, Rinehart & Winston.

Peterson, P., Carpenter, T., & Fennema, E. (1989). Teachers' knowledge of students' knowledge in mathematics problem solving: Correlational and case analyses. *Journal of Educational Psychology. 81*(4), 558–569.

Schifter, D. (1993) . Mathematics process as mathematics content: A course for teachers. *Journal of Mathematical Behavior. 12*, 271–283.

Schifter, D. (Ed.) (1996a). *What's happening in math class: Envisioning new practices through teacher narratives.* (Vol. 1.) New York: Teachers College Press.

Schifter, D. (Ed.) (1996b). *What's happening in math class: Reconstructing professional identities.* (Vol. 2.) New York: Teachers College Press.

Schifter, D., & Fosnot, C.T. (1993). *Reinventing mathematics education: Stories of teachers meeting the challenge of reform.* New York: Teachers College Press.

Schifter, D., & Simon, M. A. (1992). Assessing teachers' development of a constructivist view of mathematics learning. *Teaching and Teacher Education., 8*(2), 187–197.

Shulman, L. S. (1986a). Paradigms and research programs in the study of teaching: A contemporary perspective. In M. C. Whittrock (Ed.), *Handbook of research on teaching.* New York: Macmillan.

Shulman, L. S. (1986b). *Those who understand: Knowledge growth in teaching. Educational Researcher, 15*(2) 4–14.

Shulman, L. S., & Elstein, A. S. (1975). Studies of problem solving, judgment, and decision making: Implications for educational research. In. F. N. Kerlinger (Ed.), *Review of research in education* (Vol 3). Itasca, IL: F. E. Peacock.

Spiro, R. J., Coulson, R. L., Feltovich, P.J., & Anderson, D. K. (1988). Cognitive flexibility theory: Advanced knowledge acquisition in ill-structured domains. In *Tenth Annual Conference of the Cognitive Science Society* (pp. 375–383). Hillsdale, NJ: Lawrence Erlbaum Associates.

Spiro, R. J., Vispoel, W., Schmitz, J., Samarapungavan, A. M., & Boerger, A. (1987). Knowledge acquisition for application: Cognitive flexibility and transfer in complex content doamins. In B. S. Britton (Ed.), *Executive control processes* (pp. 177–199). Hillsdale, NJ: Lawrence Erlbaum Associates.

Tharp, R., & Gallimore, R. (1988). *Rousing minds to life: Teaching, learning and schooling in social context.* Cambridge: Cambridge University Press.

Thompson, A. G. (1991). *The development of teachers' conceptions of mathematics teaching.* Paper presented at the annual meeting of the International Group for the Psychology of Mathematics Education, Blacksburg, VA.

Thompson, A. G. (1992). Teachers' beliefs and conceptions: A synthesis of the research. In D. A. Grouws (Ed.), *Handbook of research on mathematics learning and teaching.* New York: Macmillan.

Wasley, P, (1990). Stirring the chalkdust: Changing practices in essential schools. *Teachers College Record*, 93, 28–58.

Wood, T., Cobb, P., & Yackel, E. (1991). Change in teaching mathematics: A case study. *American Educational Research Journal, 28* (3), 587–616.

Zimpher, N. L., & Howey, K. R. (1990). Scholarly inquiry into teacher education in the United States. In R. P. Tisher & M. F. Wideen (Eds.), *Research in teacher education: International perspectives.* New York: The Falmer Press.

II

THEORETICAL PERSPECTIVES ON STUDYING TEACHER CHANGE

2

Understanding Teachers in Transition: Characteristics of a Model for the Development of Mathematics Teaching

Lynn T. Goldsmith
Deborah Shifter
Education Development Center, Inc.

The current mathematics reform movement has recognized that new forms of mathematics teaching will be needed to support proposed curricular changes. These new forms extend beyond the acquisition of new teaching techniques and strategies to the reconstitution of fundamental notions of teaching, learning, and the nature of mathematics as a discipline, and also to the creation of different classroom opportunities for learning. The means by which teachers effect this kind of transformation are as yet little understood. This chapter suggests looking to developmental psychology for guidance in constructing models of the process of reconstructing new forms of mathematical practice. Drawing from theories of cognitive development, the chapter focuses on three characteristics of developmental processes: (a) qualitative reorganizations of understanding; (b) orderly progression of changes; and (c) mechanisms and sociocultural contexts that support transitions. The chapter also suggests adding a fourth factor to accounts of development: (d) individual motivational and dispositional factors.

Whereas past mathematics education reform movements focused almost exclusively on changing curriculum, the current movement recognizes the need for new forms of mathematics teaching as well as new curricular efforts (California State Department of Education, 1991; Mathematical Association of America [MAA], 1991; Mathematical Sciences Educational Board [MSEB], 1989, 1990; National Council of Teachers of Mathematics [NCTM], 1989, 1991). If students are to learn mathematics for understanding, they must be taught in a way that encourages them to experience mathematics as a subject area that can, in fact, be understood. Traditional mathematics instruction has tended, by relying heavily on rote memorization and routine drill and practice, to reinforce the perception that mathematics is mysterious and conceptually inaccessible. Thus, conventional teaching strategies need to be supplanted by new modes of instruction that instill in students the expectation that mathematics should be sensible and that encourage them to engage deeply with mathematical ideas and reasoning.

The mathematics education community is beginning to develop a radically revised picture of what kind of instruction should take place in the classroom. Teachers, together with their students, create a culture of mathematical inquiry aimed at developing deep and flexible understanding of the domain. Posing questions, making and proving conjectures, exploring puzzles, solving problems, debating ideas, describing and predicting patterns are all part of the new mathematics classroom.

Because this picture is a significant departure from traditional instruction, teachers cannot realize these new images by simply adjusting a bit of practice here and there or by importing a new teaching technique or curriculum package. For many teachers, these changes involve reconstituting fundamental notions of teaching, learning, and mathematics in addition to inventing different kinds of classroom opportunities for learning. The motivation for helping teachers develop new forms of practice is high, but the means by which teachers actually do so are currently not well understood. If we are to succeed in stimulating significant change on a wide scale, it is critical that we develop models for the growth of teaching practice.

The work of the past decade can be roughly categorized into three conceptual approaches to the issue of teacher development (Fennema, Carpenter, Franke, et al., 1996; Nelson, 1995). Fennema, Carpenter, Franke, and colleagues have taken a knowledge-based approach, seeking to effect changes in teachers' practice by offering them research findings about how children develop an understanding of certain mathematical concepts. They then invite teachers to reflect on how this research can inform their work with students, and provide support for their efforts to incorporate this knowledge into their classroom teaching (Carpenter, Fennema, & Franke, 1996; Fennema, Carpenter, Franke, et al., 1996; Knapp & Peterson, 1995). Other teacher educators and researchers have taken a sociocultural approach, focusing on the process by which teachers and students negotiate a "mathematical community" in which mathematical understanding is constructed by all the participants (Cobb, Wood, & Yackel, 1993; Cobb & Yackel, 1995; Cobb, Yackel, & Wood, 1992; Stein & Brown, chap. 7, this volume). The third approach can be characterized as a developmental one, investigating the experi-

ceived by practicing the demonstrated procedures. The teacher and text provide the source of this information, and hence have the mathematical authority for determining right and wrong, "good" and "bad" mathematics. Classroom instruction is organized around the transfer of information from knowledgeable teacher to uninformed student. In Lipinski's recollection, Miss Tiderman's modeling of the correct procedures for solving problems, her passing on to students the algorithmic tools for solving problems through talk and demonstration, and her focused, "crisp" explanations were all intended to give her students the mathematical knowledge that they did not yet have.

Subsequent stages in all of the current frameworks involve moving away from beliefs and behaviors based on the transmissibility of knowledge, and toward beliefs and behaviors granting students greater agency in their own learning. Teachers' relationships with their students and with mathematics itself begin to change as they become less intent on helping students acquire facts and procedures, and more involved in building on what (and how) their students understand.

The final stages of these frameworks generally describe the kind of teaching currently endorsed by the reform movement (NCTM, 1989, 1991). The images of "reformed" teaching vary. Our own image of this end point is a form of teaching based on deep understanding of the mathematical ideas underlying the curriculum, beliefs about knowledge as actively constructed by the learner, and the use of teaching "moves" that create opportunities and challenges for students to build deeper and fuller mathematical understanding. Mathematics teaching derived from this vision places great emphasis on developing firm conceptual understanding by building on students' current states of knowledge and skill. Classrooms are organized around students' active explorations of mathematical topics, with an emphasis on "knowing why" as well as "knowing how." Instruction is informed by students' current understandings and requires flexible lesson plans in order to respond to an unpredicted but important question, conjecture, or confusion raised in class. Conversation is discursive as well as informational as teachers and students, together, work to understand mathematical ideas.

These descriptions of changed and changing practice focus largely on the ways that teachers help make mathematical learning possible for their students. Teachers intrigued by the call to reform are moved to make changes in their practice because they want to make their teaching better. They hear that there are new materials, teaching strategies, and curricula available, and they want to learn to use these new tools to help their students become better mathematicians. The focus is on what teachers can *do* in the classroom. Teachers' commitment to changing practice begins, and eventually ends, with action—in their classrooms working with their students.

Embedded in this process of reshaping classroom activity, interactions, and expectations is the opportunity to examine fundamental issues about teaching, learning, and mathematics. Some of the frameworks currently being developed focus heavily on teachers' inquiries into these fundamental beliefs; others focus more on teaching behaviors. Our own position is that the two are tightly interwoven. Once the process of reformulating practice has begun, changes in belief and changes in practice are difficult to distinguish. In the following passage, for example, sixth-grade teacher Alan Gagnon (1993) writes about how he has come to question many of his fundamental beliefs about the teaching of mathematics:

> Teaching has become a struggle for me. When I started teaching over twenty years ago, it was so simple: I took the book and went section by section to explain the concept(s) and skills needed to learn the material in that section. I prepared thoroughly and always reviewed the material before attempting to introduce it. I answered questions both on the material and on my presentation. I had strategies and alternative approaches ready to provide clarification if necessary. I thought if I presented a concept clearly and the students listened, then they should "get it." "Telling it right" was enough. I provided students with homework and testing situations to practice the skills they learned. . . .I was, I felt, an effective teacher. My successes far outweighed my failures. . . .

> I have begun to question just what it meant to be an effective teacher. I have discovered that my students, who appeared to be successful, were often lacking insight and true understanding of the very concepts that I thought they had successfully learned. This realization caused me to question what it means to teach for understanding.

> I have come to realize that my old view of teaching (presenting the material in a clear and concise manner) was too narrow in scope and did not take into consideration how learning takes place. As I struggle to gain insights into how my students learn, my teaching changes.

> In considering how to teach there are many questions that must be answered. What is learning? How does learning occur? What is the role of the teacher in the learning process? What is the role of the student in the learning process? How do I assess what my students understand and how do I use what I learn to provide them with experiences that allow them to advance those understandings? What are my obligations to all my students, including the best and the so-called worst? Where does the need to follow the "curriculum" fit into the puzzle?

> These questions are a source of great concern to me. If I am going to continue to feel effective in the classroom then these issues must be given both thought and action. Reflection has become a powerful tool in my daily attempts to bring about a metamorphosis in my teaching. Yet, in reflecting on these questions other concerns surface. Should students work regularly

in groups? Do they need to be active in the exploration of math concepts? Should they be encouraged to develop problem-solving strategies? Do I need a better understanding of the mathematics I am attempting to teach? Am I required to make better connections between the ideas and concepts I deal with? Where is the time to accomplish all of this going to come from? (p. 1)

Gagnon wrote of needing to rethink what it means to learn mathematics and what kinds of mathematics his students should be learning. As he struggled to develop his new ideas about the learning process and the domain of mathematics, he also wrestled with issues of pedagogy and practice: *How* can he help significant mathematical learning occur in his classroom? Figuring out just what his classroom should be like in its daily structures and details is a complicated understanding in and of itself. It does not derive automatically from having taken a critical stance toward his practice, nor from changing some of his beliefs about teaching.

Teachers seeking to change their practice may not have useful images from their personal experiences to guide the creation of a focused and productive classroom culture that emphasizes inquiry and the exchange of ideas. Because most teachers were themselves mathematics students in traditional classrooms, their own points of reference give them little insight into how teaching—or learning—mathematics might be different from what their own experiences would dictate. It is one thing for teachers to accept the current wisdom about what students should be doing in "good" mathematics classes (e.g., exploring and experimenting with mathematical ideas, engaging in mathematical discourse, working with concrete materials, and learning to work both collaboratively and independently). It is another thing entirely to develop classroom structures and activities that actually stimulate mathematics learning in such ways. Descriptions of the development of mathematics teaching will have to capture the process by which teachers (re)invent their teaching practice to create classroom cultures that promote learning for understanding.

Part of this process does involve learning to use new activities, techniques, and materials. A number of years ago Hall and his colleagues proposed a series of stages through which teachers progress as they assimilate innovative programs into their practices, and described a corresponding set of stages with respect to the focus of their "concern" in their teaching (Hall & Loucks, 1978; Hall, Loucks, Rutherford, & Newlove, 1975). Although these stages track the process by which innovations are integrated into a teacher's current practice, they do not necessarily reflect qualitative changes in the practice itself. In fact, they are more likely to reflect teachers' success in making room for innovations within their existing modes of teaching.

Schifter and Simon (1992) took the position that learning to implement new instructional materials and strategies is but one aspect of a much deeper change in teaching. In fact, without concomitant changes in fundamental beliefs about the nature of classroom activities, it is possible for teachers to assimilate new materials or strategies into traditional instruction or poorly defined instructional goals. A teacher's practice can become a pastiche of techniques, strategies, and materials appropriated over the years. These may be based in different—and even inconsistent—theoretical positions about learning, and may have been modified or used by the teacher in ways that preserve little of the intent of those who originally designed the materials or techniques.

Making the deeper, more substantial changes in the fabric of one's teaching practice is a complex and time-consuming process. As Cohen and Ball (1990) noted, "It's not like changing your socks" (p. 163). We suggest that such changes are more like redoing your entire wardrobe to create a whole new look. Such change requires developing some guiding image of what that new look should be, careful consideration of all of the elements of your existing wardrobe, decisions about which pieces will still serve and which need to go, and expeditions to shops, boutiques, and yard sales to look for items and outfits to build a new one. Changing your socks may be part of the necessary transformation, but rarely will new socks alone carry off a new style.

Similarly, developing a new form of mathematics practice involves more than acquiring some new instructional techniques, although acquiring those techniques is an important part of the reconstitution of practice. These techniques represent just the beginning, not the end, of this process. In addition to acquiring new strategies, resources, and techniques, teachers need the time and opportunity to reflect on their beliefs about teaching and learning mathematics, to observe their students, to try to understand students' thinking, and to examine their own teaching practice. They need time to develop a sense of the important mathematical ideas for their grade level, and to learn to guide class discussion and activity toward the productive exploration of significant mathematical issues. Developing the whole of one's mathematics practice involves more than just asking students to use manipulatives, setting up cooperative work groups, or adding "problem solving" to the standard array of mathematics problems. It also involves examining currently held beliefs and practices, discarding elements that no longer seem to serve the practice well, making room for new ones, and reorganizing them into a new, coherent whole.

This process neither involves the wholesale acquisition of new strategies nor the rejection of old ones, but the thoughtful consideration and choice of pedagogical "moves" based on the particulars of the moment (Chazan & Ball, 1995). Teachers beginning to work on their practice often interpret the call to reform as an injunction to add new strategies and techniques (for example, cooperative group work, hands-on explorations, eliciting multiple solution strategies) and to abolish old ones (telling things to students, using paper-and-pencil worksheets, requiring students to learn number facts). As teachers learn to focus on the mathematical meanings that their students are constructing, they can be more reflective and discriminating about the kinds of experiences that help students deepen their understanding. They can decide when to ask and when to tell, when to focus on the concrete and when to move toward the general case, when to practice skills and when to engage in open-ended investigation. They no longer need to adopt structures or strategies simply because they are *au courant* but rather can begin to assess how, in specific instances, particular pedagogical decisions affect students' thinking. This critical stance toward the instructional tools of the trade allows teachers to make considered decisions about how to accomplish the goal of helping their students develop deep mathematical understanding. The issue is not simply one of having available a range of instructional strategies, but of knowing how and when such strategies can be most effectively employed.

These changes in teachers' classroom behaviors serve as the matrix within which changes in belief and understanding are embedded. Making the transition from traditional mathematics instruction to a constructivist-based mathematics practice requires changes not only in teachers' classroom strategies, but also in the beliefs and understandings that ground and shape the practice itself. It is the dynamic between changing practice and changing belief that results in substantial reorganizations of teaching. Without changes in instructional strategies, decisions, and techniques, teachers will be unable to "walk the walk and talk the talk." In turn, these new ideas, beliefs, and understandings develop further as teachers try to enact them in their classrooms and reflect on the pedagogical and content issues that they raise.

Developmental models of mathematics teaching will therefore need to account for qualitative change in a belief–behavior complex. Changes in classroom practice are accompanied by qualitative reorganizations in various "strands" of belief and knowledge that underlie the craft of teaching mathematics. We propose to begin exploring two: epistemology as it is enacted in classroom practice, and personal understanding of mathematics as enacted in classroom practice. Further work will most likely isolate additional strands to consider. The following is a brief discussion of our current knowledge about how these initial two strands change over time. We believe that current evidence supports the view that developing new forms of mathematics practice does involve restructuring of knowledge and action. The characteristics of the different levels of teaching that make them *qualitatively* different from each other, however, remain to be defined.

Enacted Conceptions of Epistemology

Teachers who are encouraged to listen to and observe students working on mathematical problems, or to explore mathematical problems themselves and reflect on their own processes of understanding, often reconsider their notions of how people learn mathematics (Fennema, Carpenter, Franke, et al., 1996: Schifter, 1996a, 1996b). By watching students grapple with different conceptual issues or by grappling with these issues themselves, teachers come to believe that deep mathematical understanding comes not from being told how to get "right" answers, but rather from active engagement in the posing and solving of problems. Learning is seen less as the result of information provided to the students by the teacher, and more as the result of students' active efforts to make things comprehensible for themselves.

Ms. Sayer, a fifth-grade teacher, describes how a simple request to her students that they explain their work led her to question what they were really understanding:

> Even the kids that can perform the algorithms don't truly understand what they are doing....they're bright little kids, but they're bright little robots who do exactly what we tell them to because that's how they were taught and that's how I was taught....The eye-opener for me was last year when Manuel did [a] subtraction problem. There was a zero in the middle of the problem [in the 10's place]....He could do [the problem] but when he had to tell me what he did, he got upset. [He said] "I don't know what to do with the zero...I don't know how to tell you what to do with that zero," which said to me, this kid truly doesn't understand (Interview, 9/94).

This reconceptualization of the learning process implies a reconceptualization of the teacher's role as well. If teachers begin to question the quality of learning that occurs with traditional teaching, then they must begin to question what the teacher can do to help students develop more substantive understanding. Rather than thinking of themselves as authoritative sources of information, teachers begin to recast their roles to be guides and directors of students' learning, selecting activities and posing questions to help students examine and rework their current mathematical understandings.

Thinking differently about the locus of agency for learning represents a significant shift for many teachers, and this new conceptualization of teachers' and students' roles and responsibilities for learning seems to develop over an extended period of time. Near the beginning of the process, many teachers tend to have one foot in each of two conflicting paradigms. One set of beliefs about learning (often implicitly, rather than explicitly held) formed the basis of their past instructional practice and frequently is well-entrenched. The new notions that they begin to develop as they reflect on both their own and their students' conceptual understandings, however, contradict some of these old assumptions. These contradictions are reflected in a practice that necessarily includes many structures and habits that are based on the old paradigm and are inconsistent with new goals.

Consider, for example, Ms. Gale's comments. She has some idea of the kind of mathematical inquiry she would like her sixth grade special education students to undertake, but acknowledges that she cannot always help to sustain productive investigation among her students. She recognizes when she is teaching "in the old way," but doesn't yet know how to teach consistently in the "new" one. She notes:

> I find it hard to ask good questions ....I'm acutely aware when I am feeding it [i.e., information]. I'm very aware when I'm doing it the old way, or when I'm trying something a little more on the exploratory end. And sometimes I feel that I don't have the...skill myself, to present a concept in an exploratory fashion....and ask the right questions, and have them work through it. And sometimes I have a problem understanding what [the students] are talking about. (Interview, 6/94)

Over time, some teachers are able to resolve the contradictions by sorting out which elements of their past practice fail to support the kind of mathematical understandings they now want their students to achieve. They are able to design and conduct lessons that fit their new vision of classroom practice. At this point, however, teachers remain more focused on lesson design and their own beliefs than on the close details of their students' thinking.

It seems to take yet another conceptual shift for teachers to realize that student understanding can be both the guide and the goal of their practice. Reflected in this shift is a changing view of agency in learning. Rather than feeling the burden of responsibility for presenting clear, comprehensible material to their students, teachers come to see students themselves as the source of their own sense-making and understanding. At this point, teachers become less concerned with the particulars of their own behaviors ("What is the right question to ask?" or "How do I get the students to work productively together?") and focus instead on trying to learn about students' constructions ("What is the student trying to understand?"). Although most teachers will say that they have always listened to their students, they begin to attend to students' thinking in a new way, which allows them to develop a coherent picture of students' underlying ideas about mathematics. Ms. Marsh, a sixth-grade teacher, describes how she has learned to shift her focus and develop a new ear for her students' comments:

> I might try orchestrating a discussion that I think will get [the students] there [i.e., to an idea] and it still doesn't get them there and I think it's because I'm not necessarily seeing where they're coming from. It's one

thing I've had to do a lot of—stay away from my own perception of math, what I believe it is. . .and really say, "what are *they* seeing it as?" As much as in traditional math we orchestrate what we want them to see and what we want them to perceive and what we want them to understand . . . but we're missing what they're really thinking. I'm kind of forced with that a lot to looking back to what they're thinking. I've changed my role to being sort of a listener, asking "what do you mean?" and I find delight in sitting back and listening to what they have to say. If they're willing to share that. There are still some kids who are reserved or who think you have to be the math expert. But gradually we get to that comfort level where we can say, "Hey, what do you think of this?" and kids are comfortable saying what they think....You really need to listen. And if you don't listen, it doesn't mean they're learning math any better. If you don't *know* that they're confused, are they confused? Yes, they are. (Interview, 6/94)

These changing views of the development of knowing are crucial for opening teachers' attention to their students' understanding. In addition, they have strong implications for the social organization of learning in the classroom. When a conception of learning is predicated on students' receiving information and on the teacher as the sole intellectual resource, the sociology of the classroom reflects a hierarchical and unidirectional set of intellectual relationships (see Fig. 2.1a). The important opportunities for learning are believed to reside in the teacher's having important things to say or show, and the students being ready and able to take this all in and use it when called on to do so.

Like Ms. Sayer, teachers who come to believe that students' understanding is not reflected solely in their ability to execute rote procedures can begin to consider students as active agents in the constitution of their own knowledge. This premise about learning provokes a significant shift in the social dynamic of the classroom toward greater intellectual interaction between teacher and student. Not only do students need to think about what their teacher says, but the teacher must try to understand what her students are saying (see Fig. 2.1b). Teachers are less intent on telling and more mindful of what their students are thinking. Yet the balance of intellectual power and authority in the classroom remains largely with the teacher.

Another change in the social organization of the class occurs when teachers reposition themselves as orchestrators, rather than conductors, of mathematical inquiry in the classroom (see Fig. 2.1c). This happens as teachers discover that their students can learn from each other by working together on mathematical ideas, and not only when the teacher is closely managing the children's interactions and explorations. In fact, teachers often note that their students see intriguing mathematical possibilities and solutions that they, themselves, have never seen before. This is not to suggest that the teacher's role is identical to that of the student members of the class, for this is surely

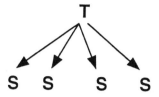

Figure 2.1 a

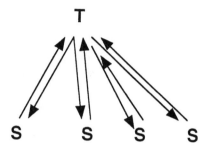

Figure 2.1 b

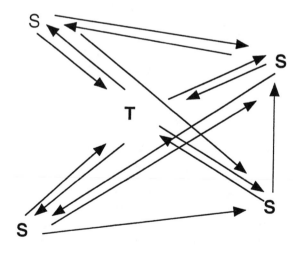

Figure 2.1 c

FIG. 2.1. Changing intellectual relationships among teachers and students in the classroom.

not true. As a more knowledgeable, experienced member of the group, and the acknowledged educational leader of the class, it is his or her responsibility to assess students' understanding, monitor their progress, and stimulate continued growth in mathematical understanding. However, the teacher need not be the only person in the classroom who creates opportunities for the development of mathematical ideas. As students share their thoughts, puzzle over questions, debate ideas advanced in class, and think together about the mathematics they are studying, they can provide much of the intellectual energy and substance for mathematical learning themselves.

However, teachers' listening to students' mathematical reasoning and having students listen to each other should not be an end in itself. Although it is a necessary part of organizing instruction to address the mathematical issues that students are encountering, it is not sufficient. Teachers must also understand the mathematical terrain that they are making available to their students.

Enacted conceptions of mathematics

To help students build deeper and richer mathematical ideas, teachers must have some understanding of the central mathematical ideas embedded in the curriculum for their grade level (Schifter, 1995), knowledge of the ideas that children bring to their learning (Carpenter, Fennema, & Franke, 1996), and notions about the kinds of experiences that they can create to help stimulate students to develop mathematically (Schifter, 1996a, 1996b). In addition, it has been suggested that teachers must reexamine their own understanding of mathematics both in terms of mathematical content and in terms of their assumptions of what properly constitutes the domain of mathematics itself (Ball, 1989; Even & Lappan, 1994; Schifter, 1995; Schifter & Fosnot, 1993; Thompson, 1991). The opportunities for mathematical learning that teachers can create depend in part on their images of what mathematics is all about.

Traditionally, the goal of most mathematics instruction has been to teach students to become fluent in applying a set of discrete procedures in order to solve problems. Within this orientation, mathematics is considered to be a set of memorized rules and procedures for correctly solving particular quantitative problems. Helping students become conversant with these rules and procedures has involved providing them with many chances to practice applying mathematical facts and strategies so they can become as efficient and accurate as possible.

In contrast, the reform movement is advocating new goals for mathematics instruction. These goals involve students becoming actively engaged in efforts to make sense of the mathematics they study. They invite a reconsideration of the nature of the domain of mathematics itself. Rather than considering mathematics to be a set of absolute and immutable truths, for example, teachers begin to think about it as a body of knowledge that has been created, refined, challenged, modified, and appended by hundreds of generations of men and women who have been intrigued by its workings. This view, in turn, leads to a shift away from the notion that learning mathematics involves becoming proficient at applying procedures or rules for arriving at "the" correct answer to a problem. Learning mathematics comes to be viewed as a process of conjecturing, discussing, testing, playing with, revising, and extending ideas about mathematical objects. Doing mathematics becomes something that takes more than 30 seconds of solitary computation—it becomes a textured conversation that illuminates how people reason about a variety of quantitative and spatial relationships.

Some teachers interpret this perspective as a mandate for making "problem solving" the centerpiece of their mathematics instruction. Problem solving, conjecturing, and discussing are treated as ends in themselves, rather than as tools for investigating particular mathematical structures. This can happen if teachers are particularly uncertain themselves about what the fundamental mathematical ideas are that underlie the mathematics they teach. Students' methods of solving problems can become the primary focus of the lesson partly because teachers are surprised to discover that their students have richer approaches than previously credited, or because teachers cannot envision any goal for their lessons other than developing generic reasoning skills. If teachers do not have a strong enough grasp of the mathematics they teach, they may not be able to engage their students in an exploration of mathematical ideas beyond calling attention to a variety of possible solution strategies. They themselves may not be able to distinguish valid from invalid reasoning. This can leave them with no way to assess the various solutions offered.

As teachers think more about the relationship between problem solving and the creation of deep understanding, they may come to consider discussion and debate as a means of examining and learning about mathematical structure. The problems students work then serve as a starting point for discussion of more general mathematical questions, rather than simply as the opportunity to present the students' own ideas. In this view, the teacher's role is to challenge students' thinking about important mathematical connections, not to preside over mathematical "show and tell."

In the following example, second grade teacher Lisa Seyferth describes a lesson that focused on encouraging her students to think about different strategies for solving an addition problem that required regrouping. Toward the end of the school year she wrote:

Last week I prepared to approach addition with regrouping again by making a poster showing five different methods of adding 38 and 25. The first four ways were methods which second graders had articulated when explaining their thinking in November, three of which involved adding the tens first. One way showed counting onto the first number by ones. And finally the poster showed the traditional algorithm. (See Fig. 2.2.)

I met with a group of ten children....I gave them this word problem and asked them to pay attention to how they solved it, and to please write something down that would explain their thinking:

Ms. Walker and Ms. Seyferth were watching kids playing outside. They counted 38 children in and around the structure. They saw 25 kids playing Freeze Tag on the field. How many kids did they see?

...When I showed the poster, they excitedly said "I did it that way!" or "I solved it the green way!"

...We looked at the methods shown on the poster, trying to understand what was happening in each. Out of the ten children, eight solved the problem by adding the tens first. One child, Jim, solved the problem using the traditional algorithm .... Another, Bill, said that his grandmother tried to show him "the pink way."... So we looked at "the pink way" and tried to make sense of it.

Jim described how he used it. He said he started with the ones. He added 8 and 5 and got 13. Since you can't write 13 in the ones you write the 3

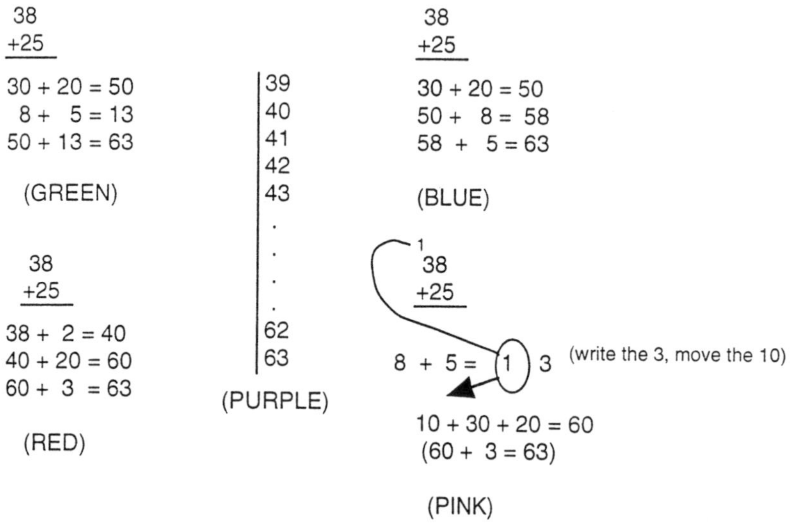

FIG. 2.2. Methods for adding double digit numbers (poster from a second grade classroom).

there, and put the 1 over the tens. Then you add the tens and it's 60, so it's 63. When I asked him why you can't write 13 in the ones he said because "fifty-thirteen" doesn't make sense. Guy added that it looks like five hundred thirteen. I asked "What is this one?" indicating the "carried" one. He said it was the ten from thirteen....

By the time these ten children were exposed to the traditional algorithm they had pretty well constructed their own understandings of addition with regrouping. They were comfortable thinking of numbers in terms of tens and ones; it had meaning for them. Therefore their task was different. I was asking them to reconcile a new method with what they *already knew*. (Seyferth, 1994. p.1–2, emphasis in original)

To be able to design lessons for underlying mathematical issues, as Seyferth did for the idea of grouping into tens, teachers must be fluent with the mathematics they teach. Similarly, the ability to respond spontaneously to students' ideas and to take advantage of teachable moments in mathematics class requires an understanding both of the important mathematical ideas for the grade level and of the typical ways that children think about these ideas. Teachers must develop a more expanded view of the nature of mathematics, as well as a map of the terrain to be explored by their students. This does not mean that they must already have answers to all mathematical questions that might arise in class, but they must have enough of a sense of the mathematics to guide their students toward important aspects of the domain (see also Simon, 1995).

A tension exists between honoring students' own constructions of mathematical ideas and introducing students to the canons of the mathematical domain (Ball, 1989). Teachers changing their practice must find a balance between valuing students' individual constructions of their mathematical understanding and guiding them toward the shared understandings, principles, and structures that make up the domain of mathematics. The goal of mathematics education is not for each student to develop his or her own idiosyncratic view of mathematics. It is not a matter of "anything goes." Good mathematical education should acculturate students into the structure, language, and ways of reasoning about quantitative and spatial phenomena. These are the tools of the discipline of mathematics. Each student will necessarily develop a personal understanding of mathematics and an individual relationship to it, but these should fall within the bounds created by a shared understanding of the domain. Teachers who have developed clear and reasoned ideas about the essential aspects of the discipline will be in a far better position to guide students productively through the mathematical terrain.

As teachers work to recognize the major conceptual issues that their students confront during the year, they further refine and organize their focus on the central mathematical content of the curriculum. The big ideas that underlie the curriculum are those that students invariably encounter and must construct for themselves.

Consider, for example, Deborah Carey O'Brien's (1995) description of her lessons about exploring perimeter and area with her third-grade students. Not only does she attend to her students' efforts to understand these two attributes, but in thinking about their work, she recognizes that her lesson has also raised issues about some "old" ideas as well:

> I asked the class to measure some cards that were 3 x 4. They needed to find out the . . . area and the perimeter....[As I checked in with groups of students,] two girls were in a lively disagreement about the perimeter. Lin said she was sure it was 7 inches while Theresa was just as sure it was 10 inches.... [I could see that Lin was counting only two of the four sides, but] all the while [the girls were discussing the problem] I was trying to figure out how [Theresa] was counting and coming up short....Theresa counted only one side of each block on the corners. I listened while Theresa explained as she held her finger on a corner block, "This is just one block so you can't count it twice...."
>
> Counting one thing as more than one does go counter to what young mathematicians have just learned and practiced about one to one corre-spondence. I wondered how many children were working through this new twist on the old idea of counting. I was pretty surprised to see about a third of the class grapple with this issue....
>
> By noticing this difficulty some of the students were having, I was able to examine for myself what I thought the problems were and then ask questions or set up tasks which would help people find their way out of their confusions. (p. 1–2)

O'Brien had not been expecting her students to have difficulty counting the sides of tiles. However, when she noticed the counting "errors," she was prepared to recognize in them mathematical ideas that her students needed to confront. After the class discussed the 3 x 4 rectangle, she next asked them to work on a 12 x 1 rectangle:

> By focusing attention on this particular rectangle, I knew we would need to address the "end" blocks counting as more than one—in this case three. And I expected some students would point out that the "inner" blocks are counted twice. (p. 2).

Once O'Brien identified the source of confusion, she chose to draw attention to the part of the task over which there had been most disagreement—to lead them through, not around, their puzzlement. This orientation helped her to focus her teaching on helping her students refine their notions of both measuring and counting.

Having an image of the fundamental mathematical ideas underlying a grade's curriculum can also help teachers organize and focus their assessments of students' progress. Teachers working to change their practice begin to rethink their ways of evaluating student performance (NCTM, 1995). As teachers move away from an image of learning as the retention and application of facts and procedures, their criteria for judging the development of their students' mathematical thinking will change. We currently know little about how this process plays out, but imagine that it is related to changes in teachers' own understanding of mathematics and appreciation of mathematically powerful concepts.

Qualitative reorganizations in mathematics teaching involve reformulating aspects of classroom practice in the context of new mathematical understandings and changing beliefs about learning and teaching. The research community has begun to gather evidence of teachers' reorganizations of belief and practice. Further investigations clarifying and elaborating the character of these changes will help create a fuller picture of whether there are, in fact, qualitatively different levels to teachers' practice.

There has yet to be much attention in the mathematics community to exploring dynamic characteristics of the change process, the issues of orderliness and transition mechanisms, which represent important features of cognitive developmental theories. These are the focus of the following sections of this chapter, as we consider how these notions might be applied to studying teachers' development of new forms of practice.

ORDERLY PROGRESSIONS OF STAGES

A second characteristic of developmental theories is that the progression of stages is assumed to be sequential and invariant (Case, 1985, 1992; Erikson, 1950; Fischer, 1980; Langer, 1969; Piaget, 1970; Werner, 1948). These theories posit that growth proceeds according to a single, fixed order, whereby the challenges to be faced and resolved in the present stage become the base from which the next stage's challenges are created.

The view of stage progression as unitary and invariant holds when considering some phenomena but not others. Seen from a broad perspective, it might be possible to characterize development in terms of movement along a single, general pathway. Piagetian theory, for example, which focuses on the universal development of logical thought and considers very general kinds of changes, may reasonably claim a fixed sequence of restructurings. When the focus is on the development of understanding at a more detailed and specific level, many variations can be noted in the ways knowledge is constructed. For example, more microscopic analyses of cognitive systems reveal what appear to be regressions in functioning of systems that are generally moving forward (Case, 1985; Strauss, 1982), thus challenging the notion of steady forward progression. Gruber (1985) observed that, despite the universality of achievement of certain cognitive milestones (of the Piagetian variety), there is also a great deal of variability in the particulars of the pathways people take to get from one milestone to the next. He suggested that, instead of thinking of knowing in terms of static milestones, we might think of the process of coming to know in terms of the variety of pathways people take toward these common intellectual "way stations."

Formulating developmental models of mathematics teaching should include some treatment of this general issue of progressive movement. However, the level at which analysis should proceed remains an open question. Mathematics teaching is a complex domain that combines thought and action. It involves a coordination of internal, psychological constructions of mathematics, epistemology, and pedagogy that guide a multitude of on-the-spot practical decisions and external actions made in the context of the specific classroom conditions that prevail on a given day and time. We argue that the very fact of its complexity requires a level of analysis which is too fine-grained to support broad claims for invariant patterns of change.

Rather than searching for strictly ordered change, we propose that models of mathematics teaching investigate the *orderliness* of change. By this we mean looking for aspects of the transition process that are predictable, given an understanding of a teacher's current profile with respect to the strands of epistemology and mathematical understanding. In particular, we could consider tracking the patterns of issues teachers confront and resolve as a function of these two strands. We expect that there are a relatively small number of pathways for teachers to take in developing their mathematics practice. These pathways would depend on the prior status of the contributing strands, on the kind of external support and encouragement teachers receive for making changes, and on teachers' own motivational and dispositional makeup. Research directed toward mapping the issues teachers confront as they enact their new beliefs and understandings in the classroom will help to create a fuller picture of how teachers move through the terrain of creating a reformed mathematics practice.

Some elementary school teachers, for example, seek to examine their mathematics teaching because they see this as the weak link in their practice. Often they feel that they, themselves, can solve mathematics problems in a rote way, but don't understand what they are doing. Some teachers do not even feel that they are good mechanical problem solvers and are looking for ways to address their intense discomfort with doing mathematics themselves. Many of these teachers are familiar with "process" approaches to teaching other parts of the curriculum such as writing and language arts, and feel that their students would also benefit from mathematics instruction oriented toward developing their mathematical voices. Yet, because of their own mathematical limitations, they are unable to envision mathematics lessons as anything other than doing activities and working problems from a text. Although the idea of attending to their students' mathematical ideas may make sense, some teachers have no way of knowing how to do this. Often they find that they need to deepen their own mathematical understanding before they can really follow their students' thinking. As these teachers learn more about thinking mathematically themselves, they become better able to make principled judgments about the purpose and value of the mathematical activities and problems they choose for their students. Ms. Carpenter, a third-and fourth-grade teacher, captured some of these issues as she traced three years' worth of changes in her stance toward mathematics in her classroom:

> I have been teaching the combined third and fourth grades for two years, this is my third....The first year, I was involved in [an in-service mathematics project] and during that year I taught math in a very random way. I was rediscovering math for myself in the [in-service] classes and each time we did something new and interesting I would do it with my class of kids, too. We had fun, but I was not convinced that I knew what I was doing. We were experimenting with ideas. The problem was: I didn't know enough math myself to find the links between the ideas, the patterns or the energy that holds particular notions together. The next year, that was my quest. To find a rhythm to the teaching of mathematics. To have a solid sense of why we were doing what we were doing and to build the community in my classroom around the communal investigation of how the number system functions and how we communicate mathematical ideas with each other. This year I want to go deeper into the meat of number. I am convinced that there is a richness and a purpose to the investigation of "number" and how we speak the language of mathematics and number with each other. So this year I am going to dig deeper into the construct of the number system and the manipulation of it. (Written reflection, 9/94)

A different set of issues initially confronts those teachers who have a well-developed understanding of the mathematical terrain they teach, but little sense of what, exactly, their students are taking away from math lessons. Teachers in this situation often question the idea that clear explanations will ensure student learning. Learning to take a careful look at what their students actually understand and what they know only in superficial and procedural ways becomes important, as does exploring ways of structuring activities and discussions to help students develop firm and flexible understandings.

As a high school teacher enrolled in an in-service institute, for example, Ms. Roberts found herself entering a new territory after 20 years of teaching. She began to wonder about her *students'* mathematical ideas, and over the next few years thinking about her students' understanding was the key issue driving changes in her practice. As she reflected on her growth as a teacher, she noted:

> As I look back on myself as a teacher before [I entered the program]...I believe that...I had already incorporated non-routine problems, pursuing alternate solutions, grouping students for cooperative problem solving and using diagrams to some degree into my teaching style....What I experienced at the Institute that first summer was an overall...framework for classroom instruction upon which to hang these strategies. It was very clear to me...that I was experiencing a program which was founded, or based, on some unifying principles—I could not articulate these (and in fact, I still have difficulty speaking in general terms about these beliefs. I need the context of school and my own classes to help) but I "felt" their presence.
>
> What I sensed that I "got" out of the Institute was a structure which would give me reasons for using a particular strategy at a particular time, based on the mathematical concepts I was teaching....I would not describe my philosophy of learning [prior to entering the project] as constructivistic. As a matter of fact I would describe myself as having a philosophy of teaching but not a philosophy of learning. I developed a philosophy of learning over the two year period after [the Institute]. It was during those years that I moved from making classroom decisions based on my intellectual understanding of the math concepts to making classroom decisions based on my students' understandings. The biggest single factor that enabled me to make this change was my reflection on what was happening in the classrooms, and the skill I worked hardest at developing was listening to my students. (Written reflection, 9/89, emphasis in original)

Investigations seeking to identify alternative pathways toward new forms of practice would substantially fill out our understanding of the terrain of teachers' development. The value in investigating the orderliness of progressions lies not only in lending support to a theoretical perspective on the cognitive restructuring that occurs for mathematics teachers, but also in supporting teacher education. The practical value of having such work lies in offering teacher educators an empirically based resource for guiding their pedagogical decisions as they work with teachers to improve their mathematics teaching. In addition, such a mapping can focus attention on understanding the *conditions* that stimulate these orderly progressions, that is, for understanding the mechanisms that help teachers move from stage to stage.

TRANSITION MECHANISMS

A third characteristic of developmental theories is that they propose mechanisms to account for transitions from one level of understanding to another. The mechanisms offer a view of how development proceeds and are key theoretical elements for those seeking to facilitate change, because engaging these mechanisms stimulates growth. Attention to both psychological and sociocultural mechanisms can be found in current theories of cognitive development. Psychological mechanisms promote individuals' reorganization of their own knowledge and understanding. Sociocultural mechanisms serve two purposes: They provide the context and stimulus for individual change, and they support the creation of new social and intellectual forms themselves.

At the psychological level, a number of different mechanisms have been proposed. Over the past few decades the Piagetian notions of assimilation and accommodation have received the most attention as descriptions of the means by which individuals develop thought. According to Piaget, these processes help the individual to adjust and expand his or her current understanding by taking into account new, challenging features of experience. Sometimes the adjustments needed to meet a new challenge are quite small, as, for example, when a child can apply an already developed strategy to a new situation. For the girl who can add "4 + 6" by counting up, adding "5 + 7" offers minor challenges. To count up five from seven, the child must start the count from a slightly larger number and must keep track of two additional counts as she coordinates the running sum with the number of remaining counts. She may do so by gesturing with each of five fingers (instead of four), or perhaps by mentally imaging five objects as she counts up. The adjustments she makes to her knowledge about counting up are relatively small, and she is likely to solve "5 + 7" with little or no difficulty. Often the adjustments are somewhat more significant. For example, were the child asked to solve "14 + 27," she would need to develop new ways to keep track of the count. If she chooses to monitor her counting up with her fingers, she will need to decide what to do when she has used all ten digits: does she count some fingers twice, move on to her toes, or look for other objects to count? If she adds on the 14 in her head, she must monitor the count as well as the running sum: Does she begin to image groupings of counts instead of individual elements, or does she find other ways to keep track (one child we know would count, "28, 1; 29, 2; 30, 3...41, 14.")?

At other times, new experiences or challenges are so different from individuals' current knowledge and skill that they have few resources for operating on these experiences in a cognitively productive manner. For example, without an understanding of infinity, it is virtually impossible to make sense of the idea of infinite sets of different magnitudes.

Ideas or activities that offer little possibility of connection between current understanding and the intellectual demands of the situation do not tend to promote intellectual growth.

From a Piagetian perspective, developing new and more sophisticated understandings involves resolving challenges to current ways of thinking. Piaget proposed that the mechanisms of assimilation and accommodation, working in concert, resolve these challenges and move individuals' systems of knowing toward greater coherence and stability. The challenges themselves grow out of individuals' activities in the world. They may derive from interactions with friends, parents, or teachers, or they may originate in more solitary explorations of objects or ideas. Challenges to one's current ways of understanding are always intrinsic to the individual, for they derive from the person's recognition, not necessarily explicit, that he or she does not understand something. Thus, from a Piagetian perspective, the construction of knowing is an individual, internal process driven by perceived disparities or conflicts between the individual's existing ways of thinking and the intellectual demands and opportunities of the environment. If development is predicated on perturbations in knowing, as Piaget proposed, teachers' professional development would proceed through confronting and resolving problematic aspects of their practice.

Karmiloff-Smith (1992) proposed an additional mechanism based on reflection on intellectual *successes* rather than on cognitive conflicts. Her model of representational redescription described intellectual development as proceeding by representing knowledge in increasingly explicit and organized forms. By making implicit understandings explicit, knowledge that is originally tied to acting in a narrow set of instances can be broadened and applied to a wider variety of situations.

It remains to work out how this process would account for changes in a complex domain such as mathematics teaching, but it is an intriguing notion that development is driven by processes of "explicitation" and borrowing across areas of understanding, as Karmiloff-Smith argued, rather than solely by processes that redress deficiencies in understanding. One can imagine, for example, that teachers would learn much about teaching mathematics by thinking about other areas of their teaching that they find satisfying and effective. In reflecting on aspects of the curriculum that they feel they are teaching well, they can make explicit those principles of pedagogy, epistemology, and command of content that define good teaching for them. This process would give teachers an initial purchase for thinking about how to rework these features specifically for the teaching of other parts of the curriculum. It is not unusual, for example, for teachers to observe that they are committed to using a whole language approach to literacy, but do not know how to create an analogous whole math approach to learning mathematics. In trying to understand what they might learn about teaching mathematics by thinking about what they already know about teaching language, teachers might be undertaking a form of representational redescription of the sort Karmiloff-Smith described.

Still other theorists take a more sociocultural view of cognitive development, arguing that the construction of knowing is not a matter of individual, solitary construction of understanding, but a dialectical process firmly grounded in a system of social relations (Broughton, 1987; Cole, 1985; Lave, 1988; Vygotsky, 1978; Wertsch, 1985a, 1985b). These theorists emphasize that *all* knowledge is socially constructed, regardless of whether it is an individual's personal understanding, the very intellectual disciplines that we seek to learn, or the social organizations in which we study, work, and play.

It is Vygotsky's writings about culture, thought, and development that have received the most attention within the American psychological community over the past two decades (see, for example, Cole & Scribner, 1978; John-Steiner & Souberman, 1978; Rogoff, 1990; Wertsch, 1985a, 1985b). Within a Vygotskian perspective, qualitative restructurings of thought are related to the acquisition and use of powerful new tools and signs for mediating thought (Luria, 1976; Vygotsky, 1978; Wertsch, 1985a). These tools and signs are cultural creations and help to shape the structure and organization of individual thought by emphasizing particular, socially valued relationships and processes of reasoning. The means for intellectual change lies in the individuals' appropriation and exercise of these socially constructed mediators, as the tools and signs help to organize and shape their experiences and interpretations of the world.

Writing, for example, can serve as a powerful tool for intellectual growth by helping to hold an idea or experience still for reflection. The very process of writing provides opportunities for revisiting the phenomenon as we seek to capture it in prose. When we write, we can examine our thoughts and actions. We ask ourselves what we *really* mean, what we really understand, and what connections and implications we are still trying to develop. Writing allows us to stop, reflect, think, reflect again, and struggle to articulate further. Having a physical record of the thinking process also broadens the opportunities for sharing ideas and engaging in dialogue with a wide variety of others (as well as with the self), thus expanding the possibilities for developing further understanding.

The emphasis on the cultural and historical matrix in which individuals function seems to have most attracted American scholars to Vygotsky's work. The fact that individual development is heavily determined by the cultural supports available in a particular society at a particular point in its history means that it is essential to recognize the broader social context in which individual thinking and learning develops.

Although there is an increasing interest in describing mathematics classrooms in terms of sociocultural phenomena (Cobb, Wood, & Yackel, 1993; Cobb & Yackel, 1995; Stein & Brown, this volume; Wood, 1995), there is currently little work in mathematics education that focuses specifically on elaborating sociocultural mechanisms of teachers' developing practice. There are, however, a number of intervention projects currently exploring different models for in-service professional development that may yield information about this. A number of investigators have also written more generally about sociocultural aspects of reconstructing mathematics practice (see, for example, Borko et al., 1992; Britzman, 1991; Cobb, Wood, & Yackel, 1990, 1993; Fennema, Carpenter, & Peterson, 1989; Hart, 1992; Maher & Alston, 1990; Schifter & Fosnot, 1993).

We encourage systematic study of both psychological and sociocultural mechanisms when investigating the process by which teachers develop new forms of mathematics practice. An initial task for guiding inquiry at the psychological level might be to articulate the kinds of experiences that stimulate teachers to reflect on their practice and begin to make changes in their teaching. If we can understand what catalyzes the process of development for teachers, we may be able to encourage more teachers to undertake the process. A second potentially fruitful area is the investigation of the dynamic between teachers' beliefs and their classroom practices. We have asserted that the development of new forms of mathematics teaching involves a continuous interplay between thought (teachers' beliefs and knowledge) and action (teachers' classroom moves). This dynamic perspective would lead to research questions such as: How do beliefs at any given time in a teacher's development constrain or enable classroom moves? How do teachers reflect on their classroom experiences in order to make changes? What kinds of resources (either material or interpersonal) can influence teachers' process of reflection and subsequent action?

There are several different ways in which the research community might attend to sociocultural factors influencing the development of teaching. We might choose to explore the ways that sociocultural processes can have an impact on the work of individuals. This orientation could lead us to ask, for example, whether there are new mediators of thought and activity that are acquired as teachers develop new forms of practice. If, as Vygotsky posits, significant change is linked to the acquisition of new mediating tools and signs, we might ask how this applies to the context of teachers developing their practice. Are developing images of new forms of mathematics instruction (Schifter, 1995; 1996a; 1996b) functioning as such mediators? If so, how do they function as mediators? Do opportunities for collegial exchange provide the "zone of proximal development" within which teachers receive support and guidance for developing their practice?

The process of becoming acculturated to new forms of mathematics teaching includes the development of new ways of thinking about mathematics learning and new ways of communicating those thoughts and ideas. The language that teachers develop to talk about their work may be another productive place to look for evidence of sociocultural mechanisms. Teachers who seek to change their mathematics practice often find themselves in need of a different vocabulary and set of categories for thinking about teaching and learning. Their use of language itself helps them to reflect on specific classroom events, abstract important principles from their experiences, and draw generalizations and implications for their practice as a whole. Without teachers' developing new ways for describing classroom practice, it is often difficult for them to consider and discuss how particular classroom events might relate to developing a pedagogy of mathematics teaching. (Certainly, however, acquiring a different vocabulary without having the opportunity to experience their classrooms in a new way will not help teachers to develop their practice. There must be a strong connection among thinking, talking, and doing.)

A second kind of mediator may be found in the different types of educational cultures in which teachers work. Taking this perspective, we are directed toward explorations of the nature and functioning of the communities in which teachers work (Borko et al., 1992) and to considerations of what it means for teachers to work together to develop their practice (Hammerman, 1995a, 1995b; Stein & Brown, chap. 7, this volume). Teachers' efforts to construct new forms of mathematics teaching can be affected considerably by the images they have of good teaching, the nature of collegial relationships, the criteria and procedures for job evaluations, and the kinds of professional development that prevail in their schools and districts. How, for example, do teachers work together to develop supportive communities for inquiry and discussion about teaching? What are the conditions and processes that foster teachers' exploration and experimentation with new forms of teaching? How do parents and administrators facilitate or impede this process? How do teachers interpret and use the images, materials, and support that are being created to stimulate and sustain professional development? How are these materials themselves changed in the process?

Finally, we might ask how teachers' professional development is influenced by interactions with their students. Some researchers have begun to examine the process by which teachers and students work together to create new classroom cultures for mathematics learning (Ball, 1993; Cobb, Wood, & Yackel, 1993; Cobb, Yackel, & Wood, 1992). Investigations that would extend ongoing work could include studying teachers' responses to students who resist the changing roles and responsibilities of reformed mathematics classes, the ways that teachers' development is influenced by working with students who have already had experience engaging in mathematical inquiry and discussion, and the ways that teachers and students develop mathematics communities in classrooms where some of the students are familiar only with traditional mathematics instruction and others have been acculturated to a view of mathematics as exploration and investigation.

THE MISSING ELEMENTS:
MOTIVATION AND DISPOSITION

Modern theories of cognitive development have paid little attention to factors that occupy more prominent positions in other branches of psychology: the influence of motivational factors on learning and individual differences in behavior (Adorno, Frenkel-Brunswick, Levinson, & Sanford, 1950; Allport, 1955; Dweck & Leggett, 1988; Escalona, 1968; White, 1959). There have been some recent efforts to integrate emotional factors into discussions of intellectual development (Case, 1988; Fischer & Lamborn, 1989; Shapiro & Weber, 1981), but there has yet to be a well-developed account of what sustains people as they undertake the often difficult and frustrating task of reconstructing their understanding (Goldsmith & Davenport, 1995). A complete model for the development of mathematics teaching would include more detailed considerations of both motivational processes and the ways in which individual dispositional factors influence the course of development.

Perhaps people become motivated to undertake change when they feel some discomfort or dissatisfaction with their current ability to act on the world in desired ways, or perhaps simply when they become curious about other ways of thinking or doing. In the case of mathematics teachers, this "felt need" for change can originate in many places—a desire to be current pedagogically, a sense that existing teaching methods are not adequately serving some students, or a recognition that students have a considerable amount of intuitive understanding that is not being invoked in traditional curricula or activities. This initial motivation is extremely important, and those who seek to provide professional development need to know how to encourage teachers to find a compelling reason to undertake the task of transforming their practice. Beyond this, however, is the importance of understanding more about what *keeps* teachers motivated to work on their teaching during those times that perservering may be terrifying, seemingly unproductive, frustrating, or boring. Schifter and Fosnot's (1993) case studies of mathematics teachers in transition suggested that courage is an important ingredient in the motivation equation.

In addition to understanding more about these motivational factors, we propose that certain individual dispositional characteristics are likely to influence teachers' course of development. Teachers' particular interpersonal and intellectual orientations to the world will influence the ways in which they approach and resolve certain kinds of issues about students, relations with parents, colleagues, administrators, classroom structure and functioning, and use of curriculum materials and resources. All teachers will encounter these issues in some form or another, but the nature of their experiences may vary, in part as a function of their own internal psychologies. What provides a welcome opportunity for reflection and development for some teachers may become a serious stumbling block for others, and perhaps a nonissue entirely for still others.

One of these issues relates to teachers' comfort in allowing students to be confused, puzzled, or frustrated as they learn. It is perhaps a legacy of behaviorist-based theories of learning that we have a tendency to want students' learning to be painless and continually progressive. The Piagetian view allows for a somewhat less relentlessly rosy picture of the process, maintaining that cognitive development occurs as individuals necessarily find themselves in periods of relative uncertainty about their understanding. Rarely does significant learning feel as if it is constantly progressive, and part of the territory of reconstructing understanding includes being stuck, frustrated, and uncomprehending. An important question for teachers is whether they try to minimize these aspects of the process, or whether they are able to find ways to encourage and support students as they struggle with the limitations of their current ways of knowing. Those teachers who feel responsible for safeguarding their students from feelings of frustration or temporary lack of success may find it difficult to watch students struggle with ideas. Teachers who are comfortable with others' frustration and are able to trust students to make sense of the mathematics they are learning may find it easier to leave students time and space to wrestle with challenging ideas or problems[3].

A second factor involves teachers' comfort with a greater degree of ambiguity and uncertainty in their teaching lives. Because the kind of teaching envisioned by the reform movement is more exploratory and responsive to students' needs and interests than the traditional, drill-and-practice classroom, teachers seeking to change their practice must be willing to rely on a more flexible level of planning for lessons and activities. Those who find this degree of ambiguity uncomfortable may need extra support for opening their classrooms to a more exploratory and opportunity-driven mode of teaching and learning.

Supporting this kind of classroom environment may put the authoritarian teacher out of a job—or at least a role. Creating a classroom that

---

[3]Teachers, themselves, are likely to experience all of these emotions as they try to rework their own practice (Goldsmith & Davenport, 1995). A further question for teacher educators to consider, then, is the degree to which we let teachers struggle as they dismantle and reassemble their teaching (Schifter & Fosnot, 1993).

focuses on students' active participation in the construction of their own knowledge will be more difficult for teachers who find comfort and power in being the ultimate arbiter and judge of success and progress. Some teachers may find it difficult to soften their position as primary intellectual authority; others may find it liberating to recognize that they can be effective educators without having to feel that they always know more than their students do.

Still other teachers may have difficulty assuming more authority for the mathematics they do with their students. Teachers who seek external sources of authority for themselves—who are most comfortable when they know that someone else will have an answer, a preferred way of doing things, or an agenda to be followed—may find it uncomfortable to think about creating mathematics classrooms that favor developing methods for students themselves to evaluate the adequacy of mathematical arguments and solutions. Teachers who tend to look to others as the source of authority and power may have difficulty with the issue of shifting the locus of intellectual authority from textbook or expert to actively inquiring student, colleague, or to themselves.

GENERAL DIRECTIONS
FOR FUTURE RESEARCH

By identifying that which is orderly about the development of mathematics teaching, researchers will be able to create a general road map of the process. This mapping, together with an understanding of the mechanisms of change and their interaction with motivational and dispositional factors, can help to guide the design and planning of intervention programs aiming to help teachers develop new forms of mathematics practice.

Currently, there is little systematic information about how teachers in the process of changing their mathematics practice encounter and resolve the kinds of issues described in this chapter. At present, therefore, we have little general guidance for characterizing the processes of developing practice, or for recognizing familiar dilemmas, crises, or choice points as familiar signposts along pathways for change. If we are to develop such information systematically, we will need to supplement the current case-study approach with longitudinal studies of larger cohorts of teachers engaged in changing their practice. These will be particularly useful for providing information about the range and variation of ways that teachers use to reformulate their practice.

Future investigations might focus on further articulating reorganizations in particular teaching strands. We have opened the conversation with a discussion of two strands, offering first-order descriptions of teachers' enacted conceptions of epistemology and mathematics. Subsequent work could focus on exploring these strands more deeply and on identifying other major strands and describing reorganizations in them. As the descriptions of the development of mathematics teaching become richer, they will offer better guides for teacher educators and reflective teachers who seek to reformulate their practice.

As teachers begin to move toward new forms of practice, the disparity between vision and daily classroom reality often becomes a source of discomfort for teachers who become frustrated at being unable to teach consistently in the way they would like. Investigation of factors that influence the implementation of consistent classroom practice could inform our efforts to reduce the tension for teachers in transition. Some possible candidates for investigation are the kind of support and feedback necessary for promoting continued development of teaching practice, how reflection influences the transition process, how teachers' sense of obligation to students to be good teachers interacts with their uncertainty that relinquishing traditional views of teaching and learning will best serve their students' educational needs, and the kinds of pedagogical and content knowledge necessary to teach effectively within the new paradigm.

We close this chapter with some general observations about constructing investigations of teachers' development. Just as teachers are being called on to reflect on their roles and relationships in the classroom, so too are researchers being invited to reconsider the assumptions and methods that guide their work. The prevailing intellectual *zeitgeist*, with its emphasis on the social construction of meaning, has stimulated a reassessment of the relationship between subject and object, knower and known, across a wide variety of disciplines. Neither teachers nor researchers have license to presume they can judge what the other understands without listening carefully. Researchers must work closely and collaboratively with teachers so they can investigate, together, the dimensions of teachers' changing practice. The researcher brings a unique perspective to this process—a theoretical and analytic stance and the opportunity to observe the phenomenon across a large number of individuals. Each individual teacher brings to such collaboration the living of the phenomenon itself—the important particulars of his or her own case and insights about the process that help to keep inquiry firmly grounded in the realities of the experience. We stand to learn the most about the ways teachers reconstruct their mathematics practice through the thoughtful and respectful interplay of these two perspectives.

ACKNOWLEDGMENTS

The authors would like to thank Sophia Cohen, Elizabeth Fennema, Ilene Kantrov, Barbara Scott Nelson, Terry Wood, and Alan Schiffmann for commenting on earlier drafts of this paper. Support for research reported here and for the preparation of this paper was provided by the Dewitt–Wallace Readers Digest Fund and the National Science Foundation under grant numbers TPE–9050350, ESI–9254393, ESI–9254477, and RED–9353820. Any opinions, findings, conclusions, or recommendations expressed in this paper are those of the authors and do not necessarily reflect the views of the funding organizations.

REFERENCES

Adorno, T. W., Frenkel-Brunswik, E., Levinson, D. J., & Sanford, R. N. (1950). *The authoritarian personality*. New York: Harper.

Allport, G. (1955). *Becoming: Basic considerations for a psychology of personality*. New Haven, CT: Yale University Press.

Ball, D. L. (1989). Research on teaching mathematics: Making subject matter knowledge part of the equation. In J. Brophy (Ed.), *Advances in research on teaching: Vol 2. Teachers' subject matter knowledge and classroom instruction*. (pp. 1–48). Greenwich: JAI.

Ball, D. L. (1993). With an eye on the mathematical horizon: Dilemmas of teaching elementary school mathematics. *The Elementary School Journal, 93* (4), 373–397.

Borko, H., Eisenhart, M., Brown, C. A., Underhill, R. G., Jones, D., & Agard, P. C. (1992). Learning to teach hard mathematics: Do novice teachers and their instructors give up too easily? *Journal for Research in Mathematics Education, 23*(3), 194–222.

Britzman, D. (1991). *Practice makes practice: A critical study of learning to teach*. Albany: State University of New York Press.

Broughton, J. M. (Ed.). (1987). *Critical theories of psychological development* . New York: Plenum.

California State Department of Education. (1991). *Mathematics framework for California Public Schools, kindergarten through Grade 12*. Sacramento: California State Department of Education.

Carpenter, T. P., Fennema, E., & Franke, M. L. (1996). Cognitively guided instruction: A knowledge base for reform in primary mathematics instruction. *Elementary School Journal, 97*(1), 3–21.

Case, R. (1985). *Intellectual development: Birth to adulthood*. New York: Academic Press.

Case, R. (1988). The whole child: Toward an integrated view of young children's cognitive, social, and emotional development. In A. D. Pelligrini (Ed.), *Psychological bases for early education* (pp. 155–184). New York: Wiley.

Case, R. (Ed.), (1992). *The mind's staircase: Exploring the conceptual underpinnings of children's thought and knowledge*. Hillsdale, N.J.: Lawrence Erlbaum Associates.

Chazan, D., & Ball, D.L. (1995). *Beyond exhortations not to tell: The teacher's role in discussion-intensive mathematics classroom*. East Lansing: College of Education, Michigan State University, National Center for Research on Teaching and Learning.

Cobb, P., Wood, T., & Yackel, E. (1990). Classrooms as learning environments for teachers and researchers. In R. B. Davis, C. A. Maher, & N. Noddings (Eds.), *Constructivist views on the teaching and learning of mathematics. Journal for Research in Mathematics Education Monograph #4*. (pp. 125–146). Reston, VA: National Council of Teachers of Mathematics.

Cobb, P., Wood, T., & Yackel, E. (1993). Discourse, mathematical thinking, and classroom practice. In E. A. Forman, N. Minick, & C. A. Stone (Eds.), *Contexts for learning* (pp. 91–119). New York: Oxford University Press.

Cobb, P., & Yackel, E.(1995). Constructivist, emergent, and sociocultural perspectives in the context of development research. In D. T. Owens, M. K. Reed, & G. M. Millsaps. (Eds.), *Proceedings of the seventeenth annual meeting of the North American Chapter of the International Group for the Psychology of Mathematics Education. vol. 1.* (pp. 3–29). Columbus, OH: Eric Clearinghouse for Science, Mathematics, and Environmental Education.

Cobb, P., Yackel, E., & Wood, T. (1992). A constructivist alternative to the representational view of mind in mathematics education. *Journal for Research in Mathematics Education, 23*(1), 2–33.

Cohen, D. K., & Ball, D. L. (1990). Relations between policy and practice: A commentary. In D. K. Cohen, P. L. Peterson, S. Wilson, D. L. Ball, R. Putnam, R. Prawat, R. Heaton, J. Remillard, & N. Weimers (Eds.), *Effects of state-level reform of elementary school mathematics curriculum on classroom practice* (Research Report 90-14). East Lansing: College of Education, Michigan State University, National Center for Research on Teacher Learning and the Center for Learning and Teaching of Elementary Subjects.

Cole, M. (1985). The zone of proximal development: Where culture and cognition create each other. In J. V. Wertsch (Ed.). *Culture, communication and cognition: Vygotskian perspectives* (pp. 146–161). New York: Cambridge University Press.

Cole, M., & Scribner, S. (1978). Introduction. In L. S. Vygotsky, *Mind in society: The development of higher psychological processes* (pp. 1–14). Cambridge, MA: Harvard University Press.

Cooney, T. (1993). On the notion of authority applied to teacher education. In J. R. Becker & B. J. Pence (Eds.), *Proceedings of the fifteenth annual meeting of the North American chapter of the International Group for the Psychology of Mathematics Education. Vol. 1* (pp. 40– 46). San Jose, CA: San Jose State University.

deRibaupierre, A. (Ed.). (1989). *Transition mechanisms in child development: The longitudinal perspective.* New York: Cambridge University Press.

Dweck, C. S., & Leggett, E. L. (1988). A social-cognitive approach to motivation and personality. *Psychological Review, 95*(2), 256–73.

Erikson, E. H. (1950). *Childhood and society.* New York: Norton.

Escalona, S. K. (1968). *The roots of individuality: Normal patterns of development in infancy.* Chicago: Aldine.

Even, R., & Lappan, G. (1994). Constructing meaningful understanding of mathematics content. In D. Aichele & A. Coxford (Eds.), *Professional development for teachers of mathematics: 1994 NCTM Yearbook* (pp. 128–143). Reston, VA: National Council of Teachers of Mathematics.

Fennema, E., Carpenter, T. P., Franke, M. L., Levi, L., Jacobs, V. R., & Empson, S. B. (1996). A longitudinal study of learning to use children's thinking in mathematics instruction. *Journal for Research in Mathematics Education, 27*(4), 403–434.

Fennema, E., Carpenter, T., & Peterson, P. L. (1989). Learning mathematics for understanding: Cognitively Guided Instruction. In J. Brophy (Ed.), *Advances in research on teaching* (Vol. 1; pp. 195–217). Greenwich, CT: JAI.

Fischer, K. W. (1980). A theory of cognitive development: The control and construction of hierarchies of skills. *Psychological Review, 87,* 477–531.

Fischer, K. W., & Lamborn, S. D. (1989). Mechanisms of variation in developmental levels: Cognitive and emotional transitions during adolescence. In A. deRibaupierre (Ed.), *Transition mechanisms in child development: The longitudinal perspective* (pp. 33–67). New York: Cambridge University Press.

Gagnon, A. (1993). *Struggling.* Unpublished manuscript.

Goldsmith, L. T., & Davenport, L. R. (1995). Affective issues in developing mathematics practice. In B. S. Nelson (Ed.), *Inquiry and the development of teaching: Issues in the transformation of mathematics teaching* (pp. 27–36). Newton, MA: Center for the Development of Teaching, Education Development Center.

Goldsmith, L. T., & Sassi, A. M. (1996, April). *Teachers in transition: Describing the terrain for developing mathematics teaching.* Paper presented at the annual meeting of the American Educational Research Association, New York.

Gruber, H. E. (1985). Divergence in evolution and individuality in development. In G. Butterworth, J. Rutkowska, & M. Scaife (Eds.), *Evolution and developmental psychology* (pp. 133–147). New York: St. Martin's.

Hall, G. E., & Loucks, S .F. (1978). Teacher concerns as a basis for facilitating and personalizing staff development. *Teachers College Record, 80*(1), 36–53.

Hall, G. E., Loucks, S. F., Rutherford, W. L., & Newlove, B. W. (1975). *Levels of use of the innovation: A framework for analyzing innovation adoption.* Austin, TX: The Research and Development Center for Teacher Education.

Hammerman, J. K. (1995a). Teacher inquiry groups: Collaborative explorations of changing practice. In B. S. Nelson (Ed.), *Inquiry and the development of teaching: Issues in the transformation of mathematics teaching* (pp. 47–56). Newton, MA: Center for the Development of Teaching, Education Development Center.

Hammerman, J. K. (1995b). Creating a culture of intellectual inquiry in teacher inquiry groups. In D. T. Owens, N. K. Reed, & G. M. Millsaps (Eds.), *Proceedings of the seventeenth annual meeting of the North American chapter of the International Group for the Psychology of Mathematics Education* (Vol 2; pp. 268–274). Columbus: The Ohio State University.

Hart, L. (1992, April). *Looking for evidence of teacher change in the Atlanta Math Project: Waiting for Godot?* Paper presented at the SIG/RME Research Pre-session of the annual meeting of the National Council for Teachers of Mathematics, Nashville, TN.

John-Steiner, V., & Souberman, E. (1978). Afterword. In L. S. Vygotsky, *Mind in society: The development of higher psychological processes* (pp. 121–33). Cambridge, MA: Harvard University Press.

Karmiloff-Smith, A. (1992). *Beyond modularity.* Cambridge, MA: MIT Press.

Knapp, N. F, & Peterson, P. L. (1995). Teachers' interpretations of "CGI" after four years: Meanings and practices. *Journal for Research in Mathematics Education, 26*(1), 40–65.

Langer, J. (1969). *Theories of development.* New York: Holt, Rinehart, & Winston.

Lave, J. (1988). *Cognition in practice: Mind, mathematics, and culture in everyday life.* New York: Cambridge University Press.

Lipinski, M. (1992). *Looking at math with stars in my eyes.* Unpublished manuscrpit.

Luria, A. R. (1976). *Cognitive development: Its cultural and social foundations.* Cambridge, MA: Harvard University Press.

Maher, C. A., & Alston, A. (1990). Teacher development in mathematics in a constructivist framework. In R. B. Davis, C. A. Maher, & N. Noddings (Eds.), *Constructivist views on the teaching and learning of mathematics. Journal for Research in Mathematics Education Monograph #4* (pp.147–166). Reston, VA: National Council of Teachers of Mathematics.

Mathematical Association of America. (1991). *A call for change: Recommendations for the mathematical preparation of teachers.* Washington, D.C.: Author.

Mathematical Sciences Educational Board. (1989). *Everybody counts.* Washington, D.C.: National Academy Press.

Mathematical Sciences Educational Board. (1990). *Reshaping school mathematics: A philosophy and framework for curriculum.* Washington, D.C.: National Academy Press.

National Council of Teachers of Mathematics. (1989). *Curriculum and evaluation standards for school mathematics.* Reston, VA: Author.

National Council of Teachers of Mathematics. (1991). *Professional standards for teaching mathematics.* Reston, VA: Author.

National Council of Teachers of Mathematics. (1995). *Assessment standards*. Reston, VA: Author.

Nelson, B. S., & Hammerman, J. H. (1996). Reconceptualizing teaching: Moving toward the creation of intellectual communities of students, teachers, and teacher educators. In M. W. McLaughlin & I. Oberman (Eds.), *Teacher learning: New policies, new practices*. (pp. 3–21). New York: Teacher's College Press.

Nelson, B. S. (1995). Introduction. In B. S. Nelson (Ed.), *Inquiry and the development of teaching: Issues in the transformation of mathematics teaching* (pp. 1–8). Newton, MA: Education Development Center, Center for the Development of Teaching.

O'Brien, D. C. (1995). *One doesn't always equal one*. Unpublished manuscript.

Piaget, J. (1970). Piaget's theory. In P. Mussen (Ed.), *Carmichael's handbook of child psychology*. New York: Wiley.

Rogoff, B. (1990). *Apprenticeship in thinking: Cognitive development in social context*. Oxford, England: Oxford University Press.

Schifter, D. (1993). Mathematics process as mathematics content: A course for teachers. *Journal of Mathematical Behavior, 12*(3), 271–83.

Schifter, D. (1995). *Enacted conceptions of mathematics*. Paper submitted for publication.

Schifter, D. (Ed.). (1996a). *What's happening in math class? Volume 1: Envisioning new practices through narrative*. New York: Teachers College Press.

Schifter, D. (Ed.). (1996b). *What's happening in math class? Volume 2: Reconstructing professional identities*. New York: Teachers College Press.

Schifter, D., & Bastable, V. (1995, April). *From the teachers' seminar to the classroom: The relationship between doing and teaching mathematics, an example from fractions*. Paper presented at the annual meeting of the American Educational Research Association. San Francisco, CA.

Schifter, D., & Fosnot, C. T. (1993). *Reconstructing mathematics education: Stories of teachers meeting the challenge of reform*. New York: Teachers College Press.

Schifter, D., & Simon, M. (1992). Assessing teachers' development of a constructivist view of mathematics learning. *Teaching and Teacher Education, 8*(2), 187–197.

Schifter, D., Russell, S. J., & Bastable, V. (in press). Teaching to the big ideas. In M. Solomon (Ed.), *Reinventing the classroom*. New York: Teachers College Press.

Schram, P., Wilcox, S., Lappan, G., & Lanier, P. (1989). Changing preservice beliefs about mathematics education. In C. A. Maher, G. A. Goldin, & R. B. Davis (Eds.), *Proceedings of the eleventh annual meeting of the North American chapter of the International Group for the Psychology of Mathematics Education* (pp. 296–302). New Brunswick, NJ: Rutgers University, Center for Mathematics, Science, and Computer Education.

Seyferth, L. (1994). *Second graders and their teacher grapple with double digit computation*. Unpublished manuscript.

Shapiro, E. K., & Weber, E. (Eds.). (1981). *Cognitive and affective growth: Developmental interaction*. Hillsdale, NJ: Lawrence Erlbaum Associates.

Siegel, A. W., Bisanz, J., & Bisanz, G. L. (1983). Developmental analysis: A strategy for the study of psychological change. In D. Kuhn & J. Meacham (Eds.), *On the development of developmental psychology* (pp. 53–80). Basel, Switzerland: Karger.

Simon, M. A. (1995). Reconstructing mathematics pedagogy from a constructivist perspective. *Journal for Research in Mathematics Education, 26*(2), 114–145.

Strauss, S. (Ed.). (1982). *U-shaped behavioral growth*. New York: Academic Press.

Thompson, A. G. (1991). The development of teachers' conceptions of mathematics teaching. In R. G. Underhill (Ed.), *Proceedings of the thirteenth annual meeting of the North American Chapter of the International Group for the Psychology of Mathematics Education*. (Vol. 2; pp. 8–14). Blacksburgh, VA: Virginia Polytechnic Institute.

Vygotsky, L. (1978). *Mind in society: The development of higher psychological processes*. Cambridge, MA: Harvard University Press.

Werner, H. (1948). *Comparative psychology of mental development.* New York: International Universities Press.

Wertsch, J. V. (1985a). *Vygotsky and the social formation of mind.* Cambridge, MA: Harvard University Press.

Wertsch, J. V. (Ed.). (1985b). *Culture, communication and cognition: Vygotskian perspectives.* New York: Cambridge University Press.

White, R. W. (1959). Motivation reconsidered: The concept of competence. *Psychological Review, 66,* 297–333.

Wood, T. (1995). From alternative epistemologies to practice in education: Rethinking what it means to teach and learn. In L. P. Steffe & J. Gale (Eds.), *Constructivism in education* (pp. 331–339). Hillsdale, NJ: Lawrence Erlbaum Associates.

3

Developing New Models of Mathematics Teaching: An Imperative for Research on Mathematics Teacher Development

Martin A. Simon
The Pennsylvania State University

The National Council of Teachers of Mathematics' (NCTM) *Curriculum and Evaluation Standards for School Mathematics* (1989) heralded a national mathematics education reform effort. The success of this mathematics education reform is dependent on the development of teachers to prepare them to carry out the reform agenda. (I use *development* to include not only the learning of concepts, skills, and information, but also the development of dispositions, awareness, and sensitivities.) Critical to the success of teacher development efforts is the generation of a research base on the development of teachers, development that is in line with the goals of the mathematics education reform. The reform has its roots in constructivist views of knowledge development and two decades of research on students' mathematical thinking. In this chapter, I argue that the articulation of new models of mathematics teaching, which build on these theoretical and empirical contributions, is essential for research in mathematics teacher development. I identify recent contributions to the generation of such models, discuss my own emerging model of teaching, and use it as an example of how a model of teaching might contribute to research on teacher development.

The term *model of teaching* allows me to focus on an underdeveloped aspect of a greater whole, an integrated model of mathematics teaching and learning. Jan de Lange (1995) argued articulately that the ultimate aim is not a theory of teaching that is independent of a theory of learning,

55

but rather an integrated theory that encompasses mathematics, learning, teaching, curriculum, and the functioning of classrooms. An integrated model would have two important characteristics, a compatibility between perspectives on teaching and learning, and an interdependence between these perspectives. By interdependence, I mean that as one develops, it influences the other. This contrasts with a static view of learning that influences the view of teaching, but not vice versa.

In this chapter, I am concerned with models of teaching in two different, but related, contexts. The first is teachers' personal models of teaching. These models are evolving sets of images, beliefs, concepts, and modes of action that comprise what it means to be a (mathematics) teacher. Some aspects of teachers' models are conscious, whereas other aspects may not be. Teachers' own models of teaching identify as well as restrict possibilities for the teachers' actions. (Here *action* includes not only physical action, but also thought and communication.) The teachers' models are not independent of the situations in which teachers find themselves. Rather these models are constrained by the teachers' participation in relevant communities, for example, the classroom and school communities. Teachers, as part of these communities, are engaged in ongoing negotiation of what it means to be a teacher. This view of the interdependence of the evolving knowledge of the individual and the knowledge and practices of the social group is based on the emergent perspective articulated by Cobb and his colleagues (Cobb, 1989; Cobb & Yackel, in press) and discussed later in this chapter.

The second context in which I am concerned with models of teaching is research on teacher development, where models of teaching constitute a key piece of the conceptual framework that guides the research. In this context, models of teaching contain the same components as teachers' personal models of teaching. However, as part of conceptual frameworks, these models are conscious, articulated, and evolving. They are generally taken as shared by a research team, and are constrained and guided by the researchers' participation in the mathematics education research community.

EVOLVING VIEWS OF TEACHING AND LEARNING

I begin with a description of why new models of teaching are necessary, which includes a look at changing views of mathematics learning and their potential impact on models of teaching. I consider not only researchers' models, but also teacher educators' models of teaching, because research on teacher development can involve the researcher as teacher educator (Simon, in press; cf. Simon & Blume, 1994).

Traditional school mathematics teaching is based on a lecture–demonstration model in which teaching is predominantly telling and showing. If we want someone to know what we know, we tell them and/or show them. Unsuccessful teaching tends to be remediated by repeating the curriculum content, breaking the communication into smaller parts, and finding different ways to express the idea to be grasped. The role of the teacher in this process is clear. However, the model of learning on which traditional teaching is based is not explicit. Many teachers have developed their models of teaching in the context of thousands of hours as students in traditional classrooms. Their personal models derive from what they view as appropriate and effective teaching based on their observations of teachers in classrooms, not on explicit models of learning: "As a consequence, learning to student (verb) necessarily involves learning about teaching (expectations, values, suppositions, assumptions, etc.) in particular situations. I would argue that what is learned is a way of acting and construing within the institutional setting of the classroom" (Cobb, personal communication).

Constructivism: A New Paradigm

The observer can infer a model of learning implicit in traditional teaching, one of filling up the learner with knowledge, what Freire (1971, cited in Belenky, Clinchy, Goldberger, & Tarule, 1986) called the "banking" perspective. In recent years, a substantial body of theoretical and empirical work has led a significant segment of the mathematics education community to question this view of learning and to shed it in favor of a view of learners as active constructors/organizers of their own learning.

Constructivism represents a change in perspective on what knowledge is and how knowledge is developed. According to von Glasersfeld (1989), "This view differs from the old one in that it deliberately discards the notion that knowledge could or should be a representation of an observer-independent world-in-itself and replaces it with the demand that the conceptual constructs we call knowledge be *viable* in the experiential world of the knowing subject" (p.122).

From a constructivist perspective, knowledge is not passively received from the world, from others, or from authoritative sources. Rather, all knowledge is created as individuals (and groups) adapt to and make sense of their experiential worlds (von Glasersfeld & Steffe, 1991). In explicating the ideas of the eighteenth-century philosopher, Vico, von Glasersfeld (1989) wrote, "The human knower can only know what the human knower has constructed" (p. 123). *Knowledge*, therefore, "refers to conceptual structures that epistemic agents, given the range of present experience within their tradition of thought and language, consider viable" (p. 124).

Applying these ideas to mathematical knowledge, mathematics is viewed as an ongoing creation of human minds, not an aspect of the external world waiting to be discovered. Whereas the history of mathematics represents the collective constructions of mathematicians, each individual learner of mathematics is engaged in making sense of his or her own experiential world. Von Glasersfeld emphasizes, "It is this *construction* of the individual's subjective reality which...should be of interest to practitioners and researchers in education" (p. 139).

According to Piaget (1977), the learner's construction of knowledge is a self–regulating process. Individuals' cognitive schemes allow them to establish an orderliness and predictability in their experiential worlds. When experience does not fit with the individual's schemes, a cognitive disequilibrium results, which triggers the learning process. This disequilibrium leads to adaptation. Reflection on successful adaptive operations (reflective abstraction) leads to new or modified concepts (accommodation), contributing to re-equilibration.

Constructivism and Pedagogy

Constructivism has given us a fundamentally different way to think about knowledge and its development. It has redefined our perception of the human learner and offered us a framework for understanding the complex processes of learning. These changes in our concepts of mathematical knowledge, learner, and learning lead us to question the adequacy of traditional models of teaching.

Constructivism, as a general theory, is used to explain knowledge development in diverse situations (including teacherless situations). Mathematics teaching in schools is a particular situation in which *intentional interventions* are made to promote the construction of powerful mathematical ideas. These intentional interventions can be labeled "pedagogy" and include the actions of teachers as well as the design of curriculum. However, constructivism does not describe the role of (nor the potential role of) pedagogy in knowledge development. Although it provides an orienting perspective, it does not define a particular teaching practice. Thus, mathematics educators are faced with the challenge of developing new models of teaching that are consistent with constructivist perspectives.

The Need for New Models of Mathematics Teaching

The key question is, Assuming that constructivism provides a viable theory of knowledge development, how do we best assist learners to construct powerful mathematical ideas? My search for answers to this question stems from the following reasoning:

1. We need an alternative to the lecture–demonstration model of teaching. Lecture and demonstration can be useful as *tools*. As with any tools, however, they should be used only when their use is indicated.

Constructivism makes us skeptical about trusting that students' constructions will be similar to what we tell them. Constructivism makes us aware that learners build new knowledge on the basis of previous knowledge, and that each student brings to any situation a unique web of knowledge. Therefore, individual students will make different sense of the same message. Furthermore, there seems to be an inherent inadequacy in telling every student the same thing.

Our ability to understand students' current knowledge and thinking is (and likely will always be) limited at best. Therefore, a model of teaching that requires the teacher to provide each student with what he or she needs at each point in time cannot succeed.

2. We need to develop approaches to instruction that harness the students' inherent ability to learn and to self–regulate. Before students attend school, they develop complex knowledge and skills without formal instruction. The best example of this is learning to speak, an example of the inborn self–regulatory mechanisms of individual children in the context of their participation in a community of practice, a community in which effective participation involves proficiency with the language. The role of pedagogy is to increase the depth and scope of what can be learned and the efficiency with which it is learned. Effective pedagogy requires first understanding how humans learn in the absence of formal instruction, as a foundation for developing effective instruction. Traditional teaching does not make adequate use of the learning potential of the individual (or of groups).

3. Leaving students alone or asking them what they want to learn is a naive application of constructivism and is inadequate to guide mathematics teaching. Left alone, students will not reconstruct the major advances in the history of mathematics:

> The suggestion that students can be left to their own devices to construct the mathematical ways of knowing compatible with those of wider society is a contradiction in terms. A teacher who actually took this caricature of constructivism seriously would be abrogating his or her obligations to students, to the school as a social institution, and to the wider society. (Cobb, Yackel, & Wood, 1992a, p. 27)

Rather, we must develop approaches to teaching that increase the likelihood that students will construct powerful mathematical ideas. These approaches must be informed by careful study of students' mathematical concepts and how these concepts develop.

Although many teachers have not explored constructivist theory deeply, there is a growing commitment to teaching in ways that are more responsive to a view of learning as an active process. Some teachers are telling and showing less, questioning more, and giving answers less in an effort to nurture students' abilities to come to their own answers. Collaborative small groups and the use of hands–on materials are also seen as ways of supporting students' active learning. The problem, however, is that these modifications do not constitute an intentional approach to helping students develop new concepts. Whereas the traditional approach to teaching a new idea is clear, the approach to replace it is not at all clear. Of what might this reconceptualization of mathematics teaching consist? In what ways might a teacher interact with students to foster their construction of increasingly powerful mathematical ideas?

In recent years, these questions have remained relatively unexplored. Many mathematics educators and teacher educators have focused on teaching strategies (e.g., collaborative groups, manipulatives) without engaging in reexamining the underpinnings of teaching, the bases for choosing particular strategies. Many have begun to talk about "constructivist teaching." This vocabulary has contributed to confusion about constructivism, implying that constructivism prescribes a particular model of teaching, thus obscuring the need to generate new models (Simon, 1995a, 1995b). Although constructivism can serve as a strong foundation for new models of teaching, it does not determine or prescribe such models. (The notion of constructivism as a foundation is not meant to suggest that constructivism is static, rather that constructivism and models of learning mutually influence each other.) Consider the following analogy. Although the foundation of a house supports and constrains the above–ground structure, a wide range of houses can be built on any given foundation. A builder who attempts to build a house based solely on the constraints of the foundation is unwise. An architectural drawing that specifies a particular way of meeting the future residents' space demands is necessary. Likewise, it is ineffective to proceed with teaching, teacher education, and research on teacher development with only the foundation of constructivism, without particular models of teaching that outline particular approaches to fostering learning.

So far I have argued that new models of teaching are necessary but lacking and have identified my assumption that teachers are guided and constrained by their personal models of teaching. Let us now examine the relevance of new models of mathematics teaching to teacher education and research on teacher development.

Models of Teaching in Mathematics Teacher Education. Because a necessary component of some research on teacher development is the creation of effective contexts for teacher development, it is important to articulate the function of models of teaching in mathematics teacher education.

1. Teacher educators need to be successful teachers of mathematics who confront the challenges of mathematics teaching. It is not enough for teacher educators to learn about mathematics teaching; they must themselves engage in the ongoing struggle of developing a successful mathematics teaching practice. In this way, they are not only developing their own conceptions of practice, but are participating in a community of mathematics educators who are engaged in developing more effective ways to promote students' mathematical learning. (Some of the teaching of mathematics might be done in the context of teaching mathematics to teachers in mathematics education courses.) Teacher educators cannot effectively teach someone else to teach mathematics if they cannot teach mathematics themselves. Being able to teach mathematics presupposes some experience in doing so, struggling with the inherent challenges that teaching presents.

2. Teacher education includes teaching mathematics to teachers. All faculty who teach mathematics to teachers are teacher educators because of the significant impact that they have, directly on the teachers' knowledge of and about mathematics, and indirectly on their conceptions of how mathematics is learned and taught. Even those who teach only mathematics education courses need to be able to teach mathematics lessons as part of their courses. (See Simon, 1994 for a model of teacher education that builds on mathematics learning opportunities for teachers.)

3. The teacher educator's model of mathematics teaching contributes to defining the goals of mathematics teacher education. A mathematics teacher educator without a model of teaching is in a situation analogous to a mathematics teacher without a clear vision of what mathematics is about. Without a clear vision of the role of the teacher in promoting mathematical learning, mathematics teacher education is a smorgasbord, a mix of that which is thought to be helpful. However, key elements of teacher development and key connections between those elements may be overlooked without an explicit (and evolving) model of mathematics teaching to guide the curricular and instructional decisions of teacher education.

4. Teacher educators engage in fostering teachers' development of new and personally meaningful models of mathematics teaching. Although the goal is not to infuse the teachers with the teacher educator's model, the teacher educator's model guides his or her decisions on how to assist the teachers in developing useful models. Teacher educators who attempt to foster such models without having a model themselves are in a similar situation to teachers who try to teach the concept of ratio without understanding it.

5. New models of mathematics teacher education can serve as templates for new models of mathematics-teacher education. Mathematics teacher education is a complex endeavor, the goal of which is the

confident and competent functioning of its students in an area of challenging conceptual issues and constant non routine problem solving (i.e., mathematics teaching). As such, mathematics teacher education has similar (although more complex) demands to those of mathematics teaching. New models of mathematics teaching can provide a template for new models of teaching teachers to teach mathematics.

Models of Teaching in Research on Mathematics Teacher Development. M o d e l s of teaching are an essential component of conceptual frameworks for research on teacher development:

> A conceptual framework is an argument that the concepts chosen for investigation or interpretation, and any anticipated relationships among them, will be appropriate and useful, given the research problem under investigation....conceptual frameworks are based on previous research and literature ...an array of current and possibly far–ranging sources. The framework may be based on different theories *and* various aspects of practitioner knowledge, depending on exactly what the researcher thinks (and can argue) will be relevant to and important to address about a research problem, at a given point in time and given the state–of–the–art regarding the research problem. (Eisenhart, 1991, p. 209)

Quality research on mathematics teacher development requires researchers to identify appropriate conceptual frameworks; models of teaching are a key component of these conceptual frameworks. A fundamental problem in the study of mathematics teaching and mathematics teacher development is figuring out what to look at. When one studies teachers' actions, knowledge, abilities, and the processes of their professional development, there are infinite possibilities on which to focus; all are not equally useful. Choosing among the possibilities is the result of either an explicit conceptual framework or a tacit set of beliefs and concepts. In this sense, no research is free of a conceptual lens, the concepts that determine what a researcher attends to and sees.

Models of teaching are essential components of conceptual frameworks for research on mathematics teacher development. The researcher's model of teaching, whether implicit or explicit, defines what counts as teacher development in the research. Studying development requires identifying those aspects of teacher change that are of interest, (i.e., relevant to the model of teaching).

CONTRIBUTIONS TO NEW MODELS OF TEACHING

Some important work has been done in recent years with respect to identifying the roles of mathematics teachers and describing the nature of "pedagogical deliberations" (Ball, 1993a). *Professional Standards for*

School Mathematics (NCTM, 1991) provided a broad foundation by identifying teachers' responsibilities in four areas:

- Setting goals and selecting or creating mathematical *tasks* to help students achieve these goals;
- Stimulating and managing classroom *discourse* so that both the students and the teacher are clearer about what is being learned;
- Creating a classroom *environment* to support teaching and learning mathematics;
- *Analyzing* student learning, the mathematical tasks, and the environment in order to make ongoing instructional decisions. (p. 5)

Cobb, Yackel, and Wood (1993), building on the notion of the classroom as a developing mathematics community, pointed out that the teacher's actions are in service of two broad social goals: to facilitate the development of shared mathematical knowledge, and to participate in and guide the conscious development of classroom norms and practices. Regarding the first goal, classroom mathematical conversations facilitated by the teacher result in taken–as–shared mathematical knowledge. The second goal is served by a second type of conversation that focuses on what constitutes appropriate and effective mathematical activity in the classroom. Brousseau (1981), on the other hand, suggested that the establishment of the *contrat didactique* (didactical contract), which comprises norms, practices, and roles of teacher and students, is largely an implicit process. The nature of classroom mathematical activity and the interactions among classroom community members result in implicit agreements, expectations, and understandings that define the *contrat*. These two perspectives may highlight two aspects of the same phenomenon. Brousseau oriented us to the importance of classroom activity for establishing classroom norms, whereas Cobb, Wood, and Yackel's investigations demonstrated the power of teacher–managed discussion of classroom activity, and pointed to the potential of teachers using this power in conscious ways. This last point is probably particularly important when the teacher is trying to establish a "mathematics tradition" (Cobb, Wood, Yackel, & McNeal, 1992) different from the one with which the students are familiar, a frequent occurrence in this era of reform.

Brousseau's (1983, 1987) theory of situations provides a framework for thinking about the teacher's role in planning for and guiding mathematical activity. The first step involves identifying a mathematical idea that can be learned by the students. Next, the idea is embedded in a problem context for student exploration, *situation a–didactique*. Such a context should be meaningful to the students, allowing them to solve problems using their knowledge of that context and their prior mathematical knowledge. The solution of the problem might be a specific instantiation of the idea to be learned. Tzur's (1995) "task–oriented approach" seems consistent with Brousseau's *situation a–didactique*.

Ball (1993b) discussed how teachers create contexts for students to explore mathematical ideas. She identified three responsibilities of teachers related to "representations" of mathematical content:

> To probe and analyze the content so that they can select and use representations that illuminate critical dimensions of that content for their students. Threaded throughout must be thoughtful consideration of students' current ideas and interests. A teacher must also figure out how to support and use the representational contexts that students construct. And teachers need alternative models[1] to compensate for the imperfections and distortions in any given representation. (p. 384)

Engaging the students in appropriate problem contexts (*situations a–didactiques*) is not sufficient for learning. Brousseau indicated that situations must be created for the decontextualizing, generalizing, and abstracting of ideas (*situations didactiques*) beyond the narrow context of the original problem situation. Balacheff (1990) noted that "The teaching process should allow for this shift of pupils' interest from being practitioners to becoming theoreticians" (p. 264). Lampert (1990) chose her problems with this goal in mind:

> The most important criterion in picking a problem was that it be the sort of problem that would have the capacity to engage all of the students in the class in making and testing mathematical hypotheses. These hypotheses are imbedded in the answers students give to the problem, and so comparing answers engaged the class in a discussion of the relative mathematical merits of various hypotheses, setting the stage for the kind of zigzag between inductive observation and deductive generalization that Lakatos and Polya see as characteristic of mathematical activity. (p. 39)

Following the *situations didactiques*, the teacher endeavors to create "situations for institutionalization" (Brousseau, 1987; Douady, 1985) in which ideas constructed or modified during problem solving attain the status of knowledge in the classroom community. This is consistent with Cobb, Yackel, and Wood's (1993) notion of mathematical knowledge as knowledge that is taken as shared by the classroom community.

Pedagogical thinking, such as that displayed by Lampert, is built on knowledge of mathematics, of students, and of the ways in which students learn mathematics. According to Ball (1993a), teachers must have a "bifocal perspective—perceiving the mathematics through the mind of the learner while perceiving the mind of the learner through the mathematics" (p. 159). This reflects the two "imperatives of respon-

---

[1]Ball uses "models" to refer to mathematical representations, not to models of teaching.

siveness and responsibility" (Ball, 1993b, p. 374). The former is a sensitivity to the students' thinking, knowledge, and interests, the latter to the teachers' obligation to carry out the curricular expectations of the school district and to teach consistent with their own sense of the "ideas and traditions growing out of centuries of mathematical exploration and invention" (p. 375).

Steffe and Tzur (1994) and Steffe (1991) stressed that the teachers' plans must be based on the mathematics *of* students. Steffe and Wiegel (1992) noted, "The most basic responsibility of constructivist teachers[2] is to learn the mathematical knowledge of their students and how to harmonize their teaching methods with the nature of that mathematical knowledge" (p. 17). For Steffe and D'Ambrosio (1995), the goal of such inquiry was teachers' development of evolving models of their students' mathematical understanding. Ball (1993a) underscored the investigative theme, "Teaching is essentially an ongoing inquiry into content and learners and into ways that contexts can be structured to facilitate the development of learners' understandings" (p. 166).

Ball and Chazan (1995) characterized their view of teaching as creating and maintaining a climate of "intellectual ferment" in which problematic issues are raised, diverse ideas are valued, and disagreements are managed. Such a climate is seen as generative for learning, as students struggle to make sense of and evaluate diverse viewpoints and construct arguments to convince themselves and their peers. It is also consistent with Ball's (1993b) commitment (in her role as teacher) to represent the discipline of mathematics in "intellectually honest" ways. Lampert (1992) pointed out that it is not just the concepts and procedures of mathematics that must be learned, but also where mathematical knowledge comes from and what makes it true. She advocated classrooms in which students learn about mathematical activity by engaging in it. She saw the teacher as an "ambassador" between the mathematical world of the classroom and the mathematical world of the wider culture.

Dutch mathematics education researchers have been engaged for more than two decades in the ongoing development and application of an integrated model of mathematics learning and teaching that they call Realistic Mathematics Education (RME; Streefland, 1991; Treffers, 1987). RME, which focuses on the design of curriculum, is based on a view of learning mathematics as "proceeding from one's own informal mathematical constructions to what could be accepted as formal mathematics" (Streefland, 1990, p. 1). The RME pedagogy promotes such mathematical development through "guided reinvention" (Freudenthal, 1991), a process that is shaped by five teaching/learning principles:

---

[2]Steffe did not eschew the term "constructivist teacher." However, his views are compatible with those expressed in this chapter (cf. Steffe & D'Ambrosio, 1995).

1. Constructions stimulated by concreteness [similar to Brousseau's *situations a–didactiques*].
2. Developing mathematical tools to move from concreteness to abstraction.
3. Stimulating free productions and reflection.
4. Stimulating the social activity of learning by interaction.
5. Intertwining learning strands in order to get mathematical material structured [for students to develop a connected knowledge of related ideas and operations] (Streefland, 1990, p. 4)

I amplify the second and third of these principles because they illustrate the unique contribution made by RME.

Developing Mathematical Tools to Move from Concreteness to Abstraction

Perhaps the most unique aspect of the RME pedagogical approach is its use of mathematical tools. Using a cyclical developmental research methodology, RME researchers analyze and identify spontaneous, informal strategies generated by mathematics students. Based on these informal strategies, researchers develop particular tools (often representational systems) designed to serve as models for the students to represent their thinking. Gravemeijer (1995) referred to this approach to developing models as "bottom–up" because the models are based on students' strategies (albeit with an eye on an abstract goal), rather than built to embody the abstract or algorithmic structure as in base–ten blocks. By capturing key aspects of the mathematical structure of the students' strategies, these models—for example, the empty number line (Gravemeijer, 1994) and the arithmetic rack (Gravemeijer, 1995)—provide an opportunity for students to reflect on that structure, affording an increase in level of abstraction.

Stimulating Free Productions and Reflection

Although reflection was highlighted in the last section, the role of students' free productions merits further comment. Free productions are student–invented strategies. They are encouraged both at the initial level, as responses to the original context problem, and at the next level, working with tools that have been provided. Although the use of the tools constrains students' productions, there is still room for independent thinking within those constraints.

AN EMERGING MODEL
OF MATHEMATICS TEACHING

The emerging model of mathematics teaching discussed here builds particularly on the work cited earlier, and has taken shape in the context of two major research projects on mathematics teacher education (Simon & Blume, 1994; Simon & Schifter, 1991). A discussion of the empirical basis for aspects of this model can be found in Simon (1995a). That discussion also demonstrates how empirical work can be used to develop models of teaching.

The emerging model discussed here responds to the challenge referred to earlier: If we give up telling and showing as the primary model of teaching, how do we enable students to learn mathematics that they do not know? The model described in this section builds directly on the emergent perspective on knowledge development (Cobb & Yackel, in press). After a brief description of this perspective, I highlight particular aspects of cognitive and social perspectives on learning, that have guided the development of this model and the principles of teaching that derive from them, and then present the Mathematics Teaching Cycle, which describes the interaction among different functions of the role of the teacher.

The Emergent Perspective

The emergent perspective on mathematical knowledge development, articulated by Cobb and his colleagues (Cobb, 1989; Cobb & Yackel, in press), combines a constructivist psychological perspective with an interactionist social perspective (Bauersfeld, Krummheuer, & Voigt, 1988). According to the emergent perspective, learning is both an individual constructive process and a social process in which learners are members of communities that develop taken–as–shared knowledge, norms, and practices in line with their purposes. Cobb (in press) described the application of this perspective to the mathematics classroom:

> The basic relation posited between students' constructive activities and the classroom social processes in which they participate is one of reflexivity in which neither is given preeminence over the other. In this view, the students are considered to contribute to the evolving classroom mathematical practices as they reorganize their individual mathematical activities. Conversely, the ways in which they make these reorganizations are constrained by their participation in the evolving classroom practices. (p. 4)

Thus, the emergent perspective eschews debate over whether learning is primarily psychological or social. Rather it asserts the usefulness of coordinating the analyses that result from taking each perspective (psychological and social) as primary.

The Emergent Perspective in Relation to Teaching

If we give up *showing* and *telling* as the teacher's principal means for promoting students' mathematical development, what do we have to replace them? I suggest *posing problems* and *facilitating classroom discourse* as principal means for promoting mathematical development. In this section, I examine how cognitive and social theoretical frameworks can provide a foundation for the establishment of pedagogical frameworks that guide the use of these two aspects of teaching .

The Teacher's Role From a Cognitive View

Assimilation and accommodation.   Aspects of equilibration theory (Piaget, 1985) serve as a foundation for key aspects of my emerging model of teaching. (Note that how to make use of these aspects of learning theory for teaching is a contribution of the model of teaching and not inherent in the learning theory itself.) Piaget viewed cognitive growth as an equilibration process, a continual adaptation of cognitive structures to new experiences. Equilibrium is sought but never attained. The cycles of disequilibration/re–equilibration lead to greater knowledge (greater cognitive power). The equilibration process is often thought of as being made up of two processes, assimilation and accommodation. *Assimilation* is defined as "the incorporation of an external element, for example, an object or event, into a sensorimotor or conceptual scheme of the subject" (Piaget, 1985, p. 5). *Accommodation* is the modification of schemes in response to an object that does not fit with prior schemes. However, I propose a view of assimilation and accommodation that is not generally held, wherein they represent a single polarity. Piaget (Bringuier, 1980) explained that, "There is no assimilation without accommodation because the scheme of assimilation is general, and as soon as it's applied to a particular situation, it must be modified according to the particular circumstances of the situation....Actually adaptation is a whole whose two poles can't be dissociated. Assimilation and Accommodation" (pp. 42–44).

Thus, the act of assimilating a new object requires some degree of accommodation; the scheme is modified by incorporation of the object. The reverse argument can also be made. Accommodation, the development of a new or modified scheme, cannot happen in a vacuum. It always results from reorganizing and/or connecting preexisting schemes. Thus, accommodation is assimilation into evolving schemes; the set of relevant, available schemes defines the range of possible accommodations that can be made.

Assimilation and accommodation are part of the natural functioning of the organism, that is, part of the individual's adaptive mechanisms that unfold without instruction. However, in redefining the role of the teacher, we can explore the possibility of the teacher intentionally promoting and supporting these aspects of the equilibration process. Considering assimilation and accommodation as two poles of the same process, each pole invites a different perspective of the teacher as problem poser (or task designer). From the perspective of assimilation, the teacher focuses on what tasks might be undertaken successfully (but not trivially), given her model of the students' schemes. From the perspective of accommodation, the teacher focuses on what tasks might challenge the limitations of current schemes. Piaget (1985) asserted, "One sort of equilibration is that which occurs between assimilation of objects to schemes of action and accommodation of schemes of action to objects.... When assimilation and accommodation succeed, they form a whole, each aspect of which implies the other " (p. 7).

The teacher's challenge is to identify student tasks that result in an appropriate balance between assimilation and accommodation. The balance point is ever–changing as a result of a range of situational variables. This search for the appropriate balance point is illustrated in Example One.

Example One.   In a recent whole–class teaching experiment with pro- spective elementary teachers, I had as my goal that my students come to understand the multiplicative relationships in evaluating the area of a rectangle:

> Instruction in the first class began with a small [nonsquare] cardboard rectangle being given to each of the small groups of students seated at the classroom's six large rectangular tables. The problem was to determine how many rectangles of the size and shape [of the rectangle] that they were given could fit on the top surface of their tables. Rectangles could not be overlapped, could not be cut, and could not overlap the edges of the table. Students were instructed to be prepared to describe to the whole class how they solved this problem. (Simon & Blume, 1994, p. 477)

The students all chose to measure along the width and the length using the small rectangle (maintaining its orientation throughout) and to multiply the two resulting numbers. A lengthy discussion ensued as to why that was a reasonable way to solve the problem. This demand for justification invited conceptual connections between students' knowledge of multiplication and the counting of the rectangles. Once the students seemed to have made these connections, I (the teacher) demonstrated an alternative way to measure the table, in which the small rectangle was rotated 90° to measure the second side, thus measuring both length and width of the table with the same side of the small rectangle. The students were persuaded that my method of measuring would not be helpful in finding the number of rectangles that would fit on the table. I then asked the question, "Does the number obtained when I measure this way and multiply the two numbers have *any* meaning. Does it tell us anything about this particular table?" The students responded that my method of measuring would produce over-lapping rectangles and, therefore, the number that I obtained would be nonsense. (See Simon & Blume, 1994, for detailed analysis of the students' understandings.)

> I responded to the students' claims by trying to engender disequilibrium: Out in the hall I have two [rectangular] tables of different sizes. I used this method, where I measure across one way, turn the [rectangle], measure down the other way, and multiply. When I multiplied using [this] method, on table A I got 32 as my answer, and [when I measured] table B [using the same rectangle and the same method], I got 22. Now what I want to know is, [having used] the method of turning the rectangle, is table A bigger, is table B bigger, or don't you have enough information from my method to tell? (Simon & Blume, 1994, p. 480)

The students agreed that table A was larger than table B, because 32 is greater than 22. I then asked, "32 *what* and 22 *what*?" The students continued, however, to assert that the numbers obtained by this method were meaningless because of the overlapping of the rectangles. I had attempted to cause disequilibrium (to promote accommodation), yet those schemes of interest remained unshaken.

> In subsequent class sessions, I took a different approach. I posed the following problem: Problem 4: Two people work together to measure the size of a rectangular region. One measures the length and the other the width. They each use a stick to measure with; the sticks, however, are of different lengths. Louisa says, "The length is four of my sticks." Ruiz says, "The width is five of my sticks." What have they found out about the area of the rectangular region? (Simon & Blume, 1994, p. 487)

In this problem context, the students were able to identify the rectangular area units that were generated. After considerable discussion of this problem, I reposed the earlier task in a somewhat different manner:

> Problem 5: I used your rectangle and my method (rotating the rectangle) to measure two rectangular regions; one was 3 x 4 and the other was 5 x 2. Draw these regions (real size). Record all that you can determine about their areas. (Simon & Blume, 1994, p. 487)

This time half of the small groups were able to identify square units of area measure. Their descriptions of their thinking persuaded many of their classmates of the reasonableness of that solution.

Example One can be thought of as demonstrating the two aspects of the assimilation–accommodation polarity. My original attempts to promote a modification in the students' conceptions were too far toward the accommodation end of the polarity. The schemes to which the students were assimilating (c.f., Simon and Blume , 1994) did not allow them to reconsider what was being measured and what units were being generated. As I focused more on what they might be able to assimilate (with accommodation), a greater opportunity for conceptual change ensued. Their experience with the sticks problem seemed to result in relevant assimilatory schemes.

In this discussion, the focus has been on the teacher's role as problem poser to promote assimilation and accommodation on the part of students. The teacher's role in guiding classroom discourse, however, can also serve this function effectively. Verbalization of different ideas and solution strategies among the students often leads to opportunities for cognitive restructuring as students make sense of, validate, compare, and contrast these diverse contributions. Furthermore, teachers' spontaneous questions, such as "Will that always work?" or "How could you modify that conjecture to make it true?" contribute to cognitive restructuring and could be considered to exist in the overlap between problem posing and discourse facilitation.

Reflective Abstraction.   An important part of this cognitive restructuring or learning is reflective abstraction, reflection on successful adaptive operations. The teacher as problem poser can generate reflective tasks (Tzur, 1995), which focus on generalization and abstraction and organize classroom activity to promote and orient reflection. In the role of facilitator of discourse, he or she can pose questions that invite students to make their mathematical activity explicit and, thus, a potential object of reflection. Instigation of whole class and small group discussions, which involve students in the problems of communication of and interaction among ideas, and instigation of written reflections (journals, focused writings) can all contribute to the opportunities for reflective abstraction.

The Teacher's Role From a Social View

Just as a cognitive lens on learning allowed for the identification of useful sites for teacher intervention, a social lens can be similarly generative. From a social perspective, the classroom is seen as a mathematics learning community that constitutes its own norms and practices in service of developing (taken–as–) shared mathematical knowledge (Cobb, Yackel, & Wood, 1992b; Streeck, 1979). Much of what it means to do and learn mathematics, and what one comes to believe about the nature of mathematics, results from one's experience in communities of practice. The classroom mathematics community is of primary importance in this respect. Mathematics classes, no matter how they are taught, affect students' conceptions of mathematics.

In the model described here, intentional interventions are made by the teacher to contribute to establishing a classroom community in which particular conceptions about mathematics are more likely to be developed and particular norms and practices established. Note that the mathematics classroom culture is viewed as interactively constituted by the teacher and students. The teacher, who is not only a member of the classroom community, but also a member of other communities that practice mathematics and/or mathematics education, can be purposeful in contributing to a classroom culture that fosters useful conceptions of mathematics (e.g., compatible with those of mathematicians, the general public, and others).

The teacher as facilitator of the classroom discourse has a major effect on what issues are explored, which significantly influences what is seen as *of mathematical interest*, which in turn influences views of what constitutes mathematics (e.g., what is central to the discipline). Further, the teacher's role in orchestrating discussion, as well as his or her initiation of particular conversations about students' mathematical activity contributes to establishing what it means to be an effective member of this mathematical community, including the valuing and appropriateness of certain types of reasoning and communication.

The teacher is also instrumental in the establishment of how mathematical validity is determined in the classroom. Where does mathematical authority reside? The teacher, by consistently avoiding the role of arbiter of mathematical validity and by fostering discourse that focuses on mathematical justification, can promote acceptance of the classroom community's responsibility for determining mathematical validity.

During the lesson described in Example One, the students were confident in their multiply–length–times–width strategy, but their initial justifications were not consistent with the mathematics tradition that I (as teacher) wanted to foster. In Example Two, excerpts from Simon and Blume (1996) show a negotiation of what constitutes mathematical justification, part of the larger process of establishing norms for appropriate mathematical activity in this classroom. I use "negotiation" to signal a situation in which members of the classroom community, who begin from different perspectives, participate in ongoing cycles of responding to and being affected by each other's language and/or actions. This mutual influencing is key to what I call negotiation. Most frequently, I refer to negotiations between the teacher and the students.

Example Two.   In response to the teacher's inquiry about why students multiplied the number of rectangles along the width of the table by the number of rectangles along the length, Bobbie replied,

All right, it seemed like the easiest way to come up with an answer... alls [sic] we would have to do is multiply two numbers and come up with one answer."

Bobbie's response described his motivation for multiplying but lacked an attempt to persuade others in the class that multiplication worked, that it was an appropriate operation to perform. Bobbie's interpretation of the teacher's question differed from the teacher's. The teacher ("Simon" in the transcript) then attempts to focus the class on justifying their solution method and to describe what would constitute justification.

Simon: Why is it—You said it was an easy way to get an answer. Is it, is it an easy way to get a *correct* answer? Now why, why measure along an edge and another edge? How is doing that and multiplying two numbers related to covering this whole table with rectangles? You seemed to all think that was a good way to go about the problem. Why do you think that was?

Deb then appealed to authority to justify the use of multiplication: "Because, um, in previous, previous math classes you learned the formula for area is length times width. So probably everybody has the idea."

In previous mathematics classes, these students likely accepted mathematical validity as being established by the teacher or the textbook. Using a humorous reference to an earlier discussion, the teacher attempts to shift authority for judging validity to the class: "All those evil math teachers you were talking about before, and now you are taking their word for it? How do we know if they are right?"

Several students then respond with descriptions of how their teachers demonstrated to them that multiplying length by width produces the same result as counting squares.

Molly: The teachers. They showed us how it worked.

[Students give] evidence that the method works. The teacher then focuses the discussion on whether the procedure always works, attempting to create a need for a deductive argument.

Simon: So it worked. And it worked on the ones you had in school before. Does that always work? [pause] All the time, most of the time, some of the time?

Molly: In rectangles or squares.

Simon: It always works for rectangles or squares?

Molly: From what I've seen.

Simon: From what you've seen. There might have been some rectangles you haven't met yet?

Molly now considers the question, "Will it always work?" in a different way. She articulates the connection between counting the rectangles and the use of multiplication:

Well, it would work because, um, multiplying and adding are related in that multiplying is, is like adding groups, and so it would always work, because you add them up to see how many is in the square and to multiply the, the groups that go like that, that'll always work. You would get the same number, I'm saying if you added them or if you multiplied that side times that side. Because you're adding, I mean, you're multiplying the number of groups by the number in the groups, which is the same as adding them all up. (Simon & Blume, 1996, pp. 11–12)

In Example Two, I, as the teacher, worked within a tension between responding to the students' contributions (by accepting, clarifying, monitoring other students' understanding of the contributions) and promoting the type of mathematical activity that I see as important (deductive justification). I continually accepted their answers as appropriate to their understanding of my questions, yet continued to modify my probing questions to fit with their most recent contributions while promoting a need for deductive justification. This session was the beginning of the negotiation of norms for validation and justification. This negotiation was mostly *implicit*, a theme within the classroom mathematical conversations. Later in the semester, it was not unusual to hear a student asking "How do we know that will always work?" or challenging classmates in other ways to justify their ideas, an indication that these norms had indeed been established.

Cobb, Yackel, and Wood (1993) indicated the significance of the teacher's instigation of and participation in *explicit* discussion of classroom norms and practices. In Example Three, transcript data from the Construction of Elementary Mathematics Project (Simon, 1995a; Simon & Blume, 1996) portrays such a conversation:

Example Three. Early in the course described in the previous examples, students complained that they never knew if their mathematical ideas were correct because I did not tell them. This seemed to represent a different perspective on knowing from the one motivating my actions. I chose to respond by initiating a game that I thought would advance this discussion.

In What's in the Bag, the students try to determine what is hidden inside a bag held by the teacher. They may ask any question that can be answered *yes* or *no* except for a question that identifies the object (e.g., Is it a pencil?). Key to this game is that the object is never shown and the teacher never evaluates the validity of what the students think it is. Students may continue to ask questions until they are *sure* that they know what is in the bag. Note that knowing is determined by each student, not by the teacher.

In this particular trial of the game, the students received affirmative responses to questions such as "Can you measure with it?", "Does it go 1 to 12?", "Is the majority of it wood?", and "Can you use it to draw straight lines?" When I asked the students if they were sure about what was in the bag, all but a couple said that they were:

Simon: How many of you need to see it? [many hands raised] Why?

Tammy: To know if we're right or not.

Lilly: I think that's poor teaching strategy.

Simon: That's a poor teaching strategy?

Lilly: You're not showing it to us creates frustration.

Simon: Causes frustration.

Lilly: Whether we're right or not.

Molly: We need immediate feedback.

Simon: OK. Let's uh, the purpose of this is not just to play the game, but as I said I wanted to get a point across, and the point I want to get across is the following: Most of you had the experience, during this little game, that you were able to get to a point through your own thinking and asking of questions, collecting information—you were able to get to a point where you're absolutely sure you know what's in this bag, without me telling you whether you're right or not, and without seeing what's in the bag. Now, I think that's wonderful. Okay. And it seems to me that you, that you've shown an ability of investigation and thought. That's the reason I play this game with my kids, is that I want them to develop those abilities and most of you seem to be able to do that fairly, fairly readily. OK. Now I view what we're doing in mathematics the same way, but I want you to begin to know things in mathematics not because I tell you they're so, not because I say, "Right. Good job," but because you understand it so well that you're sure this is the way it works. "I collected enough information, I thought about it enough, I thought about what other people said, I responded to questions, and, boy, I know this. I don't know it because Dr. Simon said 'right' at some point. I know this because I really understand it." So we're involved in trying to get to that point. Now, there's a problem with this, which is that most of you have never had this experience before in mathematics. So I reckon that you don't have a whole lot of idea about how long it takes, what it takes, what it feels like along the way. All this stuff is new.

During the remainder of this class and part of the next, considerable discussion ensued as to the respective roles of teacher and student, the appropriate level of confusion in learning, and how knowing and understanding come about.

The teacher's role as problem poser also affords opportunities to contribute to what is seen as important and central in the activity of doing mathematics. Thus, pursuing understanding, looking for patterns, conjecturing, mathematizing, and justifying come to be seen as paramount when they are consistently the focus of classroom tasks and assessments. The problems and tasks in Example One are examples of problems that contribute to establishing a conceptual focus. Note that in none of the four problem contexts was a number the answer to the problem. Each problem phrasing can be viewed in terms of what it says about what is important in that mathematics class.

The Mathematics Teaching Cycle

The Mathematics Teaching Cycle (Simon, 1995a) refers to a conceptual framework that describes the relationships among teacher's knowledge, goals for students, anticipation of student learning, planning, and interaction with students. It is represented schematically in Fig. 3.1. Central to the Mathematics Teaching Cycle (MTC) is the inherent tension between responding to the students' mathematics and creating purposeful pedagogy based on the teacher's goals for students' learning.

I have adopted Steffe's term, "students' mathematics," (Steffe & D'Ambrosio, 1995) because it acknowledges the importance of recognizing the students' ideas and practices as a coherent system that allows students to make sense of and operate within their experiential worlds. It is incumbent upon the teacher (and researcher) to endeavor to understand the students' mathematics, not just to determine how the students' knowledge differs from some target knowledge (e.g., the teacher's or researcher's knowledge). On the one hand, the teacher follows students' ideas and questions, departing from his or her own notions of where the classroom activity should go. On the other hand, the teacher poses tasks and manages discourse to focus on particular mathematical issues. Teaching is inherently a challenge to find appropriate balance between these two poles. The MTC represents a conception of teaching that is purposeful *and* responsive. The teacher pursues a mathematical agenda that is a result of a "bifocal perspective," constantly orienting between his or her view of the relevant mathematics and his or her view of the students' mathematics. Because these views are constantly changing, the teacher's agenda is correspondingly changed.

I will comment on the MTC beginning at the lower left of Fig. 3.1. Inquiring into students' mathematics is an ongoing process because the students' mathematics can never be known directly (only inferred) and

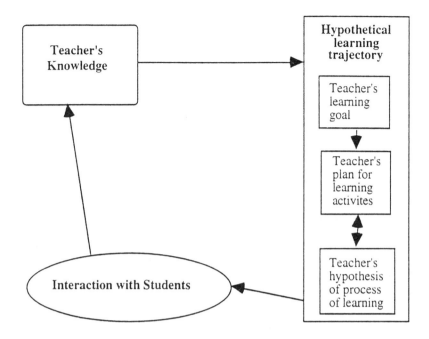

FIG. 3.1.   Mathematics Teaching Cycle.

because it is constantly changing. The inquiry process is one of listening to and watching the spontaneous mathematical activity of the students, eliciting mathematical activity through selected tasks and questions, developing hypothetical models of the students' mathematics, and further inquiring to refine these developing models.

In the MTC, knowledge of the students' mathematics is derived from interaction with students and is part of the teacher's knowledge that is brought to bear on pedagogical decisions. This knowledge, as well as other aspects of teacher knowledge, serves as a basis for choosing appropriate goals for the students' learning. (Of course, factors external to the classroom, such as school curricular demands, may influence the choices made.) According to the MTC, the mathematics teacher's actions are at all times guided by his or her current goals for student learning, which are continually being modified based on interactions with students. Goals may be altered on the spot during instruction or in the context of subsequent planning. The teacher's goals for students' learning provide direction for the *hypothetical learning trajectory*, the teacher's prediction of the path by which students' learning might proceed.

The hypothetical learning trajectory is made up of three components: the learning goal, the learning activities, and the hypothetical learning process—a prediction of how the students' thinking and understanding will evolve in the context of the learning activities. The bidirectional arrows in Fig. 3.1 between the development of a hypothetical learning process and the development of the learning activities indicate a symbiotic relationship; the generation of ideas for learning activities is dependent on the teacher's hypotheses about the development of students' thinking and learning; however, the generation of hypotheses of student conceptual development also depends on the nature and sequence of anticipated activities.

The generation of a hypothetical learning trajectory prior to classroom instruction is the process by which the teacher develops a plan for classroom activity. However, as the teacher interacts with the students, the teacher and students collectively constitute an experience. This experience, by the nature of its social constitution, is different from the one anticipated by the teacher. The interaction with students leads to a modification in the teacher's ideas and knowledge as he or she makes sense of what is happening and what has happened in the classroom. The diagram in Fig. 3.1 indicates that the adaptations in the teacher's knowledge lead to a new or modified hypothetical learning trajectory.

Fig. 3.2 gives a fuller picture of the Mathematics Teaching Cycle by identifying some of the relevant aspects of the teacher's knowledge and the connections between the teacher's knowledge and the teacher's thinking described in the model. Beginning at the top of the diagram, the teacher's own mathematical understandings and ability to analyze the conceptual field in question guide the teacher's identification of potential student learning. Observation of and communication with students lead the teacher to form models of the students' mathematics. These two interacting sources of knowledge are the basis for the teacher's choice of learning goals for the students: "Using their own mathematical knowledge, mathematics teachers must interpret the language and actions of their students and then make decisions about possible mathematical knowledge their students might learn" (Steffe, 1990, p. 395).

Three aspects of teacher knowledge, in addition to knowledge of mathematics and knowledge of students' mathematics discussed above, contribute to the teacher's approach to working towards the learning goals. First is the teacher's sense of how students learn. It is here that a constructivist or emergent view of knowledge development is important and has a direct impact on the teacher's consideration of what might be useful interventions. In addition, the teacher's understanding of how particular mathematics is learned, derived from formal research in the field and from reflection on the teacher's own work with students, informs his or her choice of intervention. Finally, the teacher's vision of

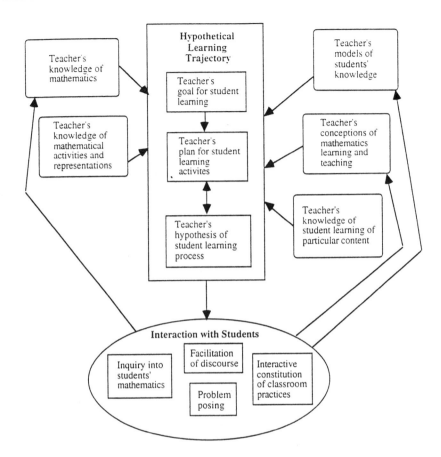

FIG. 3.2. Mathematics Teaching Cycle, expanded. Arrows indicate direction of influence. Connections and directions of influence are absent from the diagram to reduce complexity and to focus attention on relationships that are of particular interest in this discussion.

the role of the mathematics teacher contributes to defining his or her choice of actions with respect to the students. Thus, the teacher's model of teaching is part of this model of teaching.

Because the goals and actions taken by the teacher are guided by all of the relevant areas of teacher knowledge, and because all of these areas of knowledge change as the teacher interacts with the students, the goals and related actions are constantly being modified. Thus, the process of teaching represented by the Mathematics Teaching Cycle does not follow a linear progression from goals to actions. Consider a teacher, Mr. Smith, who has planned a particular lesson: Mr. Smith begins the lesson by posing problems to the students. As he observes the students and listens to their verbalization of their ideas, several changes can take place in his knowledge. Mr. Smith's understanding of what his students understand and do not understand may change. He may see aspects of the mathematics or the interrelationship of mathematical ideas that he had not previously seen. He may become aware of other mathematical representations or new ways to adapt familiar ones. His understanding of how the particular mathematics is learned may change. Mr. Smith might get new ideas for useful problem contexts for working on the mathematics. Each of these changes may result in on-the-spot or post lesson modification of his goals and actions. For a reflective teacher who is attentive to the mathematics of his students, it is likely that all of these changes in the teacher's knowledge (and more) are taking place during teaching on a regular basis. Sometimes fine–tuning of the lesson is in order, whereas at other times the whole thrust of the lesson may be altered. Regardless of the extent of modification, changes may be made in any or all of the three components of the hypothetical learning trajectory: the goal, the activities, and the hypothetical learning process.

A particular iteration of the cycle may range in time from a brief moment to several weeks. In practice, the teacher may be simultaneously at different points in a variety of different cycles (some of them interconnected) reflecting multiple goals. A wide–angle view of this complex reveals a web of knowledge, thought, and action. However, zooming in on particular areas of this web, we see the organizing principles of the MTC.

Thus, the mathematics teaching that I am describing is an inquiry process, one in which the teacher is involved in model building and hypothesis generation (e.g., models of students' mathematical understanding, predictions of how learning might progress). The teacher's learning is a key aspect of teaching. Teaching is goal directed, yet the goals are constantly being modified. The teacher's relationship with the students is one of both direction setting and following. At each point in the interactive process between teacher and students, the teacher functions within the tension among his or her current goals for student learning and commitment to respond to the mathematics of the student. The principal currencies of teaching according to this model are problem posing and facilitation of discourse.

IMPLICATIONS FOR RESEARCH
ON THE DEVELOPMENT
OF MATHEMATICS TEACHERS

In this section, I identify eight aspects of the model described in the last section and discuss briefly their potential impact on research on mathematics teacher development. Note that these aspects are overlapping and often interdependent:

1. *Knowledge of and about mathematics.* According to this model, the teacher is engaged in ongoing inquiry, learning, and decision–making. These activities are dependent on the teacher's understanding of the mathematics involved and his or her conceptions of the domain of mathematics. This knowledge defines what is worth learning and the activities that are appropriate to the enterprise. Thus, the model suggests that teacher development research focus on significant changes in this area.

2. *A personally meaningful model of mathematics learning.* Central to this model are a teacher's concepts of how mathematical knowledge is developed. What is deemed appropriate teaching rests on beliefs about learning and learners. (This particular model is grounded in constructivism and social perspectives on learning.) Thus, a key site for research is the teacher's construction and refinement of useful models of learning.

3. *Knowledge of students' development of relevant concepts.* The teacher's ability to make sense of the students' mathematics depends on his or her knowledge of students' learning of relevant concepts. Research can focus on the development of such knowledge, which seems to derive from reading research studies, watching tapes of students engaged in mathematics, and interacting with students in the classroom.

4. *Relationship to students' mathematics.* A teacher's relationship to students' mathematics encompasses commitment to understanding his or her students' mathematics, ability to elicit and probe their mathematics, and ability to analyze students' mathematical activity and form useful models of their knowledge. These are individually and collectively appropriate foci for research.

5. *A personally meaningful model of mathematics teaching.* In the model that I described, the model is itself recursively embedded. That is, according to the model, the teacher's personal model of teaching guides and constrains instructional decision making and defines the teacher's role in relation to students' learning. For the teacher who is moving away from a traditional model, considerable growth is needed to constitute a new model consistent with reform principles (Simon & Mazza, 1993). Thus, the teacher's developing model of teaching is an important site for study. Note that a model of teaching is not acquired, but rather is constantly in a state of construction and renovation. (This does not imply that individuals must or should invent it entirely on their own; structured educational opportunities are useful in this respect.)

6. *Ability to define appropriate learning goals for students.* A teacher's ability to define appropriate learning goals for students, longer range goals as well as goals for spontaneous interventions, implies the ability to identify key mathematical ideas in the mathematics being considered, as well as to make use of knowledge of students' concept development and knowledge of that teacher's own students' mathematics. This development is likely to involve a change in teacher thinking

that focuses increasingly on articulating goals for students' learning. Research can focus on these issues.

7. *Ability to anticipate how students' learning might ensue.* The hypothetical learning trajectory of the MTC suggests that learning to anticipate how student learning might progress is a key aspect of lesson planning and of on–the–spot decision making during teaching. Also, development is necessary in the teacher's ability to modify the hypo-thetical learning trajectory in response to new insights. A research focus on the generation and modification of hypothetical learning trajectories is likely to reveal aspects of development that are not apparent when different constructs are used.

8. *Ability to construct lessons consistent with one's model of teaching.* As his or her new model of teaching develops, the teacher's challenge is to find ways to implement this model in particular mathematical and classroom contexts. Doing so means constituting new forms of practice both by adapting new techniques and by rethinking the role of familiar ones. This is an important focus for research.

Although this discussion of sites for study of mathematics teacher development deriving from the model is not exhaustive, it demonstrates how a model can provide focus for such inquiry.

CONCLUSION

The articulation of a model of teaching can guide research on the development of teachers. As such, it contributes both focus and justifi-cation for the foci chosen. However, these models, components of the researchers' conceptual frameworks, must be used in ways that do not restrict the researcher's ability to learn from the research process. Eisenhart (1991) stated that conceptual frameworks "must be timely [reflecting the current state of research knowledge and] may have short shelf–lives; they may be revised or replaced as data or new ideas emerge" (p. 210). Effective research programs attend to data that do not seem to fit their frameworks and use such data to modify these frameworks.

Research on mathematics teacher development is intended to identify and describe both the nature and extent of teacher development (and the context in which it occurs) and the key issues in, and obstacles to, that development. However, the range of teacher knowledge and activity is so vast that the challenge is to make useful choices about what to focus on: What constitutes development? Certainly, all teacher change would not be deemed development. Earlier in the chapter, I noted that to the extent that a model highlights relevant areas of teacher knowl-edge and skills, it identifies specific foci for the study of teacher devel-opment. A model of mathematics teaching, as part of a research project's conceptual framework, can provide much of this needed definition and focus. We are not looking for a unique or monolithic view of teaching. Rather, we need to elaborate models that can provide useful conceptual frameworks for research on teacher development. Each model that is developed will provide its own unique set of lenses and foci, although there may be significant overlap between models. The complex domain of mathematics pedagogy is not likely to be captured comprehensively by a single model. Different models will emphasize different aspects of the teaching enterprise and provide different lenses for viewing the same aspects. The challenge is to develop useful ways to think about mathematics pedagogy, and to be able to articulate these ways of thinking as part of a framework for research and practice.

This chapter is not only a call for the articulation of short–lived models for individual research projects, but an encouragement to the mathematics education community to commit to the process of building new models of mathematics teaching, a process that will afford the development of more useful models and contribute to theory building with respect to mathematics teaching and learning.

ACKNOWLEDGMENTS

This material is based on work supported by the National Science Foundation under Grant No. TPE–9050032. Any opinions, findings, conclusions, or recommendations expressed in this material are those of the author and do not necessarily reflect the views of the National Science Foundation.

REFERENCES

Balacheff, N. (1990). Towards a *problematique* for research on mathematics teaching. *Journal for Research in Mathematics Education, 21*, 258–272.

Ball, D. L. (1993a). Halves, pieces, and twoths: Constructing representational contexts in teaching fractions. In T. Carpenter, E. Fennema, & T. Romberg (Eds.), *Rational numbers: An integration of research* (pp. 157–196). Hillsdale, NJ: Lawrence Erlbaum Associates.

Ball, D. L. (1993b). With an eye on the mathematical horizon: Dilemmas of teaching elementary school mathematics. *The Elementary School Journal, 93*, 373–397.

Ball, D. L., & Chazan, D. (1995). *In the aftermath of the standards: Reconceiving the teacher's role in classroom discourse.* Manuscript in preparation.

Bauersfeld, H., Krummheuer, G., & Voigt, J. (1988) Interactional theory of learning and teaching mathematics and related microethnographical studies. In H-G. Steiner & A. Vermandel (Eds.), *Foundations and methodology of the discipline of mathematics education* (pp. 174–188). Antwerp, Belgium: Proceedings of the TME Conference.

Belenky, M., Clinchy, B., Goldberger, N., & Tarule, J. (1986). *Women's ways of knowing: The development of self, voice, and mind.* New York: Basic Books.

Bringuier, J-C. (1980). *Conversations with Jean Piaget.* Chicago: University of Chicago Press.

Brousseau, G. (1981). Problemes de didactique des decimaux [Problems in teaching decimals]. *Recherches en Didactiques des Mathematiques, 2.1* 37–125.

Brousseau, G. (1983). Les obstacles epistemologiques et les problemes en mathematiques [Epistemological obstacles and mathematical problems]. *Recherches en Didactiques des Mathematiques, 4.2,* 164–198.

Brousseau, G. (1987). *Les differents roles du maitre* [The different roles of the teacher]. Angers, France: P.E.N. Colloquium.

Cobb, P. (1989). Experiential, cognitive, and anthropological perspectives in mathematics education. *For the Learning of Mathematics, 9,* 32–42.

Cobb, P. (in press). *Conducting teaching experiments in collaboration with teachers.* In R. Lesh & E. Kelly (Eds.), *Innovative research designs in mathematics and science education.* Dordrecht, Netherlands: Kluwer.

Cobb, P., Wood, T., Yackel, E., & McNeal, B. (1992). Characteristics of classroom mathematics traditions: An interactional analysis. *American Educational Research Journal, 29(3),* 573–604.

Cobb, P., & Yackel, E. (in press). Constructivist, emergent, and sociocultural perspectives in the context of developmental research. *Journal of Educational Psychology.*

Cobb, P., Yackel, E., & Wood, T. (1992a). A constructivist alternative to the representational view of mind in mathematics education. *Journal for Research in Mathematics Education, 23,* 2–33.

Cobb, P., Yackel, E., & Wood, T. (1992b). Interaction and learning in mathematics classroom situations. *Educational Studies in Mathematics, 23,* 99–122.

Cobb, P., Yackel, E., & Wood, T. (1993). Learning mathematics: Multiple perspectives, theoretical orientation. In T. Wood, P. Cobb, E. Yackel, & D. Dillon, (Eds.), *Rethinking elementary school mathematics: Insights and issues. Journal for Research in Mathematics Education Monograph Series, 6,* (pp. 21–32). Reston, VA: National Council of Teachers of Mathematics.

de Lange, J. (April, 1995). *Developing theory of mathematics teaching.* Symposium presentation at National Council of Teachers of Mathematics Research Presession, Boston, MA.

Douady, R. (1985). The interplay between different settings, tool–object dialectic in the extension of mathematical ability. In L. Streefland (Ed.), *Proceedings of the ninth international conference for the Psychology of Mathematics Education* (Vol. II, 33–52). Utrecht, The Netherlands.

Eisenhart, M. (1991). Conceptual frameworks for research circa 1991: Ideas from a cultural anthropologist; implications for mathematics education researchers. In R. Underhill (Ed.), *Proceedings of the thirteenth annual meeting of the North American Chapter of the International Group for the Psychology of Mathematics Education* (Vol. I, pp. 202–219). Blacksburg, VA.

Freire, P. (1971). *Pedagogy of the oppressed.* New York: Seaview.

Freudenthal, H. (1991). *Revisiting mathematics education: China lectures.* Dordrecht, The Netherlands: Kluwer.

Gravemeijer, K. (1994). Symbolizing from a developmental–research perspective. Draft of paper presented at the Symposium on Symbolizing, Communicating, and Mathematizing, Vanderbilt University, Nashville, TN.

Gravemeijer, K. (1995). Educational development and developmental research in mathematics education. *Journal for Research in Mathematics Education, 25,* 443–471.

Lampert, M. (1990). When the problem is not the question and the solution is not the answer: Mathematical knowing and teaching. *American Educational Research Journal, 27,* 29–63.

Lampert, M. (1992). Practices and problems in teaching authentic mathematics. In F. Oser, A. Dick, & J. Patry, (Eds.), *Effective and responsible teaching: The new synthesis*, (pp. 295–314). San Francisco: Jossey–Bass.

National Council of Teachers of Mathematics (1989). *Curriculum and Evaluation Standards for School Mathematics*. Reston, VA: Author.

National Council of Teachers of Mathematics (1991). *Professional standards for teaching mathematics*. Reston, VA: Author.

Piaget, J. (1977). *The principles of genetic epistemology*. London: Routledge & Kegan Paul.

Piaget, J. (1985). *The equilibration of cognitive structures: The central problem of intellectual development*. Chicago: University of Chicago.

Simon, M. (1994). Learning mathematics and learning to teach: Learning cycles in mathematics teacher education. *Educational Studies in Mathematics*, 26, 71–94.

Simon, M. (1995a). Reconstructing mathematics pedagogy from a constructivist perspective. *Journal for Research in Mathematics Education*, 26, #2, 114–145.

Simon, M. (1995b). Elaborating models of mathematics teaching: A response to Steffe and D'Ambrosio. *Journal for Research in Mathematics Education*, 26, #2, 160–162.

Simon, M. (in press). Research on mathematics teacher development: The teacher development experiment. In R. Lesh & E. Kelly (Eds.), *Innovative research designs in mathematics and science education*. Dordecht, Netherlands: Kluwer.

Simon, M., & Blume, G. (1994). Building and understanding multiplicative relationships: A study of prospective elementary teachers. *Journal for Research in Mathematics Education*, 25, 472–494.

Simon, M., & Blume, G. (1996). Justification in the mathematics classroom: A study of prospective elementary teachers. *Journal of Mathematical Behavior*, 16, 3–31.

Simon, M., & Mazza, W. (1993). From learning mathematics to teaching mathematics: A case study of a prospective teacher in a reform–oriented program. In B. Pence (Ed.) *Proceedings of the fifteenth annual meeting of the North American Chapter of the International Group for the Psychology of Mathematics Education*, Asilomar, CA.

Simon, M. & Schifter, D. (1991). Towards a constructivist perspective: An intervention study of mathematics teacher development. *Educational Studies in Mathematics* 22, 309–331.

Steffe, L. (1990). Mathematics curriculum design: A constructivist perspective. In L. Steffe & T. Wood (Eds.), *Transforming children's mathematics education : International perspectives*, (pp. 389–398). Hillsdale, NJ: Lawrence Erlbaum Associates.

Steffe, L. (1991). The constructivist teaching experiment: Illustrations and implications. In E. von Glasersfeld (Ed.), *Radical constructivism in mathematics education*, (pp. 177–194). Dordrecht, The Netherlands: Kluwer.

Steffe, L., & D'Ambrosio, B. (1995). Toward a working model of constructivist teaching: A reaction to Simon. *Journal for Research in Mathematics Education*, 26, #2, 146–159.

Steffe, L., & Tzur, R. (1994). Interaction and children's mathematics. *Journal of Research in Childhood Education*, 8, #2, 99–116.

Steffe, L., & Wiegel, H. (1992). On reforming practice in mathematics education. *Educational Studies in Mathematics, 23*, 445–465.

Streeck, J. (1979). Sandwich. Good for you. In J. Dittman (Ed.), *Arbeiten zur konversations analyse* [Work toward analysis of conversation]. (pp. 235–257). Tubingen, Germany: Niemeyer.

Streefland, L. (1990). Realistic Mathematics Education (RME). What does it mean? In K. Gravemeijer, M. van den Heuvel, & L. Streefland (Eds.), *Contexts free productions tests and geometry in Realistic Mathematics Education* (pp. 1–9). Utrecht, the Netherlands: Research group for Mathematics Education and Educational Computer Centre State University.

Streefland, L. (1991). *Fractions in Realistic Mathematics Education: A paradigm of developmental research*. Dordrecht, Netherlands: Kluwer.

Treffers, A. (1987). *Three dimensions: A model of goal and theory description in mathematics instruction–The Wiskobas Project*. Dordrecht: Reidel.

Tzur, R., (1995). *Interaction and children's fraction learning*. Athens: GA: University of Georgia, unpublished doctoral dissertation.

von Glasersfeld, E. (1989). Cognition, construction of knowledge, and teaching. *Synthese, 80*, 121–140.

von Glasersfeld, E., & Steffe, L. (1991). Conceptual models in educational research and practice. *The Journal of Educational Thought, 25*(2), 91–103.

4

On Understanding the Structure of Teachers' Beliefs and Their Relationship to Change

Thomas J. Cooney
University of Georgia

Barry E. Shealy
University at Buffalo, SUNY

There is much ado in the present literature about reform in mathematics education. Reform necessitates change, that is, doing things differently. For many teachers, changing their teaching of mathematics is problematic and fraught with difficulties. Change of the sort suggested by the National Council of Teachers of Mathematics (see, for example, NCTM, 1989, 1991, 1995) and the Mathematical Association of America (see, for example, MAA, 1991) involves fundamental shifts in reconceptualizing both mathematical activity and the role of the mathematics teacher. For example, fundamental to the recent calls for reform is the notion that mathematics is a human endeavor in which the ability to reason, communicate, and solve problems is of paramount importance. In some sense, teacher education is about enabling preservice and in-service teachers to move toward this vision of mathematics so they can better enable their students to engage the complexities and technologies of the 21st century.

The notion of teacher change has had many dimensions and emphases over the years. One can envision change in terms of teachers' effective use of time as, for example, suggested by the model of effective teaching posited by Good, Grouws, and Ebmeier (1983). Alternately, one can think of change along a continuum from novice to expert teacher where, for example, lesson organization and explanation of content moves toward the effectiveness generally associated with the expert teacher (see McKinney, 1986). For example, Leinhardt (1988) found that expert teachers were better able to weave lesson segments and routines together and provide a broader array of concept representations (specifically fractions) than were novices. Within the context of the Cognitively Guided Instruction (CGI) project, Fennema and Franke (1992) argued that teachers can develop the ability to base their instruction on what the child knows by acquiring both into the child's cognitive processes and developing a knowledge base of how instruction can be based on those processes. We see, then, that there are numerous perspectives that can serve as a basis for conceptualizing teacher change.

Our focus on teacher change is from the perspective of developing teachers' belief structures in such a way that autonomy in evaluating alternatives in teaching mathematics is commonplace. We want teachers to develop the ability to see themselves as authorities, in that they can evaluate materials and practices in terms of their own beliefs and practice, and be flexible in modifying their beliefs when faced with disconfirming evidence. Although there are many factors involved in conceptualizing teacher change, we maintain that such an orientation is critical to the professional development of teachers. Without it, teachers can be buffeted and bandied about by proclamations stemming from local or national organizations. In this chapter, we describe changes in beliefs that have occurred in mathematics and mathematics education—changes that are likely to influence our notions of change and reform.

CHANGES IN BELIEFS

In this section we consider changes in beliefs about mathematics and mathematics education and possible connections between them and research related to changes in teachers' beliefs. We begin with a look at how the field of mathematics has changed regarding the question of what constitutes mathematical activity.

Mathematics

Tymoczko (1979) suggested that a paradigm shift in the way we view the nature of mathematics and mathematical activity occurred during the 1970s. The proof of the Four-Color Theorem (Appel & Haken, 1977), based on a computer experiment, sent rumblings through the field of mathematics and created a cleft in mathematicians' beliefs regarding the nature of proof. Mathematical activity had been considered an a priori activity in which the mathematician chooses an axiomatic system and then, working in isolation, follows formal deductive methods to produce irrefutable conclusions. These methods and results were considered timeless. The Four-Color Theorem proof presented a "substantial piece of pure mathematics which is known by mathematicians only *a posteriori*" (Tymoczko, 1979), that is, on the basis of a particular experience. Although this feat has fostered debates about the nature of mathematical proof, it is noteworthy that the conclusion was generally accepted, a fact Tymoczko suggested would not have been the case 25 years ago.

Tymoczko (1979) raised the issue of a Kuhnian paradigm shift in mathematics in which the accepted virtues of intuition, logic, and various heuristic strategies are supplemented by empirical investigations aided by the computational abilities of the modern computer. Furthermore, the shift is from a private view of mathematical activity to a public one in which the activity of the mathematician is not isolated but consists of conjecture and public critique, critique being the critical process that shapes subsequent inquiry (Lakatos, 1976). Lakatos (1976) described this process in terms of "proof-ideas." Tymoczko (1986), in summarizing Lakatos, said that the activity of the mathematician consists of developing ideas for investigation or generating persuasive and probabilistic arguments that invite criticism. This criticism may include local counterexamples that challenge lemmas within a proof but leave the larger conjecture alive, or global counterexamples that challenge the primary conjecture but leave component lemmas alive for further investigation. This process eventually leads to mature proofs. It is these mature proofs that have been traditionally accepted as mathematics, rather than the activities of conjecture and investigation that preceded their development.

Not only has the accepted view of mathematical activity been broadened, but the very nature of mathematics has been challenged. Traditionally, mathematics is seen as a well-defined field of inquiry that is timeless and unchanging, its bedrock being a reasoning process considered infallible (Tymoczko, 1986). Mathematics is often taken for granted and rarely questioned. This view of mathematics provides a sense of security and certainty. According to Davis and Hersh (1986), "the very existence of the characteristic features of mathematics attracts the world and invites the world to apply them, come what may" (p. 282). A different, more prominent view held currently is that mathematics can be seen as a way of thinking about the external world, a category of constructing meaning. This view introduces uncertainty into a field where certainty was previously a hallmark. Not only do we now see mathematics as tentative and uncertain, but we also see that mathematics actually introduces uncertainty or problems into our interpretation of the world. As Davis and Hersh (1986) put it, "mathematics is one of the crucial ways in which meaning is transformed and sometimes lost" (p. 281). For example, abstraction, an important mathematical activity, "is extraction, reduction, simplification, elimination. Such operations must entail some degree of falsification" (p. 281). It follows that mathematics is a function of our experience and is far more tentative than previously thought. We could argue that this shift in conceptualizing mathematical activity has far-reaching consequences for how we construe reform in mathematics education in general and the teaching of mathematics in particular.

Mathematics Education

Concurrent with changes in views about the nature of mathematics, we are undergoing vigorous reform in mathematics pedagogy. In connecting these shifts, the issue arises of whether the shifts in philosophy of mathematics fueled changes in mathematics pedagogy, or whether changes in pedagogical philosophy fueled changes in the philosophy of mathematics. In any event, our philosophy of mathematics and our views of mathematical pedagogy are closely intertwined. Tymoczko (1986) argued, in fact, that a key but often missing consideration in the philosophy of mathematics is the pedagogy of mathematics. The answers to the questions of what and how we teach will strongly reflect our beliefs about mathematics and mathematical activity. As Thom (1973) once put it, "Whether one wishes it or not, all mathematical pedagogy, even if scarcely coherent, rests on a philosophy of mathematics" (p. 204). Furthermore, Tymoczko (1986) noted that shifts in teaching practices might provide an "accurate seismograph for recording shifts in the foundations of mathematics" (pp. 46–47). Several researchers in mathematics education have connected beliefs about the nature of mathematics to beliefs about teaching mathematics (Brown, Cooney, & Jones, 1990; Ernest, 1991; Thompson, 1984, 1992). Ernest (1989) described three views of the nature of mathematics as manifested in models for teaching mathematics, the mathematics curriculum, and the learning of mathematics—instrumentalism, Platonism, and problem solving. His analysis emphasized the pervasive influence of various philosphical perspectives of mathematics on creating models in mathematics education.

Although the issue of which fueled which may be problematic, it is clear that current reform in mathematics education (NCTM, 1989, 1991, 1995; Mathematical Sciences Educational Board, 1989, 1990) reflects the shifts in thinking about mathematical activity and the nature of mathematics that Tymoczko (1986) and Davis and Hersh (1986) described. These shifts might be characterized as movement away from the instrumentalist model and toward Ernest's problem-solving view (Ernest, 1989). It is illustrative that the shift involves not only instructional issues, but assessment ones as well. For example, when mathematics is believed to be well defined and its teaching straightforward, assessing achievement is simply a matter of assessing product-oriented outcomes—a point contrary to reform. But this static view of mathematics is giving way to a more constructivist one, which suggests that students' mathematical understandings are complex, problematic, and difficult to assess. Although it may be questionable how much the developments in the field of mathematics fueled this change in perspective about the teaching and learning of mathematics, these developments are at least compatible with current calls for reform. It can be argued that reform is grounded in the constructivist epistemology, thereby suggesting that change in the teaching of mathematics requires greater attention to reflection and to the individual child's mathematics.

But such change does not come easily. Parents and students often have a more static view of mathematics. Consider, for example, the document *Reshaping School Mathematics* (Mathematical Sciences Education Board, 1990) which pointed out two "outdated public assumptions" about mathematics:

- Mathematics is a fixed and unchanging body of facts and procedures.

- To do mathematics is to calculate answers to set problems using a specific catalogue of rehearsed techniques. (p. 4)

As Donovan (1990) pointed out, parents often define what mathematics is, at least in terms of what they want their children to learn. Students often share a rather static view of mathematics as well (see Schoenfeld, 1992). Consequently, the expectations of both the general public regarding quality mathematics teaching and the consumers of that instruction may comprise a view of instruction that is inconsistent with a constructivist perspective. To then ask teachers to change may place them in an uncertain if not untenable position. At the very least, it requires that teachers be self-directed, autonomous, and resolute that their teaching of mathematics is both consistent with changes in mathematics and in mathematics education, and is in the best interests of students and society. We contend that teachers need to be not only reflective in their practice, but also capable of internalizing many voices into a coherent philosophy of teaching mathematics.

Teachers

With reform in mathematics and mathematics education confronting us, the notion of teacher change is critical. How can teacher education promote teachers' professional development in accordance with these reform movements? What types of experiences provide a context for teacher change? Ernest (1989, 1991) and Bauersfeld (1980) argued that the social context in which teachers learn to teach can be a significant factor in what they learn about teaching. Further, the teachers' own level of consciousness about their beliefs influences their disposition to realize change.

In the literal sense, the notion of teacher change is applicable only to those who have already been teaching. We maintain, however, that the seeds for change can and should be planted early in teachers' professional lives, taking advantage of the social contexts in which teachers learn to teach. Many preservice teachers enter teacher education programs expecting, even seeking, to be told how to teach. They have spent years being told what they need to know and do in school and consequently are accustomed to a receiving mode of learning, which is easily translated into a telling mode of teaching. Their experiences as students have made them receivers of information from authorities; consequently they are quite willing to accept the broadcast metaphor of teaching. Yet, there is a felt need for learning how to teach. As one of Ball's (1988) participants said after a field experience, "One thing I learned from this experience is that I am not qualified to teach math yet. Once I have the math methods class, then I will be much more ready" (p. 46). Other participants in studies of preservice teacher education programs have expressed similar sentiments (cf. Feiman-Nemser & Buchmann, 1986; Shealy, Arvold, Zheng, & Cooney, 1994). As a star student in one of the author's classes proclaimed in a bittersweet moment, "Now I know the right way to teach!" Planting seeds of reform necessitates challenging teachers' beliefs. Unfortunately, many teacher education programs do little to challenge previously held beliefs (Zeichner & Gore, 1990).

Over the past several years, research on the beliefs of preservice secondary mathematics teachers has been conducted at the University of Georgia as the teachers progress through their teacher education program. The research is longitudinal in nature, usually following students over a four-quarter sequence in mathematics education and perhaps into their first year of teaching. The methodologies are anthropological in nature, using both structured and unstructured interviews based on course work, field activities, and observations of teaching. This research suggests that when teachers enter their first year of teaching unprepared for the uncertainty inherent in practice, they tend to either blame themselves for failure (cf. Nancy in Shealy, 1994) or take control of their classroom by denying uncertainty, sometimes accusing reform-minded teacher educators of being unrealistic (cf. Henry in Shealy et al., 1994). Nancy (Shealy, 1994), for example, was dependent on her teacher educators and other teachers she revered for making sense of her role as a mathematics teacher. When she began teaching and experienced difficulty, she tended to place blame for her perceived failure on herself and felt she had let her students, her mother, and her instructors down. For Nancy, the world of teaching was perceived as relatively simple and unproblematic. Beliefs constructed during her teacher education program dissolved when she was faced with the problematic nature of the classroom. Like Nancy, Rust's (1994) participant, Nina, became distraught and did not want to be observed by the researchers, feeling she had failed people who had respected her. Given the inadequacy of their beliefs to assist them in dealing with classroom difficulties, both Nancy and Nina were left vulnerable in terms of defining their own identity as classroom teachers.

Another first-year teacher, Todd (Shealy, 1994, 1995), began his teacher education program by investigating mathematics in the context of problem-solving situations in a course on problem solving. He participated in open-ended investigations in other mathematics education courses when learning to use technological tools. Todd saw these investigations as reinforcing his emphasis on making mathematics interesting and providing him a perceived vehicle for accomplishing this goal when he began teaching. We say "perceived" because observations of his early teaching experience revealed a very traditional teaching style. Todd, like many teachers, did not make his beliefs explicit and consequently failed to challenge the implications of his beliefs when faced with the reality of classroom teaching. He was overwhelmed with the practical considerations of getting school started. Perhaps it was not surprising, then, that his teaching did not reflect the reform-minded views he expressed during his preservice program.

Todd's orientation toward teaching and learning were constructed in what were, for him, isolated contexts. For example, he wanted to make mathematics interesting through the solving of problems, a perspective that reflected his own experiences in learning mathematics. Throughout his teacher education program, the focus of his attention was on his doing of mathematics. Yet these experiences were never connected in any substantial way with his emerging theme of wanting to help students avoid frustration. Perhaps because of his participation in a research program, Todd began to reflect on his teaching style, traditional as it was, and slowly to connect his learning experiences with his desire for students to learn mathematics by solving problems.

Greg (Shealy, 1994, 1995), a first-year teacher, provides an interesting contrast to the other teachers mentioned. Greg was an unusual first-year teacher in that he took risks to provide a more open classroom. He went out of his way to approach and listen to other teachers. He said that even if you disagreed with a particular teacher's approach to teaching, you could always find something that was helpful. This valuing of others led him to appreciate students' input as well. Much of his planning time centered on creating activities to involve students in constructing and sharing their mathematical understandings. At one point Greg found a new tool he had never used before (a Mira), learned how to use it on his own, and then used it extensively for one of his class activities. Greg was willing to take risks, fail, and try again because he felt these types of activities were essential for his students. When classes did not go well, he tried to learn from the experience and use it to modify the next activity. The ingredients for change in Greg's teaching were a willingness to take risks, to listen, and to be reflective.

In general, the secondary preservice teachers revealed different levels of being reflective, which may account for the various ways they internalized their experiences. Some held rigidly to what they believed about mathematics and teaching when they entered their teacher education program. Others were receptive but provided little interpretation to what they had learned; they accepted whatever their instructors communicated. Both of these types of teachers experienced difficulty in adjusting to the demands of the classroom and in using whatever they learned in their teacher education programs during that first year of teaching. The question arises as to whether they developed a strong enough philosophy or vision of teaching to sustain what they learned when they began teaching. A few were able to examine what they believed about mathematics and teaching and to modify those beliefs into a stronger, more cohesive set of beliefs. These teachers seemed to experience the greatest success in their first year of teaching.

Experienced teachers may have more consistency between their stated beliefs and their actual practices, as was the case for Thompson's (1984) Lynn, Jeanne, and Kay, who fit nicely into Ernest's (1989) three categories. Lynn saw mathematics as a static collection of facts to be transferred verbally to the students. Mathematics was characterized by certainty, predictability, absoluteness, and freedom from emotional content. Lynn believed that her students learned primarily by watching the teacher's demonstrations attentively and then practicing the presented procedures. She sought to produce students who could "perform the mathematical tasks specified in the curriculum, using standard procedures or methods" (p. 117). In her instruction, Lynn was concerned with managerial aspects of teaching and allowed little interaction. She also had low expectations for her students, blaming difficulties in learning on the students' dispositions and backgrounds.

Jeanne (Thompson, 1984) was closer to Ernest's Platonist (1989). She emphasized mathematics as a logical system with concepts coherently related. She, like Lynn, saw mathematics as fixed and predetermined, but emphasized concepts and structure rather than facts and procedures. For Jeanne, instruction meant providing a logical, coherent presentation emphasizing justification and reasoning, relating new concepts to previous ones. Jeanne talked about the importance of students participating during class, but student participation generally involved responding to her questions. In contrast, Kay demonstrated some aspects of Ernest's (1989) problem-solving approach to mathematics. She tended to see mathematics as a mental exercise and involved students in problem-solving sessions, encouraging them to "guess, conjecture, and reason on their own" (p. 113). She emphasized the creation of an open and informal classroom atmosphere and the importance of being receptive to suggestions, ideas, and intuition. Although Thompson (1984) did not address the issue of teacher change per se, her study suggests that reform-oriented teachers are more likely to have a broader view of mathematics and to hold beliefs consistent with this view, thus demonstrating the importance of linking teacher change to the beliefs teachers hold about mathematics and mathematics education.

Projects that have resulted in significant change in experienced teachers have placed considerable emphasis on the teachers' experiences as a context for reflection, noting change in the teachers' beliefs as an important outcome. Simon & Schifter (1991) involved teachers in reflecting on their mathematical experiences, then provided support as the teachers implemented their newly acquired understandings in the classroom. The authors noted changes in teachers' "views of how children learn, their understanding of the nature of mathematics, their feelings about doing mathematics, and their ideas about what constitutes good teaching" (p. 327). Similarly, Cobb, Wood, and Yackel (1990) noted teachers reconceptualizing their role as teacher from one to "provide and sanction the official way to solve problems" (p. 137) to using "her authority to guide and sustain mathematical communication by listening, offering suggestions, and clarifying children's meanings" (p. 137). In a longitudinal study of teachers involved in the CGI project, Fennema et al. (in press) noted changes in teachers' beliefs about the ability of students to solve problems and corresponding changes in instructional approaches.

Teachers with many years of experience also undergo change, contrary to conventional wisdom. At some point an experienced teacher may begin a process of reevaluating his or her role as a teacher of mathematics (consider the case of Sue in Cooney, 1994a). For example, as much as a teacher loves teaching mathematics to children, the teacher may find he or she also enjoys the role of mentor to other teachers. Perhaps a teacher's classroom experiences or his or her own mathematical investigations trigger a desire to reassess the role of a teacher of mathematics. Perhaps the teacher will pursue curriculum development, research, educating other teachers, or trying to have an impact on peers or school programs. Regardless of the form, the reevaluation of commitments entails risks and requires the teacher to have belief structures that are resolute yet permeable (Kelly, 1955) when faced with the uncertainty of change.

USING THE CONSTRUCT OF AUTHORITY
TO CONCEPTUALIZE CHANGE

In conceptualizing the notion of teacher change, metaphors can be very helpful, despite the fact that their use in educational research is sometimes controversial. Some question the importance and role of metaphors for comprehending, communicating, or coming to know. For the skeptic, metaphors are seen as occasionally useful in a heuristical sense, but essentially ornamental and, in some cases, misleading. Others argue that metaphors are epistemologically necessary for the acquisition of new knowledge (Petrie & Oshlag, 1993). Snow (1973) argued that metaphors can provide an important form of theorizing when used from a realistic perspective. It is in this sense of theorizing that we have adopted various writings about authority as an orientation to conceptualizing the notion of teacher change.

Theoretical Perspectives on Authority

There have been a number of scholars who have addressed the issue of authority from a variety of perspectives. We draw primarily on the work of Perry (1970); Belenky, Clinchy, Goldberger, and Tarule (1986); Green (1971); and Rokeach (1960). We do so in a metaphorical way as we consider the structure of belief systems and the means by which people come to know. Using a metaphorical analysis, Green (1971) provided the following conceptualization of how beliefs are structured:

> We may, therefore, identify three dimensions of beliefs systems. First there is the quasi-logical relation between beliefs. They are primary or derivative. Secondly, there are relations between beliefs having to do with their spatial order or their psychological strength. They are central or peripheral. But there is a third dimension. Beliefs are held in clusters, as it were, more or less in isolation from other clusters and protected from any relationship with other sets of beliefs. Each of these characteristics of belief systems has to do not with the content of our beliefs, but with the way we hold them. (p. 47–48)

Green distinguished quasilogical from psychological strength in the following way. A teacher may hold that the use of alternate assessment items is an important way to assess learning, yet rarely uses such items because of the difficulty in creating them or concern over the amount of time it takes to grade them. His or her belief in the use of such items may be primary and consequently yield derivative beliefs about the importance of students demonstrating their ability to reason and communicate. But this belief may not be psychologically central, that is, its intended actions dissipate in the face of other demands that are valued more highly, for example, coverage of content. Cooney and Shealy (1995) found that in studying teachers' assessment practices, some teachers incorporated their originally held peripheral beliefs about alternate assessment into their central core of beliefs about mathematics and the teaching of mathematics. For these teachers, their use of alternate assessment methods was exhibited consistently throughout their teaching. But others never incorporated these peripheral beliefs into their central core of beliefs, despite the fact that they had indicated the importance of using alternate assessment methods. Consequently, their use of such things as open-ended questions was sporadic and highly dependent on whether they felt students had already mastered other, more basic material.

Beliefs that are psychologically central in one context may not be psychologically central in another context—as in the case when clusters of beliefs are isolated. For example, Jones (1991) found that Darla, a middle school teacher, believed strongly in different perspectives about teaching mathematics, yet this psychologically central belief was peripheral with respect to her limited beliefs about mathematics. Indeed, teachers' beliefs about mathematics may be held more strongly than their beliefs about the teaching of mathematics (cf. Cooney, 1985; Eggleton, 1995; Wilson, 1994). By considering the origins and intensity with which beliefs are held, we can better understand why some beliefs tend to manifest themselves in practice whereas others do not. This kind of analysis can help us determine why some teachers change their instructional approach whereas others do not, despite participation in the same teacher education program and rhetoric about reform that may be strikingly similar.

Rokeach (1960) talked about beliefs being psychologically central and about the notion of primary beliefs. He wrote, "The concept 'primitive belief' is meant to be roughly analogous to the primitive terms of an axiomatic system in mathematics or science" (p. 40). From these primitive beliefs stem other, more peripheral, beliefs. Like Green, Rokeach discussed the notion of beliefs held in isolation from each other. Thus, according to both Green and Rokeach, it is possible for a teacher to hold simultaneously that problem solving is the essence of mathematics and that students best learn mathematics by taking copious notes and mastering every detail (cf. Fred in Cooney, 1985) or by having the teacher explain each step (cf. Todd in Shealy et al., 1994). Isolation occurs when contradictory beliefs are not explicitly compared, perhaps reflecting the existence of beliefs held from a nonevidential perspective, a perspective immune from rational criticism (Green, 1971). Nonevidentially held beliefs encourage one to see the world in terms of polarities, in contrast to Bauersfeld's (1988) state of fundamental relativism.

Another orientation that enables us to understand teachers' thinking processes and actions in the classroom is the way that teachers construct their knowledge about mathematics and the teaching of mathematics. Perry (1970) and Belenky, Clinchy, Goldberger, and Tarule (1986) wrote about various ways people position themselves with respect to authority. The two schemes are similar in that they range from a person who sees the world as one in which an authority dictates truth, to one in which truth is seen as contextual and the individual is a, perhaps the, determiner of truth. Perry's scheme is developmental, based on his analysis of the way men, specifically, think and come to know. The elements of his scheme consist of dualism, multiplism, relativism, and commitment. Roughly speaking, a dualistic perspective is rooted in seeing truth as that which emanates from an authority. Multiplism involves recognizing a variety of opinions but not evaluating them analytically. There is a recognition of differences in opinion, but such a difference is tolerated either because the authority has not yet revealed the "correct" position or because "everyone is entitled to his own opinion." Relativism involves an ability to see the relative merits of various perspectives; that is, different perspectives are not of equal merit. Commitment involves a personal commitment to a particular perspective because of its perceived merits.

Belenky et al. (1986) did not posit a stage theory, but they did explicate various ways that women come to know that are not unlike Perry's (1970) basic scheme. Whereas Perry's research involved only men, Belenky et al.'s research involved only women. These authors used the metaphor of voice to describe women who are representative of the authors' seven positions. For example, a woman is a received knower if what she knows is what she has received from others (not unlike Perry's notion of dualism) or a constructed knower if she has integrated various voices, including her own, into a cohesive web of knowledge based on the contexts in which she lives. Ernest's (1991) categories of beliefs about mathematics and the teaching of mathematics are also related to the notion of authority in that he utilizes a scheme based on an absolutist–fallibilist scale. His categories range from a perspective of mathematics as a given subject to a perspective of mathematics as a subject created by human inventiveness. These categories are related to Perry's scheme in that one's perception of authority is at the heart of how one comes to know.

We are not taking the position that one scheme applies only to men and the other only to women. Rather, we wish to focus on what we see as common to these two theoretical orientations, namely, how an individual positions himself or herself with respect to authority, and the ability of that person to see authority as dependent on context and self. For teachers, authorities beyond self could be professors, school administrators, parents, textbooks, or proclamations from professional organizations such as the National Council of Teachers of Mathematics (NCTM). The location of self within these various types of authorities determines where the person's orientation lies on a continuum ranging from dualism to relativism.

In Perry's (1970) scheme of nine stages, a critical point occurs in positions 4–6 in which individuals dramatically restructure how they see the world as they begin a "radical reperception of all knowledge as contextual and relativistic" (p. 109), rather than "assimilate the new, in one way or another, to the fundamental dualistic structure with which they began" (p. 109). For Belenky et al. (1986), the third of their seven positions describes a person for whom "truth eventuates in a new conception of truth as personal, private, and subjectively known or intuited" (p. 54). Such "revolutionary points" are particularly important in considering the professional development of teachers. Although it is likely that these points emerge in an evolutionary sort of way, they do suggest a transition from the teacher being dependent on others in a consensual sense to one in which the teacher evaluates different perspectives in terms of what he or she values, attending to empirical evidence as part of the construction process.

The revolution seen in this transition is critical for understanding teacher change. Many teachers who move toward these revolutionary points are troubled as they recognize the implications of their development. In a sense, the teachers are being asked to make their lives more problematic, less certain. Some teachers are not ready for this transition and, rather than continue their process, retreat to a more dualistic position, often with ambivalence (cf. Henry in Arvold & Cooney, 1994; Shealy et al., 1994), or temporize (Perry, 1981) by postponing further movement until they have more experience (cf. Todd in Shealy, 1994, 1995).

The relevance of the notion of dogmatism as a characteristic of a dualistic perspective is reflected in Green's differentiation between indoctrination and teaching, the latter being a matter of helping an individual coming to know based on rationality, the former relying on proclamations from an authority. The basic issue is one of how we come to believe that something is "true" or "false." Indoctrination, as applied to the teaching of mathematics, minimizes the impact of rationality in favor of memorization. Here we see a connection between Green's (1971) analysis and that of Perry (1970) and Belenky et al. (1986). Nonevidentially held beliefs are more likely to be dualistic as they are not the result of any sort of analysis that attends to context. They are held because someone has said it is so (cf. Nancy in Shealy et al., 1994; Nina in Rust, 1994).

The epistemology behind techniques such as telling, memorizing, and following predetermined and prescribed algorithms, which we so often deplore at least in their extreme, is based on the existence of dogmatism and the absoluteness of authority. Denied is a sense of fundamental relativism. It follows that considering how teachers position themselves with respect to authority can provide a means of conceptualizing teacher development and a means of conceptualizing activities to promote that development. Although it is surely the case that evolution is implicit, it is, nevertheless, fundamental to developing a reform-oriented perspective. Teachers on different sides of the "crossover" are likely to view documents such as the NCTM *Standards* in quite different ways.

At present, there is considerable discussion concerning possible implications of the constructivist epistemology for the teaching of mathematics. Although there is much debate about the clarity or even the strength of those implications (see Simon, 1995; Steffe & D'Ambrosio, 1995), it seems unlikely that teachers can adopt much in the way of constructivist principles if their orientation is essentially dualistic. Principles of teaching rooted in constructivism rely on an ability to reflect, to analyze, and to question what might be in terms of another's cognition. Such reflection requires the individual to decenter and see the world through another's lens. von Glaserfeld's (1994) notion of *viability* is relevant here in the struggle to determine whether our explanations of another's actions seem plausible. This struggle is predicated on the notion that an individual sees the world as a contextual place and not a place of absolute truths. If we accept the notion that reflective abstraction is essential for learning new concepts (see Simon, 1995), then we can argue that reflective abstraction is also essential for reformulating and reconceptualizing our meanings of both mathematics and the teaching of mathematics.

The importance of reflection in reconceptualizing one's role can be found in many places, not the least of which are von Glasersfeld (1991) and Schön (1983, 1987). Inherent in any notion of reflection is the ability of the individual to "step out of the stream of direct experience, to re-present a chunk of it, and to look at it *as though* it were direct experience, while remaining aware of the fact that it is not" (von Glasersfeld, 1991, p. 47). A precondition for the act of reflection is the ability of the person to decenter and view his or her actions as a function of the context in which he or she is acting. Schön's (1983) reflective practitioner, a notion that enjoys so much credence in the field of education, cannot exist unless the individual is willing to step out of himself or herself and view his or her actions from a relativistic perspective. Such an act seems unlikely to occur when the individual holds a dualistic view of the world.

Reformulation and reflective abstraction applied to pedagogical matters require, even demand, that reflection occur in a social context. Our ideas, our visions about teaching have their origins in our experiences as participants in the schooling process. Although there may have been a "burning bush" that influenced us, there is still the context of our schooling experiences, which provides the backdrop for understanding the implications of that defining moment. More likely, the process is less dramatic and more evolutionary. Nevertheless, it is clear that the act of reflection is central to any reform process that values teachers as adaptive agents (Cooney, 1994b; cf. Steffe, 1990). The preservice teacher Nancy (Shealy et al., 1994) exemplified the difficulty of this evolutionary progress. Involved in activities that challenged, even required, her reflectivity, Nancy caught a vision of what she wanted for her students.

She recognized a reliance on self (which she called "imagination") in some of her peers and wished she had the same herself. She hoped to design instruction so her students could develop this inner voice, but was skeptical about herself growing in this way.

It is not unusual for preservice teachers to exhibit the following two orientations about teaching: Teaching is both a matter of finding effective ways of communicating mathematics and of treating students fairly and humanely. These orientations, which fit Shealy's (1994, 1995) notion of *naive idealism*, characterize an individual who is waiting to "hear the word" on how mathematics should be taught. "Just tell us the right way to teach," is the cry from many such preservice teachers. Their search for the "right way" brings them to their teacher education program with the expectation that they will receive the necessary information and skills to become an effective teacher of mathematics. This is surely a reasonable expectation. Nevertheless, the orientation is one of receiving, not to be confused with one in which they have to unpack and repack many of their ideas about mathematics and its teaching (see Ball, 1988). If the naive idealist remains in a searching mode, professional development and change become difficult. Cooney and Wilson (1995) described a teacher who was quite confident in her ability to become a successful teacher and who was looking for field experiences and activities in her teacher education program that would strengthen what she was already sure was the right way to teach. The teacher's emphasis was on confirmation of her beliefs rather than consideration of "partial solutions," that are context dependent. Similarly, Henry, a first-year teacher, was steadfast in his belief that the teaching of mathematics was a matter of efficient telling (Arvold & Cooney, 1994). His dualistically held beliefs were structurally different from what Shealy (1994, 1995) called naive idealism. Henry was not searching for an authority to reveal truth, but rather for confirmation of what he had already determined to be truth. His beliefs were held nonevidentially (Green, 1971) in that evidence, for Henry, consisted only of confirming evidence. Henry was unlikely to change because the only evidence acceptable to him was that which confirmed his current beliefs. All other evidence was dismissed as "nonsense."

It seems wise to separate Shealy's notion of the naive idealist in which the individual has a receiving orientation couched in a set of evidentially held beliefs, from that in which beliefs are held nonevidentially. The latter type of teacher might better be termed a "dogmatic idealist," as this brand of idealism stems from a dualistic orientation. The "missionary" teacher, that is, one who sees himself or herself as the one who will transform the teaching of mathematics from the boring and irrelevant to the exciting and insightful, often fits this category. In contrast, a student of one of the authors indicated that her use of cooperative learning groups early in her first year of teaching did not go well,

"Because I don't yet have the experience and confidence." Here we see a teacher who is holding to a belief about teaching but sees the context (lack of experience and confidence) as impeding her realization of what she values. Such realization is an indication of movement toward relativistic thinking.

Developing Connections Between Authority and Change

To illustrate the connections between authority and change, consider the case of Peterson's (1994) Annie Keith. According to Peterson, Keith was a CGI first-grade teacher who epitomized the reform-minded teacher. Peterson (1994) provided the following analysis of Keith's teaching:

> Ms. Keith makes visible through her words and actions that she learns from her children. Because learning includes all parties—teachers and students—Ms. Keith is not the only authority for knowledge in the classroom. Their [sic] are multiple authorities and multiple ways of knowing. In her classes, students "prove" their mathematical solutions to themselves and to others, explain why they think something is true, and give reasons and justify their thinking.ƒ

> Annie creates a learning environment where students bring up mathematical ideas, choose and create problems and mathematical tasks that interest and challenge them, and justify their mathematical thinking to themselves and their community. Authority for knowing and learning rests with the students and the community rather than only with the teacher. Such a learning environment seems designed to foster mathematical power in the ways suggested by the NCTM *Standards*. (pp. 22–23)

Annie Keith typified the position that knowledge is not a function of telling by an external being, but rather is a socially constructed phenomena. In her case we can see a teacher helping students work through their ideas so that they can judge the merit of their ideas themselves. This strongly suggests a relativistic perspective.

There is one caveat, however. Keith adhered to the position that "Mathematicians never say 'can't'" (Peterson, 1994, p. 23), a position questioned by Schoenfeld (as cited in Peterson, 1994, p. 26). In part Schoenfeld maintained that when certain mathematical stipulations are made, consequences follow that render some conclusions illogical. This raises the issue of how teachers should react when students put forth erroneous conclusions that nevertheless exhibit certain mathematical insights. In a series of interviews one of the authors directed, the question was explored as to whether increasing the perimeter of a rectangle ensured that its area would increase. One interviewee was quite adamant that such was the case. "It just seems like common sense," was the student's response, supported by examples in which the width of the rectangles remained constant while lengths of the rectangle varied. Sure enough, as the perimeter increased, so did the area. There is a certain tension here between honoring the discovery and enabling the student to realize the misconception. This tension is part of the experiences of reform-minded teachers, who are faced with similar situations on an almost daily basis. Consider the case of Ball's (1993) Sean who discovered numbers that were both odd and even. The value of this discovery lies in the ingenuity the child exhibited in recognizing characteristics and patterns of numbers. Ball's response was to support Sean's discovery by designating such numbers as "Sean numbers." Ball's perspective is clearly one of honoring context and construction—rather than bowing to an absolute authority that claims that a number cannot be both odd and even. As was the case with Peterson's Keith, it signifies a teacher who values knowledge construction within an individual even when the construction is flawed in some absolute sense. There is a certain valuing of mathematical inventions yet realizing that not "everything goes." We see a similar emphasis with Thompson's (1984) Kay. She communicated an expanded view of mathematics, as opposed to Lynn and Jeanne, whose views of mathematics were different yet narrow. For Kay, teaching mathematics was a matter of providing multiple representations, whereas for Lynn and Jeanne, teaching mathematics was a matter of focusing on a single interpretation. These more limited views of mathematics precluded an emphasis on a more relativistic view of mathematics with the classroom dialogue confined to a particular mathematical interpretation.

Let us return now to some of the preservice teachers we discussed earlier (Shealy et al., 1994). Nancy internalized what consisted of consensual knowing, a version of what Belenky et al. (1986) called "received knowing." Reform for Nancy will be difficult until she elevates her own voice to one of importance and starts to reconstitute her own belief structures. Reform is not a matter of accommodating others, but rather is a matter of accommodation in the Piagetian sense. Henry, in contrast, tended to hold his beliefs in a dogmatic and nonevidential way. Unless he allows evidence to influence his beliefs, change is unlikely. Attention to the problematic had different effects for these two teachers. For Nancy, it was a matter of "taking a vote." For Henry, it was a matter of finding an existence proof; that is, finding someone who believed as he did. In the absence of this, he began to doubt whether he should become a teacher. His beliefs, however, were confirmed during his student teaching because his cooperating teacher also believed in effective telling. Consequently, Henry's beliefs became even more resistant to change as he became convinced he had been correct all along. The notion of reflection might facilitate Nancy's growth, but it seemed only to solidify Henry's conviction that he knew the "right" way to teach.

Greg's belief structures were permeable (Kelly, 1955) in that he was willing to accept originally held peripheral beliefs into his core beliefs. For example, initially he rejected the use of technology—as did Henry. But when he saw technology as a means of helping students develop intellectually, his beliefs about the use and role of technology were incorporated into his more centrally held belief that the role of the teacher is to help students prepare for life. Progress for Todd was a matter of connecting previously held beliefs with his experiences as a teacher. It might be argued that his reflective experiences during his preservice program facilitated his development, however slow it was in coming.

It seems clear that reflection is not a product of dualistic thinking. Reform, by its very nature, necessitates the asking of questions, the posing of the contrary, and consideration of what is not presently the case. Such a perspective is central to seeing the world in contextual terms, to appreciating that other perspectives are possibilities. Reform is not the product of inertia nor of blind acceptance. To the contrary, it requires a commitment to integrate many varied voices in a rational way. Although reform in general is not necessarily a product of consensuality (there are many examples of reform dominated by strong personalities), reform of the sort suggested by the NCTM *Standards* requires a relativistic orientation.

AUTHORITY, CHANGE, AND TEACHER EDUCATION

We have argued that reform in the classroom requires that teachers see themselves as part of a system in which analysis of context and constraints are an integral part of their teaching. Teachers who hold absolutist views about mathematics or mathematics teaching are unlikely candidates to conduct such analyses. Consequently, teaching becomes the byproduct of inertia from years gone by or the unquestionable acceptance of the latest educational proclamation instituted in a mechanistic way. Neither results in the kinds of fundamental teacher change suggested in the current reform literature. The "crossing over," in terms of Perry's (1970) or Belenky et al.'s (1986) schemes, into a more relativistic world is central to realizing fundamental change in the way mathematics is taught.

The question then arises as to how teacher education programs for both preservice and in-service teachers can enable teachers to engage the kind of fundamental analysis suggested here. Brown (1982) suggested that the metaphor of therapy is relevant for conceptualizing teacher education as a problematic activity. He provides the following analysis.

Much of therapy is focused not so much upon the provisions of answers by an expert, but rather upon the understanding that wisdom begins with each of us learning to generate a fresh set of questions on our own—questions themselves (and not answers) that may enable us to understand ourselves in a new light. In fact much of therapy is about enabling a person to understand that a perceived problem might profit from being redefined or reconceptualized. (p. 12)

The key ingredients implied by Brown (1982) are that of reflection and attention to context, for these are the cornerstones for analyzing and reconceptualizing. Both are consistent with the notion that addressing issues in the teaching and learning of mathematics provides opportunities to view classroom situations from a variety of perspectives. This process necessitates an ability to shift focus away from one's own ego in order that new questions can be posed and the classroom can be seen from a different perspective.

Cooney (1994b) spoke of pedagogical power as the essence of intelligent problem solving within the context of teaching mathematics. But how can we engender such an orientation among the teachers with whom we work? Our perspective suggests we ought not to be searching for the "right" approach, but rather be searching for means of enabling teachers to see themselves as part of a system wherein alternatives and "partial solutions" are considered and valued. Unfortunately, a dogmatic idealist such as Henry, who rejects alternative perspectives, is unlikely to prosper in such a program.

We contend that the introduction of problematics applies to both mathematical and pedagogical situations. Given that students often see mathematics as a subject consisting of isolated algorithms that yield single right answers (Schoenfeld, 1992), it is not surprising that the task is formidable. For example, we have found that it is not uncommon for preservice teachers to indicate that they "can't remember" how to solve an equation such as $2^x = 135$ and therefore are left void of a strategy such as graphing or constructing tables to generate at least an approximate solution. When "the" solution strategy cannot be recalled, the solution process quickly comes to a halt. In part, this is due to their limited view of mathematics; a broader view might suggest that there are many ways to solve equations other than the traditional, mechanical method. But if equation solving is seen solely as a procedural activity, it is not surprising that once that procedure is forgotten, the ability to solve the equation also disappears. The simplistic but conceptual notion that an equation is an expression involving two quantities (left member and right member) seems relevant here. Solving equations then becomes a matter of generating values so that the left and right members yield the same numerical value. Tools for doing so consist of spreadsheets, graphing calculators, and other technologies, in addition to the mechanical procedure typically taught in schools. The point is that even the most mechanical aspect of school mathematics can be placed in a broader, more problem-solving context.

The preceding example deals with a very simple mathematical situation, but we can focus on pedagogical situations as well. Lyons' (1990) Margaret, a teacher with 15 years' teaching experience, expressed concern about how to help students take risks, ask questions, or simply raise a hand. The key seems to be that students need help "knowing what they are knowing" so that they can "work up to (their) real, true questions" (Lyons, 1990, p. 172). This process requires the passing of intellectual authority from the teacher to the students so that students are empowered to find their own intellectual voices. Our concern as teacher educators is to help teachers take risks as teachers—or at least understand the process by which teachers can take risks so that they can work up to their own "real, true questions." Maybe, for some teachers, the issue is one of helping them find their own voices (recall Nancy) and of providing a context by which they develop a vision of self as an integrated knower. We can see a certain symmetry here. If teachers are to enable students to develop their own voices, then it seems reasonable to assume that the teachers must also have developed such voices.

The process of teacher change is risky and can be uncomfortable. Retreating to a dogmatic world where right is right and wrong is wrong is a tempting fate. Teacher education provides a context for enabling teachers to develop the voice and the breadth of conceptual thinking about both mathematics and pedagogy that is required for significant change in teaching mathematics. We expect some teachers will change and others will not, despite our best efforts, and that some will change regardless of whether there are any external efforts at all. But consideration of what teachers believe and how their beliefs are structured provides us a means of conceptualizing teacher education in ways that promote change in something other than a random manner. That is, after all, what teacher education is all about.

REFERENCES

Appel, K., & Haken, W. (1977). The solution of the four-color map problem. *Scientific American, 237*(4), 108–121.

Arvold, B., & Cooney, T. J. (October, 1994). *A first year secondary mathematics teacher's orientation toward authority: Implications for professional development.* Paper presented at the sixteenth annual meeting of the North American Chapter of the International Group for the Psychology of Mathematics Education, Baton Rouge, LA.

Ball, D. L. (1988). Unlearning to teach mathematics. *For the Learning of Mathematics, 8,* 40–48.

Ball, D. L. (1993). With an eye on the mathematical horizon: Dilemmas of teaching elementary school mathematics. *The Elementary School Journal. 93,* 373–397.

Bauersfeld, H. (1980). Hidden dimensions in the so-called reality of a mathematics classroom. *Educational Studies in Mathematics.*, *11*, 23–41.

Bauersfeld, H. (1988). Interaction, construction, and knowledge: Alternative perspectives for mathematics education. In D. A. Grouws & T. J. Cooney (Eds.), *Perspectives on research in effective mathematics teaching* (27–46). Hillsdale, NJ: Lawrence Erlbaum Associates.

Belenky, M. F., Clinchy, B. M., Goldberger, N. R., & Tarule, J. M. (1986). *Women's ways of knowing: The development of self, voice, and mind.* New York: Basic Books.

Brown, S. I. (1982). On humanistic alternatives in the practice of teacher education. *Journal for Research and Development in Education, 15*, 4, 1–12.

Brown, S. I., Cooney, T. J., & Jones, D. (1990). Mathematics teacher education. In W. R. Houston (Ed.), *Handbook of research on teacher education* (pp. 639–656). New York: Macmillan.

Cobb, P., Wood, T., & Yackel, E. (1990). Classrooms as learning environments for teachers and researchers. In R. Davis, C. Maher, & N. Noddings (Eds.), *Constructivist views on the teaching and learning of mathematics. Journal for Research in Mathematics Education Monograph No. 4* (pp. 125–146). Reston, VA: National Council for Teachers of Mathematics.

Cooney, T. J. (1985). A beginning teacher's view of problem solving. *Journal of Research in Mathematics Education, 16*, 324–336.

Cooney, T. J. (1994a). In-service programs in mathematics education. In S. J. Fitzsimmons & L. C. Kerpelman (Eds.), *Teacher enhancement for elementary and secondary science and mathematics: Status, issues, and problems* (pp. 8.1–8.36). Cambridge, MA: Abt Associates, Center for Science and Technology Policy Studies.

Cooney, T. J. (1994b). Teacher education as an exercise in adaptation. In D. B. Aichele (Ed.), *Professional development of teachers of mathematics* (pp. 9–22). Reston, VA: National Council of Teachers of Mathematics.

Cooney, T. J., & Shealy, B. E. (1995). Teachers thinking and re-thinking assessment practices. In D. T. Owens, M. K. Reed, & G. M. Milsaps (Eds.), *Proceedings of the seventeenth annual meeting of the North American Chapter of the International Group for the Psychology of Mathematics Education*, (Vol. 2, pp. 109–114). Columbus, OH: ERIC Clearinghouse for Science, Mathematics, and Environmental Education.

Cooney, T. J., & Wilson, P. S. (1995). On the notion of secondary preservice teachers' ways of knowing mathematics. In D. Owens, M. Reed, & G. Millsaps (Eds.), *Proceedings of the seventeenth annual meeting of the North American Chapter of the International Group for the Psychology of Mathematics Education*, (Vol. 2, pp. 91–96). Columbus, OH: ERIC Clearinghouse for Science, Mathematics, and Environmental Education.

Davis, P. J., & Hersh, R. (1986). *Descartes' dream: The world according to mathematics.* San Diego: Harcourt Brace Jovanovich.

Donovan, D. (1990). Cultural power and the defining of school mathematics: A case study. In T. Cooney (Ed.), *The teaching and learning of mathematics in the 1990's* (pp. 166–173). Reston, VA: National Council of Teachers of Mathematics.

Eggleton, P. J. (1995). *The evolving mathematical philosophy of a preservice mathematics teacher.* Unpublished doctoral dissertation, University of Georgia, Athens.

Ernest, P. (1989). The impact of beliefs on the teaching of mathematics. In C. Keitel, P. Damerow, A. Bishop, & P. Gerdes (Eds.), *Mathematics, education, and society* (pp. 99–101). Paris: UNESCO.

Ernest, P. (1991). *The philosophy of mathematics education.* London: Falmer.

Feiman-Nemser, S., & Buchmann, M. (1986). The first year of teacher preparation: Transition to pedagogical thinking? *Journal of Curriculum Studies, 18*, 239–256.

Fennema, E., Carpenter, T. P., Franke, M. L., Levi, L., Jacobs, V. R., & Empson, S. B. (in press). Mathematics instruction and teachers' beliefs: A longitudinal study of using children's thinking. *Journal for Research in Mathematics Education.*

Fennema, E., & Franke, M. L. (1992). Teacher's knowledge and its impact. In D. A. Grouws (Ed.), *Handbook of research on mathematics teaching and learning* (pp. 147–164). New York: Macmillan.

Good, T., Grouws, G., & Ebmeier, H. (1983). *Active mathematics teaching.* New York: Longman.

Green, T. (1971). *The activities of teaching.* New York: McGraw-Hill.

Jones, D. L. (1991). A study of the belief systems of two beginning middle school mathematics teachers (Doctoral dissertation, University of Georgia, 1990). *Dissertation Abstracts International, 51,* 3353A.

Kelly, G. A. (1955). *Psychology of personal constructs* (Vol. 1). New York: Norton.

Lakatos, I. (1976). *Proofs and refutations.* New York: Cambridge University Press.

Leinhardt, G. (1988). Expertise in instructional lessons: An example from fractions. In D. Grouws & T. Cooney (Eds.), *Perspectives on research on effective mathematics teaching* (pp. 47–66). Reston, VA: National Council of Teachers of Mathematics.

Lyons, N. (1990). Dilemmas of knowing: Ethical and epistemological dimensions of teachers' work and development. *Harvard Educational Review, 60,* 159–180.

Mathematical Association of America. (1991). *A call for change: Recommendations for the mathematical preparation of teachers of mathematics.* Washington DC: Author.

Mathematical Sciences Education Board. (1989). *Everybody counts: A report to the nation on the future of mathematics education.* Washington, DC: National Academy Press.

Mathematical Sciences Education Board. (1990). *Reshaping school mathematics: A philosophy and framework for curriculum.* Washington DC: National Academy Press.

McKinney, K. (1986). How the experts teach math. In N. Paulu (Ed.), *Research in Brief.* Washington, DC: US Department of Education, Office of Educational Research and Improvement.

National Council of Teachers of Mathematics. (1989). *Curriculum and evaluation standards for school mathematics.* Reston, VA: Author.

National Council of Teachers of Mathematics. (1991). *Professional standards for the teaching of school mathematics.* Reston, VA: Author.

National Council of Teachers of Mathematics. (1995). *Assessment standards for school mathematics.* Reston, VA: Author.

Perry, W. G. (1970). *Forms of intellectual and ethical development in the college years.* New York: Holt, Rinehart & Winston.

Perry, W. G. (1981). Cognitive and ethical growth: The making of meaning. In A. W. Chickering (Ed.), *The modern American college* (pp. 76–116). San Francisco: Jossey-Bass.

Peterson, P. (1994). Learning and teaching mathematical sciences: Implications for in-service programs. In S. J. Fitzsimmons & L. C. Kerpelman (Eds.), *Teacher enhancement for elementary and secondary science and mathematics: Status, issues, and problems* (pp. 6.1–6.36). Cambridge, MA: Abt Associates, Center for Science and Technology Policy Studies.

Petrie, H., & Oshlag, R. (1993). Metaphor and learning. In A. Ortony (Ed.), *Metaphor and thought* (pp. 579–609). Cambridge, England: Cambridge University Press.

Rokeach, M. (1960). *The open and closed mind.* New York: Basic Books.

Rust, F. O. (1994). The first year of teaching: It's not what they expected. *Teaching and Teacher Education, 10,* 205–217.

Schoenfeld, A. (1992). Learning to think mathematically: Problem solving, metacognition, and sense making in mathematics. In D. Grouws (Ed.), *Handbook of research on mathematics teaching and learning.* (pp. 334–370). New York: Macmillan.

Schön, D. A. (1983). *The reflective practitioner: How professionals think in action.* New York: Basic Books.

Schön, D. A. (1987). *Educating the reflective practitioner.* San Francisco: Jossey-Bass.

Shealy, B. E. (1994). Connecting orientation towards authority to first-year teachers' thinking about teaching. In D. Kirshner (Ed.), *Proceedings of the sixteenth annual meeting of the North American Chapter of the International Group for the Psychology of Mathematics Education*, (Vol. 2, pp. 176–182). Baton Rouge: Louisiana State University Press.

Shealy, B. E. (1995). Conceptualizing the development of two first-year secondary mathematics teachers' beliefs. Doctoral dissertation, University of Georgia, Athens, 1994. *Dissertation Abstracts International, 56–3A,* 856.

Shealy, B. E., Arvold, B., Zheng, T., & Cooney, T. J. (1994, April). *Conceptualizing the professional growth of preservice secondary mathematics teachers.* Paper presented at the annual meeting of the American Educational Research Association, New Orleans, LA.

Simon, M. A. (1995). Reconstructing mathematics pedagogy from a constructivist perspective. *Journal for Research in Mathematics Education, 26,* 114–145.

Simon, M. A., & Schifter, D. (1991). Towards a constructivist perspective: An intervention study of mathematics teacher development. *Educational Studies in Mathematics, 22,* 309–331.

Snow, R. (1973). Theory construction for research on teaching. In R. Travers (Ed.) *Second handbook of research on teaching* (pp. 77–112). Chicago: Rand McNally.

Steffe, L. (1990). Adaptive mathematics teaching. In T. Cooney (Ed.), *The teaching and learning of mathematics in the 1990's* (pp. 41–51). Reston, VA: National Council of Teachers of Mathematics.

Steffe, L. P., & D'Ambrosio, B. S. (1995). Toward a working model of constructivist teaching: A reaction to Simon. *Journal for Research in Mathematics Education, 26,* 2, 146–159.

Thom, R. (1973). Modern mathematics: Does it exist? In A. G. Howson (Ed.), *Developments in mathematical education* (pp. 194–212). Cambridge, England: Cambridge University Press.

Thompson, A. G. (1984). The relationship of teachers' conceptions of mathematics and mathematics teaching to instructional practice. *Educational Studies in Mathematics, 15,* 105–127.

Thompson, A. G. (1992). Teachers' beliefs and conceptions: A synthesis of the research. In D. A. Grouws (Ed.), *Handbook of research on mathematics teaching and learning,* (pp. 127–146). New York: Macmillan.

Tymoczko, T. (1979). The four color problem and its philosophical significance. *The Journal of Philosophy, 76*(2), 57–83.

Tymoczko, T. (1986). Making room for mathematicians in the philosophy of mathematics. *The Mathematical Intelligencer, 8*(3), 44–50.

von Glasersfeld, E. (1987). *The construction of knowledge.* Seaside, CA: Intersystems Publications.

von Glasersfeld, E. (1991). Abstraction, re-presentation, and reflection: An interpretation of experience and Piaget's approach. In L. P. Steffe (Ed.), *Epistemological foundations of mathematical experience* (pp. 45–67). New York: Springer-Verlag.

Wilson, M. R. (1994). One preservice secondary teacher's understanding of function: The impact of a course integrating mathematical content and pedagogy. *Journal for Research in Mathematics Education, 25,* 346–370.

Zeichner, K. & Gore, J. (1990). Teacher Socialization. In R. Houston (Ed.), *Handbook of research on teacher education* (pp. 329–348). New York: Macmillan.

5

The More Things Change . . . Gender, Change, and Mathematics Education

Patricia B. Campbell
Campbell-Kibler Associates

Standards, reform, mathematics for all, "authentic" assessment, increasing diversity—the words of change surround mathematics education and mathematics educators including those who work in gender equity. However, as change occurs, too often educators and other "mathematics change agents" don't reflect on what change has already occurred and what further change should occur. Nor is enough time spent defining the goals this change seeks to achieve. In the case of gender equity in mathematics, there is a need not only to look critically at goals but to reflect on what we think gender equitable mathematics teaching is, and even on whether there is a feminist mathematics.

The goal of this chapter is to do some of that exploration and reflection while reviewing both the current status of gender equity in mathematics and current gender equity efforts. The chapter seeks to provide information on change within a context of current gender equity efforts, to examine areas of success and lack of success, and to explore some implications for future gender equity efforts in mathematics education.

AREAS OF GREATER AND LESSER SUCCESS IN GENDER EQUITY AREAS

The past 20 years have been areas of great change in terms of gender equity and mathematics. Girls are now taking mathematics in numbers equal to boys up to the precalculus level, and gender differences in general mathematics achievement have declined to almost nothing. Girls remain less apt to take advanced mathematics courses like calculus, to take mathematics-related courses or physics, to consider math-related careers, or to like math.

The impact of gender equity on mathematics has been mixed. At one level efforts have been successful. For example, in 1972 one-tenth of one percent (.1%) of high school senior girls were interested in engineering, whereas eight years later that number increased to 1.9%! In 1972, boys were 68 times more apt to be interested in engineering; by 1980 the number had been reduced to 4.5! (National Science Foundation, 1993).

Change has also occurred in girls' (or at least middle class girls') understanding that they need to take high school math courses to increase their college and career options. Lucy Sells' message in her 1973 classic *High School Math As The Critical Filter* was heard. Middle class girls now take enough high school math to "get into a good college." Girls take algebra, geometry, and third year-math in numbers equal to boys. At the same time, mean gender differences in general math achievement are declining. With the exception of the Scholastic Achievement Test: Math (SAT: M) scores, meta-analysis has found overall math gender differences decreasing by one half to two thirds in the past 20 years, to be "almost negligible" at this point (Friedman, 1989; Hyde, Fennema, Ryan, Frost, & Hopp, 1990).

Indeed the National Assessment of Educational Progress (NAEP) mathematics data indicate minimal overall gender differences in mathematics scores at Grades 4, 8, and 12. Between 1978 and 1990[1], 9- and 13-year-old boys gained on girls, decreasing the already small-9-year-old gender gap and actually changing the 13-year-old gender gap from favoring girls slightly to favoring boys. Seventeen-year-old girls gained on boys, decreasing that gender gap by about half. The gender gap favoring boys decreased among top scoring[2] 9- and 17-year-olds, while it increased among 13-year-olds (Mullis, Dossey, Owen, & Phillips, 1993).

There have been changes in affective areas as well. Girls' images of girls who do math appear to be quite positive, at least among girls who applied for a free summer sports, computer, and math program. Of over 200 girls from five geographically diverse sites, nationally no girl gave a negative response to the sentence: "Girls who do math are. . . ." Girls did not see girls who do math as nerds, geeks, or as unfeminine; rather they saw them as "no different from anyone else," "smart," and "awesome" (Campbell, Bachmann Acerbo, & Storo, 1995).

Yet the changes have gone only so far. For example, 40% of the girls who did not continue in mathematics in high school stopped because they didn't like mathematics, compared to 27% of the boys. Similarly,

---

[1]The change in NAEP samples from age to grade in 1990 made it impossible to compare 1972 data with 1992.

[2]Top students are defined as those who score at one or more levels above that expected for their grade.

35% of girls and 22% of boys didn't continue in science because they didn't like it (National Science Foundation, 1994).

While none of the girls gave negative responses to "Girls who do math are . . .," only around 65% gave positive responses to "When I do math I feel . . . ." Disturbingly, the 200+ girls described earlier, whether they attended a special math/sports program or not, became more interested in taking math and science courses during the summer, when they were out of school. After returning to school, girls' interest in math and science courses tended to decrease. The finding is particularly strong because of the geographic, ethnic, and socioeconomic diversity of the girls (Campbell, Bachmann Acerbo, & Storo, 1995).

In addition, there is some indication that gender differences favoring boys are greater in more advanced math areas, such as problem solving, than they are in areas such as computation (Hyde et al, 1990). Although gender gaps in the SAT: M are decreasing slowly, in 1995, boys' scores were still 40 points higher than girls' (503 vs. 463; Ponessa, 1995). Also underrepresentation of girls in math classes starts occurring in fourth year math and calculus level (boys 23%, girls 18%; Mullis et al., 1993; National Science Foundation, 1994). At the college level, inequities are even worse. One such example is the fall 1994 University of Chicago honors analysis course, where nine times more men than women were enrolled (45 men and 5 women)[3].

Impact of these changes on career choice appears to be mixed. Among those taking advanced math and science courses, there is some indication that most girls are not continuing in these fields. For example, a study of Rhode Island high school seniors found that 64% of the young men who had taken physics and calculus were planning to major in science or engineering in college, compared to only 18.6% of the young women who had taken these courses (Dick & Rallis, 1991). In 1990, boys were more than three times as likely as girls to be planning careers in math, science, or engineering (10% for boys vs. 3% for girls; National Science Foundation, 1994).

After the initial surge of women in math and math-related careers, the numbers and percentages plateaued, and interest in mathematics and math-related fields is down for both girls and boys. Between 1980 and 1990 the percentage of high school senior girls interested in engineering decreased from 1.9% to 1.4%, whereas the percentage of high school senior boys interested in engineering stayed about the same (8.5% to 8.6%; National Science Foundation, 1993). However, after remaining at around 16% for 10 years, the percentage of women entering engineering at the college level has been slowly increasing, to reach 18.5% in 1994 (Daniels, 1995).

---

[3]By the third quarter this number of students had been reduced to 13 men and 4 women, but as one woman student explained, "The women had been screened out [of mathematics] much earlier than that." (Campbell-Kibler, 1995 personal communication).

There has been change, a great deal of change, in a short period of time. However, the areas of change have been selective. The best way to describe the situation appears to be "practicality not passion." Girls (and many boys) have been convinced of the practicality of mathematics, but they have not been given the passion—the excitement and joy of doing mathematics.

THE "PROBLEM" OF GIRLS AND MATHEMATICS

There has been a focus in gender equity efforts in mathematics on what doesn't work rather than what does, on what should be eliminated rather than on what should be added.

Most efforts to "change teachers" to increase gender equity have targeted the "girl problem" in mathematics. Work with both preservice and in-service teachers has tended to focus on "the problem." Programs tend to focus on increasing educators' awareness of stereotypes such as who does mathematics, girls' lower scores on the SAT: M, girls' under-representation in advanced math and physics courses, and women's underrepresentation in math-related fields.

A national survey of math, science, and technology professors' educational methods found the gender equity topics that they were most apt to cover were:

- math and science stereotypes,
- teacher interaction patterns favoring boys,
- the underrepresentation of girls in math and science courses and activities,
- the underrepresentation of women in math and science careers.

All of these topics were related to the "problems" of gender equity (Campbell, Sanders, & Imig, 1997). The "problem" orientation of this sample of professors was also reflected in an analysis of the gender equity efforts of 61 professors of math, science, and technology methods, who were part of a multiyear gender equity training program. After participating in the program, the gender equity activities they were most apt to do with their students covered:

- mathematics/science/technology as a male domain,
- classroom interaction and atmosphere,
- biased and inappropriate curriculum materials.

The most popular activity the professors did with their methods students was "Draw a scientist, mathematician, technologist," where the point of the activity is to use the drawings to show that children and adults perceive (and stereotype) people in math, science, or technology as white, male, and stereotypically "nerdy" (Campbell, 1995). This activity was so popular that some students at some participating universities commented that they ended up drawing a "scientist/mathematician/technologist" in each of their methods courses. In addition, most speeches and short-term workshops for in-service teachers also focus on awareness of the "problems" of gender equity in mathematics. Speakers and workshop leaders, too, have teachers, parents, and students draw a "scientist, mathematician, technologist" on a regular basis[4].

There are a number of possible reasons for the focus on gender equity problems. One major reason is that equity goals have tended to focus on stopping things that shouldn't be done, including stereotyping, using linguistic bias, perpetuating unreality, making groups or their members invisible or excluded, providing one view of an issue or group, causing imbalance, and separating the contributions of women and minorities from the mainstream (McCune & Mathews reported in Wilbur, 1995). Currently, gender equity in classrooms still tends to be defined as the absence of negatives. Still needed is an articulation of what should be done to create equal educational opportunity and what equal educational opportunity means (Wilbur, 1995, p. 17).

A second reason for the focus on problems is that it is efficient. Very little time is spent on gender equity in preservice and in-service education, at least in math, science, and technology methods. Although gender equity is covered in most methods classes (72% of professors cover gender equity), most professors (67%) spend 2 hours or less per semester on it (Campbell, Sanders, & Imig, 1997). Gender equity efforts for most in-service teachers also tend to be short, usually a 1–2 hour workshop or presentation as part of an in-service day.

When there is only a short amount of time spent on gender equity, it is understandable that the focus is on problems. Information abounds about girls' lower SAT scores and women's underrepresentation in math related fields. In addition, much of the media attention to gender equity issues in mathematics has been based on *The AAUW Report: How Schools Shortchange Girls* (Bailey et al., 1992) and David and Myra Sadker's (1994) *Failing At Fairness,* and has centered on problems reported there on girls' and women's underrepresentation and on teachers' unequal treatment of girls. Targeting problems and their related facts is relatively easy, can be done quickly, and, perhaps most importantly, is not controversial, and it does have an impact—it increases awareness and helps teachers, parents, and even students understand

---

[4]This is not to denigrate Draw A Scientist and it's variations—it is a useful, fun tool that quickly points out stereotypes. The activity is a good way to build awareness of an equity problem in mathematics.

the importance of taking mathematics. However, the focus on problems without a focus on solutions doesn't change the classroom environment nor does it generate excitement about mathematics.

BEYOND PROBLEMS: PROGRAMS THAT LOOK FOR GENDER EQUITY SOLUTIONS

Although the involvement that most teachers have with gender equity is "one shot" and problem oriented, there are programs that go a step beyond the awareness of problems to look toward solutions. These existing programs or their components can help teachers now to make their efforts more gender-equitable and to involve more girls (and many boys) in mathematics.

Longer term gender equity training, such as EQUALS and GESA, goes beyond the problem level to explore solutions. Targeted toward volunteer teachers with an existing interest in gender equity, these programs involve teachers in several days of training, often with later follow-up. Although research and evaluation on impact is thin, there is, as the following suggests, some indication that these programs do have an impact.

EQUALS

EQUALS is a teacher training program, developed by Lawrence Hall of Science at University of California, Berkeley, that trains teachers in techniques that can be used to overcome gender stereotyping and to sustain the interest of girls and other underrepresented students in mathematics and science. A controlled study of EQUALS-trained teachers found that middle school students taught by EQUALS-trained teachers increased their problem-solving skills significantly more than other students. Although no overall differences in problem solving were found in elementary and high school EQUALS classes, White girls and African American boys in EQUALS classes had the largest increases in problem-solving skills. Furthermore, following their first year in EQUALS, elementary school students became less likely to see mathematics as a male domain, and in both elementary school and high school, EQUALS students had higher beliefs in the intrinsic value of mathematics than did control students (Sutton & Fleming, 1995). A second controlled study of the impact of the EQUALS program focused on preservice teachers and found EQUALS participants increasing their mathematics competence compared to a control group (Amodea & Enslie, 1985).

Current Students/Future Scientists and Engineers

Current Students/Future Scientists and Engineers (CS/FSE) is a program from the Clark Science Center of Smith College. Each year, teams of middle school and high school teachers/administrators meet for several days of training and planning on ways to encourage girls in math and science. At the end of the session, each team has to develop a plan to be implemented during the upcoming school year. Nine-month follow-up of CS/FSE found teams doing a mean of 2.8 activities to encourage girls in math and science, including providing role models/guest speakers, having discussions with faculty on gender issues, providing students with information on gender issues and increasing student awareness of math, science, and engineering careers. In addition, almost two thirds of the teachers felt that their own behaviors had changed, causing them to call more on females and to encourage all (Campbell & Storo, 1994).

GESA

GESA (Gender/Ethnic Expectations, Student Achievement) is a more general teacher training program, developed by the GrayMill Foundation, to train teachers in ways to overcome gender and ethnic stereotyping. GESA also provides teachers with specific techniques to use in all subject areas to increase student expectations and achievement. The results of research on the impact of GESA are mixed. One study comparing teachers at a GESA and a nonGESA elementary school concluded GESA training did not effect teacher–student interaction patterns (Stoddard, 1993). However, a second study found that after GESA training, teachers were more aware of gender issues and had more interactions with female students, although no significant differences were found in the self-esteem of GESA and non-GESA students (Levitt, 1992). A third study compared GESA-trained and nonGESA-trained fifth-grade teachers on student self-esteem and reading. GESA-trained teachers were found to be more effective in increasing student reading achievement. GESA-taught low achieving students made greater gains than nonGESA-taught low achievers in reading and in self-perception (Feeney, 1992). No studies were found that looked at the impact on GESA in math areas.

Playtime Is Science

Playtime Is Science (PS) is a training program that targets preschool and primary teachers. Although billed as a hands-on science training program with an emphasis on equity and on parent involvement, the activities have a strong focus on problem solving and spatial skills development. A study on PS's impact on teachers found that PS was successful in increasing the number of hands-on math and science activities teachers did (Campbell, Bachmann Acerbo, & Storo, 1994). In addition, whereas both girls and boys in PS became more science aware and better problem solvers, in some areas PS participation reduced gender differences. After PS the gender gap in terms of children saying they did science and that they did science at home was eliminated (Campbell, Bachmann Acerbo, Storo, & Sprung, 1995).

WHAT'S MISSING?: GENDER EQUITY SOLUTIONS

To be successful, gender equity needs to be part of the mainstream of mathematics and needs to move beyond awareness of problems and the "counting" of female/male interactions into looking at what and how mathematics is taught. To do this well, educators need to examine what we know about change.

Gender equity efforts and programs have made a difference in mathematics education, but for a number of reasons, the success of these efforts has been limited. For gender equity efforts to be successful it is important to:

- infuse gender equity concerns and awareness into mainstream teaching;
- move beyond gender equity awareness and problems;
- apply what is known about change to gender equity efforts.

Infusing Gender Equity[5]

Gender equity tends to be an "add on." In a college methods class, that means a session or two on gender equity and then on to the real business of teacher eduction—teaching students to become good teachers. "Good teaching" is not enough. There is danger in the popular idea that "a rising tide lifts all boats," that the use of manipulatives and other hands-on activities along with small group cooperative learning will help all students. Although improved mathematics education is an important and laudable goal, for gender equity it is not enough for all to gain; the gaps between girls and boys must decrease while all gain. Without special attention to gender the hands that will be doing the hands-on will tend to be male.

---

[5]Gender equity has been outside the mainstream of educational reform. An analysis of 35 educational reform reports found "most of the reports do not define the educational issues under review in terms of gender, nor do they include sex as a separate category in their data analysis and background information" (Bailey et al., 1992, p. 6). The NCTM Standards are an exception. They deal with gender equity issues implicitly in the curriculum standards and explicitly in the teaching standards.

In teaching in general, and within gender equity efforts, it needs to be asked if one can one be a good teacher without taking into account issues of gender, without attempting to meet the needs of half the class, or without reflecting on the impact of one's own behavior. It is obvious that a teacher who actively discourages girls, allows a small number of predominately male students to dominate the class, or allows a classroom environment where girls are put down or disrespected is neither a good nor an equitable teacher. The answer could be less clear when good teaching strategies are applied inequitably or in ways that have inequitable results. Yet pedagogy that leaves out large numbers of children is *not* good pedagogy. Even when activities and methods are done to be equitable, Rosser (1995) was concerned that an application of equity strategies in science and math without gender and race components can actually end up hurting women and men of color. She cited the instructor who made sure that each small group in his predominately male science class had one girl and several boys in it, because spreading the girls out "was equitable." In this case, under the guise of equity, there could be increased isolation for the girls. By just putting the students in groups without setting up rules and structures to ensure that all students participate, it can be practically guaranteed that the girls will have fewer opportunities and will participate less. Indeed Koehler (1990) found that in mixed sex math groups girls were less likely to receive help from boys, and if there was only one girl, she was ignored.

Similarly, another high school teacher explained that in her classes if four boys and one girl raised their hands, then she called on girls 20% of the time, because to do anything else "would not be fair." (Campbell, 1993). This definition of fairness left girls as second class citizens in the math class of a teacher who was strongly committed to encouraging girls.

Most teachers are not opposed to special efforts to encourage girls in math and science, but they have few ideas of what to do. The major strategy they report using is "treating all students equally" (Campbell & Acerbo, 1994; Campbell & Shackford, 1993), but what this means can vary greatly from teacher to teacher. Teachers need to collect data about their own teaching to become aware that they don't treat all students equally and that no one treats all students equally. This helps us all move to the next step of actively determining how one wants to treat individual students and checking to see if, under the teaching methods being used, this is happening.

Moving Beyond Awareness and Problems

As mentioned earlier, equity is now seen as the absence of negatives. There needs to be a movement beyond that to see equity as the presence of positives in a domain-specific way. The gender equity model has, in many cases, been content-free with the same "generic" gender equity activities for all the content areas. Looking at how women and girls are portrayed in textbooks, providing role models, and exploring how teachers interact with female students and with male students are all important activities that need to be done, but they are limited because they are not specific to the content area being taught.

It is important to move beyond "one model fits all" and explore what gender equity means, not just for teaching math, but in specific mathematics areas. In the biological sciences some of this work has been done already. For example, Rosser (1995) suggested that it could be good science and good equity in biology to switch from considering the male body as the norm to using the female body. There are a number of scientific justifications for this including:

- the female body could be more accurate for the norm because of its cyclicity;
- if the female body is more complex, a standard reason for limiting research to males[6], then if more complex is the norm, there will be fewer reasons to exclude both sexes from research and theory ;
- all human zygotes start out as female.

Of course the gender equity implications of such a switch could be great as well.

A second example targets methodology. Now, in part thanks to the work of people like Barbara McClintock in botany and Sarah Hrdy in primatology, an alternative scientific method is being used. In this method of studying animal and human behavior, researchers immerse themselves in the animal culture and determine patterns from what they see. As a consequence, the traditional scientific method of hypotheses testing is not the only method being used and increasingly is not the only method being taught.

Although it would be wonderful to provide examples such as these in mathematics, at this point it is difficult. Fennema (1990) asserted that, based at least in part on what teachers know and believe about gender differences in mathematics, decisions are made about what each female or male learns in the classroom. These decisions in turn, influence what that female or male learns in mathematics. However, it is not clear what this means in terms of content.

The concept of "feminist science" has been with us for a while and many of the issues of feminist science have become part of mainstream science and can, and should, be a part of good science teaching. It is not

---

[6]A more recent example was reported in the 10/15/95 Boston Globe justifying the exclusion of women from a study of eating patterns in the elderly because of females' greater complexity.

clear if there is such a thing as feminist mathematics[7]. Neither is it clear if such gender laden variables as the toys children play with influence how mathematics is constructed. For example, if your primary play-things are individual units (i.e., trucks), or pieces that are put together to make a unit (i.e., train cars or Legos), do you construct mathematics differently than if your primary toys are related families (i.e., dolls, tea sets, cook sets and cleaning equipment)?

While the concept of feminist or gendered mathematics is being explored and debated, gender equity efforts in mathematics need to become more content specific. This may mean, for example, if one problem is going to be used in a middle school math class over a several-day period, teachers need to check in advance if the problem context is one that interests girls and boys. The context in which the problem is put—be it nuclear war, music, or just abstractions—should be equally attractive to and involve both girls and boys.

As there is a movement away from generic gender equity activities, educators need to listen to what students say about math and math teaching. The following quotes from high school girls who could perform in math class but weren't planning to continue in it provides some clues to what needs to be done.

> I want real problems. When is the last time you called someone up and asked them how old they were and they said " I am twice as old as my brother. . . ." Give us real problems.

> I do math in my own way. Nobody else in my class does it this way . . . [and the teacher] doesn't understand. [Teachers] don't like that, if you have your own way, if that isn't their way. A good teacher says "oh that is another way" and brushes it aside. Teachers are really upset at having to admit that you have another way.

> We liked the rods—even if they were an ugly color, they were fun and, I got to see how multiplication worked. You can prove to a little kid how 2+2=4 with the rods. You could see that it worked. You could really know it, those little rods were proof that it worked. For little kids this represents the real life (Campbell & Campbell-Kibler, No date).

These girls wanted math that was real, that allowed for a variety of methods to get to answers, and that helped them get to the "whys" behind the "hows". By listening to their students, teachers can get clues on how to reach students and keep them interested in math.

Going beyond generic gender equity may mean that along with dealing with issues related to classroom interaction and classroom

---

[7]Historically there has been gendered mathematics. For example, Pythagoreans considered odd numbers male and good, and even numbers female and evil (Wertheim, 1995, p 25).

climate, math teachers may work together using examples specific to the content. For example, calculus and precalculus teachers might discuss the following vignette: "Calculus teachers are concerned that the increasing emphasis on graphing calculators will turn more girls off calculus. What can be done so that doesn't happen?"

Similarly as part of a math methods course, elementary preservice teachers might work on the following problem: "Elementary school teachers feel that the increasing emphasis on problem solving and the decreasing emphasis on computation and rule-based mathematics will further turn girls off to mathematics. What can be done so that doesn't happen?"

Moving beyond the generic also means that, just as mathematics educators are increasingly realizing the importance of students constructing their own knowledge, it must be realized that teachers must also construct their own knowledge. Preservice and in-service teachers need to examine what equity means to them and what, for them, a gender equitable classroom is. For in-service teachers this also means collecting data on what they are doing and reflecting on that data: "Am I doing what I want?" "Is it having the impact I want?" "Am I serving most, if not all, of my students?" These are questions that math teachers need to be asking and answering regularly.

Being explicit about goals, collecting information as to the degree to which those goals are being met, and trying out new ways to reach those goals are key to good mathematics teaching and gender-equitable teaching. Originally it was thought that good pedagogy is good for all students; in reality, it is the reverse—that which is good for all students is good pedagogy.

Applying What Is Known About Change

Applying gender equity to the mainstream and moving beyond generic gender equity involves a great deal of change, both within the mathematics education community and within the gender equity community. Yet, too often what has been missing in gender equity efforts has been an analysis of what is known about change and the change process that can be applied to gender equity efforts.

Perhaps the single most important key to making change is having a goal—an explicit goal or set of goals. What do gender equity advocates and math educators want to happen, what are the goals? In gender equity and math education, goals aren't always clear. Goals often may conflict, as does "mathematics for all" versus "mathematics for the best and the brightest" (Tobias, 1990). Similarly, goals may be so general as to be of little value—what does "mathematics for all" mean? Some might also ask what the choices for goals are. Within gender equity, goals tend to fall into three separate areas—equal access, equal treatment, and equal outcomes.

Within equal access, goals center around breaking down legal and psychological barriers to courses, schools, activities, or careers. With some exceptions (such as publicly supported, all-male military academies), the legal barriers have been broken. The psychological barriers such as "real girls don't do advanced mathematics" still exist.

Equal treatment goals, as the name suggests, focus on providing girls as a group, and boys as a group, with the same treatment and opportunities. Goals in this area often center around eliminating stereotypes and equalizing teacher/student interaction.

Equal outcome goals don't necessarily assume equal access and treatment. Indeed, to have equal outcomes it might be necessary to have unequal access or treatment. Travis (1992) maintained that there is a confusion between equality and sameness that must be untangled, because it has now become clear that in many domains the assumption of sameness has lead to unfair and unequal results[8].

She went on to espouse an equity goal that evaluates policies and classroom behaviors by directing attention to their results, not their intentions.

If the goals in an individual classroom or in a profession are in access, treatment, or outcome, the processes to reach those goals may be quite different and the measures to see if the goals have been met are sure to be different.

Although there is room for individual differences, there is a need for some consensus in the math education and equity communities. In the meantime, "the absence of integrated outcomes has overwhelmed teachers as they are confronted with reams of related but disconnected recommendations for each discipline and social cause" (Wilbur, 1995, p. 8).

One possible goal for equity and mathematics education is "to reduce the gaps while all gain," namely that gender and racial differences in student math participation, interest, and achievement should be decreasing while all gain. This may mean unequal access or unequal treatment while one group "catches up," as long as all groups are gaining.

As goals are being defined, an examination needs to be made of what is known about the change process that can assist efforts to make mathematics more gender equitable. There has been a great deal of writing on change—both in and out of education—some of which challenges preconceptions.

For example, it was earlier assumed, based in part by a Rand study of educational innovation, that in order for change to occur, there had

---

[8]While Travis' example focused on the unequal outcomes of giving women and men the same number of toilet stalls, there are education examples as well dealing with such issues as previous experience with activities that develop spatial skills.

to be an initial commitment to that change. This was, in part, a reason for gender equity's focus on problems and awareness—there was a need to "hook" the teachers before they would change in more gender equitable ways. A 10-year follow-up to the Rand study found that whereas initial commitment to the desired change is useful, it is not the only or even the major influence on individual response to change. It was found that belief could follow practice and that individuals required to change could become believers (McLaughlin, 1991).

Although initial commitment is not the major component of an individual's willingness to accept a change, the impact of the change on an individual is. Hall (1979) found that teachers had intense concerns about what an educational change "means for me," whereas their concerns about the impact of the change on students was relatively low. Similarly, Liker, Roitman, and Roskies (1987) found that employees' reactions to change could be in great part explained by how the changes influenced the individual's job prospects. The impact on the individual is strong enough that Carnall (1986) felt that the key to successful change is the sketching out of the impact of change in terms of the relative advantage or disadvantage involved for members of different interest groups involved.

In addition, in the early 1980's Little (1982) found that in examples of successful change, teachers and administrators planned, designed, researched, and evaluated the change together. Stressing the importance of collegiality and partnership to teacher ability to implement change, Little (1982) also found it was key that teachers talked with each other about the teaching practices being implemented, and that teachers and administrators observed each other and provided to each other useful evaluations and feedback. McLaughlin (1991) found that teacher participation mattered, especially in designing implementation strategies, whereas Fullan (1991) found that change worked when teachers interacted with each other about the changes being made.

Participating in change also involves values and beliefs. In education, change "requires not only new and revised materials and new teaching approaches but also most importantly an alteration of beliefs" (Fullan, 1991, p. 37). "Significant educational change consists of changes in beliefs, teaching style, and materials which can come about only through a process of personal development in a social context" (Fullan, 1991, p. 127). Solutions "come through the development of shared meaning" (Fullan, 1991, p. 5).

Wilbur (1995, p. 12) agreed, maintaining that

> shifting the norms of the culture launches a process that must include, if not begin, by teasing out the values that dignify self-determination, collaboration, critical thinking and democratic action. Too often this step is passed over with claims that value inquiry is only an exercise in

philosophy with little relevance for what teachers do on Monday. In the "make it and take it" world of staff development, the underpinnings of authentic decision-making are frequently ignored. Consequently, tacit beliefs about the learner, the growth process and motivation go unquestioned, leaving teachers powerless to make substantive change or to evaluate decision in light of educational aims.

RECOMMENDATIONS

As with most efforts, there are more questions than answers. However, there are also some guideposts. The starting point is with goals—what gender equity advocates and math educators want to happen. Collectively and individually a search needs to be made for goals. Mathematics teachers need to ask themselves what their goals are for their classes, what it would take for them to feel that their class had been a success, and then if or how equity is related to that success.

Defining and redefining goals, collecting data about the degree to which those goals are being met, reflecting on the data, and making changes as necessary is a process that every teacher should be doing. Because few teachers want to have inequitable classrooms and most want what is best for their students, this process could be a major step toward mainstreaming equity.

Although it is important to stress the negative behaviors of students and teachers that need to be stopped, it is even more important to look at the behaviors that need to be started so that students, both girls and boys, learn, use, and, yes, even like mathematics.

Although there is increased awareness of equity in mathematics methods and teaching, there needs to be, as well, an increased awareness of mathematics in gender equity. The goal is for the two to intersect so completely that good mathematics education is equitable mathematics education.

Of course there are policies that can facilitate these efforts. One of the most valuable is to develop a reward structure for teachers that includes positive incentives for moving toward gender equity and negative consequences for not doing so. Criteria used for teacher evaluation and tenure decisions could and should include specific measures of gender equity (Bailey & Campbell, 1992-93). Important as well is the provision of in-depth, ongoing professional development opportunities for teachers, parents, and administrators that focus on working from their own personal and professional experiences toward a clearer understanding of the ways in which gendered assumptions and power imbalances affect the opportunities available to students, and that assist them in developing procedures for successfully addressing these issues (Bailey & Campbell, 1992-93).

As work is continued toward making things better, reflection needs to be done on the progress that has been made, from the girls who think girls who do math are "awesome" to the "nerd power" movement at MIT; from the increasing test scores to the increasing participation in math courses. Educators have been doing many things right. However, just as in mathematics few interesting things are linear, so is the case in equity. We need to learn from what we have done and expand in more complex, challenging ways.

REFERENCES

Amodea, L. B., & Enslie, J. (March, 1985). *The effects of a mathematics intervention program on the computational skills and attitudes of pre-service elementary and secondary teachers.* Paper presented at the American Educational Research Association Annual Meeting. Chicago, IL. (ERIC Document ED 270247)

Bailey, S., Burbidge, L., Campbell, P. B., Jackson, B., Marx, F., & McIntosh, P. (1992). *The AAUW report: How schools shortchange girls.* Washington, DC: AAUW Educational Foundation/NEA.

Bailey, S., & Campbell, P. B. (1992-93). *"Gender equity: The unexamined basic of school reform." Stanford Law and Policy Review.* Vol. 4.

Campbell, P. B. (1995). *Teacher Education Equity Project Evaluation Report.* Groton, MA: Campbell-Kibler Associates.

Campbell, P. B. & Acerbo, K. (1994). *Evaluation report.* Groton, MA: Campbell-Kibler Associates.

Campbell, P. B., Bachmann Acerbo, K., & Storo, J. (1994). *Playtime Is Science: 1994 evaluation report.* Groton, MA : Campbell-Kibler Associates.

Campbell, P. B., Bachmann Acerbo, K., & Storo, J. (1995). *Math, science, sports and empowerment: Girls incorporated replication and expansion of the EUREKA! model.* Groton, MA : Campbell-Kibler Associates.

Campbell, P. B., Bachmann Acerbo, K., Storo, J., & Sprung, B. (1995). *Small children and fun science: The impact of Playtime Is Science on young children.* Groton, MA: Campbell-Kibler Associates.

Campbell, P. B. & Campbell-Kibler, K. (No date). *Math, education and life: A daughter and mother speak to parents and children.* Unpublished document.

Campbell, P. B. & Imig, D. (1997). Uniformed but interested: Findings of a national survey on gender equity in pre-service teacher education. *Journal of Teacher Education, 48*(1), pp. 69–75.

Campbell, P. B., Sanders, J., & Imig, D. (in press). Uninformed but interested: Findings of a national survey on gender equity in pre-service teacher education. *Journal of Teacher Education, 48*(1), 69–75.

Campbell, P. B. & Shackford, C. (1993). *FAMILY SCIENCE 1991-93: Final evaluation report.* Groton, MA: Campbell-Kibler Associates.

Campbell, P. B. & Storo, J. (1994). *Smith college Current Students / Future Scientists and Engineers (CS / FSE): 1994 evaluation report.* Groton, MA : Campbell-Kibler Associates.

Campbell-Kibler, K. B. (June, 2, 1995). Personal communication.

Carnall, C. A. (1986). Toward a theory for the evaluation of organizational change. *Human Relations, 39,* p. 745.

Daniels, Jane Z. (Fall, 1995). Increasing undergraduate engineering enrollments. *WEPAN News,* Vol. 4, No. 2, p. 1.

Dick, T. P. & Rallis, S. (July, 1991). "Factors and influences on high school students' career choices." *Journal of Research In Mathematics Education, 22,* 281–92.

Feeney, N. J. R. (1992). The effects of the Gender/Ethnic Expectations and Student Achievement program (GESA) on the self-perceptions and reading achievement of fifth grade students. *Dissertation Abstracts, 53,* 07A. DA #01250288.

Fennema, E. (1990). Teacher beliefs and gender differences in mathematics. In E. Fennema, and G.C. Leder (Eds.), *Mathematics and Gender,* (pp. 169–187). New York: Teachers College Press.

Friedman, L. (1989). Mathematics and the gender gap: A meta-analysis of recent studies on sex differences in mathematical tasks. *Review of Educational Research, 59,* (2), 185–213.

Fullan, M. (1991). *The new meaning of educational change.* New York: Teachers College Press.

Hall, G. (Summer, 1979). *The concerns-based approach to facilitating change.* Austin, TX: Research and Development Center for Teacher Education, Educational Horizons.

Hyde, J., Fennema, E., Ryan, M., Frost, L., & Hopp., C. (1990). Gender comparisons of mathematics attitudes and affect: A meta analysis. *Psychology of Women Quarterly, (14)*3, pp. 20–25.

Koehler, M. S. (1990). Classrooms, teachers and gender differences in mathematics. In E. Fennema, & G. C. Leder (Eds.) *Mathematics and Gender,* (pp. 128–148). New York: Teachers College Press.

Levitt, I. S. (1992). *An evaluation of an intervention program for teachers to improve gender equity in classrooms.* Dissertation Abstracts. 1992, 52, 09A # DA 01203591.

Liker, J. K., Roitman, D. B. & Roskies, E. (1987). Changing everything all at once: Work life and technological change. *Sloan Management Review, 28,*(19), 29.

Little, J. (1982). Norms of collegiality and experimentation work place conditions of school success. *American Educational Research Journal, 19,* 325–40.

McLaughlin, M. W. (1991). The Rand change agent study: Ten years later. In A. R. Odden (Ed). *Education Policy Implementation,* (pp. 143–155). Albany, New York: SUNY Press.

Mullis, I. V. S., Dossey, J. A., Owen, E. H. & Phillips, G. W. (1993). *NAEP 1992: Mathematics report card for the nation and the states.* Washington, DC: Office of Educational Research and Improvement, US Department of Education.

National Science Foundation. (1993). *Women and minorities in science and engineering an update.* Washington, DC: Author.

National Science Foundation. (1994). *Women and minorities and persons with disabilities in science and engineering:* 1994. Arlington, VA (NSF 94-333).

Ponessa, J. (Sept. 6, 1995) Math and verbal scores up on revamped SAT. *Education Week.* p. 13.

Rosser, S. (Aug., 1995). *Teaching to reach the majority.* A speech to the participants of the Teacher Education Equity Project, City University of New York, Seattle, WA.

Sadker, M., & Sadker, D. (1994). *Failing at fairness.* New York: Scribner.

Sells, L. (1973). *High school mathematics as the critical filter.* Berkeley: University of California. (ERIC Document Reproduction Service No. ED 080351).

Stoddard, C. B. (1993). Investigation of the effectiveness of a teachers' training program Gender/Ethnic Expectations: Student Achievement (GESA) for reducing disparity in teacher-student interactions. Dissertation Abstracts. 54, 04 A. # DA 01306375.

Stebbins, M. W. & Shani, A. B. (Winter, 1989). Organization design: Beyond the 'mafia' model. *Organizational Dynamics, 17,* (13), 18.

Sutton, R. E. & Fleming, E. S. (1995). Evaluating an intervention program: Results from two years with EQUALS. In C. Heid (Ed.), *Sex equity: Knowledge and practices.* Bloomington, IN: Center for Urban and Multicultural Education, Indiana University Press.

Tobias, S. (1990). *They're not dumb, they're different*. Tucson, AZ: Research Corporation.

Travis, C. (1992). *The mismeasure of woman*. New York: Simon and Schuster.

Wertheim, M. (1995). *Pythagoras' trousers*. New York: Random House.

Wilbur, Gretchen (1995). *Transforming schools into equity cultures*. Unpublished manuscript.

III

CONTEXT AND TEACHER CHANGE

6

A Conceptual Framework for Studying the Relevance of Context to Mathematics Teachers' Change

Doug Jones
University of Kentucky

Context is an elusive but common concept. Although most people have an intuitive notion of what context is, they cannot clearly define it. They caution against taking statements *out of context*, assert that actions must be understood *in context*, and argue that context can be productively used in teaching. Context is said to have something to do with environment, something to do with conditions, something to do with the actors in a given situation. But regardless of whether context is treated as an intuitive concept or a productive construct, it has definite implications for teaching and teacher change. As Dewey (1931/1985) stated, "The most pervasive fallacy of philosophic thinking goes back to the neglect of context."

This chapter begins with an examination of three characteristics of context that are pertinent to a study of teacher change— context is functional, explanatory, and interactively constructed. This examination leads to a discussion of three faces of context: interpretation of policy, school norms and expectations, and conceptions of mathematics. Relationships between these faces of context and teaching are then discussed. Finally, I suggest direction for investigations of the relationship between context and teacher change.

CHARACTERISTICS OF CONTEXT

Two fundamental characteristics of context and its relationship to teaching and learning mathematics are that context is both *functional* and *explanatory*. To illustrate these characteristics, we look to linguistics and anthropology.

131

Context Is Functional

Linguistically, context can be defined as the text in which a statement, phrase, or symbol is embedded and from which its meaning must be inferred. For example, in mathematics, the literal symbol x can refer to multiplication, as in 3 x 4 = 12; it can stand for an unknown, as in $3x + 4 = 19$; it can represent an element of a domain set for a function, as in $f=\{(x,y)\,|\,y=5x\text{-}2;\,x \in \mathbb{R}\}$. Those who are successful in dealing with literal symbols like x in mathematics know to look at them in context in order to discern the appropriate meaning for the symbol. That is, the meaning for the literal symbol must be derived from its relationship to the surrounding text and the way in which it is used. This is a functional interpretation of context. When viewed from this perspective, context helps people build meaning from their experiences. Although this example is rather straightforward in its dealings with literal symbols, the functional characteristic of context plays a significant role in complex teaching and learning environments. Examples of this role are discussed later in the chapter. (For related discussion, see Stein & Brown, chap. 7, and Secada & Adajian, chap. 8, this volume.)

Context Is Explanatory

Context is also used to refer to setting and environment. When someone says that you have to look at his or her teaching *in context*, he or she often means to look at it in relationship to the conditions that support or limit that teaching. These include the conditions of the classroom; the educational emphases of the school; the political, social, and educational relationship between the school and the community; the financial resources available; the educational policies that govern teaching; and so on. Nespor (1984) and Brown, Collins, and Duguid (1989) used context in this manner. Interpreting context to refer to conditions that support or limit also is common in anthropology. Indeed, in his discussion of context, Warren (1987) included a culture's norms, expectations, mechanisms for determining what is and is not acceptable in given situations, and the ways in which a person forms his or her identity. In fact, Geertz (1983) asserted that any attempt to understand a group of people must take account of what is known locally—that is, what is accepted, negotiated, or considered to be common knowledge among a particular group. This use of context is explanatory; understanding such conditions helps one to better understand teaching. (For related discussion, see Stein & Brown, chap. 7, and Campbell & White, chap. 12, this volume.)

Context also carries the connotation of being a "conceptual trash can" that justifies experimentally observed effects, or a powerful "phenomenon" that makes possible the distinction between figure and ground (see, e.g., Davies & Thomson, 1988). Although common, neither the trash can nor the phenomenon interpretation is likely to help us think more deeply about the relationship between context and teaching.

A bigger problem with these characteristics, and one that is recognized by authors in this volume, is that they make context out to be separate from individuals. From the perspective that context is external, it is tempting to think of context as unaffectable—as only a limiting force—and, thus, to think of teachers as being victims of context. As with any victim, the educator who is limited by an external, "imposition" form of context learns to be helpless or feels persecuted (or both). With regard to studying teacher change, context would be more usefully conceived as having some personal character. Taking this into account leads to a third characteristic of context.

Context Is Interactively Constructed

Any productive interpretation of context includes the methodology a teacher employs, his or her instructional goals, and his or her perspectives on mathematics and on what is appropriate or inappropriate to do with students. It includes the meanings a teacher has for approaches such as using cooperative groups, the extent to which there is agreement between the teacher's orientation and that of the students, the school community, and the professional community. In these attributions, context *is* seen to have a personal character. In effect, context is intertwined with perspective (Cobb, 1986; Easley, 1980). But perhaps the most important characteristic of context with regard to teachers' change is that context is interactively constructed. A constructive context arises through discussion and reflection on action, whether taken or imagined. (A developmental process through which context is affected and constructed is discussed by Goldsmith & Schifter in chap. 2 of this volume.)

For a personal example of ways in which context might be constructed, we turn to student teachers' reactions to their field placements. It is not uncommon for student teachers to feel somewhat limited in what they can do in their placements. They are unfamiliar with school policies regarding discipline, they do not teach the students or the curriculum for a full year, they have had limited experience anticipating students' questions, and so on. However, the biggest concern they report is that their teaching styles are different from that of their cooperating teachers. In some situations, student teachers are advised to just "hang in there" and accommodate their teaching actions to what already is in place. However, sometimes student teachers are confident enough, and have enough support, to be able to take action that ultimately changes the classroom climate, the students' expectations, and to some extent, the cooperating teacher's style or goals. For instance, one of my student teachers consistently engaged her students in exploratory activity. She had them collect, analyze, and present data (from outside the classroom) that was related to the content she was teaching; she had them investigate mathematical relationships with computers, graphing calculators, and physical representations; and she engaged them in discussion about the sense they were making of concepts. At the end of her placement, her cooperating teacher indicated that for the first time in 25 years he was thinking of doing things differently in his classroom. For the cooperating teacher, the teaching and learning context changed as a result of his interactions and reflections with the student teacher.

Another student teacher was convinced of the value of questioning and asking students to justify their mathematical actions. Although he met with resistance from the students for the first two months, he persisted with his emphasis on questioning, and students eventually came to expect, if not value, his stream of "Why does that work?," "What does it mean?," and "Where have you seen something like this before?" Because questioning and justification came to be expected, they provided guidance to this teacher as he contemplated his lesson preparation, his interaction with colleagues, and his future professional development.

Having the support of their supervisors and being pushed to reflect on and analyze their teaching actions was instrumental in helping these beginning teachers mold their teaching experiences into something they felt made a difference. Although this kind of change is a rare occurrence, it clearly illustrates the claim that the context of the classroom can be interactively constructed and can help individuals and groups frame and give meaning to their actions, ideas, and experiences.

There is a tension in this construction, though—the tension between the constructed and imposed aspects of context. Although setting, policy, and conditions may be imposed principally by external forces, they are not unaffected by a teacher's goals and perspective. (Witness the teachers who have successfully fought to get school policies regarding textbook adoption changed.) Similarly, although teachers' goals, beliefs, and perspectives are fundamentally internally constructed, they are definitely affected by conditions and policies. (Witness the teachers who, because of district or state policy, are forced to integrate their teaching and come to believe in its value—see for example, Appalachia Educational Laboratory [AEL], 1993b, 1996. For related discussion see Cooney & Shealy, chap. 4 in this volume.) There is a dynamic relationship between the primarily imposed and the primarily constructed faces of context. At any given time, context may appear to have more of one kind of character than the other; it should not be conceived as only constructed or imposed.

Before going any further, though, we need to turn to three faces of context: interpretation of policy, support or limitations due to school norms and expectations, and perspective on mathematics. For each of these faces of context, two examples pointing out ways in which it affects teaching are presented.

FACES OF CONTEXT

Interpretation of Policy

There is considerable evidence to suggest that interpretation of policy is an important variable in teacher change of the general sort now under consideration (AEL, 1993a, 1993b, 1996; Corrigan & Haberman, 1990; Feiman-Nemser & Floden, 1986). Analyses of curriculum reform, alternative or emergency certification policies, school-based decision making, and the like all point to variation based on local or regional emphases.

Example 1a. Some of the curricular reforms of the late 1950s and 1960s attempted to move teachers away from textbook-based teaching toward experience-based learning and to engage students in informal, exploratory activities, rather than in rote learning. Teachers and students alike were to be inspired by a new view of learning as individual insight and discovery, rather than as the accumulation of facts. But the impact on American schooling was less than had been hoped for (Weiss, 1978). A variety of reasons, ranging from changing social values to differing views of the nature of the process of policy implementation (see Atkin & House, 1981), were given for the relative failure of the reforms. However, these attributions rely on treating context as an external constraint—that is, that the context of these reforms had top-down imposition of policy as a principal component.

On the other hand, there is a substantial and well-regarded body of analysis that supports the view that the difference between success and failure depends on local implementation and the degree to which local concerns either fit, or can be accommodated to, those of the reform (Atkin & House, 1981; Berman & McLaughlin, 1978; Elmore & McLaughlin, 1988; The Ford Foundation, 1972). The bulk of the curriculum projects were examples of a center–periphery model of knowledge diffusion, in which the innovation, in this case the new curriculum, was developed in one place by specialists but was viewed as broadly applicable, existed fully realized prior to its diffusion, and was disseminated through the movement of the innovation from the center outward to the user. Teachers and administrators were viewed as eager and pliable recipients of new knowledge.

In fact, local concerns and characteristics often overshadowed designers' priorities; teachers acted like the creators of their own norms of good practice rather than as uncritical consumers. Further, the participation of building principals and teachers in decision-making about implementation proved to be an important variable: "Teachers were influenced by external factors only to the extent that it suited them and their circumstances allowed it" (Atkin & House, 1981, p. 13). Implementation turned out to be more a process of negotiation between local actors and the innovation than a matter of compliant adoption of ideas formulated elsewhere. Local variability was the rule; local context mattered.

Example 1b. In 1991, Newtown High School[1] in rural Kentucky (AEL, 1993a) was faced with the mandate of establishing a school council for making decisions about the operation of the school (curriculum policy, school scheduling, budget oversight, the hiring of personnel, and so on). The state had legislated that such a council was to be made up of the school principal, representatives from the faculty, and representatives from the parents. In effect, this council was charged with constructing a school that was responsive, within the limitations of the state's education goals, to the community's values, needs, and concerns. The intent was to promote balanced decision making and to provide for a large measure of local control of the school. To some extent, this happened. For example, the Newtown High School council devoted substantial time to parents' concerns that the mathematics department was not meeting students' needs.

Council members tried to work with the department to address the concern. The mathematics department conducted a self-study regarding its difficulties and issued a one-page handout on problem solving. Although the resulting changes in teaching were not dramatic, there would have been no change without the interaction and involvement of the faculty, the council, and the parents. Orange County High School, a comparable school (also in rural Kentucky), was faced with a similar problem, but handled it quite differently (AEL, 1993a). In order to alleviate the problem, the principal recommended offering lower-level classes. Parents were concerned that such action would not really address the problem and that it would further weaken the mathematics program. Nevertheless, the principal's recommendation was adopted. Effectively, this school council served only as an advisory board to the principal. Although state policy granted shared decision-making, local interpretation and implementation determined what that policy meant.

Commentary on Implementation of Policy Examples. The policies discussed in these examples were externally imposed on schools and, in that regard, contributed in a functional way to the educational contexts of the affected schools. Understanding the local concerns and the ways and degree to which local participants were prepared to implement the policies helps to explain these contexts. However, it was the interaction among the people in those schools that determined the meaning and application of the policies. In effect, they re-created policy in a way that was usable for them. They then had the refined policy to use as guidance.

---

[1]All names used in these episodes are pseudonyms.

It is likely that through interaction the *implemented* policies were refined several times.

Similarly, the process of *doing* mathematics often begins with refining and extending existing mathematical ideas. Through this process, the mathematician, whether elementary or advanced, experienced or inexperienced, creates new and often richer mathematical ideas. The constructive process helps mathematics become more meaningful and usable. The constructive process also helps *context* become more meaningful and usable.

School Norms and Expectations

Schools and classrooms also are a point of focus for studies of the influence of context on teachers' change. The well-known work of Goodlad (1984), Jackson (1968/1990), Lortie (1975), and Ryan (1970), and the continuing stream of books (e.g., Bullough, 1989; Kidder, 1989; Schifter & Fosnot, 1991; Schofield, 1982) dealing with particular classrooms and schools point to the dynamics of classroom interaction and how crucial an understanding of these dynamics is, even if only implicit, for a teacher's success. Further analyses by Bauersfeld (1980), Jackson (1968/1990), and Voigt (1985) showed that there are numerous regularities in schooling, some of which constitute hidden agendas or implicit expectations, that structure teachers' and students' interactions and experiences. The following examples illustrate the explanatory characteristic of context.

Example 2a. Fred (Brown, 1985; Cooney, 1985) was a first-year teacher who had professed an interest in making problem solving a focus in his classroom. He wanted to motivate his students with recreational mathematics—puzzles, cleverly-stated questions—and problem solving activities. On one occasion he asked his General Mathematics class to explore probability and applications to the insurance industry by rolling dice. But with these kinds of activities, Fred violated his students' expectations. Where Fred saw mathematical activity, the students saw games which really had no place in the serious business of learning basic arithmetic and algebraic facts. They felt that Fred was abrogating some of his responsibility as a teacher. They expected him to present new information, have them work a few problems for practice, then assign textbook exercises for homework. Even though he had the support of his building principal (Brown, 1985), Fred was unable to continue to use his motivator problems. The students exerted such pressure that he eventually restructured his class to better fit their expectations. Reflecting on this classroom, we find that students' expectations were both functional and explanatory parts of the context of Fred's classroom. And, although the classroom that evolved was not what Fred indicated he wanted, Fred and his students constructed the context through interaction.

Example 2b. Statewide education reform in Kentucky brought a new primary program to the elementary schools. According to the state department of education, there are several critical attributes that must be emphasized in the program: (a) developmentally appropriate instruction, (b) multiage, multiability classrooms, (c) authentic assessment, (d) qualitative reporting of students' progress, (e) professional teamwork among the teachers, (f) parental involvement, and (g) continuous student progress (as opposed to progress through the program by completing separate grade levels; Kentucky Department of Education, 1993a).

In a study of eight elementary schools, researchers with Appalachia Educational Laboratory (AEL, 1993b, 1996) found great differences in the success with which the program was being implemented. Two major factors, teacher work load and a supportive principal, were found to be important to successful implementation of the program. Teachers reported that time was the major barrier to successful implementation. Typically the teachers at these schools worked hard at preparing themselves to teach in the new primary program. They attended two to three times the required number of professional development workshops; they continually spent long hours in the evenings and weekends getting materials ready to use in their classes; they spent much more time documenting students' progress; and they still had to try to make time for collaborative planning for instruction. Extra time commitments took their toll on teachers and schools in many ways. First, teachers spent time on school responsibilities at the expense of their families. Second, some schools put off instituting their school councils (see Example 1b) because the primary teachers did not have time to be representatives to the councils. In the absence of these teachers, it was feared that the primary program would not be fairly represented. Third, due to time constraints, many teachers at these schools were not able to keep up with all seven of the critical attributes and had given up trying to implement the primary program as designed. Although many of the teachers initially were excited about all of the critical attributes, they experienced a great deal of frustration as a result of the time problem. Finally, teachers tended not to think about the reforms as anything but a collection of several attributes. Although several of the critical variables, particularly developmentally appropriate instruction, were successfully implemented individually, the primary program was not implemented systemically (AEL, 1996). The decision to try seriously to implement the primary program was functional in the educational context of these schools; however, the time constraint effectively prevented teachers from developing a big picture of the primary program.

The second major factor, the extent to which the principal provided support, goes a long way toward explaining the educational context in these schools and was manifest in numerous ways. Supportive principals were well versed in the primary program and provided direction for the teachers on their faculties. They found resources and released time for teachers to collaborate in planning for their classes and for alternative assessments. These principals also kept informed about what their teachers were doing with the primary program and modeled appropriate instructional practices at teachers' requests. On the other hand, unsupportive principals tended to avoid workshops on the primary program, did not provide for collaborative planning, tended to stay away from the primary area of the school building, and discouraged parental involvement in the program.

Commentary on School Norms and Expectations Examples. Although state and district policies set up some of the differences among schools, much was still determined by individual schools. In effect, it was a combination of beliefs and expectations that created the teaching and learning context in these schools. Fred (Example 2a) and his students had expectations of one another; the primary teachers (Example 2b) had beliefs about education and expectations of themselves in regard to the profession; principals had beliefs and expectations regarding what was important to do for their teachers.

Teachers like Fred are apt to feel caught between conflicting sets of expectations. Schoenfeld (1988) argued that teaching that meets goals of the professional community at large, beginning with exploration and leading to justification and rigor, may be at odds with good teaching that conforms to typical school norms. Indeed, the literature of teacher socialization (see, e.g., Eisenhart et al., 1993, Ryan, 1970; Zeichner & Gore, 1990) points out that many teachers, particularly beginners, experience tensions between what they would like to do and what they feel constrained to do in their classrooms. On the other hand, Lampert (1987) and Ball (1991) described the ways in which students' ideas about what counts as legitimate activity in a mathematics classroom are an important factor when considering changes in teaching. Expectations of the students, the teacher, the school, and the community are important parts of the context of teaching and learning and, thus, are relevant to examinations of teacher change. (For related discussion, see also Cooney & Shealy, chap. 4, and Franke, Fennema, & Carpenter, chap. 10, in this volume.)

Conceptions of Mathematics

Context extends beyond policies, school settings, and classroom norms. In the past 20 years, a number of studies have made it clear that the view a teacher has of mathematics has a significant impact on his or her classroom interactions and teaching goals (e.g., Ball, 1988; Jones, 1990; Marks, 1987; Schoenfeld, 1983; Shaw, 1989; Shirk, 1972; Thompson, 1984). For many, a focus on computations and algorithmic procedures stems from a belief that mathematics is concerned with preexisting truths, that it always is straightforward, that there always are clearly identified correct answers, and that it is created, discovered, or outlined by someone else: The student's job is to receive what the teacher gives. As the following contrasting episodes illustrate, this perspective has definite implications for the richness of students' understanding.

Example 3a. Sarah (Jones, 1991) had been a second-grade teacher for more than 15 years. She viewed mathematics as a collection of rules to be followed; doing mathematics meant privately working the textbook exercises. Over the years, she became bored and dissatisfied with her teaching. In an effort to change, she got involved with a teacher enhancement program. Six months into the program, Sarah's view of mathematics had changed significantly, and her teaching was beginning to reflect the program's emphasis on mathematics as an active, sense-making endeavor. After one particular class period during which children worked in cooperative groups using physical models, she said, "I think they learn a lot from [their activity] and from their conversation with each other . . . a lot more than they would learn with me standing up there telling them. They're experiencing what they're saying instead of me telling them what they need to experience" (Jones, 1991, p. 4). Sarah's commitment to her new view of mathematics and mathematical activity was nourished by her experiences with her students. In return, her vision of teaching and learning mathematics provided the foundation for those experiences.

Example 3b. Ms. Daniels (Borko et al., 1992; Eisenhart et al., 1993; Jones, 1990) was a beginning middle school mathematics teacher. She entered teacher education with a substantial background in college mathematics. Throughout her teacher education program and first year of teaching, she professed a desire to teach mathematics so that students would understand both concepts and procedures. She believed that each was taught somewhat differently, but could not clearly articulate how to teach for conceptual understanding. She made vague references to the need for students to discover mathematical results, but had difficulty providing conceptual explanations. In her student teaching and first year of teaching, Ms. Daniels taught, and believed she was better prepared to teach, for procedural understanding more than for conceptual understanding. Eisenhart et al. (1993) pointed out numerous reasons why this would be expected, given her university and school experiences. But by briefly examining her perspective on mathematics, we can more deeply understand its role as part of the context of her teaching.

Ms. Daniels' experiences in college mathematics emphasized procedures more than concepts. In fact, it was because of difficulty with an introductory proof course, for which conceptual understanding was vital, that she switched her major from mathematics to education. Still, she claimed to have a mathematical perspective on life, using its logical procedures and discernible organization as a standard to which other disciplines and activity were compared (Jones, 1990). For example, she stated that playing the piano was related to doing mathematics in that the player had to interpret symbols, play correctly, and sequence the music. Things that she did not consider to be mathematical were those for which little thinking was involved or for which organization and procedure were not important. Such a focus on organization and procedure contributed explicitly to her belief that practice was vital to understanding mathematics (Eisenhart et al., 1993) and to her belief that her teaching needed to help students set up a definite organization for mathematical ideas (Jones, 1990). The richness she found in mathematics was due to the connections she saw. Although she recognized the need for personal interpretation and meaning-making in mathematics, she felt ill-prepared to help her students understand concepts by making connections. She became frustrated trying to teach for conceptual understanding.

Commentary on Conceptions of Mathematics examples.   Lakatos (1976), Davis and Hersh (1981), Tymoczko (1986), and Ernest (1991) discussed a view of mathematics that is very different from that experienced in most school programs. In this view, mathematics is seen as a social and human endeavor. The mathematician gets an idea, perhaps through abstraction of experience, through collaboration, or by reflecting on his or her own or others' prior work, and works on the idea in private for a while. At some point, the mathematician checks his or her ideas with colleagues in the mathematical community. Based on any feedback received, he or she works again in private, then again invites public reaction. This toggling back and forth between private and public venues continues until the mathematical community finds the idea acceptable or sensible. At that point, the idea becomes a mathematical result. It takes on an existence that does not depend principally on individual interpretation and becomes more "object-like" (Hawkins, 1985). Ernest (1991) refered to this as the site at which personal, subjective knowledge is transformed into socially negotiated objective knowledge. The meaning and connotations of the mathematical result, however, still are personal. The construction, refinement, and playing with ideas constitutes mathematical activity, and leads to mathematical results. According to Greeno (1991) and the National Council of Teachers of Mathematics (NCTM, 1989), activity is necessary for conceptualizing in mathematics. The strength of this view for teaching and learning is that there is room for mathematical growth and real-life mathematical actors with real and personal experiences from which to abstract meaning. In short, it recognizes the need to couple mathematical results with meaning and context.

Ms. Daniels (Example 3b) struggled with a view of mathematics that resembled the view described by Lakatos, and, by participating in the teacher development project, Sarah (Example 3a) began to experience this kind of mathematics. Although it caused problems for Ms. Daniels, a changed view of what it means to do and understand mathematics was definitely linked to a dramatic change in Sarah's classroom interaction and goals. Beyond the case of Sarah, case study literature, tracing the effects of changes in mathematics teachers' ideas about mathematics on their teaching, is becoming substantial (see Ball, 1989; Franke, Fennema, & Carpenter, chap. 10, this volume; Lampert, 1987; Schifter & Fosnot, 1991).

On the other hand, this mathematical face of context may appear different from the policy and school or classroom faces. When we think of mathematics, we often think about mathematical results, as noted previously. Once validated by a mathematical process, these results tend not to change, whereas policies and expectations do tend to change. The philosophy and emphases from which the field of mathematics receives direction, however, do change (see McCleary & McKinney, 1986), just as mathematical ideas under development normally change (see Davis & Hersh, 1981). Similarly, the identifiable faces of context may change over time or with different people or circumstances, but the fact that context influences teaching and learning does not change.

Summary of Context

The examples of this section point to a number of fundamental characteristics of context: It is functional, it is explanatory, and it is interactively constructed. As the examples point out, context is partially internal and partially external, in its construction and refinement there is considerable local variability, and it can provide guidance and direction. Faces of context include interpretations of policy, school expectations and norms, and perspective on mathematics. These faces are influenced by teachers' relationship to the profession, the community's relationship to the profession, and the community's perspective on mathematics. In that they are identifiable, these faces have the potential to be examined as influences on teachers' change. In that the faces of context are not all of a kind, there is an element of personal or social construction to the contexts of teaching and learning mathematics. Over the long haul, there is change in these faces of context.

CONTEXT AND TEACHER CHANGE

Many changes are being proposed—change in teaching methods, change in what counts as curriculum content, change in perspective on what it means to teach and learn mathematics, change in who is responsible for policy and instructional decisions, and a host of other changes. Indeed, reform is fundamentally about change (Kuhn, 1970), and numerous documents have made explicit calls for these kinds of changes (e.g., California State Department of Education, 1985; Kentucky Department of Education, 1993b; Mathematical Association of America, 1991; Mathematical Sciences Education Board & National Research Council, 1991). Making such changes can be very exciting (AEL, 1993a; Schifter & Fosnot, 1991), but it requires considerable effort (Example 2b), understanding (Example 3b), and commitment (Example 3a). In this section, I briefly discuss the kinds of change currently being promoted, referring the reader to other chapters in this volume for fuller discussion of changes in teaching, mathematics, and epistemology.

Change in Teaching

For 100 years, reform efforts have called for significant change in the way we teach and learn mathematics (NCTM, 1970). The "Perry movement" at the turn of the century urged teachers to make mathematics more concrete and to stress interrelationships between mathematics and science. The 1920s connectionists (e.g., Thorndike) emphasized practicing and developing tightly defined skills, but this gave way to calls from Dewey and Brownell for meaningful instruction in the 1930s. The New Math reforms of the 1950s and 1960s emphasized mathematical structure and discovery learning. (For discussion of these reform movements see Jones & Coxford, 1970.) In 1980, NCTM issued a directive that problem solving should become the centerpiece of teaching and learning mathematics (NCTM, 1980). Most recently, the *Professional Standards for Teaching Mathematics* (NCTM, 1991) called for five major shifts in mathematics instruction: (a) toward classrooms as mathematical communities, (b) toward logic and mathematical evidence as verification; (c) toward mathematical reasoning; (d) toward conjecturing, inventing, and problem solving; and (e) toward connecting mathematics, its ideas, and its applications.

Producing such classrooms requires that teachers make several related changes—in their ideas about mathematics, in their views of teaching and learning, and in their daily practice of teaching. Case studies of mathematics teachers who are moving toward such a view of teaching reveal numerous beliefs that begin to change (see Cooney & Shealy, chap. 4, this volume; Etchberger & Shaw, 1992; Fennema, Carpenter & Loef, 1993; Franke, Fennema, & Carpenter, chap. 10, this volume; Lampert, 1987; Jaberg & Lubinski, chap. 9, this volume; Romberg, chap. 13, this volume; Schifter & Fosnot, 1991; Thompson, 1984).

However, we all have personal experience with teachers who are not making these kinds of changes. For some, as with the teachers in the AEL (1993a) study of primary program implementation, the absence of support is the major hindrance to change. For others, the view that a teacher's relationship to the profession requires good faith compliance with directives passed down from professional organizations is in conflict with the message that teachers are in charge of instructional decisionmaking. But a fundamental reason that change is difficult is that it forces an unfamiliar, and perhaps uncomfortable, interpretation of teaching and learning mathematics. Changes in emphasis lead to change in the context of teaching and learning, and that change can lead to significant tension.

Change in Mathematics

It is important to note that what counts as mathematics often varies from culture to culture and from setting to setting, reflecting differences in social expectations. Carraher, Carraher, and Schliemann (1985), Ginsburg (1982), Lave (1988), and Saxe (1991) reported numerous cases of people engaged in mathematical activity in their daily lives that is very different from what they would identify as mathematical from a school perspective. The methods these people use typically are invented, very ingenious, and show a good understanding of the mathematics involved in their problems and activities.

Beyond differences attributable to culture and social expectations, the nature of mathematics has varied even within the mathematical community. For example, the introduction of Arabic numerals changed forever the way we experience arithmetic. Descartes' coordinatization of the plane significantly changed the way we think about geometry and algebra. Lobachevsky's pioneering work in non-Euclidean geometry helped us understand more deeply the nature of axiomatic systems. Cantor's work in set theory changed the way we think about rigor, and Gödel's incompleteness theorem changed the focus of philosophers of mathematics from foundationalism to what it means to *do mathematics*. Finally, recent work on the four-color problem and Fermat's last theorem have made us think harder about justification.

Although these represent significant changes in mathematicians' orientation to the discipline of mathematics, changing the face of the discipline is not done capriciously. As McCleary and McKinney (1986) reported,

> Mathematicians do not reject the results of former communities of mathematicians; indeed, they try to bring as much of the past as is reasonable

into their present picture of the discipline. Though mathematics is cumulative in this sense, initiation into a mathematical community involves the acceptance of a set of criteria that determine what constitutes proper mathematics, and these criteria *do* change over time. (p. 51, emphasis in original)

Clearly any framework that intends to account for the ways in which context is relevant to teacher change must pay attention to the potentially different connotations teachers, students, and communities may have for what is mathematical.

Change in Epistemology

It is likely that in order to align with the vision of the profession, many of the changes in mathematics teachers' knowledge, beliefs, and practice will be rooted not only in changes in particular classroom practices or views of mathematics, but also in their understanding of the nature of knowledge. The epistemological position that underlies the National Council of Teachers of Mathematics' *Professional Standards for Teaching Mathematics* (NCTM, 1991) is a socioconstructivist one. It holds that knowledge is the dynamic product of the work of individuals operating in intellectual communities, not a solid body of immutable facts and procedures independent of mathematicians. In this view, learning is considered more a matter of meaning-making and of constructing one's own knowledge than of memorizing mathematical results and absorbing facts from the teacher's mind or the textbook; teaching is the facilitation of knowledge construction, not the delivery of information.

The examples in the previous sections present a strong case that teachers' beliefs, knowledge, and practices are heavily influenced by their epistemologies. Current understanding of teaching and learning argues for an epistemology that begins with activity and perception, one that is embedded in world experiences (Brown, Collins & Duguid, 1989; Greeno, 1991). In like manner, I assert that for teachers, change is rooted in teaching activities. Knowledge, beliefs, and practices are examined because of perceptions of teaching experiences with real people in real places. Although significant changes are being proposed, the extent to which they will be manifest depends a great deal on the ways in which teachers respond to the reforms.

Context, Tension, and Change

As was the case with Fred, Ms. Daniels, and the teachers in the primary program, a fundamental impact on teaching was made by their response to the tensions they felt. Some of these tensions result from conflict between personal goals and interpretations of policy or expectations;

some result from conflicting messages about the relationship between the teacher and the profession; some result from the difficulties associated with putting beliefs into practice. Ideally, ideas about what counts as mathematics, mathematics instruction, mathematics learning, typical classroom routines and behavior, typical school structures, and the larger society's expectations of what schooling will produce would be internally consistent. However, given that successful negotiation of the everyday world does not require that ideas and practices match (see von Glasersfeld, 1984), inconsistencies in an individual's conceptual scheme are not surprising.

When tensions arise, whether they are between beliefs about mathematics and beliefs about teaching or between goals and policies, it is what is done in striving to resolve the tensions that has the greatest relationship to context. In particular, tension manifest in any of the several faces of context may be an indicator of changes in teachers' ideas about mathematics, mathematics learning, mathematics teaching, classroom life, and the nature of school. However, what it is that prompts the teacher to consider reconstructing his or her ideas and actions regarding teaching, rather than assimilating the cause of the tension, and what is the nature of the supports necessary for change to occur, is a question currently receiving considerable attention (Duckworth, 1987; Fennema, et al., 1993; Fosnot, 1989; Schifter & Fosnot, 1991). Whether or not lasting changes result, the mere fact of responding to tension changes context, future interactions, and, thus, teaching.

METHODOLOGICAL IMPLICATIONS

How then do these ideas help us to conceptualize context and its role in mathematics teachers' change? In what ways will they be useful in structuring and guiding investigations? In this chapter I have asserted that there are several potential faces of context: policies, school norms and expectations, perspectives on mathematics, beliefs about oneself as a teacher or as a mathematician, participation in teacher development projects, presence or absence of reform initiatives, existence and effectiveness of school councils, classroom resources, colleagial relationships, and so on. I have described three characteristics of context—that it is functional, explanatory, and interactively constructed—all of which are important to consider when investigating teachers' change. I have asserted that although conceiving of context as being constructed is fundamental, at any given time context may be seen to have some existence apart from the individuals who constructed it and can provide guidance to those individuals. I have argued that interaction with, and response to, tension play a significant part in teachers' change. Finally, I have asserted that some aspects of context seem to support change, whereas others promote maintaining the status quo. This discussion generates a number of research questions for studying the relevance of context to mathematics teachers' change and has several methodological implications.

Research Agenda

A research agenda regarding context needs to include the following. Fundamentally, studies are needed that provide rich descriptions of context. Given the varied characteristics and faces of context discussed in this chapter and the complexity of context and its relationship to teaching and teachers' change, such studies are of paramount importance. They will provide the groundwork on which theoretical perspectives regarding context can be built.

Second, studies are needed that explore the interactive nature of context described in this chapter. Although it is easy to conceive that context is constructed, the ways in which this may happen are not so clear. Although it is easy to conceive that context affects *and is affected by* teaching and learning, the kinds of changes in teaching or in context are not so clear. Several kinds of studies would be useful here:

1. A potentially tension-producing experience for teachers can be their observation of students' mathematical thinking. Under certain conditions, students have the opportunity to display their thinking, and teachers have reason to take note of it, not dismiss it. Because change in knowledge, beliefs, and practice occurs over time, it would be valuable to investigate the nature of the interaction between teachers' knowledge and beliefs, their growing skill at providing opportunities for students to demonstrate their thinking, and subsequent tensions. Longitudinal studies are imperative.

2. Many of the instances in which mathematics teachers are changing their ideas about mathematics, mathematics learning, teaching, classroom life, and the nature of schooling are mediated by explicit staff development programs (e.g. Bush, 1992; Franke, Fennema, & Carpenter, chap. 10, this volume; Schifter and Fosnot, 1991). Some of these are programs that take place predominantly outside the normal school setting (e.g., Summermath for Teachers); others are school-based changes (Cognitively Guided Instruction); still others are statewide interventions (Kentucky), which take place both in and out of school. Comparative studies of the degree to which differences in the intensity or comprehensiveness of the contextual change are related to teacher change would be useful. Furthermore, the theoretical underpinnings of these programs are different. For example, Summermath for Teachers is grounded in a constructivist view of conceptual change. The Coalition for Essential Schools, on the other hand, begins with school change,

arguing, in effect, that the social scaffolding for change must be in place if change is to last. Comparative studies of programs with differing theoretical orientations would be useful. In particular, the question of to what extent, and in what ways, the programs and their participants affect one another are in order.

3. A third set of questions that derives from the interactive view of context would probe the characteristics of contexts that support change. For example, if change needs to be socially scaffolded, what are the characteristics of that social scaffolding? What parts of the change process need social scaffolding? Are the needs for scaffolding universal, or are there individual and group variations among teachers? Does social scaffolding need to be explicit and intentionally provided, or can teachers use naturally occurring features of their teaching context as scaffolding? If so, how does this happen?

4. Finally, to what extent and in what ways are the functional, explanatory, and interactive characteristics of context related? In what kinds of circumstances does one of these characteristics overshadow the others in teachers' perceptions? Are teachers more likely to change if they perceive context to be interactively constructed? In what ways might the functional and explanatory characteristics of context be productively used?

Third, in order to be in concert with the reforms, mathematics teachers are being asked to move to a position that may be quite different from that of their students, their colleagues, and the larger community. Therefore, as teachers change we expect to find increased tension in these social systems. Increased tension may occur in teachers' ideas about mathematics, teaching, learning, and classroom and school, as well as in the multitude of interactions that teachers regularly have with students, other teachers, administrators, and parents. In studying the role of context in teachers' change, it would be interesting to investigate how tension at any of these levels is handled. In what contexts, and in what ways, is tension resolved? In what contexts is the cause of tension ignored or assimilated? In what contexts does tension cause teachers to fundamentally reconstruct their ideas about the very nature of mathematics education?

Finally, the question "What aspects of the broader culture should be considered as we study teacher change?" needs to be addressed. Policy, norms and expectations, and perspective on mathematics clearly are not the only faces of context; investigations intended to identify and discuss other faces of context are needed. Teaching is a complex endeavor, and the varied ingredients of the contextual soup are mutually influential. However, because an epistemological shift of ideas about what constitutes mathematics knowing, learning, and teaching is fundamentally at issue, any place where epistemologies run into each other will be a research site. Tension will show us where to look in any particular case. Accumulating case studies of teachers dealing with tensions might give us a picture of which aspects of the larger culture matter in the business of teacher change.

Based on evidence from earlier studies there are a number of variables of interest—communities with high achievement goals for students; communities where top-down control is an important element of school administration; communities where achievement of basic skills in mathematics has been held as an important goal; groups, such as Latinos and girls, where active participation in mathematics class may run against norms of acquiescence; and so on. However, because the change at issue is one that moves our ideas about mathematics education in a direction that allies them with human growth and development, there may be other variables that prove more salient. For example, degree of flexibility in the environment, norms of nurture and support in the school and local community, the existence and effectiveness of school councils, or views of mathematics as an inherently interesting activity may prove to be important variables.

Research Methodology

There are several concerns regarding research methodology. What methods are likely to either facilitate or hinder investigations of the relationship of context to teachers' change? How can we find out what "insiders" and "outsiders" find to be relevant? As Munby (1982) plainly stated, "Ask them." However, he went on to warn against what Brown and Cooney (1986) refered to as "motivated blindness"—certain aspects of the environment and assumptions about teaching and learning mathematics, say the parsing of teaching into distinct courses, may be so important to a teacher that he or she may not be able even to conceive of teaching in a different environment. In the absence of such a conception, the teacher will not notice that aspect of context. From that teacher's perspective, his or her teaching is not bound by courses; from an outsider's perspective, that teacher's actions may be all but completely defined by the need to teach distinct courses. In light of the fact that context varies from one person to another, even in the mathematics classroom (Nickson, 1992), it seems clear that investigations must take account of context as the participant perceives it and as observers perceive it. Investigations must include a substantial amount of interpretive research.

Further, we must deal with a variation of the uncertainty principle. If context is vitally important to the meaning of a teacher's actions, then we must be concerned about our own poking about at contextual factors. In a study of beginning middle school mathematics teachers, Borko et al. (1992) found that simply being asked questions about what went on in their lessons made participants question their teaching. For these beginning teachers, a questioning environment made for a different context; different context spawned different interactions and possibly different experiences in their teaching. Asking a teacher about district policies, student expectations, or views of mathematics may artificially make him or her notice them and wonder about their effect on his or her teaching. It seems clear that understanding how context relates to teachers' change requires a certain amount of exploration and drawing attention to aspects of context that might affect teachers. We must explore both imposed and constructed aspects of context. However, it also seems clear that any such investigations will affect the teachers, the context, and what is learned.

SUMMARY

This chapter has been a discussion of context, change, and possible relationships between them. I have discussed context as a constructive and interactive concept, presented examples that show how context influences education in general and teachers in particular, and discussed changes currently being promoted in teaching, mathematics, and perspective. I have asserted that it is the way in which teachers respond to tensions that is most directly related to potential relationships between context and teacher change. Finally, I have proposed a tentative research agenda for investigating context and teacher change.

I have asserted that reform initiatives are predicated on significantly changing what it means to teach and learn mathematics. Fundamentally, the changes being proposed are due to an epistemological shift in which learning mathematics depends on constructing meaningful mathematical relationships. I also assert that a natural result of this shift is the view that context also is constructed. In particular, in a productive context of teaching and learning mathematics, theories and practice interact, ideas are communicated, tested, contradicted, and refined. In short, context is recognized and cultivated.

Ernest (1991) argued that individual, subjective knowledge and corporate, objective knowledge are mutually renewing. In like manner, I assert that the external, object-like aspect of context and the internal, constructed characteristic of context contribute to the renewal of each other. In the exploratory and empirical search for which aspects of context affect teachers as teachers change what they are about and the ways aspects of context affect teachers, any noticeable part of the environment may be studied in any number of ways. But I must agree with Feyerabend (1975) that "anything goes" does not mean "everything goes." It is not productive to begin such a study with preexisting ideas about context, which will be verified if only the researcher is clever enough. Any aspect of context may bear significant study. It is not productive, however, to set out to study something just because it may be noticed. Rather, I argue for an eclectic methodology that is purposefully constructed. I believe that by investigating possible relationships between context and teacher change, we will learn how to think smarter about research, about context, and about teachers' change.

ACKNOWLEDGMENTS

The preparation of this chapter was supported in part by the National Center for Research in Mathematical Sciences Education, University of Wisconsin–Madison. All ideas, findings, and recommendations expressed herein are those of the author and do not necessarily reflect those of the National Center for Research in Mathematical Sciences Education.

An earlier version of this chapter was prepared for the Second Conference on Methodologies for Studying Teacher Change in the Reform of School Mathematics, Nashville, TN, March, 1992. Special thanks is given to Dr. Barbara Scott Nelson and Dr. Elizabeth Fennema for their helpful comments and assistance in the preparation of this chapter.

REFERENCES

Appalachia Educational Laboratory (1993a). Kentucky's primary program. *Notes From the Field: Education Reform in Rural Kentucky, 3*(1), 1–6.

Appalachia Educational Laboratory (1993b). School-based decision making after two years. *Notes From the Field: Education Reform in Rural Kentucky*, 3(2), 1–6.

Appalachia Educational Laboratory (1996). Five years of education reform in rural Kentucky. *Notes From the Field: Education Reform in Rural Kentucky, 5*(1), 1–6.

Atkin, J. M., & House, E. R. (1981). The Federal role in curriculum development, 1950–1980. *Educational Evaluation and Policy Analysis, 3*(5), 5–36.

Ball, D. L. (1988, April). *Prospective teachers' understandings of mathematics: What do they bring with them to teacher education?* Paper presented at the annual meeting of the American Educational Research Association, New Orleans, LA.

Ball, D. L. (1989). Teaching mathematics for understanding: What do teachers need to know about the subject matter? In *Competing visions of teacher knowledge: Proceedings from an NCRTE seminar for education policy makers, February 24–26.* East Lansing, MI: The National Center for Research on Teacher Education.

Ball, D. L. (1991, February). *Students making math: Creating a mathematics-making culture in your classroom.* Paper presented at "Teaching & Schooling for a New Vision of Secondary Mathematics: Starting with Geometry." Education Development Center, Newton, MA.

Bauersfeld, H. (1980). Hidden dimensions in the so-called reality of a mathematics classroom. *Educational Studies in Mathematics, 11,* 23–41.

Berman, P., & McLaughlin, M.W. (1978). Implementing and sustaining innovations. In *Federal programs supporting educational change*. Santa Monica, CA: The RAND Corporation.

Borko, H., Eisenhart, M., Brown, C., Underhill, R., Jones, D., & Agard, P. (1992). Learning to teach hard mathematics: Do novice teachers and their instructors give up too easily? *Journal for Research in Mathematics Education, 21*, 194–222.

Brown, C. (1985). *A study of the socialization to teaching of a beginning secondary mathematics teacher*. Unpublished doctoral dissertation, University of Georgia, Athens.

Brown, J. S., Collins, A., & Duguid, P. (1989). Situated cognition and the culture of learning. *Educational Researcher, 18*(1), 32–42.

Brown, S. I., & Cooney, T. J. (1986). *Research on teaching: Towards meaning making*. Unpublished manuscript, University of Georgia, Athens.

Bullough, R. V. (1989). *First-year teacher: A case study*. New York: Teachers College Press.

Bush, W. S. (1992). *The Kentucky K-4 mathematics specialist program: Year Two report*. Washington, DC: National Science Foundation.

California State Department of Education (1985). *Mathematics framework for California public schools*. Sacramento: California State Department of Education.

Carraher, T. N., Carraher, D. W., & Schliemann, A. D. (1985). Mathematics in the street and in schools. *British Journal of Developmental Psychology, 3*, 21–29.

Cobb, P. (1986). Contexts, goals, beliefs, and learning mathematics. *For the Learning of Mathematics, 6*(2), 2–9.

Cooney, T. J. (1985). A beginning teacher's view of problem solving. *Journal for Research in Mathematics Education, 16*, 324–336.

Corrigan, D. C., & Haberman, M. (1990). The context of teacher education. In W.R. Houston (Ed.), *Handbook of research on teacher education* (pp. 195–211). New York: Macmillan.

Davies, G., & Thomson, D. (1988). Context in context. In G. M. Davies & D. M. Thomson (Eds.), *Memory in context: Context in memory* (pp. 335–345). Chichester, England: Wiley.

Davis, P., & Hersh, R. (1981). *The mathematical experience*. New York: Houghton Mifflin.

Dewey, J. (1985). *Dewey: The latter works (Vol.6)*. London: Feffer and Simons. (Original work published 1931)

Duckworth, E. (1987). *"The having of wonderful ideas" and other essays on teaching and learning*. New York: Teachers College Press.

Easley, J. (1980). Alternative research metaphors and the social context of mathematics teaching and learning. *For the Learning of Mathematics, 1*(1), 32–40.

Eisenhart, M., Borko, H., Underhill, R., Brown, C., Jones, D., & Agard, P. (1993). Conceptual knowledge falls through the cracks: Complexities of learning to teach mathematics for understanding. *Journal for Research in Mathematics Education, 24*, 8–40.

Elmore, R. F., & McLaughlin, M. W. (1988). *Steady Work: Policy, practice, and the reform of American education*. Santa Monica, CA: The RAND Corporation.

Ernest, P. (1991). *The philosophy of mathematics education*. London: Falmer.

Etchberger, M. L., & Shaw, K. L. (1992). Teacher change as a progression of transitional images: A chronology of a developing constructivist teacher. *School Science and Mathematics, 92*(8), 411–417.

Feiman-Nemser, S., & Floden, R. E. (1986). The cultures of teaching. In M. C. Wittrock (Ed.), *Handbook of research on teaching* (3rd ed., pp. 505–526). New York: Macmillan.

Fennema, E., Carpenter, T., & Loef, M. (1993). Learning to use children's mathematical thinking: A case study. In C. Maher & R. Davis (Eds.), *Schools, mathematics, and the world of reality*. Boston: Allyn & Bacon.

Feyerabend, P. (1975). *Against method*. London: New Left Books.

The Ford Foundation (1972). *A foundation goes to school*. New York: Author.

Fosnot, C. T. (1989). *Enquiring teachers, enquiring learners: A constructivist approach for teaching*. New York: Teachers College Press.

Geertz, C. (1983). *Local knowledge*. New York: Basic Books.

Ginsburg, H. (1982). The development of addition in contexts of culture, social class, and race. In T. P. Carpenter, J. M. Moser, & T. A. Romberg (Eds.), *Addition and subtraction: A cognitive perspective*. Hillsdale, NJ: Lawrence Erlbaum Associates.

Goodlad, J. I. (1984). *A place called school: Prospects for the future*. New York: McGraw-Hill.

Greeno, J. G. (1991). Number sense as situated knowing in a conceptual domain. *Journal for Research in Mathematics Education, 22*, 170–218.

Hawkins, D. (1985). The edge of Platonism. *For the Learning of Mathematics, 5*(2), 2–6.

Jackson, P. W. (1990). *Life in classrooms*. New York: Teachers College Press. (Original work published in 1968.)

Jones, D. L. (1990). *A study of the belief systems of two beginning middle school mathematics teachers*. Doctoral dissertation, University of Georgia, Athens.

Jones, D. (1991). Monitoring reform efforts: Studying change in Kentucky's teachers. In E. Fennema & B. S. Nelson (Eds.), *Methodologies for studying teacher change in the reform of school mathematics*. Madison: University of Wisconsin Press.

Jones, P. S., & Coxford, A. F. (1970). Mathematics in the evolving schools. In National Council of Teachers of Mathematics (Ed.), *A history of mathematics education in the United States and Canada* (pp. 11 – 89). Washington, DC: National Council of Teachers of Mathematics.

Kentucky Department of Education (1993a). *State regulations and recommended best practices for Kentucky's primary program*. Frankfort, KY: Author.

Kentucky Department of Education (1993b). *Transformations: Kentucky's curriculum framework*. Frankfort, KY: Author.

Kidder, J. T. (1989). *Among schoolchildren*. New York: Avon.

Kuhn, T. S. (1970). *The structure of scientific revolutions* (2nd ed.). Chicago: University of Chicago Press.

Lakatos, I. (1976). *Proofs and refutations*. London: Cambridge University Press.

Lampert, M. (1987). *Teachers' thinking about students' thinking about geometry: The effects of new teaching goals*. (Issue paper TR-88-1.) Cambridge, MA: Educational Technology Center, Harvard Graduate School of Education.

Lave, J. (1988). *Cognition in practice: Mind mathematics and culture in everyday life*. Cambridge, England: Cambridge University Press.

Lortie, D. C. (1975). *Schoolteacher: A sociological study*. Chicago: University of Chicago Press.

McCleary, J., & McKinney, A. (1986). What mathematics isn't. *Mathematical Intelligencer, 8*(3), 51–52, 77.

Marks, R. (1987). *Those who appreciate: The mathematician as secondary teacher. Joe: A case study of a beginning mathematics teacher*. Stanford University: Knowledge Growth in Teaching Project.

Mathematical Association of America (1991). *A call for change: Recommendations for the mathematical preparation of teachers of mathematics*. Washington, DC: Author.

Mathematical Sciences Education Board & National Research Council (1991). *Counting on you: Actions supporting mathematics teaching standards*. Washington, DC: National Academy Press.

Munby, H. (1982). The place of teachers' beliefs in research on teaching and decision making, and an alternative methodology. *Instructional Science, 11*, 201–225.

National Council of Teachers of Mathematics. (1970). *A history of mathematics education in the United States and Canada*. Washington, DC: Author.

National Council of Teachers of Mathematics. (1980). *An agenda for action: Recommendations for school mathematics of the 1980s*. Reston, VA: Author.

National Council of Teachers of Mathematics. (1989). *Curriculum and evaluation standards for school mathematics*. Reston, VA: Author.

National Council of Teachers of Mathematics. (1991). *Professional standards for teaching mathematics*. Reston, VA: Author.

Nespor, J. (1984). *The interaction of school context and teachers' beliefs* (R & D report No. 8023). Austin, TX: Research & Development Center for Teacher Education, University of Texas at Austin.

Nickson, M. (1992). The culture of the mathematics classroom: An unknown quantity? In D.A. Grouws (Ed.), *Handbook of research on mathematics teaching and learning* (pp. 101–114). New York: Macmillan.

Ryan, K. (1970). *Don't smile until Christmas: Accounts of the first year of teaching*. Chicago: University of Chicago Press.

Saxe, G. B. (1991) *Culture and cognitive development: Studies in mathematical understanding*. Hillsdale, NJ: Lawrence Erlbaum Associates.

Schifter, D., & Fosnot, C. T. (1991). *Reinventing mathematics education: Stories of teachers meeting the challenge of reform*. New York: Teachers College Press.

Schoenfeld, A. (1983). Beyond the purely cognitive: Belief systems, social cognitions, and metacognitions as driving forces in intellectual performance. *Cognitive Science, 7*, 329–363.

Schoenfeld, A. (1988). When good teaching leads to bad results: Disasters of well-taught mathematics classes. *Educational Psychologist, 23*, 145–166.

Schofield, J. W. (1982). *Black and white in school: Trust, tension or tolerance?* New York: Praeger.

Shaw, K. L. (1989). *Contrasts of teacher ideal and actual beliefs about mathematics understanding: Three case studies*. Unpublished doctoral dissertation, University of Georgia, Athens.

Shirk, G. B. (1972). *An examination of conceptual frameworks of beginning mathematics teachers*. Doctoral dissertation, University of Illinois, Champaign-Urbana.

Thompson, A. (1984). The relationship of teachers' conceptions of mathematics and mathematics teaching to instructional practice. *Educational Studies in Mathematics, 15*, 105–127.

Tymoczko, T. (1986). Making room for mathematicians in the philosophy of mathematics. *Mathematical Intelligencer, 8*(3), 44–50.

Voigt, J. (1985). Patterns and routines in classroom interaction. *Recherches en Didactique des Mathematiques, 6*(1), 69–118.

von Glasersfeld, E. (1984). An introduction to radical constructivism. In P. Watzlawick (Ed.), *The invented reality: How do we know what we believe we know?* (pp. 17–40). New York: Norton.

Warren, R.L. (1987). The school and its community context: The methodology of a field study. In G. Spindler (Ed.), *Education and cultural process* (pp. 120–135). Prospect Heights, IL: Waveland.

Weiss, I. R. (1978). *Report of the 1977 national survey of science, mathematics, and social studies education*. Research Triangle Park, NC: Center for Educational Research and Evaluation.

Zeichner, K. M., & Gore, J. M. (1990). Teacher socialization. In W. R. Houston (Ed.), *Handbook of research on teacher education* (pp. 329 – 348). New York: Macmillan.

7

Teacher Learning in a Social Context: Integrating Collaborative and Institutional Processes With the Study of Teacher Change

Mary Kay Stein
University of Pittsburgh

Catherine A. Brown
Indiana University

The purpose of this chapter is to explore a new perspective from which to think about the process of mathematics teachers' development, a perspective that is rooted in a sociocultural view of learning. Rather than focusing on the learning processes of individual teachers undergoing transformation, teacher learning can be conceptualized as a process of "transformation of participation" in the practices of a community (Rogoff, 1994). In this chapter, two illustrations are provided of how teacher learning can be examined in this more socially interactive way. Each illustration is cast within a specific sociocultural framework and uses data from practicing teachers' attempts to reform their mathematics instruction. Both frameworks—Lave and Wenger's (1991) theory of learning through legitimate peripheral participation in communities of practice, and Tharp and Gallimore's (1988) model of learning as movement from assisted performance to unassisted performance through a Zone of Proximal Development (ZPD)—share a basic perspective on learning as an inherently social and cultural activity that involves transforming the ways in which individuals participate in the practices of a community. By providing an example using each of these frameworks, we hope to demonstrate how this sociocultural perspective on learning guides us to look at aspects of the teacher change process that more traditional psychological perspectives on learning generally do not highlight.

Our overall aim is to highlight some of the distinctions between what sociocultural versus psychological perspectives of learning might contribute to the study of teacher change, not to advocate the adoption of one perspective over the other. In research in mathematics education more generally, Cobb (1994) called for the intelligent coordination of perspectives rather than wholesale allegiance to one particular theoretical framework. He argued, and we concur, that researchers should adopt the perspective that is most suited to the educational problem at hand. He also proposed that researchers have the responsibility (a) to inform readers of the perspective they are adopting and (b) to explain *why* they have chosen the adopted perspective. In this spirit, we offer this chapter as an orientation to sociocultural theory as a perspective that is complementary to, not in competition with, the more familiar psychological perspective that is usually used to study teacher change. Moreover, we make explicit reasons for choosing to use sociocultural theory, both as a *general* perspective for examining teacher change in school-based reform settings and with respect to our selection of *specific* sociocultural frameworks to examine particular instances of teacher change (see two examples explored later in this chapter).

The use of sociocultural theories to frame our thinking about teacher change has been influenced by challenges that we have faced with respect to describing and explaining teacher change in the QUASAR Project.[1] QUASAR is a national education reform project aimed at fostering the development and implementation of enhanced mathematics instructional programs in middle schools that serve students from disadvantaged backgrounds (Silver & Stein, 1996). Unlike many reform projects that focus their improvement efforts on individual teachers, QUASAR's efforts have focused on the school mathematics program as the unit of change. At each QUASAR site, the entire middle-school mathematics faculty, local mathematics educators (referred to as "resource partners"), and building administrators work together to develop instructional programs and practices that are aligned with the National Council of Teachers of Mathematics *Standards* (NCTM 1989, 1991) and that are responsive to local conditions. As such, the project's approach to teacher change relies heavily on the processes of collaboration among teachers and between teachers and resource partners. Teacher change is not viewed as happening one teacher at a time, but rather through a process that takes advantage of the synergy, support, and motivation supplied when a "critical mass" of teachers undertakes reform for all students in a given school.

---

[1]The QUASAR Project is directed by Edward A. Silver, funded by the Ford Foundation, and housed at the Learning Research and Development Center at the University of Pittsburgh.

Another unique feature of QUASAR's approach to teacher change is the manner in which teachers' learning can be viewed as embedded in the larger, more encompassing work of developing and implementing a comprehensive, schoolwide mathematics program. Unlike more conventional routes to teacher change, which often involve workshop attendance by individual teachers without commitment to programmatic reform at their home institutions, QUASAR teachers' learning can be seen as part and parcel of their schools' reform efforts. Project teachers often find immediate use for concepts, techniques, and ideas learned in workshops in the larger context of their work. Moreover, their role in the schools' overall mathematics program development efforts influences the number and kind of places in which learning might occur. In addition to attending workshops and learning through actual classroom teaching, QUASAR teachers participate in a variety of project-level, "work" activities (e.g., identifying, adapting, or developing curriculum materials, designing compatible assessments, planning parent information sessions, etc.). It appeared reasonable that we consider these as possible occasions for teacher learning, in addition to the more easily recognizable workshops and courses.

We found most currently available models for studying teacher change, which focus on teachers' cognitions and classroom behaviors, to be well suited for the study of individual teachers' learning that occurs in structured settings such as workshops and courses. However, we believe that describing and explaining teacher change in projects such as QUASAR also requires accounting for the learning that may occur as teachers interact with one another about mathematics teaching and learning in other informal and work-related settings. Although other projects and some research have noted the importance of collaborative activities and school context to successful school improvement efforts, we are not aware of models that conceptually integrate teacher change processes with these variables.[2]

This chapter attempts to address this gap by describing and illustrating the use of two socioculturally based frameworks that explicate the role of social interaction in the processes of learning. We first provide a general discussion of the ways in which a perspective of learning as transformation of participation affects how we think about teacher change. We then move into our two examples, using first Lave and Wenger's (1991) theory of learning through legitimate peripheral participation and then Tharp and Gallimore's (1988) model of learning as movement from assisted to unassisted performance. The chapter concludes with a discussion of the various aspects of teacher learning that

---

[2]Teacher colleagueship has been identified as an important variable in successful schools (Little, 1990a) and in school reform (Fullan, 1991); however, detailed descriptions of how and about what teachers collaborate, as well as of the mechanisms by which teacher collaboration leads to teacher change, have not been developed.

each of these two sociocultural frameworks illuminate and how these frameworks complement more frequently used psychological frameworks to create a more rich and complete understanding of the process of teacher change.

A SOCIOCULTURAL PERSPECTIVE
ON TEACHER CHANGE

Learning theories have traditionally characterized the processes of learning as primarily psychological, a process of intra-individual change. In contrast, sociocultural perspectives on learning propose that learning processes are primarily social in nature, "that learning and development occur as people participate in the sociocultural activities of their community" (Rogoff, 1994, p. 209). These two perspectives on the process of learning lead to different ideas about what is learned and how it is learned. When applied to the study of teacher change, they lead to different models of what to study and how to study it.

From Individual Cognition to Social Interaction

Conventional ways of viewing teacher development take the individual teacher to be the "nonproblematic unit of analysis" (Lave & Wenger, 1991, p. 47). This assumption underlies most lines of research on teacher development, including the expert–novice literature (e.g., Leinhardt, 1989), the teacher socialization literature (e.g., Lacey, 1977), and studies on teachers' ways of knowing (e.g., Calderhead, 1988). In addition, most current studies are heavily influenced by cognitive psychological theory, an approach that views learning as consisting of changes in the ways knowledge is structured and represented in individual teachers' minds. The goal of most analyses conducted within a cognitive psychological framework is to trace concomitant changes in individual teachers' knowledge, beliefs, and instructional practice:

> Learning to teach entails the acquisition of knowledge systems or schemata, cognitive skills such as pedagogical problem solving and decision-making, and a set of observable teaching behaviors. To understand learning to teach, one must study how these systems—and the relationships among them—develop and change with experience, as well as identify the factors that influence this change process. (Brown & Borko, 1992, p. 211)

This approach to studying teacher change emphasizes development of new knowledge structures and cognitive skills, entities presumed to reside within the minds of individual teachers. This approach also notes the importance of identifying factors that influence the change process, thus placing the study of learning to teach a context (e.g., staff development experiences, encounters with new policy mandates or curricula, or—relevant to this chapter—the opportunity to interact with colleagues). However, these contextual features of teacher learning are often portrayed as a stage on which teacher thought and action are enacted; contextual detail remains static and noninteractive with the analysis of learning.

Within mathematics education, the tendency to focus on teachers as individuals is readily apparent in the recent wave of teacher change and learning-to-teach studies: the case of Ms. Daniels' journey from college preparation to her initial year of teaching (Borko et al., 1992), the series of case studies of California teachers as they attempted to make sense of the reform framework (e.g., Putnam, 1992; Remillard, 1992), and the set of cases of experienced teachers' transformations after their exposure to constructivist philosophy in SummerMath for Teachers (Shifter & Fosnot, 1993). All of these investigations focused on the individual teacher as the unit of analysis. Although each investigation provides important information about the social context of teacher development, contextual detail is treated more as a catalyst for (or barrier to) the change process, than as an integral feature.

In contrast to psychological approaches that focus on the individual, sociocultural approaches focus on the groups or communities in which individuals participate. Sociocultural theorists view learning as "something that happens *between people* when they engage in common activities" (Bredo & McDermott, 1992, p. 35; emphasis ours). Learning is seen to result from the fact that individuals bring varying perspectives and levels of expertise to the work before them. As individuals work toward shared goals, they *together* create new forms of meaning and understanding. These new meanings and understandings do not exist as abstract structures in the individual participants' minds; rather they derive from and create the situated practice (or context) in which individuals are coparticipants.

Using sociocultural theories to understand teacher change, then, channels our attention away from the cognitive attributes and instructional practices of individual teachers and toward the collaborative interactions that occur as teachers attempt to develop and improve their practice. As attention is shifted from the individual to the group, the location of the phenomenon of learning changes as well. Instead of being located in the cognitive structures and mental representations of individual teachers, it becomes situated in the "fields of social interaction" (Hanks, 1991) between and among individuals. The result is that the unit of analysis shifts from the individual teacher to the social practice or activities in which teachers engage, and learning is redefined as transformations in the ways in which teachers participate in these social practices.

Learning Redefined as Transformation of Participation

From a traditional psychological perspective, learning is generally seen as occurring in one of two ways: through the transmission of knowledge from experts, or through individual acquisition or discovery. Rogoff (1994) claimed that both of these views of learning imply a rather one-sided process of learning. In the transmission view, the experts are active and the learners are passive; in the individual acquisition/discovery view, the learner is active, but the role of the expert is passive.[3] In both views, the roles of teacher and learner are clear cut, with little fluidity between and among ways of participating in the teaching/learning enterprise. When applied to the study of teacher learning, learning by transmission and learning by discovery/acquisition can be seen as representing two extremes of a pendulum swing, with respect to arguments about the amount of autonomy and control teachers should have in charting their own growth and development.

Rogoff (1994) claimed that a sociocultural perspective on learning represents an altogether different orientation toward the study of learning, one that is often difficult for people to understand because they attempt to assimilate it into the more familiar transmission/discovery dichotomy. According to Rogoff, "learning is a process of transformation of participation itself . . . how people develop is a function of their transforming roles and understanding in the activities in which they participate" (p. 209).

In this view, learning is not a compromise or balance between learning by transmission and learning by acquisition/discovery, but rather one in which both less and more mature participants are active and responsible. Learning as transformation of participation is most easily recognizable in informal and apprenticeship settings where, for example, children learn by working alongside adults in community activities. In these settings, the distinctive features of learning as transformation of participation include the following: (a) learners participate with an understanding of the *purpose* of the overall activity in which they are involved, (b) the instructional discourse is *conversational* rather than didactic, and (c) individuals with varying levels of expertise and experience *coparticipate*, with their roles varying according to their levels of expertise and/or experience (Rogoff, 1994). Roles are seen to vary not only across individuals at any given point in time, but also within an individual over time. As they become more experienced and skillful with the task at hand, individuals shift roles: their work becomes more independent and/or central to the overall enterprise. Transformation of

---

[3] Within mathematics education, there has been a great deal of interest recently regarding the role of the teacher in classrooms organized by constructivist principles. At this time, most individuals would probably say that the teacher's role in such classrooms is not so much passive as ill-defined.

the individual's form of participation (i.e., shifting of roles), therefore, is viewed as part and parcel of the learning process.

Learning redefined as transformation of participation can be used as a lens to look at learning in formal educational settings as well, although school-based settings provide challenges to the effective design of participatory learning for children. Schools, by their very nature, are segregated from the mature activities of the adult community and thus make coparticipation in authentic and useful community tasks difficult for students (Rogoff, 1994). With respect to the *learning of teachers*, however, schools can be seen to represent an authentic workplace. As noted by Tharp and Gallimore (1988), schools are the venues within which teachers practice their craft and have opportunities to learn how to be members of the teaching profession. Hence schools as workplaces provide relevant environments for learning through transformation of participation. The challenge is (a) to create mature teaching communities that represent the best of the teaching profession and (b) to allow learning (i.e., transformation of participation) to happen freely within these communities. In the next section, we provide more detail about teacher learning as part of ongoing, school-based community activities versus teacher learning in specially arranged events that fall outside the boundaries of in-school community activities.

Multiple Sources of Teacher Learning

Within mathematics education, the study of teacher change often focuses on changes in the knowledge, beliefs, and practices of individual teachers as a result of their experiences in courses, workshops, or institutes that are specifically designed to enhance teacher learning. Studies often begin with the examination of pedagogical events responsible for initiating and sustaining teacher growth and development. These include experiences such as preservice teacher preparation courses, in-service staff development sessions, university-based graduate degree programs, and/or summer institutes. Individual teachers' experiences in such programs and courses are described and the extent to which teachers appear to change their knowledge, beliefs, and/or practice as a result of participation is examined. Examples of such studies include the case of Ms. Daniels' journey from college preparation to initial years of teaching (Borko, et al., 1992; Eisenhart, et al., 1993), cases of experienced teachers' transformations after their exposure to constructivist philosophy in SummerMath for Teachers (Schifter & Fosnot, 1993), and investigations into the influence of workshops about children's knowledge of mathematics (Fennema, Franke, Carpenter, & Carey, 1993).

Sociocultural theories, on the other hand, tend to focus on the *learning processes of teachers*—not on pedagogical structures *for teaching*.

Arguing that learning occurs all the time, regardless of whether or not explicit teaching events have been arranged, sociocultural theories invite us to look beyond those formally structured events to other times and places during which individuals learn: "this view point makes a fundamental distinction between learning and intentional instruction. Such decoupling does not deny that learning can take place where there is teaching, but does not take intentional instruction to be in itself the source or cause of learning" (Lave & Wenger, 1991, p. 41). Hence the focus of analysis shifts away from pedagogical activity toward an analysis of the community's activities and learning resources. Rather than focusing on learning through intentionally designed instruction, learning is viewed as occurring within the ongoing work practices of the community. As such, the practices of the community can be viewed as the curriculum; learning is conceived as changes over time in social participation patterns in the work practices of the community.

This perspective on where learning occurs suggests that we need to broaden our view of what constitutes the sources or opportunities for teacher learning to include a range of activities not usually featured in more conventional analyses of teacher learning. Not only should we examine those events that have been specifically designed by teacher educators for the professional development of teachers, but we should also search for occasions during which teachers are actually engaged in the work practices of their communities.

Within mathematics education research, movement in this direction has already begun, with increased attention being devoted to the study of how teachers learn through their classroom practice. In this chapter, we expand the definition of the work practices of the teaching community to include the numerous occasions during which teachers work with each other and with outside experts to accomplish a goal related to some aspect of their mathematics program or practice. These might include developing or selecting curricular materials, designing new systems for student assessment, planning lessons, communicating with parents about a new mathematics program, making presentations about their work to other teachers, or working with administrators to adjust grading policies. Before our acquaintance with sociocultural theory, we often described these "nonteaching" and "nonworkshop" events as "informal learning opportunities," although we grew increasingly dissatisfied with this view of them as ancillary, secondary, and not integrated into a full understanding of teacher development. Sociocultural theorists call such work "joint productive activity," meaning that individuals come together with a shared goal and work toward a joint product that is meaningful to all participants. Such occasions are seen as presenting fertile ground for meaningful learning.

In the preceding paragraphs, we outlined some of the main tenets of sociocultural theory as they might be applied to the study of teacher change. A sociocultural perspective guides us to examine the interactions among teachers as they go about their day-to-day work practices, instead of focusing on the minds and behaviors of individual teachers in formal pedagogical settings. As the unit of analysis shifts from the individual to the group, teacher change is defined with respect to changes in the teachers' roles *vis-a-vis* the roles of others, that is, as *transformation of participation*. The learning of new knowledge and skills occurs hand in hand with teachers' increasingly independent and/or central roles. We turn our attention now to specific applications of sociocultural theory to the study of teacher change.

APPLYING A SOCIOCULTURAL PERSPECTIVE TO THE EXAMINATION OF TEACHER CHANGE

In this section, we explore how two frameworks based in sociocultural theory can enhance our understanding of teacher learning in specific reform mathematics settings. We begin each example with a description of the particular framework and a discussion of what it would mean to apply the framework's central constructs to the study of teacher change. We then apply the framework, drawing on data related to teacher learning at a particular QUASAR site. The goal of each example is twofold. First, we hope to explicate our rationale for selecting the specific framework by highlighting the dilemma before us in analyzing teacher change in that particular setting. Second, we aim to provide an exemplar of how the framework would guide us to examine and analyze data related to teacher learning.

Teacher Learning as Legitimate Peripheral Participation in a Community of Practice

Lave and Wenger (1991) defined the process of learning as increasing participation in the work practices of a group of people who are guided by a shared sense of value and meaning. As individuals move from newcomer to old-timer status in the group, they take on increasingly critical and complex group functions, they develop an increased sense of identity as master practitioners and, concomitantly, they gradually appropriate the knowledge and skills that are characteristic of old-timer practitioners. According to this framework, learning always occurs in *communities of practice*, with community of practice defined as a group of individuals who "share understandings concerning what they are doing and what that means in their lives and for their communities" (p. 98). The social structure of the work practices of the community defines the possibilities for learning and provides the cultural heritage necessary to interpret and support the knowledge and skills of its members.

How can analyses that focus on the participation patterns of individuals in a community of practice provide insight into teacher development or learning? Lave and Wenger (1991) viewed learning as an "integral and inseparable aspect of social practice" (p. 31). In an effort to further clarify and elaborate this somewhat nonintuitive conceptualization of *learning as practice*, Lave and Wenger characterized learning as "legitimate peripheral participation" in communities of practice:

> Learning viewed as situated activity has as its central defining characteristic a process that we call *legitimate peripheral participation*. By this we mean to draw attention to the point that learners inevitably participate in communities of practitioners and that the mastery of knowledge and skill requires newcomers to move toward full participation in the sociocultural practices of a community. "Legitimate peripheral participation" provides a way to speak about the relations between newcomers and old-timers. . . . It concerns the process by which newcomers become part of a community of practice. A person's intentions to learn are engaged, and the meaning of learning is configured through the process of becoming a full participant in a sociocultural practice. *This social process includes, indeed it subsumes, the learning of knowledgeable skills.* (p. 29, emphasis added)

From this perspective on learning, teacher change must be understood in relation to the communities of practice in which teachers participate. Examination of the teacher change process, thus, would involve the identification of the goals, values, and work practices of the community, followed by the tracing of the trajectories of newcomers as they move from peripheral to fuller and fuller forms of participation in the work practices of the community.

This framework makes clear the primacy of teachers' colleagues and the norms of the workplace to what teachers eventually learn. According to Lave and Wenger (1991), the question is not *if* learning occurs, but rather *what* learning occurs. Essentially, newcomers learn the practices, attitudes, knowledge, and skills that are valued and useful within their immediate communities.[4] Teachers-as-newcomers will learn a traditional set of practices if that is what is valued within their immediate community; likewise, they will learn a reform set of practices if granted access to a community that values and practices reform-oriented tenets.

Within this framework, teacher change would be defined as movement from peripheral to fuller forms of participation; mastery of knowledge and skills would be viewed as coinciding with increasing involvement in the practices of the community. Using the rubric of

---

[4]Indeed, Lave suggested that the true mission of education should be to make valued within communities those things that we want individuals to learn. If an individual's immediate community values a particular set of outcomes, the learning of those outcomes will happen as a natural by-product of his or her participation in community activities.

legitimate peripheral participation, a teacher who is a newcomer to a community of reform practitioners would begin by performing tasks that, although essential to the overall accomplishment of community goals, would not be the most complex, venturesome, or demanding. As the newcomer participates at the periphery, he or she would gain views of what the community is all about. What do members do? What do they care about? Where do they put their energies? How do they talk? Ideally, the newcomer's forms of participation would allow him or her "broad access to (all) arenas of mature practice" (Lave & Wenger, p. 110). For example, the newcomer would not only attend the teachers' monthly meetings and annual retreats, but also would be included in hallway conversations, work sessions that involved decisions about curriculum, and lunches held to celebrate the success of a parent information night. In these ways, the newcomer would gain multiple viewpoints or perspectives of the community members' work. He or she would begin to assemble a picture of what it means to be a practicing member of the reform community. Ideally, the newcomer's experience would allow him or her to move gradually to fuller and fuller forms of participation. For example, the newcomer might begin to plan portions of the next parent night, to take responsibility for composing a memo to the principal about their curriculum development work, and so on. As he or she moved to fuller forms of participation, the newcomer would become increasingly knowledgeable and skillful with respect to the full range of practices in which the community engages.

Within this perspective, teacher learning is not only *defined* as movement toward increasingly fuller forms of participation, but also is *measured* (or indexed) in this way. An important underlying assumption is that the most critical and relevant knowledge and skills are those that teachers evidence as they actually go about doing the work valued by their community. Hence, researchers should observe and document *what teachers do* as a measure of what they know, instead of measuring their internal cognitive attributes (i.e., assessing the contents of their minds as a measure of what they know). Teacher *learning*, in turn, is measured by transformations in their participation patterns, from peripheral to fuller forms. With each movement to fuller forms of participation, teachers are viewed as necessarily demonstrating increased knowledge and skill in the aspects of work deemed valuable by their community.

Learning Through Legitimate Peripheral Participation at Riverside Middle School

We have found the community-of-practice framework to be useful for understanding teacher learning at one QUASAR site in particular (see Stein, Silver, & Smith, in press, for a detailed account). Fairly early in the life of the QUASAR Project, the mathematics faculty at Riverside[5] formed an identifiable, reform-oriented community. The Riverside mathematics teachers viewed themselves—and were viewed by others—as a cohesive group of concerned, engaged individuals who were actively working together to create and sustain a reform-oriented mathematics program. The practices valued by this set of teachers encompassed activity both in and outside the classroom. With respect to classroom practice, the teachers shared a core set of beliefs centered around the importance of student understanding, the active construction of knowledge, and the central role of discourse in the learning of mathematics. Outside the classroom, the teachers valued the professional work of designing and improving their mathematics program (e.g., refining curricula, articulating the middle school program with the elementary and high school programs, designing compatible assessments) as well as that of explaining their program to interested audiences (e.g., parents, community members, other teachers).

Over the course of the project, a number of teachers entered this community of mathematics teachers. The newcomers included both Riverside teachers who "came on board" to teach mathematics in successive project years and new teachers hired into the school. The vast majority became practicing members of the community, taking on the community's commitment to an inquiry-based vision of teaching and learning and to continual refinement of instructional methods that would bring this vision to fruition in the classroom. A significant source of teacher learning at this site appeared to be teacher collegial interactions that occurred on a regular basis and in a variety of settings. Interview transcripts and paper-and-pencil rankings of the importance of various forms of teacher assistance point to teacher perception of the value of interactions with colleagues. Although teachers' experiences with the resource partners early in the project years (i.e., workshops, monthly staff-development sessions, retreats) were important initial sources of teacher learning, by the beginning of the third project year, our data indicate that the teachers clearly saw their interactions with each other in a variety of settings as the most important influence on their growth and development. Evidence from numerous interviews, observations, site visits, and teacher journals through the remainder of the project continued to paint a picture that highlighted the important role of communication and connection among teachers.

Given that state of affairs, we felt that our lens for viewing teacher learning at Riverside needed to bring into focus the teachers *as a group* and the ways in which their interactions in a variety of settings led to teacher learning. We concluded that the conventional models available for studying teacher learning and school improvement were not suited

---

[5]All QUASAR schools and teachers have been given pseudonyms in this chapter.

to the task. On one hand, conventional models for examining teacher development focus on individual teachers and the role that the individual's subject-matter knowledge and beliefs play in his or her instructional practice. Little or no attention is devoted to the role played by social interaction with his or her colleagues in teacher learning. On the other hand, models of school reform that *do* feature social interaction with colleagues pay little or no attention to the ways in which that interaction can lead to teacher learning. Lave and Wenger's (1991) community-of-practice framework was attractive precisely because it focused on the role of social interaction in a community as an important source of learning.

Although a community-of-practice framework appeared to be ideally suited to our needs, the exact way in which it could be used to examine teacher learning was not immediately apparent. By and large, the explication of this framework lacks specificity regarding its applications as an analytic tool, especially in formal educational settings. The following methods were developed based on our understanding of the framework.

One method for examining the Riverside teachers' participation patterns as an index of their learning is to examine all members' breadth of participation across the full range of school-based community activities. Here, we would expect old-timers to participate in a wider range of activities, to take broader responsibility for activities in which all members were participants, and to spend more time and energy on community activities overall than do newcomers. Newcomers, however, would be involved in a significant subset of activities, although in a much more peripheral manner than would be old-timers.

Figure 7.1 provides an illustration of a way to examine the breadth of participation in reform activities across time for the Riverside teachers. The teachers are identified in the left-hand column, with the most senior member (the old-timer) listed first and the remaining teachers listed in the order in which they joined the Riverside mathematics faculty. For each teacher, the first column that contains a circle diagram marks the first year he or she joined the community. The shaded portions of the circles represent the range of school-based activities in which the teacher participated. As shown in the legend, these activities included their actual teaching responsibilities and a variety of tasks related to their ongoing refinement of a comprehensive middle school mathematics program.

Close examination of the figure reveals the general pattern that, as teachers spent more time in the community, they participated in a wider range of the community's work practices. For example, examining the column for the 1991–1992 school year, we find the greatest range of participation for Teacher A, the old-timer. He taught the widest range of course offerings and was also involved with curriculum planning and

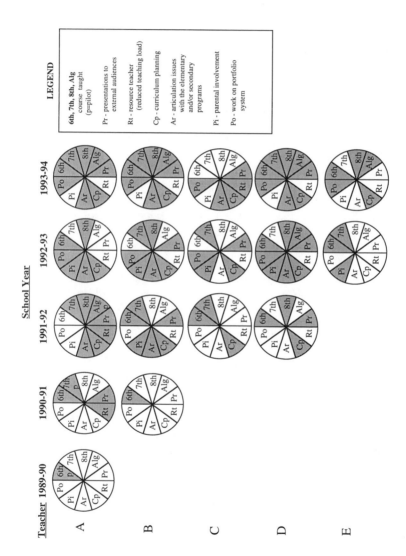

FIG. 7.1. Breadth of participation in school-based reform activities at Riverside Middle School.

with articulation issues with the elementary and secondary programs. In addition, in his role as resource teacher, he coordinated the instructional programs of the regular and special education mathematics faculties. Finally, he gave a presentation about their work at a national meeting. Teacher B, the next senior member of the community, also engaged in a fairly wide range of activities. She worked alongside Teacher A in the curriculum-planning and articulation efforts. Like Teacher A, she presented at a national meeting; she also devoted considerable effort to developing a method of involving parents with their new mathematics program. The two newcomers' activities (Teachers C & D) were somewhat more restricted, especially those of Teacher C. Teacher D participated in a fairly wide band of activities for a newcomer, mainly because she had prior experience with the innovative curriculum in a previous position in another district.

Another way to examine Fig. 7.1 is to trace the trajectory of one particular teacher over time (moving horizontally across one row). For example, Teacher B began her association with the project by teaching the sixth-grade innovative curriculum. The next year, she not only expanded her teaching responsibilities to include an additional grade level, but also began participating in a variety of programmatic and support activities. By the 1993–1994 school year, Teacher B was as "comprehensive" a participant in the community as was Teacher A.

The examination of breadth of activity, however, is only one measure of learning. Community members would also be expected to increase the *depth* of their activity over time, with depth characterized as movement from peripheral to more central roles. One way to investigate depth of participation is to examine participation patterns with respect to one particular work practice over time. This was done in some detail with respect to the practice of teaching middle school mathematics in a previous paper (see Stein, Silver, & Smith, in press). That analysis showed clear patterns with respect to form of participation and newcomer/old-timer status, most notably that newcomers always began their association with the project by teaching sixth grade, the level for which curricular materials were most complete, the mathematics the easiest, and the human support (in terms of in-house colleagues who were also teaching the course) most abundant. The opposite pattern held with respect to algebra, the most challenging and least supported course (in terms of materials and human support). As their tenure with the project grew, most individuals gradually worked their way into teaching this course.

Another work activity that showed consistent movement from peripheral to more central roles for the Riverside teachers was that of making public presentations about their work. As a community, the Riverside teachers valued sharing their experiences in implementing mathematics reform with colleagues both locally and nationally. Through presentations at annual meetings (e.g., NCTM, National Middle School Association) and local conferences, teachers talked about issues of instruction, pedagogy, and assessment, and more generally about topics such as ability grouping and parental involvement. Newcomers, however, differed from old-timers in that they did not give presentations the first year that they joined the faculty.[6] However, they often attended presentations given by their old-timer colleagues, sometimes participating at the periphery by handing out materials or placing transparencies on the overhead projector. Another way in which newcomers eased their way into making presentations to external audiences was by talking about their evolving practices—in essence giving mini-presentations about their work—in the local community. When newcomers did begin to give public presentations to external audiences, they were copresenters with more experienced presenters. Giving presentations on their own signaled that they had arrived at an old-timer status (see Stein, Silver, & Smith, in press, for a detailed description of the importance of presentation in "learning to talk" like a member of a reform community).

As the Riverside teachers increased their depth and breadth of participation in community activities, they were learning in multifaceted ways what it means to be a reform teacher of mathematics. This learning encompassed the gradual appropriation of a complex set of knowledge and skills related to valued classroom instructional practices as well as to professional work associated with building, sustaining, and explaining a reform program of mathematics instruction. Moreover, teachers were developing the attitudes, values, and orientations that underlie the central tenets of the reform movement. The learning that occurred did so without the teachers being explicitly taught in any sort of structured manner, but rather through their ongoing exposure to old-timers and the work practices of the community.

In summary, the community-of-practice framework provided us with a lens for viewing teacher collaboration as a source of teacher learning and development in the Riverside community. Riverside teachers had laid before them an unfolding of participation opportunities that allowed them to gain multiple and increasingly "inside" viewpoints on the community's work and values. These increasingly central roles were associated with increased mastery of knowledge and skills as well as heightened levels of motivation as teachers viewed themselves as becoming a particular kind of people—members of a community of reform mathematics teachers. Throughout, the tasks in which they engaged were the mature, complex tasks that formed the basis of the real work of their community.

The foregoing analysis presumed the existence of a reform community of practice—one that held goals close to those accepted by the

---

[6]The exception is Teacher D, who had experience with the curriculum before joining the Riverside community.

mathematics education community more broadly. Movement to fuller forms of participation, hence, implied becoming a teacher who embodied many of the recommendations of the *Professional Standards for the Teaching of Mathematics* (NCTM, 1991). The overall direction of change for newcomers was provided by old-timers who were seen as the master practitioners of these reform ideas. Another salient feature of the Riverside reform community was collaborative work on products that were valued by all of the middle school mathematics teachers. Many of these products (e.g., portfolio systems, parental involvement through parent nights, articulation schemes with the high school mathematics department) were associated with the community activities identified in Fig. 7.1. During many of these work activities, the Riverside teachers engaged in joint productive activity, joining forces to accomplish something about which they all cared. According to sociocultural theorists, such occasions lead to learning because individuals bring different levels of expertise and varying perspectives to the work. With high levels of motivation, participants use their differing perspectives and ability levels to move forward and learn.

Adopting a community-of-practice perspective to explain teacher learning may not be appropriate in situations where reform goals and joint productive activity have *not* taken hold. Indeed, Tharp and Gallimore (1988) painted a picture of traditional schools as places in which meaningful, shared goals and joint productive work were conspicuously lacking. Such were the conditions at Norton Middle School, another QUASAR site. Although an array of professional development activities was available at Norton, as of the beginning of the third year of the project, the teachers still had not formed a cohesive community with reform goals. Collaborative interactions among the teachers appeared to remain dependent on the presence of the resource partner(s).

In these situations, the first step in reform, according to Tharp and Gallimore (1988), is the *creation* of settings conducive to teacher learning. Tharp and Gallimore's framework of learning as assisted performance within the social organization of schools helps to explain the organizational and interpersonal factors necessary for teacher learning to occur and the obstacles that must be overcome in most schools in order for reform communities to become established. We turn now to a discussion of how this framework can help us to think about social and organizational structures of schools and ways in which time, resources, and incentives can be made available for teacher learning. We then provide an example of how this perspective can be used to examine teacher learning, drawing on data from Norton Middle School, where a community of teachers with reform goals was very slow to develop.

Teacher Learning as Assisted Performance in the Social Organization of Schools

Similar to Lave and Wenger (1991), Tharp and Gallimore (1988) defined learning as a process of transformation of participation. More specifically, learning is defined as a process of moving from assisted performance to unassisted performance, through a zone of proximal development (ZPD; Vygotsky, 1978). For Tharp and Gallimore, the provision of assistance constituted the heart of the teaching and learning enterprise as learners are guided by those more expert to participate in the complex, meaningful sociocultural practices of the community. With time and experience, learners appropriate these practices and utilize them on their own when other situations demand them.

Teacher learning from this perspective is measured as progress with respect to placement in one of four stages. First, performance is assisted by more capable others; second, peformance is assisted by the self; third, performance is independent and becomes automated. In the final stage, automated peformance may be revised, requiring a cycling back to earlier stages. Thus, movement through the ZPD is defined in terms of the transformation of the learners' participation in the performance of a task via their interactions with others.

Rather than focusing exclusively on the dyad of assistor and learner, Tharp and Gallimore (1988) widened their lens to include the social and organizational relationships that comprise settings for learning. As Minick (1985) pointed out, this is important because from a sociocultural perspective "actions are at one and the same time components of the life of the individual and the social system [and] will be defined and structured in certain respects by the broader social and cultural system" (p. 257). Whereas Lave and Wenger (1991) concretized the social context of learning as the work practices of a community of practice, Tharp and Gallimore concretized the social context of learning as *chains of assistance* and *activity settings*. Chains of assistance refer to the social and organizational structure of the schooling environment as the context for learning. Activity settings refer to the more immediate social structures within which learning occurs, marked by the specificities of time, place, participants, goals, and motivations. It is argued that the characteristics of both of these social structures—the macroorganizational structure of the schooling environment and the more microcharacteristics of activity settings—must be examined in order to fully understand the processes of learning.

Chains of Assistance

Within Tharp and Gallimore's (1988) framework, the social and organizational context for learning is examined with respect to the lines of influence (i.e., the supervisory organization) that exist in the schooling environment and the ends toward which such influence is exercised. Tharp and Gallimore refered to the lines of influence that are typically found in schools as *chains of assessment,* referring to systems that are driven by standardized achievement tests and in which district office administrators direct and assess the work of principals, who direct and assess the work of teachers, who direct and assess the work of students. In Fig. 7.2, this is represented by circles.

Under such circumstances, learners are provided little or no assistance for carrying out worthwhile, complex cognitive tasks, and there is little mutual investment in jointly valued outcomes. The goal of reforming education, according to Tharp and Gallimore, is to replace chains of *assessment* with chains of *assistance.* In school organizations that can be characterized as chains of assistance, the first responsibility of the district office administrators is to assist the principal. Similarly, the principal should assist teachers, and teachers should assist students.

With respect to teacher change efforts, the construct of chains of assistance encourages us to look at the larger social system in which we are expecting teacher development to occur. The chains-of-assistance construct also helps to identify resources for assisting teachers that lie outside formal lines of supervision. The circles in Fig. 7.2 represent sources of assistance who also have the responsibility for *formal* supervision through the exercise of authority; the rectangles represent *informal* sources of assistance by nonsupervisory others. Tharp and Gallimore (1988) noted that the provision of effective assistance does not require authority, and that the assistance of performance can sometimes be provided more effectively in its absence. Individuals altogether outside the institution (e.g., consultants, resource partners) often provide interactions with important developmental consequences for teachers. As shown in Fig. 7.2, the work of these individuals must, however, be considered in the context of the entire chain. The triangles in Fig. 7.2 indicate that persons in the chain also provide assistance to themselves, an important stage in the progression from assisted to unassisted performance.

Activity Settings

According to Tharp and Gallimore (1988), those in supervisory positions are responsible not only for providing assistance but most importantly for using their authority to create the time, resources, and incentives for teachers to participate in activity settings where effective assistance can occur. For example, principals should arrange for more expert or experienced people to interact with teachers about mathematics in settings that will be conducive to teacher learning. The providers of assistance can be from the school (more experienced "old-timers") or

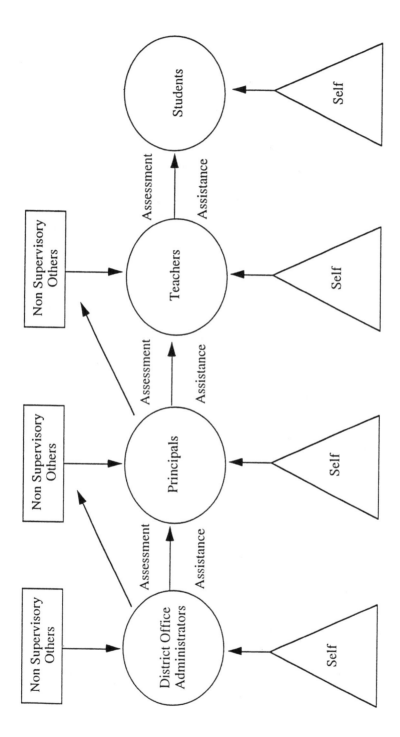

FIG. 7.2. Lines of influence in the social and organizational context for learning (adapted from Tharp & Gallimore, 1988).

from outside (the "expert" consultant). What is most important is that activity settings exist in which teachers' learning is assisted.

A full understanding of activity settings requires examination of not only *what* is learned, but also *why* it is learned, by *whom*, and *where*—in essence, an analysis of the interpersonal environment, including individuals' motivations and the larger meanings that they attach to their activities. According to Tharp and Gallimore (1988), in order for assisted performance to truly occur in an activity setting, there must be common goals and meanings as well as joint productive activity.

Common Goals and Meanings. Good assistance requires that the person assisting and the person being assisted are working for the same goal. Sometimes mutual goals can be established at the start of the relationship; more often they emerge. The presence of mutual goals is often accompanied by clear forms of communication—talk that is based on a mutually shared set of understandings and motivations, as well as shared language by which to communicate those understandings and motivations. The assistor and the assisted must build and refine feelings, motivations, intentions, and understandings that, in essence, allow them to operate as though they are both members of the same community.

Joint Productivity Activity. Instead of directing learners to accomplish a task and then assessing their ability to do so, assistors should coparticipate in the accomplishment of the task alongside the learners. Tasks should not be broken down into smaller digestible parts and "assigned" to learners. Rather, the task should remain authentic, whole, and complex, and it should be tackled jointly by the assistor and the learner. This allows assistors to better understand the learners' levels of capacity and, hence, to offer appropriate assistance. Moreover, it allows the assistor to be influenced by the contributions of the learners, thus leading to the possibility of overall adjustments to the planned learning sequence. In addition to joint participation, activity settings should be driven by a valued product. Tharp and Gallimore (1988) noted that a prime requirement of motivated activity in everyday life is the existence of a product desired by all the participants. Similar requirements hold for the activities in which teachers and others participate.

This discussion of the characteristics of good activity settings provides us with criteria for evaluating the kind of settings in which teacher learning through assisted performance might be expected to occur. It suggests that teacher learning occurs through the provision of assistance by more expert others over a period of time in a way that is responsive to the goals and motivations as well as the levels of knowledge and skill of the learners. The theory posits that such assistance is most likely to be effective if provided in the context of working on a jointly valued product.

Learning Through Assisted Performance at Norton Middle School

Norton is a middle school in Bellview Public Schools, a large urban district. During their participation in the QUASAR project, the mathematics teachers at Norton were slow to form a cohesive reform-oriented community. Interviews with the teachers at this site indicated that the Norton teachers looked to their resource partners (more-expert outsiders) rather than to their colleagues as their primary sources of assistance as they attempted to reform their instructional program. In addition, teachers perceived a number of factors in the district as constraining their reform efforts. This situation suggested to us that Tharp and Gallimore's (1988) definition of learning as movement from assisted to unassisted performance and the constructs of chain of assistance and activity settings could be used to examine teacher learning at Norton and to reveal factors present in the social organization of Bellview Public Schools that could facilitate or inhibit teacher change in a reform effort such as QUASAR.

Our illustration is divided into two time periods: the early project years (the first two years of Norton's participation in the QUASAR project) and the later project years (the second two years of Norton's participation). For each of these time periods, we describe and analyze the supervisory chain present in the Bellview School District and one of the major activity settings that was provided to assist sixth-grade teachers to reform their instructional practices: common planning time. (In this example, we limit our discussion to how common planning time played out for the sixth-grade teachers. Due to a variety of factors, common planning periods for the seventh- and eighth-grade teachers did not play out in exactly the same way, although ultimately many of the same issues were involved.) The differences in the supervisory chains and the characteristics of common planning time between the early and later project years illustrate the ways in which both the broader organizational structure of the school environment and the more microfeatures of activity settings can influence the process of teacher learning through assisted performance.

Early Project Years: Chain of Assessment. In the Bellview Public Schools, a complex system of testing was used to hold teachers and principals accountable for meeting the districts' goals for student outcomes. With respect to mathematics, these goals were very traditional, emphasizing computational skill and facility with algorithms rather than conceptual understanding and problem solving (e.g., one stated goal was, "Over 50% of the students will perform at or above the national norm on the ITBS

[Iowa Test of Basic Skills]"). The district administered at least three different assessments (the ITBS, a state-mandated competency test, and ongoing district-designed, curriculum-based tests) to determine if these goals were being met. Schools (and therefore principals and teachers) were evaluated on the basis of the results of these assessments, with scores often made public as a means of exerting pressure on schools or teachers. There is extensive documentation of the Norton teachers' and principal's perceptions of the importance of doing well on these assessments, which were frequently referred to as "high stakes." However, other than an occasional workshop on how to prepare students for the ITBS or the state-mandated competency test, teachers and principals were given very little assistance to meet district goals. In short, the supervisory context at Norton was a chain of *assessment* with little assistance provision for teachers.

As part of their application to join the QUASAR project, the district and building administrators, including the coordinator of mathematics, committed to the broad goals of the project and to the reform of the instructional program at Norton. Two resource partners, mathematics educators from nearby universities, were funded to provide assistance to the mathematics faculty at Norton. The resource partners were brought on board as "expert others" who had interactions with the teachers but no formal supervisory authority. Fig. 7.3 indicates the placement of the resource partners with respect to the overall line of district supervision.

The segment of the chain that included the resource partners, teachers, and students (the shaded area of Fig. 7.3) was intended to be a chain of *assistance* within which teacher learning would be fostered.

With the insertion of the resource partners as a new source of assistance, the principal and other administrators had taken an important step. They were providing teachers access to a form of expertise not formerly available in the building. However, additional changes in the chain of assessment were not forthcoming, at least not during the early project years. Despite their spoken "commitment" to reforming their instructional program to be more in alignment with the *Standards* (NCTM, 1989), the district office administrators continued to hold the principal and teachers accountable for student performance on computation-oriented mathematics assessments. Consequently, teachers and the principal at Norton found themselves trying to achieve goals they viewed as essentially incompatible—the student learning goals measured by the district assessments and the student learning goals they had accepted as participants in the QUASAR project.

This analysis of the larger organizational setting highlights the inconsistencies that existed between the reform efforts of the QUASAR project and the schooling environment in which the project was embedded. The inconsistencies existed along two dimensions: the goals of

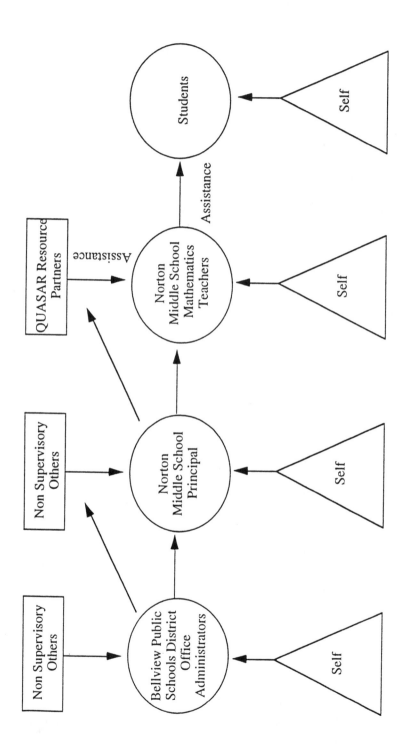

FIG. 7.3.   Lines of influence in the Norton social and organizational context for learning.

instruction (computation/basic skills vs. higher level thinking and reasoning) and the methods of working with teachers and others (direct and
assess vs. assist). In the next section, we see that these inconsistencies
trickled down and were felt at the more microlevels of activity settings
as well.

Early Project Years: Activity Setting. Although the construct of chain of
assessment/assistance helps us understand the social organization of a
school environment relative to teacher learning, the construct of activity
setting helps us to understand the social interactions within which
teachers are provided assistance—a means of examining learning as
assisted performance at a more fine-grained level of detail.

As part of the QUASAR Project, resources were made available to
create a number of activity settings that the principal and the resource
partners believed would support teacher learning—monthly workshops,
summer institutes, professional meetings, and common planning time
for mathematics teachers at a given grade level. Our analysis here
focuses on the activity setting of common planning time for the sixth-
grade teachers. The sixth-grade teachers in Norton had two consecutive
periods daily that were considered common planning time. The principal
intended that mathematics teachers would meet together two or three
times weekly and use this 90 minutes of shared time to collaboratively
plan and evaluate lessons aligned with their goals of more meaningful
mathematics instruction. One of the resource partners, Dr. O., offered
to join the teachers for these meetings once a week.

The establishment of common planning time appeared to have promise as an effective activity setting for teacher learning through assisted
performance. It provided time and resources for teacher–teacher collaboration to occur and for mutual trust and respect to develop among
teachers and between the teachers and the resource partner. The addition of the resource partner to the meetings added a level of expertise
with respect to the ideas and philosophy of the mathematics reform
movement. By working closely with the teachers, the resource partner
would become familiar with the teachers' levels of proficiency and thus
be able to provide assistance tailored to their needs. The activity setting
was deeply embedded in the day-to-day routines and responsibilities of
the teachers' everyday lives; thus, their work could remain highly
connected to practice. The planned activity of developing lessons, centered around meaningful and cognitively challenging tasks, would presumably represent work on jointly valued products that would have real
significance to their ongoing efforts to reform mathematics instruction
at Norton Middle School.

During the early project years, the promise of the common planning
time was not fulfilled for a number of reasons. The teachers and Dr. O.
met occasionally, not regularly. As time went on, the teachers com-

plained that the meetings were not helpful and took away time available for individual planning. The resource partner claimed that the teachers did not appear to be interested in the ideas that she had to offer. Examination of the characteristics of these meetings during the early project years as an activity setting for teacher learning provides some insight into the sources of teachers' and the resource partner's dissatisfaction.

1. *Common goals and meanings.* Although the teachers and Dr. O. had committed to working toward a common goal of providing an enhanced mathematics instructional program for all Norton students, as they began working together during common planning time it became apparent that, in fact, their conceptions of this goal and understandings of the means by which it would be met were quite different. Based on past work with teachers in another district, Dr. O. assumed that she could best assist the Norton teachers to develop and implement a reformed mathematics instructional program by empowering them to become reflective practitioners—individuals who could make their own instructional decisions, based on their knowledge of mathematics, curriculum, pedagogy, and learners. As such, her work with teachers during common planning time was rather open ended and was designed to raise awareness levels and to encourage the teachers themselves to construct new forms of pedagogy.

The teachers, on the other hand, described their goal for the common planning time as receiving assistance that would allow them to integrate mathematics with other content areas, implement cooperative learning groups, and use technology and manipulatives. Although they expressed uncertainty about how this all fit together to form a coherent instructional program, they believed that the role of the resource partner was to teach them instructional techniques such as those listed. Although they were seeking new techniques, it was not clear that the teachers held new goals for student learning. In fact, teachers repeatedly reminded the resource partners and QUASAR staff that they were expected to prepare students for the assessments administered by the district. The techniques teachers sought were often perceived by them as better ways to prepare students for the assessments. To the teachers, the activities in which Dr. O. tried to engage them appeared overly abstract; they had neither her vision nor the tools to begin working on the vision. To the resource partner, the teachers appeared resistant. In short, common goals and meanings were conspicuously absent.

2. *Joint productive activity.* As noted earlier, the common planning time was intended by the principal to be used to plan and evaluate lessons collaboratively. It was the principal's intention that a concrete product emerge from this activity setting—a series of lesson plans for instruction that all sixth-grade mathematics teachers would use. This

did not occur. Instead of tackling the task of jointly constructing concrete plans for instruction, teachers tended to use their meeting time to tell stories about events in their classrooms. They engaged in "storytelling and scanning" (Little, 1990b) rather than joint work. Like many experienced teachers, Norton teachers generally did little planning for lessons beyond looking over the textbook pages and seeing that worksheets were copied for students. When put in the situation of meeting together to plan, the teachers did not know what to do other than to talk about what they had been doing and what they intended to do in their individual classrooms. They did not view each other as sources of learning, only as sympathetic listeners. When the resource partner participated, she tried to focus teachers on big ideas of lessons, but because of her belief that teachers should construct their own pedagogy, she did not attempt to engage them in actually writing plans to be used.

3. *Movement through the ZPD.* In terms of initiating processes that might be conducive to teacher learning, it should be noted that, on the positive side, the principal had provided time and resources for activity settings that appeared to hold promise for assisting teacher learning. On the negative side, the incentives that were operating in the larger chain of assessment were sending mixed signals to teachers. This, in turn, influenced the degree to which common goals and meanings, as well as joint productive activity, could occur in the activity settings. Not surprisingly, teacher change during these early project years was minimal. In terms of progress through the stages of the ZPD, data suggest that the teachers and resource partner never progressed past the first stage. Indeed, it could be argued that teacher performance was never truly assisted. The lack of common goals, meaning, and joint productive work all conspired to block the provision of meaningful assistance tailored to the needs of the learners in the particular reform setting.

Later Project Years: Toward a Chain of Assistance.   Although we saw little evidence of assisted performance in the common planning time during the early project years, during the third and fourth years of participation in the QUASAR project, the Norton sixth-grade teachers made progress. During the 1993–1994 school year, the third year of Norton's participation in the QUASAR project, several events began to weaken the chain of assessment present in Bellview Public Schools, and the hazy outlines of a chain of assistance began to appear. The district mathematics coordinator gave Norton teachers permission to use curriculum materials other than those on which the district curriculum-based assessments were based. The new materials were highly compatible with the kinds of instruction advocated by the NCTM Standards and the QUASAR Project. This gave Norton "pilot project" status in the district, which resulted in the provision of a waiver of the requirement to administer the district curriculum-based assessments. At about the same time, the district announced the decision to administer a new form of the ITBS that was reported to contain items requiring less knowledge of procedures and more conceptual understanding and reasoning.

Although there was still accountability for raising student scores on the ITBS and the state-mandated competency test for the eighth-grade students, these assessments were viewed as being somewhat more aligned with reform goals than were the other tests. The Norton teachers were also asked to design an assessment process to replace the waived district curriculum-based assessments. For this purpose they decided to use assessments that accompanied the new curriculum materials, in conjunction with some assessments that they themselves constructed with the resource partner.

The changes in the assessment environment coincided with Dr. O. leaving her resource partner position due to other obligations. At the urging of the district mathematics coordinator and the building principal, she was replaced by Ms. H., a retired high school mathematics teacher from the Bellview Public Schools who was known and respected by the Norton teachers because of her leadership in district in-service work. Ms. H.'s appointment to the resource partner role can be seen as a noteworthy district-level move toward assistance provision. Ms. H. was familiar with the Bellview Public School's assessment practices *and* the reform mathematics movements. As such, she was in the position to effectively assist teachers in both of these areas.

This analysis of the organizational chain during the later project years suggests that some of the inconsistencies between the reform efforts of the QUASAR Project and the policies of the school district were beginning to break down. With respect to the goals of instruction, there appeared to be an increased focus, at all levels of the chain, on higher order thinking and reasoning skills. With respect to methods of working with teachers, there was still an emphasis on "directing and assessing" (as one form of assessment was lifted, another took its place). However, the positive impact of the approval of new curriculum materials and the removal of the oppressive district curriculum-based assessments was significant.

Later Project Years: Toward an Effective Activity Setting. After only a short time as resource partner, Ms. H. recognized that, for a number of reasons, mathematics teachers were not using the new curriculum materials in appropriate ways. It was her suspicion that teachers did not understand enough about either the mathematics or the pedagogy embedded in the new materials to use them effectively. She recognized the teachers' need for assistance and saw an opportunity to help the teachers by working with them during their common planning time to create plans that would use the new curriculum materials to engage students in higher-level mathematical activities. Thus, early in the

1993–1994 school year, Ms. H. began meeting once or twice weekly with the sixth-grade teachers during their common planning time. At the same time, she began spending considerable time in each teacher's classroom.

1. *Common goals and meaning.* The agreement to use the new curriculum materials and to assess students using the accompanying assessment materials appeared to provide a common goal for the teachers and the resource partner. Both parties wished to learn more about the ideas and methods suggested by those materials and to try them out with the students at Norton. The teachers reported that the removal of the pressure of the district curriculum-based assessments freed them up to use instructional tasks that were not aimed at improving computational skills, but they were uncertain how to teach lessons involving such tasks. The teachers also were not willing to give up computation completely, noting that high student scores on the ITBS and eighth-grade competency test were still important outcomes.

Ms. H. seemed to recognize and validate the teachers' concerns. She spent some time working with the teachers to improve their techniques for teaching students computational skills, thus addressing that concern. However, she was able to focus most of her time with teachers on their common goal of understanding and implementing the new curriculum and assessing student learning outcomes. The new curriculum materials appeared to provide both an overall picture of the learning goal and a set of tools for their work together. The goals of their work during the common planning time proved to be more concrete than the "reflective practitioner" outcome aspired to by Dr. O. and less technique-driven than the goals held by the teachers in the early project years.

2. *Joint productive activity.* During the sixth-grade common planning time, there was evidence that teachers and the resource partner were engaged in joint work. During the later project years, Ms. H. worked alongside the teachers, reviewing the curriculum materials, working through activities that teachers would later do with their students, and discussing teachers' classroom experiences with the curriculum materials. These activities were grounded in the teachers' day-to-day work practices, not in isolated forms of new knowledge whose connection to classroom practice would need to be forged. Moreover, the complete task of implementing a reform program of mathematics was retained as the overall goal toward which they were striving.

In the activity setting of common planning time, sixth-grade teachers and Ms. H. worked together to create (a) lesson plans, which all teachers agreed to use in their classroom instruction, and (b) student assessments, which all teachers agreed to administer to their students. Although common plans and assessments resulting from the common planning activities might be viewed by some as unnecessarily constraining for teachers, they were viewed by the Norton sixth-grade teachers themselves as having a number of benefits. Teachers viewed their collaborative work as providing them with an opportunity to teach well-planned lessons from which they could learn about this new form of instruction. Because the resource partner and other teachers were familiar with the materials and the purposes of the lessons, teachers felt they could receive more focused assistance both from their colleagues and from the resource partner.

  3. *Movement through the ZPD*. During these later project years, the promise of common planning time as an effective activity setting for teacher learning through assisted performance began to be realized. The activity setting was deeply embedded in teachers' day-to-day work routines and even included the production of useful products that would have real significance to their ongoing efforts to reform mathematics instruction at Norton Middle School. Clearly, teachers were engaged in assisted performance of planning.

  Examination of this activity setting indicated that as time passed, Ms. H. was able to withdraw support and hand more and more of the work of planning instruction and assessment over to the teachers. Two examples provide glimpses of how this occurred. As teachers became more familiar with the task of planning lessons using the new curriculum materials, they rotated responsibility for identifying and finding manipulatives and other resources the group would need, turning to Ms. H. only when they could not find what they needed. With respect to the design of assessments, Ms. H. constructed assessments, which teachers then reviewed, suggesting revisions. Gradually, teachers took over the task of constructing the assessments, which were then reviewed by their colleagues and Ms. H. In terms of progress through the ZPD, it appeared that teachers were on their way to unassisted performance.

CONCLUSIONS

In this chapter we used two socioculturally based frameworks to describe teacher learning in two different school-based settings. With our descriptions of the schooling environments at each of these schools, we also attempted to explain why each of the frameworks was selected. At Riverside, the challenge was to understand how teacher learning was supported by the opportunities afforded by a cohesive group of teachers who were engaged in common work toward the goal of developing and sustaining a reform program of mathematics instruction. At Norton, on the other hand, the challenge was to understand the barriers to teacher learning, given that a reform community was not established. As barriers at Norton began to be lifted, the ways in which teacher learning was productively facilitated were explored.

Use of the communities-of-practice and the assisted-performance frameworks to understand teacher learning at Riverside and Norton, respectively, enabled us to grapple with aspects of the social and organizational landscape that would not have been illuminated had we used traditional psychological frameworks. In this concluding section, we begin by describing the aspects of teacher learning that these two frameworks were especially helpful in illuminating. Then we move to a discussion of what remained in the shadows and how we might complement either of these two frameworks with analyses based in more traditional psychological frameworks.

What Sociocultural Frameworks Illuminate

Both of the frameworks employed in this chapter channeled our attention away from the cognitive attributes and instructional practices of individual teachers toward the collaborative interactions that occur as teachers (and others) attempt to develop and improve their school's mathematics instructional programs. However, the contexts for learning are concretized differently in the two frameworks. Lave and Wenger (1991) concretized context as the work practices of the local community of practice; Tharp and Gallimore (1988) concretized context as activity settings guided by common goals and joint productive activity. The learning processes that occur within communities of practice and effective activity settings are, however, similar. Learning occurs as individuals transform their forms of participation. In the communities-of-practice framework, this transformation of participation is characterized as movement from *peripheral to fuller* forms of participation in the overall work activities of the community. In the framework advocated by Tharp and Gallimore, the transformation is characterized as movement from *assisted to unassisted* performance in specific activity settings.

Another similarity between learning processes in communities-of-practice and effective-activity settings is that, in both settings, individuals "use their differences to learn" (Bredo & McDermott, 1992). By this we mean that an important ingredient in socially based learning is the gradations of expertise and experience that exist when teachers collaborate with each other or with outside experts. In fact, an overall sense of directionality to the learning process is provided by these naturally occurring asymmetries between more experienced, expert participants and novices. In the Riverside example, the old-timers provided the overall direction for change; in Norton (during the later project years) the resource partner provided this sense of direction.

It should be noted that this overall sense of directionality does not, however, imply that novice or less experienced teachers simply "imitate" or "model" precisely what old-timers or experts do. Although overall directionality is provided by old-timers and more expert others, both frameworks also acknowledge inventiveness on the part of the learner and ways in which the learner can guide the processes of learning (e.g., newcomers to a community of practice bring a fresh perspective and can question practices in insightful ways; in learning-as-assisted-performance, assistors often shift their priorities and goals in response to their ongoing assessment of the needs and contributions of the learner). In short, learners are seen to be transformed by the practices in which they engage and also to transform those practices. Indeed, we view the ways in which sociocultural frameworks allow for the establishment of socially determined directions for change as one way of responding to Richardson's (1990) call for models of teacher change that honor teacher judgments about what constitutes worthwhile and significant change, and bring to bear ways of thinking from outside an individual teacher's own experiences.

Another feature highlighted by both frameworks is the manner in which significant learning can be embedded in the actual practice of being a school mathematics teacher. In the literature, we find references to teachers' learning through their daily classroom practice (e.g., Cobb, Wood, & Yackel, 1990). The frameworks used in this chapter suggest that learning also occurs in school-based activities not immediately contained within the four walls of the classroom. For example, teachers learn by planning for and discussing lessons, by arguing over the best sequence for a curriculum, and by designing assessments. Although not actual teaching, these are part of the overall practice of being a teacher. Advantages to learning by practice include relevance, connection, and maintenance of the completeness and integrity of tasks. For example, at Norton, a primary source of teacher learning was the common planning time, which included ongoing, practice-relevant tasks such as designing lesson plans and methods of assessment. At Riverside, many of the activities that formed opportunities for teacher learning occurred when teachers met informally and/or gathered to accomplish a specific task (e.g., develop new assessment tools, refine curricular offerings, plan a parent night). In more traditional methods of studying teacher change, these activities might very well be overlooked as occasions for learning. Lave and Wenger (1991) refered to the process of learning within the ongoing work practices of a community as the "decentering of learning" or as "learning without being taught, examined, or reduced to a mechanical copier" (p. 30).

A final feature that both frameworks served to highlight is ways in which motivation and cognitive change can be examined in an integrated fashion. Studies of teacher change in mathematics tend to overlook noncognitive variables such as affect or motivation for change (Goldsmith & Schifter, 1993). The two frameworks discussed in this chapter, however, situate the learning of new knowledge and skills in the context of the larger meaning-making capacities and affective characteristics of individuals. In so doing, they integrate the study of cognitive change with the examination of goals, motivations, and identity. For example, as peripheral members of the Riverside community, newcomers were exposed to much more than the community's cognitive activities. They also learned about what life was like in the community, what members did, how they talked, what they valued. As newcomers became more experienced and moved on to positions of greater responsibility, they developed not only the requisite cognitive skills, but also the attitudes, motivations, and values of those around them. Thus, they learned tasks hand-in-hand with the development of a sense of identity as a reform practitioner of mathematics. The process of becoming part of the community is seen to be intrinsically motivating because it "confers a sense of belonging" (p. 111). As newcomers invest the increasing amounts of time, resources, and energy necessary to move toward full participation, they simultaneously develop new knowledge and skills *and*, "more significantly, an increasing sense of identity as a master practitioner." (p. 111).

Within Tharp and Gallimore's (1988) framework, much of what constitutes "learning" consists of the negotiation of goals, meanings, and motivations between individuals who begin their work together with different agendas and expectations. Therefore, a high priority is placed on understanding the goals of collaborative interactions (both initial and emergent), the meaning that individuals ascribe to their actions, and what motivated them to join the interaction in the first place. In general, socioculturally based analyses take on the "whole person acting in the world" by not separating their motivations and other affective characteristics from their cognitions and by not separating the person from his or her environment.

What Remains in the Shadows

The use of sociocultural theory to examine teacher learning might obscure certain aspects of learning. Because sociocultural theory locates the phenomenon of learning in the fields of social interaction among individuals, there is less of a tendency to examine deeply what is actually being learned by individual teachers. In this chapter, we purposefully focused both the theoretical discussion and application examples on the group, especially the patterns of participation within the group, because we adopted a definition of *learning as transformation of participation* in the practices of a community (Rogoff, 1994). By focusing on the interactions among teachers and between teachers and resource partners in the ways that we did, we were able to examine teacher learning in a social context in a manner that, to our knowledge, has not been done before. The social context, including the values, work practices, and institutional structures of the Riverside and Norton settings, were deeply interwoven into our accounts of teacher learning. In our examples, teacher learning incorporated chunks of context in a manner that pulled the social into the learning process in a far more integrated fashion than adding reference to contextual detail, almost as an afterthought. As mentioned earlier, sociocultural theories view context as much more than a static stage on which learning is enacted. In our examples, teachers used aspects of the context to do their work in much the same way as grocery shoppers use context to perform arithmetic calculations (Lave, Murtaugh, & de la Rocha, 1984).

Because of this intense focus on the social, however, readers will have difficulty putting their fingers on what was actually being learned by individual teachers as they participated in the Riverside community and/or activity settings at Norton, especially if they are looking for broad and traditional measures of what it is important for mathematics teachers to know and be able to do. In our examples, we stated that as individual teachers transformed their participatory roles, they were learning aspects of mathematics and pedagogy that were valued in their respective settings, but it has been difficult to pull these out as separate threads and identify and measure them (precisely because they are so bound up with contextual packaging). In sociocultural theory, this contextual packaging organizes what we look for and how we interpret what is found. Using context as our lens in this chapter, we found interactional patterns, motivation and goals, and changes in participation structures. Broader and more traditional indices of mathematical expertise are scattered throughout these findings, but they have not been foregrounded. Indeed, foregrounding them without their contextual entailments would defeat the purpose of the paradigm.

How might analyses, such as those provided in this chapter, that are heavily focused on learning as transformation of participation in particular communities be conducted or complemented to provide a more traditionally grounded picture of teacher change in mathematics? Our sense is that there are two ways, one that remains within the transformation of participation paradigm and one that requires a complete departure from it. In the first method, we can examine more closely an aspect of teacher's work that is conventionally seen as an important measure of their expertise, for example, classroom practice (assuming, of course, that reform teaching is a valued activity in the local setting). Rather than look at classroom practice as a separate variable that happens to coincide in time with other community efforts, however, we can examine how an individual's teaching becomes more "masterful" as his or her participation shifts from peripheral to fuller forms of participation, or from assisted to unassisted performance. We were not able to examine classroom teaching in this way at Riverside because the organization of teaching was not carried out as a collaboration among adult

professionals. By this we mean that the actual act of classroom instruction was conducted by individual teachers (as is true in most schools);
measuring teacher learning as transformation of participation hence
would be difficult—without social interaction, no transformation of
participation can occur. However, the acts of *preparing for* and *reflecting
on* teaching were very much collaborative ventures at Riverside, hence
the examination of changes in these skills, coinciding with movement
from peripheral to fuller forms of participation, could be undertaken. At
Norton, the collaborations between teachers and the resource partner
that occurred when Ms. H. spent time in teachers' classrooms could
provide an example of movement from assisted to unassisted performance of classroom practices. Although we have some data that suggest
that this indeed was the case, the documentation of these interactions
is quite limited, and we chose not to use them as examples in this
chapter.

A second way that we might address the question of what is being
learned is to step outside the sociocultural paradigm and inspect the
cognitive entailments associated with increased forms of participation.
Along these lines, Cobb (1994) contended that "sociocultural analyses
involve implicit cognitive commitments" (p. 18); that is, that learning as
portrayed by Rogoff (1994) and other sociocultural researchers implicitly assumes that individuals are actively constructing and making
sense of their activities. Sociocultural theory, Cobb argued, foregrounds
social processes, allowing the phenomenon of individual cognition to
recede into the background. Conversely, constructivist perspectives
foreground individual cognition, with social processes receding into the
background. Cobb argued that both are needed to build a complete
understanding of the development of learners: "Each of the two perspectives, the sociocultural and the constructivist, tells half a good story, and
each can be used to complement the other" (p. 17).

This approach is very different from the first because it contends that
to understand what is learned we need to step inside the minds of
individual teachers and inspect their contents. The products of learning
remain characterized as cognitive knowledge and skills, as opposed to
independent and important skilled performance in activities valued in
the individual's local setting.

In our judgment, both ways of viewing knowledge and learning are
reasonable and useful, depending on the question being addressed. In
this chapter, the questions with which we were grappling concerned
understanding the ways in which teachers learned with each other and
outside experts in the context of ongoing work activities. These questions led us to use sociocultural frameworks because they emphasized
the role of social interaction and work practices as sources of learning.
Had our questions been of a different sort (e.g., how teachers' backgrounds in mathematics were influencing their classroom practice), we

most likely would have selected a cognitive psychological framework. No doubt, the answers to both sets of questions include psychological and social dimensions, respectively. The challenge will be knowing when a coordination of both perspectives is called for and then fashioning ways to bring them together into a useful and coherent account of learning. Examples of combining sociocultural and psychological perspectives have begun to appear in the literature for the study of student learning (see Driver, Asoko, Leach, Mortimer, & Scott, 1994). We look forward to seeing similar efforts in the study of the learning of teachers of mathematics.

ACKNOWLEDGMENTS

Preparation of this chapter was supported by a grant from the Ford Foundation (grant number 890–0572) for the QUASAR project. Any opinions expressed herein are those of the authors and do not necessarily represent the views of the Ford Foundation. The authors would like to thank Ellice Forman, Barbara Nelson, and Edward Silver for their comments on an earlier draft of this chapter.

REFERENCES

Borko, H., Eisenhart, M., Brown, C. A., Underhill, R. G., Jones, D., & Agard, P. C. (1992). Learning to teach hard mathematics: Do novice teachers and their instructors give up too easily? *Journal for Research in Mathematics Education, 23*, 194–222.

Bredo, E., & McDermott, R. P. (1992, June–July). Teaching, relating, and learning. [Review of *The construction zone* and *Rousing minds to life*]. *Educational Researcher, 21*, 31–35.

Brown, C. A., & Borko, H. (1992). Becoming a mathematics teacher. In D. A. Grouws (Ed.), *Handbook of research on mathematics teaching and learning* (pp. 209–242). New York: Macmillan.

Calderhead, J. (1988). *Exploring teachers' thinking*. London: Cassell Educational, Limited.

Cobb, P. (1994). Where is the mind? Constructivist and sociocultural perspectives on mathematical development. *Educational Researcher, 23*, 13–20.

Cobb, P., Wood, T., & Yackel, E. (1990). Classrooms as learning environments for teachers and researchers. In R. Davis, C. Maher, & N. Noddings (Eds.), *Constructivist views on the teaching and learning of mathematics* (Vol. 4, pp. 125–146). Reston, VA: National Council of Teachers of Mathematics.

Driver, R., Asoko, H., Leach, J., Mortimer, E., & Scott, P. (1994). Constructing scientific knowledge in the classroom. *Educational Researcher, 23*, 5–12.

Eisenhart, M., Borko, H., Underhill, R., Brown, C. A., Jones, D., & Agard, P. (1993). Conceptual knowledge falls through the cracks: Complexities of learning to teach mathematics for understanding. *Journal for Research in Mathematics Education, 24*, 8–40.

Fennema, E., Franke, M., Carpenter, T., & Carey, D. (1993). Using children's mathematical knowledge in instruction. *American Educational Research Journal, 30*(3), 555–584.

Fullan, M. G. (1991). *The new meaning of educational change*. New York: Teachers College Press.

Goldsmith, L. T., & Schifter, D. (1993, October). Characteristics of a model for the development of mathematics teaching [Special issue]. *Reports and Papers in Progress*. Newton, MA: Education Development Center.

Hanks, W. F. (1991). Forward. In *Situated learning: Legitimate peripheral participation* (pp. 13–24). Cambridge, England: Cambridge University Press.

Lacey, D. (1977). *The socialization of teachers*. London: Methuen.

Lave, J., Murtaugh, M., & de la Rocha, O. (1984). The dialectic of arithmetic in grocery shopping. In B. Rogoff & J. Lave (Eds.), *Everyday cognition* (pp. 67–116). Boston, MA: Harvard University Press.

Lave, J., & Wenger, E. (1991). *Situated learning: Legitimate peripheral participation*. Cambridge, England: Cambridge University Press.

Leinhardt, G. (1989). Math lessons: A contrast of novice and expert competence. *Journal for Research in Mathematics Education, 20*, 52–75.

Little, J. W. (1990a). Teachers as colleagues. In A. Lieberman (Ed.), *Schools as collaborative cultures: Creating the future now* (pp. 165–193). New York: Falmer.

Little, J. W. (1990b). The persistence of privacy: Autonomy and initiative in teachers' professional relations. *Teachers College Record, 19* (4), 509–536.

Minick, N. J. (1985). *Vygotsky and Soviet activity theory: New perspectives on the relationship between mind and society*, Unpublished doctoral dissertation, Northwestern University, Evanston, IL.

National Council of Teachers of Mathematics. (1989). *Curriculum and evaluation standards for school mathematics*. Reston, VA: Author.

National Council of Teachers of Mathematics. (1991). *Professional standards for the teaching of mathematics*. Reston, VA: Author.

Putnam, R. T. (1992). Teaching the "hows" of mathematics for everyday life: A case study of a fifth-grade teacher. *The Elementary School Journal, 93*, 163–178.

Remillard, J. (1992). Teaching mathematics for understanding: A fifth-grade teacher's interpretation of policy. *The Elementary School Journal, 93,* 179–194.

Richardson, V. (1990). Significant and worthwhile change in teaching practice. *Educational Researcher, 19*(7), pp. 10–18.

Rogoff, B. (1994). Developing understanding of the idea of communities of learners. *Mind, Culture, and Activity, 1*, 209–229.

Schifter, D., & Fosnot, C. T. (1993). *Reconstructing mathematics education: Stories of teachers meeting the challenge of reform*. New York: Teachers College Press.

Silver, E. A., & Stein, M. K. (1996). The QUASAR project: The "revolution of the possible" in mathematics instructional reform in urban middle schools. *Urban Education, 30*, 476–521.

Stein, M. K., Silver, E. A., & Smith, M. S. (in press). Mathematics reform and teacher development: A community of practice perspective. In J. G. Greeno & S. Goldman (Eds.), *Thinking practices: A symposium on mathematics and science learning*. Hillsdale, NJ: Lawrence Erlbaum Associates.

Tharp, R., & Gallimore, R. (1988). *Rousing minds to life: Teaching, learning, and schooling in social context*. Cambridge, England: Cambridge University Press.

Vygotsky, L. S. (1978). *Mind in society: The development of higher psychological processes*. Cambridge, MA: Harvard University Press.

8

Mathematics Teachers' Change in the Context of Their Professional Communities

Walter G. Secada
University of Wisconsin–Madison

Lisa B. Adajian
Portland State University

Mathematics teachers' professional communities provide an important context in which to understand their practices, professional growth, and development. The general hypothesis that has guided the work of the school-level study of mathematics reform[1] is that the focus, strength, and extent of professional community helps to support teachers' practice; conversely, teaching practices help to create shared norms among teachers, which are characteristic of their professional communities. This chapter illustrates one direction of the complex interrelationship between professional community and teaching practice: Krome[2] Elementary School's teachers relied on their professional community to

---

[1] The purpose of the school-level study of mathematics reform was to better understand the nature of school mathematics reform at an organizational level higher than that of the individual, that is, at the elementary and middle school, and at the high school mathematics department. We sought schools and departments that were engaged in substantive efforts to enhance the quality of their mathematics programs. We selected cases based on evidence that (a) students were actually experiencing mathematics in ways that departed from the conventional and that were somehow consistent with the vision outlined in various reform documents, (b) teachers were acting collectively as opposed to individually in their efforts, and (c) the school or department had some commitment to equity, that is, to ensuring that all (not just a few) students were experiencing mathematics differently. The study's conceptual and methodological issues and related studies can be found in Adajian (1995), Byrd, Foster, Peressini, and Secada (1994), Peressini (1995), and Secada and Byrd (1993).

[2] All names of the school and its teachers are fictitious.

support their efforts to change and to enhance their school's mathematics program.

Before presenting the case data, we define professional community. Next is a review of selected literature showing that teachers' professional communities mediate a range of school effects from student achievement to teacher change. The combination of literature review and case data support the thesis of this chapter; that is, in order to understand the process of mathematics teachers' change, mathematics educators need to understand better the nature of teachers' professional communities.

TEACHERS' PROFESSIONAL COMMUNITY

A *community* is a group of people who have organized themselves for a substantive reason; that is, they have a shared purpose. They adopt or are assigned formal and informal roles, they organize additional structures (such as times for meeting and planning) as needed, and they take actions—all in order to achieve their purposes. Finally, they are accountable to one another in achieving their goals (i.e., they take steps to keep each other working toward their common purpose).

A *professional* community is distinguished from other forms of community in that it is organized professionally. The members of a profession (such as law or medicine) share a common base of technical knowledge. That specialized knowledge forms the profession's boundaries within the larger society, it empowers the membership with the autonomy to make decisions that fall under their purview, and it shields the profession from intrusions by others who are not themselves members of the profession. The practice of a profession's new members (for instance, junior members of a law firm) is open for review by its more senior members in what is known as the deprivatization of practice. More-senior professionals mentor newer members on the applications of the profession's technical knowledge by critiquing the new members' work and by allowing junior members to observe the mentor's own personal practices. Hence, in a profession, practice is deprivatized for instructional purposes. In addition, senior members socialize the new members into the profession's shared beliefs and norms of behavior.

What distinguishes *teachers'* professional community from other forms of professional community is that the technical knowledge, shared beliefs, and norms of behavior for the former are focused on the craft of teaching and on student learning. Our conception of mathematics teachers' professional community draws on the work of Bryk and Driscoll (1988), Little (1986, 1990), Louis, Kruse, and Associates (1994), Louis, Kruse, and Marks (1996), and Talbert and Perry (1994). It has been operationalized along four dimensions (Adajian, 1995):

1. Shared sense of purpose (i.e., the nature and extent of the school staff's shared values and goals). An elementary school's staff may share what seems like a purpose that is broadly construed (e.g., that all children learn or that they be prepared to do well in later life). Research on school restructuring (Newmann and Associates, 1996; Newmann & Wehlage, 1995) suggests that, in order to support efforts to upgrade its mathematics program, a school's shared sense of purpose must have a substantive relationship to mathematics (e.g., that mathematics is somehow central in what children are to learn or that it plays an important role in their later-life opportunities).

2. Coordinated effort to improve students' (mathematics) learning (i.e., teachers' working together and setting aside personal prerogatives in favor of shared goals).

3. Collaborative professional learning (i.e., how well and closely the teachers work together to learn about and to improve their practices as related to mathematics). The greater the depth of this collaboration (e.g., if teachers observe one another's practice), the stronger the community.

4. Collective control over important decisions affecting the school's (mathematics) program (i.e., whether teachers have the power, as a group, to focus the direction of their program).

WHY PROFESSIONAL COMMUNITY?

Since the heyday of the effective schools research, educators have known that schools exert effects on students' mathematics achievement and learning as measured by correct answers on conventional achievement tests (Good & Brophy, 1986; Goodlad, 1983; Lee & Smith, 1993; Mullis, Jenkins, & Johnson, 1994; Teddlie & Stringfield, 1993) and as measured by criteria for what has come to be called "authentic intellectual work" (Marks, Newmann, & Gamoran, 1996; Newmann, Marks, & Gamoran, 1996). What is more, restructured[3] high schools begin to close the well-documented mathematics achievement gap that is based on student social class (Lee & Smith, 1994, 1995, 1996; Lee, Smith, & Croninger, 1995).

A recurring theme of studies that have tried to better understand how schools affect student achievement has been that the strength, nature, and focus of the teachers' professional community play important roles

---

[3] *Effective* and *restructured* are somewhat misleading terms because they convey the idea that schools have achieved a particular state and/or have acquired a more or less permanent characteristic; that is, a school has become "effective" or "restructured." Current work (for example, Newmann et al., 1996) argues that restructuring is ongoing and a long-term process. Likewise, school effectiveness is not an acquired trait, but rather the result of ongoing efforts.

in mediating a school's effects on student learning and achievement (Bryk & Driscoll, 1988). For example, in an extension of their original studies (Lee & Smith, 1994, 1995), Lee and Smith (1996; Lee, Smith, & Croninger, 1995) found that teachers' sharing a collective responsibility[4] for student learning mediated the positive effects of high school restructuring on (a) student learning from eighth to tenth and on to twelfth grades in mathematics and in science and (b) the equitable distribution of that learning.[5] In its study of 24 restructured schools, the Center on Organization and Restructuring of Schools (CORS; Newmann et al., 1996; Newmann & Wehlage, 1995) found that students were most likely to perform according to the CORS standards for achievement in mathematics and social studies (Newmann, Secada, & Wehlage, 1995) in schools where teachers and other school staff maintained a sustained focus on the intellectual quality of student learning and where there was schoolwide collaboration and caring to achieve shared goals for students—in other words, where teachers formed a professional community oriented toward student learning.

The nature of teachers' professional community within high school departments also affects how faculty members in those departments respond to reform initiatives based on evolving notions of content and pedagogy. For instance, in Talbert and Perry's (1994) sample of high-school mathematics departments, the "strong technical cultures . . . [tended to] enforce attitudes counter to reform standards" (p. 7). A department's "technical culture" incorporates its shared norms and beliefs about the nature of the discipline and governs the way that the discipline relates to the actual practices of its teachers. A mathematics department's norms and beliefs give meaning to such practices as tracking, student placement in tracks, curriculum, testing, and individual teachers' instructional and assessment practices. A department's shared beliefs and practices, and the way those beliefs and practices support each other, would be considered that department's technical culture.

In the mathematics departments studied by Talbert and Perry (1994), the technical cultures were organized around teaching as the routine

---

[4] Collective responsibility, as used by Lee and Smith (1994, 1995, 1996) and Lee, Smith, and Croninger (1995), is very similar to what we mean by shared sense of purpose.

[5] Teachers' professional community (as measured through their collective responsibility for student learning) was not the only important organizational feature of restructured high schools vis-à-vis student achievement. Lee, Smith, and Croninger (1995) also found that schools' size and their academic press were important variables in explaining how high-school restructuring could enhance student achievement and start to close the social class achievement gap in mathematics and science. The highest levels of achievement were found in high schools enrolling between 500 and 1500 students. Lee et al.'s indicators of academic press included whether students tended to enroll in a narrow band of academic courses (as opposed to remedial or consumer math, for instance) and whether instruction across courses supported active learning.

telling of information, students as more or less passive recipients of knowledge, and mathematics as sequential and hierarchically organized. In contrast to the mathematics departments, Talbert and Perry found that high school science departments were not as strongly held together by their teachers' shared beliefs as were mathematics departments. Instead, science teachers tended to organize themselves around their specialty areas such as biology, physics, or chemistry. Science teachers' technical cultures tended to support teaching for understanding as outlined by the science reform documents; that is, their technical cultures tended to be organized around teaching as nonroutine (especially in the lab-based courses) and students as active learners.

· Adajian (1995) studied a national sample of high-school mathematics departments that had been nominated as places engaged in significant efforts to enhance their programs. Due to the way they were selected, it is likely that the shared beliefs of Adajian's sample were more consistent with the tenets of mathematics reform than were Talbert and Perry's sample of convenience, which would be more likely to share beliefs representative of conventional practice. Indeed, Adajian found a strong positive relationship between high school mathematics teachers' professional community (as measured by indicators along the four dimensions previously reported) and self-reported reformed-teaching practices. Taken together, Adajian's (1995) and Talbert and Perry's (1994) results suggest the important role played by a mathematics department's culture in shaping how its teachers will respond (or fail to respond) to mathematics reform.

Adajian (1995) and Talbert and Perry (1994) also found that insofar as mathematics teachers had access to new knowledge about teaching, their practices were more likely to be consistent with the mathematics education reform. Because Talbert and Perry found departmental differences in teachers' access to new knowledge about mathematics reform, they further suggested that teachers' opportunity to learn is influenced by their departments.

Rowan and his colleagues (Rowan, 1990a, 1990b; Rowan, Raudenbush, & Cheong, 1993) developed a theory that posits that nonrigid and nonbureaucratic forms of school management need to be created as teachers' work becomes more uncertain. In such schools, whose management Rowan called "organic," roles are less rigidly prescribed so that, for instance, a teacher or a group of teachers might assume a leadership role and do things that, in a more bureaucratic setting, would be seen as the proper role of the department chair or even the principal. Organic forms of management are thought to develop out of the teachers' professional communities; subsequently, both the professional community and the managerial structures that are engendered by the community support teachers by enhancing their professional opportunities to learn about teaching. Adajian (1995) applied Rowan's theory to the case of high school mathematics teachers' trying to reform their programs; she argued that those teachers' efforts would increase the uncertainty of their own personal practices.[6] Hence, according to Adajian, if mathematics teachers who are trying to reform their practices are to succeed, they need to work in departments that have strong professional communities whose focus is to support the teachers' efforts to change. Consistent with Rowan's and Adajian's analyses, Ball and Rundquist (1993) documented how Sylvia Rundquist, an elementary school teacher, experienced increased uncertainty as she tried to shift her practice to be more consistent with the vision of the reform and how, as a result, she and Deborah Ball created a supportive collaboration around professional and personal issues.

Also consistent with Adajian's elaboration of Rowan et al.'s theory, many interventions that were intended to develop new forms of teacher knowledge and practice in the teaching of mathematics and science have had to address the creation of professional communities among their teachers. One intervention that has tried to foster teacher change by creating a network of mathematics teachers is the Urban Math Collaboratives (Webb & Romberg, 1994). These networks were supposed to support teachers' professional growth and help them update their practices.

Through informal conversations with developers of many reform-oriented interventions and our reading of their publications, we have found that they had not originally intended to address issues of teachers' professional community. They were forced to deal with these and similar contextual issues—sometimes grudgingly—when they realized that, if they did not, the interventions would fail. For example, Cognitively Guided Instruction (Carpenter & Fennema, 1992; Fennema et al., 1996), QUASAR (Stein, Silver, & Smith, in press), SummerMath (Schifter & Fosnot, 1993), and *Cheche Konnen* (Warren & Rosebery, 1995) were all efforts to help teachers learn how to teach mathematics and science by having them experience and relearn these subjects via reform approaches and/or by focusing on how students reason about mathematics and science. Informal reports by the developers of these projects and by many CGI teachers suggest that the interventions resulted in teachers developing closely knit professional communities.

In summary, mathematics teachers' professional communities can influence school effects on achievement and the learning of mathematics

---

[6] Conventional mathematics instruction is often characterized as routine and procedural. In reformed mathematics teaching, on the other hand, teachers are constantly adjusting what they do based on what just happened in the class (e.g., Lampert, 1986, 1990; National Council of Teachers of Mathematics, 1991). Because the shift from conventional to reformed practice entails a shift from routinized to nonroutinized work, mathematics teachers who try to move from conventional to reformed practice experience increased uncertainty.

according to both conventional and evolving notions of student achievement. When a high school's teachers create a professional community focused on student learning, the school can enhance overall student learning and achievement in mathematics and science; also, it can begin to close the within-school achievement gap based on student social class. Finally, there is mounting evidence of a complex relationship between teachers' professional communities and their classroom practices, especially when changing those practices results in teachers experiencing increased uncertainty about the craft of teaching.

THE CASE OF KROME ELEMENTARY SCHOOL

In the previous section of this chapter, we presented evidence that the nature of a school's and/or mathematics department's professional community influences teachers' ability to teach according to the tenets of the mathematics reform and to change their practice. In this section, we present the case of Krome Elementary School to illustrate how one school's professional community was able to provide that support. We first describe the school and our data-gathering efforts in that school. Next, we provide evidence that its teachers were teaching mathematics in ways that departed from the typical stereotypes of conventional practice, and that its teachers had been changing their practices over the previous years to achieve the practices that we saw and that they spoke about in their interviews with NCRMSE visitors. Finally, based on teachers' reports, we consider how their professional community supported their efforts.

The School

Located in a suburban district, Krome Elementary School enrolled nearly 600 students in kindergarten through fifth grade. Over 70% of its student body was African American; over 50% qualified for free or reduced lunch. Enrolling the greatest concentration of poor children in the district and located in a neighborhood of high transience, Krome regularly outperformed all of the district's other schools on state assessments. Local newspaper articles featuring the school's many accomplishments were on prominent display in the teacher's lounge. Krome had won national recognition as a Blue Ribbon School of Excellence and was recognized as a model elementary school by the state. It participated with a small number of other schools from across the state in developing a performance-based science assessment system. In addition to having been officially deregulated by the state, Krome received an additional $90,000 over three years to support its innovative programs and for professional development. Due to its deregulation and participation in the state's performance-assessment project, Krome did not have to participate in either the state's or the district's regular testing programs, yet its teachers administered standardized achievement tests in reading and mathematics to all students "just to be sure" that students were learning. Krome's deregulated status allowed it freedom to design and experiment with programs that did not comply with state regulations governing, in the principal's words, "How many minutes are we spending in math? How many minutes are we spending on language arts?" Nor did the school have to document and report individual students' mastery of objectives, performance on unit tests, and its remediation efforts for every student scoring below the 50th percentile.

Because of the district's open enrollment policies, the school enrolled 70 students (about 12% of its overall enrollment) who lived outside its catchment area and did not receive district transportation. As a primary grade teacher noted: "Our school is 75% minority. But we have minority parents from other schools who bring their children here because they like what they see and like what they get." Some nonneighborhood students included the assistant principal's and some of the teachers' own children; in interviews with site visitors, these parents insisted that their choice had more to do with the quality of the school's programs than with any other consideration (such as the convenience of having their children attending school where they worked).

Despite five teachers having won district teacher-of-the-year awards in consecutive years, Krome experienced a high rate of staff turnover. Its previous principal had left to open a new school two years prior to the NCRMSE visit. When some teachers realized that the outgoing principal was recruiting some of the best staff to go with him, they banded together, decided to stay as a group, and encouraged the then-assistant principal to apply for the principal's position, which she got. The year of the NCRMSE visit, Krome had hired six new teachers (in a staff of 27; i.e., 22% new staff in a single year). At least one teacher had left because, in the words of a primary teacher, she had burned out. Others had left to pursue career opportunities elsewhere, move to a new city, or retire.

NCRMSE Data Gathering

Over the course of a two-day site visit to Krome Elementary School, NCRMSE staff observed six teachers—two from each of grades 3 (Ms. 3A and Ms. 3B), 4 (Ms. 4A and Ms. 4B), and 5 (Ms. 5A and Mr. 5B). Each teacher was observed teaching mathematics twice and was interviewed about the nature of his or her practice and professional community, among other topics. Questions about a teacher's practice were drawn from the observed lessons with the intention of discussing the specifics of that individual's mathematics teaching. We provided each teacher with a list of topics—such as planning time, pupil–teacher ratio, school leadership, opportunities for professional development, colleagues, and testing—and asked that individual to comment on how these features helped or hindered his or her teaching. Finally, we asked each teacher to discuss how his or her mathematics teaching had changed over the past five years, and whether and in what ways the school had supported or impeded that individual's efforts to change.

A group of five primary teachers was also interviewed. Like their six colleagues in the upper grades, these teachers were asked to discuss the professional community at Krome. Specific interview questions that were asked of all 11 teachers revolved around whether teachers had a shared sense of purpose and, if so, how they would describe it, what evidence they would produce to show that they in fact did have what they claimed to have, how they tried to accomplish their shared purpose, how they helped each other and held one another accountable for accomplishing it, and what school characteristics helped or impeded accomplishment of that purpose.

Krome's principal and the district's mathematics consultant also answered questions about the nature of the school's professional community. The principal and mathematics consultant were asked how they supported the teachers in their efforts to improve and to discuss the challenges teachers experienced. The teachers and the principal were asked about the teachers' roles in school governance and how they were able to maintain the school as an organization with a shared purpose. Specifically, teachers were asked whether they had any role in recruiting or hiring new colleagues, how they socialized new colleagues (whether and in what ways they made new teachers feel at home and how they helped them fit into the school), how they dealt with teachers who did not fit in, and whether anyone had ever left because he or she did not agree with the school program's (mathematics in particular) overall thrust.

Reformed Practice

In observations of and in interviews with the six teachers, the NCRMSE research team found two recurrent themes that are consistent with the various *Standards* documents (NCTM, 1989, 1991). First, the teachers were trying to make mathematics more relevant to their children's everyday lives through applications and realistic problem solving. Second, the teachers tried to focus instruction on having children explain and justify their solutions. NCRMSE researchers saw third, fourth, and fifth graders discussing and justifying their answers to one another in pairs, in small groups, and occasionally, to the whole class.

Applications and Realistic Problem Solving.   One fifth-grade class used decimal paper and other manipulatives to support their reasoning about and computations with decimals; the second class explored the various uses of the calculator. Both fourth-grade classes gathered and analyzed data about their birthdays, favorite games, fun things to do, and other topics that would interest them. They represented data via pictographs and discussed why they had chosen a certain picture to represent a specific amount. One fourth grader, for instance, did not want to draw cakes to represent two birthdays in a given month, so he drew squares instead, explaining to his teacher that half a square represented a single birthday.

Third graders created shopping lists using mail order catalogues and sales flyers. Their teacher told children that they had $15, $20, or $50 to spend (depending on the teacher's judgments of how well each child could add and subtract). Each child then figured out how much money remained after paying for her or his purchases. Some children used manipulatives to represent objects; others drew pictures. Some counted when adding and subtracting; others used invented algorithms. Many children exchanged objects when they realized they would not have enough money to buy everything on their lists.

All six teachers noted that their use of sales flyers and catalogues, data gathering on subjects that interested students, explorations with the calculator, and other lessons were efforts to make mathematics and its applications more relevant to their students. For instance, Ms. 5A explained that her long-term goal was to have her students use the calculator to attempt to apply more sophisticated mathematics than if they did everything via pencil and paper: "I've tried to explain to them that when you become an adult, you aren't going to sit down and add and subtract numbers all the time, but you need to know how to apply what we're learning in the book to other situations. I've tried to apply that more and more—help them apply what we're learning more in real life."

Echoing similar concerns, Ms. 4A tried to make mathematics relevant to children's lives: "I have always tried to make things relative [sic] for the kids. Why am I teaching this to you? Why is this important? How would you use this again?" Furthermore, she tried to help her children learn basic skills through problem solving and applications: "Instead of teaching . . . 'Okay, we are going to add $5.84 plus $2.64, what is the total?,' I give them a problem: 'If you bought this and this, and handed the lady $20.00, what would your change be?' Well, they have to do two steps to solve that." In fact, Ms. 4A's children were seeing mathematics in the world around them: "A lot of them will say, 'Oh, I went to the grocery store with my mom, and I really watched the change.'"

Not only did Ms. 4B use referents and settings that she thought would be realistic and interesting to her children, she also had children write their own problems based on in-class activities. For instance, students were told to come to class with at least two observations and problems that could be derived from the class birthday pictograph. Children spent the second day of NCRMSE observations in Ms. 4B's class discussing their observations of the data and solving the problems they had written the night before. In her analysis of this assignment, Ms. 4B noted the limitations in her students' prior experiences with mathematics problems that were supposed to be set in the real world. She

> wanted them to be able to look at a graph and figure out what types of questions can be derived from what they see—for instance, dealing with computations, how many more birthdays were in this month than in the other month. Because, I don't really know if they understand that relation. *What I'm finding out this year is that these kids, basically, what they've seen in front of them are [problems like] 5 + 6, 22 + 7.* And I wanted them to see also within the pictograph that there are other ways in which you can do computations and problem solving.

Ms. 3A alluded to her text's shortcomings in making mathematics real for her children:

> I don't think my children would do a fantastic job in math if I opened the textbook every day and said "Look at page 26." They [the children] aren't going to do it. I don't want to do it. . . . I have to teach for me and my kids, with my kids being the root of what I do. . . . What I should do is be creative enough to pull and relate the math to what the book is trying to teach, because the books don't do a good job sometimes. . . . The skill is there, but the way it is presented is not for my children; so then, I have to teach for my children. . . . Meaning that, the book says we're going to Sally's grocery store. Well, Sally's grocery store is *not* in their neighborhood [emphasis added].

Ms. 5A also referred to how she encourages students to develop their own strategies for making a problem more realistic:

> One of the things I noticed was that, when we got to solving word problems, the children didn't understand how to apply that [computations] to the problems. The book had some problems in it, but a lot of time, they still didn't [apply what they had been learning]. That's a book problem. So sometimes, I think they have to put themselves into problems and that's one of the things that I tell them to do when they are working on problems. Put your name in the problem and see if it makes more sense to you. Relate it to yourself as much as you can.

Student Justification and Autonomy.   In the lessons that were observed by the NCRMSE research team, many children explained their solutions, strategies, and reasoning to one another while working in small groups. Beyond checking on right or wrong answers, teachers often asked individual students to explain how they had figured something out and to justify their reasoning so that others in their group could understand them. In addition, four teachers asked students to explain their reasoning to the class as a whole. For instance, Mr. 5B looked for students who came up with an interesting way of determining decimal (in)equalities using decimal grids; he would then ask those fifth graders to explain their reasoning to the whole class. In their interviews with NCRMSE researchers, all six teachers said that they tried to emphasize students' explanations of how they solved a problem.

Ms. 3B relied on student explanations as a means for students to help one another: "That is purposeful. My thing is for them to rely on each other first and then come to the teacher. . . . We have learned the types of behavior to use when we help each other." Both fourth grade teachers relied on students' explanations to provide insights into their understandings of the content. Student explanations also helped Ms. 4A to better understand mathematics: "It is amazing . . . that the way I think mathematically is so different, but the ways they think has helped me. I am even building within myself because, like I said, I never enjoyed problem solving growing up. And I have grown too."

Ms. 4B interviewed children to assess their understanding, especially if, from their in-class comments, she suspected that they were not understanding the content. During class, she looked for students whose work departed from how something had been explained: "One kid in particular . . . she was designing her own [picto]graph and she wasn't representing 5s [as had been done in class], but she was doing 3s. There was another kid doing 4s. So that gives me a very good indication that those particular children know what's going on."

Teacher Change

During the five years prior to the NCRMSE visit, the teachers at Krome Elementary School reported changing their pedagogical practices along the lines of curricular content, instructional strategies, and, to a somewhat lesser extent, student assessment.

Curriculum Content.   According to the district math supervisor and Ms. 4B—the school's math specialist—the district had modified its curriculum to be in keeping with the NCTM (1989) *Curriculum Standards.* Subsequently, the district had also aligned its guide to the newly written state framework. Hence, the content that teachers were teaching was likely to have changed in recent years.

All six teachers reported using the district curriculum guide as a framework or checklist to help them make sure that children were prepared for the following grade and to be sure that there were no gaps in what was covered. Although they relied on the curriculum guide to ensure content coverage, all six teachers reported creating their own activities, which were more relevant and appropriate for their children than activities found in the guide or in their regular texts. The emphasis on realistic problems and making mathematics relevant to their students was a major change embarked on by the school's teachers during the year of the NCRMSE visit.

In a major departure from the previous year's curriculum, Krome's fifth-grade teachers completely dropped their review of addition and subtraction and started the year by reviewing multiplication and division. The teachers reasoned that their students would show what they knew about adding and subtracting when they multiplied and divided. This change allowed the fifth grade to devote more time to other content; for example, Mr. 5B planned to spend more time on decimals, fractions, percents, and metric measure—topics that were typically very difficult for Krome's fifth graders.

Instructional Practices.   Four of the six teachers claimed to have made some important changes in their personal teaching practices over the past three to five years. At one time, Ms. 3A "did more direct teaching. [But] I've seen myself go away a lot from direct teaching to more interacting with the students. And the students interacting with each other. And learning from each other." In addition to her increased attention to children's reasons, Ms. 3B had deemphasized paper-and-pencil computations because "you don't have to give a child two pages of math in order to see whether they understand a concept." In addition, Ms. 3B had begun to place greater reliance on children's discovering things for themselves and using manipulatives to support their reasoning rather than on telling them directly. Ms. 4A reported that the greatest change in her teaching had been to ask her children:

> Why? Or, did someone else figure this out a different way? Is there another way to figure this out? I used to think that it is one way and that is all. I never realized that kids can arrive at answers, all differently. And I never gave them the opportunity to explain it to me. This year I got, like I did today [having children explain and justify their answers], that happens all the time. I always say, Did anybody else figure this out a different way? So I even feel how I am teaching them money—the lessons we were into last week. I would never have thought to bring a catalogue or to bring something that they would relate to, that's real life to them. . . . For Thanksgiving, they are going to have to plan a menu, and they are going to total the cost of the menu.

Mr. 5B changed in his use of manipulatives (such as fraction bars and decimal paper) to introduce problems and in his encouragement of students to use manipulatives to help solve problems. He also said that, whereas in the past he did more straight lecture, he now tried to pose a question, allow the students to work on the problem in groups, and then to explain their own ideas to one another at the board. When going from group to group, Mr. 5B would remain alert to interesting ways of solving the problem so that he could give that student an opportunity to come to the board.

Of the teachers who claimed not to have changed their teaching practices per se, Ms. 4B stated that she had learned to teach "this way" (for example, focusing on student reasoning) while a student teacher at Krome. Her mathematics teaching had simply been maturing since she was hired (straight out of her teacher preparation program) at this school. To her, the greatest change had been in the problem-solving content and real-world connections that she now emphasized.

Ms. 5A, the other teacher who claimed not to have made any great changes in personal teaching practice during the previous five years, had been teaching for over 20 years. Though she saw a major change between where she had been as a beginning teacher 20 years earlier and her practice at the time that she was interviewed, she believed that her teaching had evolved slowly over those 20 years.

Assessment Practices.　　Two teachers reported that they had begun to rely more heavily on alternative forms of student assessment than in the past. Ms. 3B interviewed students individually because

> I feel that there are other components of a child's learning. You can tell whether they are understanding what you are doing. . . . I have a lot of kids that sometimes will not do well on the test, yet I sit down with them—one on one—and have them explain to me. Say, whatever we are doing, explain to me how they did this problem. Or, do a problem and explain to me what they have done and they understand. It's just that if you give them a test full of problems and they don't do well. Some kids don't test well. I take that into account.

What her children wrote helped Ms. 4B to understand what they knew: "I tell my kids that I want them to write out how they went about getting it [the answer]." Because she expected her children to write in complete sentences, Ms. 4B saw language arts as linked to her mathematics: "If there is a sentence or question before them, I want a complete sentence. This carries over into math and they will constantly ask me, too. They will ask, 'Ms. 4B, does this have to be in complete sentences?' They know the answer, because I won't even answer them. And then, another student will come up and say, 'What do you think?'" In addition, Ms. 4B often interviewed children to assess their understanding, especially if, from their in-class comments or work, she suspected that they did not understand the content.

Professional Community

The teachers at Krome Elementary School formed a tightly knit supportive network whose focus was the children. In varying degrees, their practices departed from the stereotype of conventional teaching. These teachers all reported emphasis on problem solving, applications, use of manipulatives, cooperative learning, and especially linking mathematics to the children's world. Our observations tended to corroborate these self-reports. Some teachers, by word and deed, demonstrated that they knew how to focus on student's understanding during instruction and through their assessment practices. In varying amounts and at varying rates, their practices had been changing over the years, with the most obvious and consistent change being their effort to relate mathematics to children's everyday worlds through applications and problem solving. Some teachers had also begun to have their children explain more to one another in class, and these teachers listened more intently to better understand their students' development.

Krome's changes were all the more stressful to its teachers because for many years running, whenever the school was judged according to conventional criteria (i.e., by student performance on standardized achievement tests), it had received awards and recognition on the local, state, and national levels. The school principal recounted how a teacher, unsure if she wanted to stay at the school, asked when the changes would end. The principal's response was that change would never end. More than one teacher left the school because working there was too difficult, and he or she simply burned out. Ms. 4B, the school's lead mathematics teacher, voiced the concerns and fears of the committed teachers who stayed:

> Last year, everything strictly came from the way it was in the book. I have to say that even this year, there has been quite a bit that has been done strictly from the book. The reason is that (in talking with a lot of teachers here and a lot of teachers within the district) there is so much emphasis on standardized testing and the score themselves, *that there are some teachers, including myself, that are really afraid to get away from teaching the way we normally have taught because fourth grade at Krome was in the 75th percentile, which is the highest in the district.. . .Our mentality has been, if it works, why change?* . . . But I'm realizing that . . . we have to change [italics added].

One of the primary reasons for change, as reported by the teachers, was that in spite of students' high scores on achievement tests, many students were simply not understanding the mathematics that they were being taught, they were forgetting what they had learned, and they could not apply their basic skills to problems. In spite of these reasons, as Ms. 4B so eloquently noted, change was difficult and stressful.

The following sections describe how the teachers' professional community, with its strong culture focused on children, their well-being, and their learning, provided support for these changes. The narrative is organized around the four dimensions of professional community: shared sense of purpose, coordinated effort, collaborative professional learning, and collective control.

Shared Sense of Purpose.   Teachers at Krome Elementary School shared a complexly interwoven sense of purpose. They believed that all their students could learn mathematics (as well as other subjects) and that the teachers, through their teaching, played a major role in ensuring that their students did learn. As a primary teacher noted during their group interview:

> Number one, number one. Children can do. All children can do. . . . And we're going to be there to help them and make sure they do. And we're going to be proud of them. And we have our trust in them and our faith in them. No question. . . . We [the teachers] set the pace. We're the role models. And they [the students] see us working our heads off and they get in there and they do it too.

This concern for the students resulted in the teachers' questioning the value of what the current principal called an excessive attention to remediation a scant five years earlier. With her support (and in some cases, prodding), teachers began experimenting with and searching for other ways of teaching. During the NCRMSE site visit, teachers focused on connecting what children were being taught to their everyday lives, on problem solving and applications, and on using manipulatives to support student reasoning. All six teachers discussed the importance of making mathematics (and indeed, all school subjects) relevant to their students' lives. Ms. 4B saw this connection as resulting in children becoming excited and enthusiastic about mathematics, "going out and saying, What did you learn in math today?"

Connecting mathematics to children's everyday world, as in the case of all these teachers' instructional efforts, resonates with and is part of a larger picture. Ms. 4B noted that,

> overall, what we want for every child at Krome is to really have that quality education. . . . I mean, getting the most out of all subjects, getting the most out of math. When they finish fourth grade, can they take what they've learned in fourth grade and use it? Not just in the future, but can they really take what they are learning now and be able to use it on their own without someone being over their heads and saying "Well, this is how you use this." But, can they take what we've given them and use it for themselves?

This larger purpose—that children be able to use what they learn in their own lives—was further elaborated by Mr. 5B:

> Our purpose is to help prepare students for the challenges that lay ahead of them. Help them improve their quality of life and to give them a better understanding of what is going on, . . . to try to build positive action, just get them ready for the challenges that they are going to be facing. Let them make good decisions. Give them the problem-solving ability to look at a problem and make decisions. . . . [Walking into a classroom] you would see people who are genuinely concerned and genuinely making an effort for their students to be successful.

Echoing Ms. 4B's and Mr. 5B's comments, Ms. 5A argued for a similar larger vision for the school's work: "That's what we are here for, so we want to adjust what we are teaching to what they are going to need later. More and more problem solving—not only in math, but in other areas. . . . We want our children to be problem solvers and be able to relate to real life situations." The belief that all children can and have to be prepared to function in their everyday world and also in the world of their future[7] resulted in teachers' questioning the utility of basic skills mastery if those skills cannot be applied.

Some teachers expressed their beliefs about their roles in their students' lives passionately. There were no hard feelings for teachers who did not share this passion and, as a result, left:

> We still see them and they're good friends; but they were just whooped. This [job] can kill you. . . . We want people who work hard, who are going to be dedicated, committed to these children. That's one reason we really pushed hard for [the hiring of] our practicum student teachers, because they already worked with these kids. And not everyone can work with these children. . . . It is attitude. . . . It *is* attitude. People who have a shared sense of purpose, who are really dedicated to what we do. We feel we're making a difference in this world. And we're—we feel it's important, what we do. We don't feel that we're "just" teachers. I don't want to be an administrator, I want to be a teacher. And that's all I want to do. And I want to be the best teacher I can. . . . I know very few people in this school who are interested in moving up to administration. We don't; we think it's a horrible job [emphasis in original].

This shared belief in the importance of their work to their students' lives helped teachers to overcome the fears alluded to by Ms. 4B and to

---

[7] Elementary school teachers who have participated in both the NCRMSE school-level mathematics reform study and in the CORS school restructuring study have often couched their shared sense of purpose in terms of (a) the "whole child," (b) that child's larger social world and future in that world, and (c) the teachers' beliefs that they have a crucial role to play in preparing each child to face that world on her or his own terms.

support one anothers' experiments with her or his practice. An equally important feature of these teachers' shared purpose was the central role that mathematics played in achieving their larger goals. If mathematics were not substantively important in their students' education, it is very unlikely that these teachers would have been so willing to change their program and their own personal practices.

Coordinated Effort. Repeatedly, the NCRMSE researchers saw evidence of teachers working together; in at least one case, a group of teachers put personal preferences aside for the greater good. Many of the teachers who, two years prior to the NCRMSE visit, had encouraged the then-assistant principal to apply for the principal's position were the ones who had been recruited by the previous principal to leave Krome and to follow him in opening a new school. When the recruits realized that only a few of their colleagues would go to the new school, they put aside the obvious personal gains of working in a new building, decided to stay, and organized themselves and their colleagues.

For at least the five prior years, the current principal had been encouraging teachers to find ways of teaching that did not depend on remediation. The curricular shift to relevant problems and applications began the year before the NCRMSE site visit as a response by a few teachers to the realization that conventional practice was inadequate. By the time of the NCRMSE visit, a clear if unspoken consensus had developed to support these efforts. Although the NCRMSE research team did not observe group decision making or how this consensus had developed, it was clear that teachers felt space to experiment within the parameters of the decisions to make the mathematics curriculum more problem oriented. Teachers had leeway in deciding how mathematics would be made relevant in their own classrooms. For example, the fifth-grade teachers thought that "relevant" included content and ways of learning that children would need to know in order to negotiate middle school; indeed, both fifth-grade teachers said that they knew and had met with sixth-grade teachers. They further said that one reason they stressed children's working independently in mathematics was that their students would not have the kind of support in later years that they had become accustomed to in Krome. On the other hand, the third- and fourth-grade teachers tried to ensure that their students' mathematics learning was relevant by placing greater emphasis on topics and problems that would interest their students right then and there.

Grade-level teams coordinated their planning and coverage of material. For example, the fourth-grade teachers met and planned their lessons together. A single teacher would plan a week's lessons in a given subject for the entire fourth grade. The teachers would then discuss the lessons and adapt them for their own classrooms. This ensured that all the fourth-graders were encountering the same content across the subjects; for example, all the fourth-graders were studying the graphical representation of data during the week of the NCRMSE site visit. The fifth-grade teachers had decided, as a group, to begin the year with multiplication and division. They made their decision based on the fact that their students would demonstrate knowledge of addition and subtraction while performing the division and multiplication algorithms and that the change would provide them with time to pursue other, more important, topics.

In a display of how much program coordination was found among the first-grade teachers, they recounted how they had spent the previous summer working together on a grant proposal. The primary grade teachers further joked that they spent more time working together on improving their program than they did with their own families. These teachers provided a compelling example of how coordinated effort takes time and involves people taking one another's concerns seriously. The primary teachers discussed how one of their number had gone to a *Math Their Way* workshop some years prior to the NCRMSE site visit. This teacher returned very enthusiastic about the program, but instead of trying to convince her colleagues of the program's value by conducting a formal workshop, she put the other first-grade teachers to work on creating the manipulatives so that she could use them in her classroom. This, of course, piqued the other first-grade teachers' interest, who went to a later workshop, began trying out the ideas that they had learned, and shared the results among themselves. When a first-grade teacher moved up to second grade, she continued to use the program and began sharing its ideas with her second-grade team.

At first, the other second-grade teachers were concerned about the fact that many *Math Their Way* activities did not culminate in formal paper-and-pencil activities. During their group-teacher interview, one second-grade teacher complained that *Math Their Way* did not take children to the "symbolic level." Instead, children spent their time manipulating objects, or at most working at what she called the "semi-concrete" level:

> And that's [where] we can see that the problem breaks down. We've worked with the concrete ... and now we can see how their [the children's] thinking moves. And that's how we often do every lesson [in] three stages [manipulating objects, semiconcrete, and symbolic]. And the last one is pencil and paper to be sure that the concept can be moved into another round.

The second-grade team then worked together to supplement the program's lessons and materials in order to address this concern. Subsequently, *Math Their Way* was adopted as the school's program from kindergarten through second grade. This thoughtful and coordinated response to resolving a significant problem in their program supported the individual teachers by providing them with the reassurance that the revised program would accomplish its goals. Moreover, while working together, the teachers also learned from one another.

Although they worked together and made common decisions about their program, all the teachers indicated that they could adapt and develop lessons to suit their own styles. A first-grade teacher described the balance between a coordinated program and teachers' individual freedom to teach according to their own styles:

> [We] breathe at the same time. The first grade program is totally the same [across classrooms]. Everyone can do the same thing in reading and math. . . . We work together, we plan together. . . . [On the other hand] you need to cover these kinds of things. Here are some ways that you can do it. But you choose which way is right for you. I don't like centers in my class. I've got mine seated. So I do it; I do whole-group instruction. Another class has it on the board—on a special board—and it's all centered. And they can go to centers at any time. So, we're all covering the same information, but not in the same way.

Similar comments about relying on the school's curriculum and coordinating the program across classrooms, but also having freedom in how the curriculum was taught, were made by every other teacher.

The teachers' coordinated efforts allowed them to pursue their shared goals by working together; no one teacher felt as if he or she were alone, out on a limb. Interestingly, no teacher mentioned the trade-offs that would seem to be part and parcel of working together—that an individual teacher might have to give something up in her or his teaching or put off pursuing a particular idea because of a common decision. How teachers negotiate such trade-offs needs to be pursued in future work.

Collaborative Professional Learning. Although coordinated effort refers to the coordination of teachers' efforts across classrooms, teams, grades, and even the whole school to achieve their common goals, collaborative professional learning refers to teachers' learning about their practice and program by working together and by sharing results and ideas.

The deprivatization of teaching practice is a strong indicator of how professionals learn from one another. The first-grade teachers spoke about often having breakfast together to plan and to share ideas; in addition, they often went to one another's classrooms to observe lessons and to discuss their common program. Four of the six individually interviewed teachers and all of the primary grade teachers spoke about feeling welcome to go into another teacher's classroom (even in another grade) to see how some idea was being presented or to work out a problem. For example, Ms. 4B planned to visit a third grade-teacher's class to observe how the third-grade teachers used the *Comprehensive*

School Math Program. Mr. 5B discussed trading classes with another teacher who seemed to be having some difficulty with a particular lesson: "There was a lesson that Ms. XXX was doing. She said, 'I sat and worked this at home and I just don't feel comfortable presenting. Would you feel comfortable doing this?' Yeah. 'Well, why don't you go do this in my class and I'll do it in yours?'"

Underlying teacher's collective learning was the norm of sharing. As Mr. 5B noted:

> If I don't have it, and somebody else does, they aren't going to say, "No, this is mine." They are going to say, "Oh sure. . . . If you can help me out, come on." I think that is unique in this school. I haven't experienced with the people that I'm working with any petty jealousies. I think that limits. What I've seen is encouragement. I've seen constructive criticism all done in good taste. Not to say that everything is perfect. When something goes wrong, there is a manner in which folks here work and discuss it.

Every single teacher and the principal agreed that anyone who participated in a professional development opportunity of any sort (workshop, conference, and/or course) was expected to share what happened, at either the next grade-level or whole-school meeting. For example, one of the school's teachers belonged to a national science reform project. She herself noted that she was always bringing back ideas to share. Similarly, the school's math specialist participated in district meetings, visited other schools and classrooms, and took part in workshops offered by the district consultant; she, too, was expected to bring back ideas to share.

The expectation to share was not limited to teachers in leadership positions. As Ms. 3A noted,

> I don't think you are required. But I figure it's part of your professionalism that you want to come back and share. You don't want to keep it all to yourself. You cannot improve your students or the faculty if I gain something and not share it with somebody else. We are all in this educational room together. That is what education is about, right? In learning and sharing. If I cannot learn something and share it with my peer groups or teachers, how can I actually effectively work in the classroom? I'm just stuck with what I know, and I'm not getting anything from anybody else. Something is going to go wrong. I'm going to miss some new trend.

The principal also privately reminded new teachers that they would be asked about what happened at a particular event. And if a teacher wished to make a formal presentation to the rest of the faculty—or if that person just needed time to think about what to present—the principal generally found some way to provide release time for that teacher. One teacher who asked for half a day of release time in order to prepare a presentation to other teachers recalled being asked by the principal if half a day would be enough time.

The principal encouraged teachers to go to conferences, participate in workshops, and take courses in teams. This allowed teachers to have colleagues with whom they could bounce ideas around during, before, and after the sessions. Groups of teachers participated in workshops and courses offered by the district math consultant. The stress on problem solving and on making mathematics (as well as all the subjects) relevant to children seems to have grown out of one such course taken by some of the school's teachers.

Collaborative professional learning is not without risk, however. When groups of teachers participate in a workshop or conference (or even when an individual presents to other teachers), teachers can also judge one another on how well they fit in and whether they take the school's norms of professionalism seriously. For instance, a group of teachers complained to the principal that one of their number had behaved in an "unprofessional" manner during a math conference that they had all participated in. As a result of this individual's behavior, the teachers decided that she was really not committed to the program and essentially froze her out. Some time later, when she went to discuss matters with the administration, the principal already knew the basis of her complaint and helped this teacher to find a position in another school.

In addition, more-senior teachers were expected to mentor new teachers. This expectation seems to have been an unspoken assumption, although the principal had been known to ask a teacher to help someone who was new to the school. Commenting about this responsibility, Ms. 5A noted that because many "new" teachers had already been teaching elsewhere, the mentor teacher also gained something from the exchange—new ideas for her or his classroom.

Collective control. NCRMSE researchers found strong evidence of teachers exerting collective control over the direction of the mathematics program. The decision by the primary teachers to adopt *Math Their Way*, the unspoken agreement of focusing on problem solving and making mathematics relevant to children, the fifth-grade teachers' decision to drop addition and subtraction from their start-of-the year review, the fourth-grade teachers' delegation of responsibility for weekly lesson planning among themselves—all these point to the teachers' ability to control the direction of their program. From every single interviewee, NCRMSE researchers heard about the support provided to their decisions by the school's administrators and the fact that the teachers felt that their voices mattered. Ms. 5A captured the tenor of her colleagues' feelings: "I'm not sure if I could override what everybody in the faculty said. But I mean she [the principal] would be willing to listen, and she would make me feel like she appreciated my opinion."

More generally, the principal conferred with the grade-level leaders on matters involving school policy. When there was a need to hire new teachers (the school hired six new teachers the summer before the NCRMSE site visit), the principal invited teachers, especially those from the affected grade, to interview the final candidates. During the interviews, teachers discussed their practices and the school's normative beliefs with each candidate. In addition, they tried to figure out how this new individual would fit into their team. By having a say in who came into the school, the teachers exerted control over the program's direction.

In the characteristics of the kind of teacher that Krome's teachers were looking for, the NCRMSE researchers could hear echoes of the school's shared sense of purpose. The primary grade teachers had strongly felt beliefs that the new hires should work hard and be committed to the school's children. These are the same qualities Mr. 5B said he looked for, as did Ms. 4B whose questions were

> primarily geared toward not so much what they knew about teaching, but geared toward: Is this someone who will be able to get along with our group? Did I have respect for this person?. . . I'm real big on kids. I ask questions concerning kids. I ask questions concerning parent involvement. Is this someone that is just going to look at whether this kid can do math or not, or is this someone who is going to be genuinely concerned about the child?

Discussion

The teachers at Krome Elementary School changed their practices in the context of a strong professional community. That professional community supported their efforts by providing them with a rationale for change through the school's shared sense of purpose, which was focused substantively on the role of mathematics as part of their children's overall well-being. The teachers worked together to achieve their goals; their efforts to enhance the quality of their mathematics program were coordinated across classrooms, teams, and grades. By their sharing and learning together, teachers had access to new ideas that entered their community, and they learned from one another. An important facet of these teachers' learning was that it took place as they worked together to solve the problems posed by their efforts to reform their practices. By risking new ideas together, the teachers were able to compare their results across their classrooms and to test new ideas against the standards of their practice. Moreover, by mentoring new teachers, they socialized them to the norms of the school. Finally, through their ability to exert control over their program—by participating in decisions about its shape, by helping teachers who had burned out to move on to other positions, and by having a say in who was hired and, hence, who would work on the program—teachers managed some of the uncertainty that came with change.

The school's professional community was also related to the school's nonbureaucratic management. The teachers and the principal worked together. The principal supported her staff but also exerted strong leadership. Teachers themselves exerted leadership among their peers, and they felt that they were heard in all important administrative decisions.

Krome Elementary School also may provide a cautionary tale to mathematics educators. It may be the case that elementary school teachers do not—some would say, cannot—focus on mathematics as their only purpose. These teachers, like many other elementary teachers who participated in the NCRMSE school level and CORS school restructuring studies, focused on the whole child as the center of their activity. Mathematics was substantially related to that concern; but it was in relationship to these teachers' concerns for the whole child that they sought to reform their mathematics program. On one hand, this focus on the child served as a practical tonic to the euphoria of reform; the teachers at Krome were willing to try something (e.g., making problems relevant to their students) if they saw that it would help their students. On the other hand, the teachers were unwilling to give up traditional practices (e.g., paper-and-pencil algorithmic work) until they were assured that to do so would not harm their students.

SUMMARY

This chapter serves more to generate than to confirm hypotheses about how professional community might support teacher change. In the first section, we defined what we meant by professional community and why we believe it is a necessary part of the school environment. We reviewed a set of correlational studies linking professional community to school effects and to changes in mathematics teachers' pedagogical practices. In the rest of this chapter, we relied on our observations of the practices of teachers at Krome Elementary School and on their self-reports on the nature of their community and of their practices to illustrate how a professional community might support teachers' efforts to improve their school's mathematics program.

Both lines of inquiry require more careful study and replication. The relationship between professional community and teachers' practices is likely to be complex. As we noted at the very start of this chapter, although teachers' professional community helps to support their practices, it is likely that efforts to teach according to evolving standards for teaching and to change practice help to create the shared norms that further define the teachers' professional community. We have argued that teachers' professional communities provide an important context in which to understand the nature of teachers' practices and of their change. Recognizing the limitations of our research methodology, we nonetheless believe that the evidence in favor of this position is compelling.

ACKNOWLEDGMENTS

The preparation of this chapter and the work reported in it were supported, in part, by the National Center for Research in Mathematical Sciences Education (NCRMSE), which was funded by the Office of Educational Research and Improvement (OERI), U.S. Department of Education (Grant No. R117G10002) and is administered through the Wisconsin Center for Education Research (WCER), School of Education, University of Wisconsin–Madison. We would like to acknowledge that much of our thinking on teachers' professional community has been shaped by our work with colleagues in the Center of Organization and Restructuring of Schools (CORS), specifically Fred Newmann, Karen Seashore Louis, and Anthony Bryk. CORS was itself funded by OERI and administered through WCER. Our thanks to Fred Newmann, Penelope Peterson, and Barbara Scott Nelson for their comments on an earlier version of this chapter. The findings and opinions expressed in this chapter belong to the authors and do not necessarily reflect the views of our colleagues, NCRMSE, OERI, or WCER.

REFERENCES

Adajian, L. B. (1995). *Teachers' professional community and the teaching of mathematics.* Unpublished doctoral dissertation, University of Wisconsin–Madison.

Ball, D. L., & Rundquist, S. S. (1993). Collaboration as a context for joining teacher learning with learning about teaching. In D. K. Cohen, M. W. McLaughlin, & J. E. Talbert (Eds.), *Teaching for understanding: Challenges for policy and practice* (pp. 13–42). San Francisco: Jossey-Bass.

Bryk, A. S., & Driscoll, M. E. (1988). *The school as community: Theoretical foundations, contextual influences, and consequences for students and teachers.* Madison, WI: National Center on Effective Secondary Schools, Wisconsin Center for Education Research, University of Wisconsin.

Byrd, L., Foster, S., Peressini, D., & Secada W. G. (1994, April). *Teachers' collective action for the enhancement of school mathematics.* Paper presented at the annual meeting of the American Educational Research Association, New Orleans, LA.

Carpenter, T. P., & Fennema, E. (1992). Cognitively guided instruction: Building on the knowledge of students and teachers. *International Journal of Educational Research, 17,* 457–470.

Fennema, E., Carpenter, T. P., Franke, M. L., Levi, L., Jacobs, V. R., & Empson, S. B. (1996). A longitudinal study of learning to use children's thinking in mathematics instruction. *Journal for Research in Mathematics Education, 27*(4), 403–434.

Good, T. L., & Brophy, J. E. (1986). School effects. In M. C. Wittrock (Ed.), *Handbook of research on teaching* (3rd ed., pp. 570–602). New York: Macmillan.

Goodlad, J. (1983). *A place called school.* New York: McGraw-Hill.

Lampert, M. (1986). Knowing, doing, and teaching multiplication. *Cognition and Instruction, 3,* 305–342.

Lampert, M. (1990). When the problem is not the question and the solution is not the answer: Mathematical knowing and teaching. *American Educational Research Journal, 27* (1), 29–64.

Lee, V. E., & Smith, J. B. (1993). Effects of school restructuring on the achievement and engagement of middle-grade students. *Sociology of Education, 66* (3), 164–187.

Lee, V. E., & Smith, J. B. (1994, April). *Effects of high school restructuring and size on gains in achievement and engagement for early secondary students.* Paper presented at the annual meeting of the American Educational Research Association, New Orleans, LA.

Lee, V. E., & Smith J. B. (1995). Effects of high school restructuring and size on gains in achievement and engagement for early secondary students. *Sociology of Education, 68* (4), 241–270.

Lee, V. E., & Smith, J. B. (1996). Collective responsibility for learning and its effects on gains in achievement for early secondary school students. *American Journal of Education, 104* (2), 103–147.

Lee, V. E., Smith, J. B., & Croninger, R. G. (1995). *Understanding high school restructuring effects on the equitable distribution of learning in mathematics and science.* Madison, WI: Center on Organization and Restructuring of Schools, Wisconsin Center for Education Research, University of Wisconsin.

Little, J. W. (1986). Seductive images and organizational realities in professional development. In A. Lieberman (Ed.), *Rethinking school improvement: Research, craft, and concept.* New York: Teachers College Press.

Little, J. W. (1990). The persistence of privacy: Autonomy and initiative in teachers' professional relations. *Teachers College Record, 91* (4), 509–536.

Louis, K. S., Kruse, S. D., & Associates (1994). *Professionalism and community: Perspectives on reforming urban schools.* Newbury Park, MA: Corwin Press.

Louis, K. S., Kruse, S. D., & Marks, H. (1996). School-wide professional community: Teachers' work, intellectual quality, and commitment. In F. M. Newmann and associates (Eds.), *Authentic achievement: Restructuring schools for intellectual quality* (pp. 179–203). San Francisco: Jossey-Bass.

Marks, H. M., Newmann, F. M., & Gamoran, A. (1996). Does authentic pedagogy increase student achievement? In F. M. Newmann and associates (Eds.), *Authentic achievement: Restructuring schools for intellectual quality* (pp. 49–76). San Francisco: Jossey-Bass.

Mullis, I. V. S., Jenkins, F., & Johnson, E. G. (1994). *Effective schools in mathematics: Perspectives for the NAEP 1992 assessment* (Rep. No. 23-RR-01). Washington, DC: National Center for Education Statistics, Office of Educational Research and Improvement, U.S. Department of Education.

National Council of Teachers of Mathematics (1989). *Curriculum and evaluation standards for school mathematics.* Reston, VA: Author.

National Council of Teachers of Mathematics (1991). *Professional standards for teaching mathematics.* Reston, VA: Author.

Newmann, F. M., & Associates (1996). *Authentic achievement: Restructuring schools for intellectual quality.* San Francisco: Jossey-Bass.

Newmann, F. M., Marks, H. M., & Gamoran, A. (1995, April). *Authentic pedagogy and student learning.* Paper presented at the annual meeting of the American Educational Research Association, San Francisco, CA. (Available from the authors at The Center on Organization and Restructuring of Schools, Wisconsin Center for Education Research, 1025 W. Johnson, Madison, WI 53706.)

Newmann, F. M., Secada, W. G., & Wehlage, G. G. (1995). *A guide to authentic instruction and assessment: Vision, standards, and scoring.* Madison, WI: Center on Organization and Restructuring of Schools, Wisconsin Center for Education Research, University of Wisconsin—Madison.

Newmann, F. M., & Wehlage, G. G. (1995). *Successful school restructuring.* A report to the public and educators by the Center on Organization and Restructuring of Schools. Madison: Wisconsin Center for Education Research, University of Wisconsin–Madison.

Peressini D. (1995). *Parents and the reform of high school mathematics.* Unpublished doctoral dissertation, University of Wisconsin–Madison.

Rowan, B. (1990a). Commitment and control: Alternative strategies for the organizational design of schools. In C. Cazden (Ed.), *Review of research in education* (Vol. 16, pp. 353–389). Washington, DC: American Educational Research Association.

Rowan, B. (1990b). Applying conceptions of teaching to organizational reform. In R. F. Elmore (Ed.), *Restructuring schools: The next generation of reform* (pp. 31–58). San Francisco: Jossey-Bass.

Rowan, B., Raudenbush, S. W., & Cheong, Y. F. (1993). Teaching as a nonroutine task: Implications for the management of schools. *Educational Administration Quarterly, 29* (4), 479–500.

Schifter, D., & Fosnot, C. T. (1993). *Reconstructing mathematics education.* New York: Teachers College Press.

Secada, W. G., & Byrd, L. (1993, April). *A conceptual framework for studying school level reform of mathematics.* Paper presented at the annual meeting of the American Educational Research Association, Atlanta, GA.

Stein, M. K., Silver, E. A., & Smith, M. S. (in press). Mathematics reform and teacher development: A community of practice perspective. In J. Greeno & S. Goldman (Eds.), *Thinking practices: A symposium on mathematics and science learning.* Hillsdale, NJ: Lawrence Erlbaum Associates.

Talbert, J. E., & Perry, R. (1994, April). *How department communities mediate mathematics and science education reforms.* Paper presented at the annual meeting of the American Educational Research Association, New Orleans, LA. (Available from the authors at the Center for Research on the Context of Secondary Teaching, School of Education, Stanford University.)

Teddlie, C., & Stringfield, S. (1993). *Schools make a difference.* New York: Teachers College Press.

Warren, B., & Rosebery, A. S. (1995). Equity in the future tense: Redefining relationships among teachers, students, and science in linguistic minority classrooms. In W. G. Secada, E. Fennema, & L. B. Adajian (Eds.), *New directions for equity in mathematics education* (pp. 298–328). New York: Cambridge University Press.

Webb, N. L., & Romberg, T. A. (Eds.) (1994). *Reforming mathematics education in America's cities: The urban mathematics collaborative project.* New York: Teachers College Press.

EDUCATIONAL REFORM PRINCIPLES

Several intertwined strands of research—together, sometimes seen as distinct—form the framework for what we call the reform approach to mathematics learning. The first of these strands has to do with individual cognitive processes and it's concerned focus on how learners actively incorporate information into an existing set of understandings. This strand of thought, often referred to as constructivism, is in the tradition of Piaget (1970, 1980). Emphasis here is put on the scaffolding of knowledge (Wood, Bruner, & Ross, 1976) and the necessity of learners building concepts in a meaningful way. It highlights the fact that learners enter any situation with preexisting knowledge and experiences that they draw on when discovering and assimilating new information. For this new information to be meaningful to learners, instructors must help them build a cognitive framework that can accommodate such information, taking into account of the initial understandings with which the learners enter the learning situation.

The other emphasis in current work in mathematics education on which we focus in this chapter has to do with the social context of learning. Mathematics education can be viewed as a process of enculturating the learner into the practices of an intellectual community (Cobb, 1994a, 1994b; Driver, Asoko, Leach, Mortimer, & Scott, 1994). This viewpoint argues that communities of practice have been constructed in different disciplines, into which a learner must be initiated in order to take part effectively in the practice of that discipline. For example, referring to science education, Driver et al. (1994) explained:

> The view of scientific knowledge as socially constructed and validated has important implications for science education. It means that learning science involves being initiated into scientific ways of knowing. Scientific entities and ideas, which are constructed, validated, and communicated through the cultural institutions of science, are unlikely to be discovered by individuals through their own empirical enquiry; learning science thus involves being initiated into the ideas and practices of the scientific community and making these ideas and practices meaningful at an individual level. (p. 6)

In this chapter we use the term *reform approaches* to refer to both of these emphases, the individual and the social. As Cobb (1994a) argued, the "analysis of mathematics learning as individual construction and as enculturation are complementary" (p.4).

IV

STUDIES OF PROFESSIONAL DEVELOPMENT PROGRAMS IN ACTION

9

Teacher Change and Mathematics K–4: Developing a Theoretical Perspective

Cheryl A. Lubinski
Patricia A. Jaberg
Illinois State University

Eleven K–4 elementary teachers' beliefs and instructional practices, both before and after they had access to research-based knowledge about children's mathematical processes, were analyzed. All teachers from one rural midwestern elementary school and their principal volunteered to attend 12 in-service sessions involving 34 hours over a 9-month period. The focus of the intervention was on developing students' understanding of mathematics by using teachers' knowledge of students' thinking processes. Comparisons made between baseline and summative data, spanning a calendar year, indicated that teachers' beliefs and instructional practices were changing. These changes reflect the degree to which each teacher internalized a theoretical perspective that embodied the belief that instructional decisions need to be based on a consideration of students' thinking. Teacher collaboration and administrative support facilitated the change process. Examples from videotapes of both first- and fourth-grade teachers are discussed in detail to illustrate specific areas of change.

BACKGROUND

Current documents such as the *Curriculum and Evaluation Standards for School Mathematics* (National Council of Teachers of Mathematics [NCTM], 1989) and *Everybody Counts* (National Research Council, 1989) advocate mathematics teaching as actively engaging students in doing mathematics. It is recommended that mathematics activities be

223

related to real-life situations and require students to use reasoning, creative thinking, and critical reflection. Furthermore, the current reform documents encourage the recognition of mathematical connections, the communication of mathematical ideas, and the development of mathematics skills that are embedded in problem-solving situations.

Reform, however, cannot be implemented simply by the adoption of a curriculum or a policy advocating change in mathematics instruction. Thompson (1992) found that teachers' interpretation and implementation of curricula are significantly influenced by their knowledge and beliefs about mathematics. In her study of preservice teachers, Ball (1988) wrote that beliefs are formed during formal education experiences and that these beliefs are deeply rooted. Teachers' beliefs affect classroom instruction and "appear to act as filters through which teachers interpret and ascribe meanings to their experiences as they interact with children and the subject matter" (Thompson, 1992, pp. 138–139).

Beliefs can be held with varying degrees of conviction, but as Cohen (1991) reported, beliefs often are persistent and don't easily change, even when they are challenged in in-service programs, by new materials, or by new policies. To promote teacher change that reflects the NCTM Standards, teacher education in-service programs and policy changes must be accompanied by long-term administrative, peer group, and university education faculty support. But even when teachers embrace new ideas and methods enthusiastically, they often do not possess the skills and knowledge necessary to implement their beliefs (Thompson, 1992).

Studies of the relationship between teachers' beliefs about teaching and instructional practices have not been conclusive. Some researchers (Grant & Shirk, as cited in Thompson, 1992) report teaching behaviors consistent with beliefs, whereas others have found that there is a disparity between teachers' beliefs about teaching mathematics and instructional practice (Cooney, 1985; Thompson, 1984). Schram and Wilcox (1988) found in case studies of two prospective elementary teachers that one changed his views (accommodation), whereas another simply modified the new ideas to fit into her existing framework (assimilation without accommodation).

Research conducted at the University of Wisconsin (Carpenter, Fennema, Peterson, Chiang, & Loef, 1989) reported an approach that offers a high degree of success in affecting teachers' beliefs and instructional practices. This research approach, Cognitively Guided Instruction (CGI), is based on the assumptions that children's thinking can be useful to teachers and "that just as children interpret and make sense of new knowledge in light of their existing knowledge and beliefs, so do teachers" (Peterson, Fennema, & Carpenter, 1991b, p. 108). Providing primary teachers with explicit research-based knowledge about developing students' understandings did influence teacher instruction and, ultimately student achievement. Findings indicate that teachers in the experimental group posed problems to students more frequently than did teachers in the control group and spent significantly more instructional time interacting with students. Results indicated that these teachers focused on student processes, listened to students' solutions and verbalization, emphasized the interrelationship of mathematical skills, and actively diagnosed students' knowledge and cognitive strategies (Peterson, Carpenter, & Fennema, 1989). Even though the original CGI project focused primarily on knowledge of addition and subtraction as part of the first-grade mathematics curriculum, that knowledge provided the key for more far-reaching changes in mathematics instruction (Carpenter & Fennema, 1992).

The intent of our research is to extend that which has been done in CGI classrooms to include Grades K–4, and to consider the role of the school principal in the change process. We want to provide descriptions of classrooms of teachers who had access to research-based knowledge on children's thinking and collaborated among themselves and with their principal about how to develop learning environments that reflect recommended changes in mathematics education.

PRELUDE TO CHANGE

The impetus for change in mathematics curriculum originated with a teacher, Ms. S., who had participated in a summer workshop on decision making and mathematics. Ms. S. communicated her experience to Ms. K., the principal, and they discussed the possibility of providing the school staff with a similar workshop at their school. It was important to Ms. K. that the change process begin with a teacher because of both the time commitment and the effects of change on the mathematics curriculum; thus, Ms. K. asked Ms. S. to explain her experience at the summer workshop to the faculty at one of the regularly scheduled faculty meetings. Ms. K. encouraged a full-staff development project rather than individual teacher involvement. In cooperation with Ms. S.'s university course instructor, Dr. L., a proposal was written and state funding granted, allowing a staff development project to begin early in the following spring.

Prior to the start of the project, Ms. K. provided the school board with a rationale for change based on current reform recommendations from the NCTM Standards. She requested the school board purchase the *Curriculum and Evaluation Standards for School Mathematics* (NCTM, 1989) for each teacher, in addition to allocating $300 for mathematics manipulatives for the school library. Ms. K. facilitated the change process from its inception by providing information to the board, to parents in school board minutes, and to the school newspaper as the project developed. The local newspaper also reported the project goal.

METHOD

Ms. K. and all 11 teachers participating in the staff development project were from a rural elementary school in central Illinois. All but one, a learning disabilities resource teacher, were in self-contained classrooms, kindergarten through fourth grade. The range of teaching experience among these teachers was from 3 to 25 years. The principal had been in education for 23 years, 6 years as an administrator. Three of the 11 teachers reported having taken some graduate courses; one had a master's degree, as did the principal. Nine of the teachers had taken general mathematics in college, five of the teachers had taken a college algebra course, and three of the teachers had taken a college geometry course.

The objectives of the staff development intervention were to:

- provide experienced K–4 teachers with research on how children learn, influencing their pedagogical content knowledge and beliefs about the teaching and learning of mathematics in order to affect their instruction, decision making, and ultimately student learning outcomes.
- assist experienced teachers in creating learning environments that encouraged teaching mathematics with understanding, by focusing on problem solving and technology as recommended in *Curriculum and Professional Standards*.

A data set that included a pre- and postintervention belief survey, a pre- and postintervention videotaped mathematics lesson, and pre- and post-lesson reflections was developed for each participant. The principal maintained a journal throughout the 9-month intervention period.

THE INTERVENTION

Project participants attended six two-hour spring sessions, an intensive summer in-service, and a culminating fall session. The entire intervention was planned and facilitated by a university mathematics educator, Dr. L., who visited each teacher's classroom in the spring (to conduct an assessment lesson) and in the fall (to observe a lesson).

The spring sessions emphasized providing research-based information on students' thinking and problem solving in the areas related to addition, subtraction, multiplication, division, place value, and fractions. Dr. L. discussed how the structure of 11 addition/subtraction problem types influences how various children determine what strategies they choose to solve them (Carpenter & Moser, 1984). Research by Peterson, Fennema, and Carpenter (1991a), which addressed how children use direct modeling, counting, or derived fact strategies and symbolic notation as they mature in their mathematical understandings, was introduced, and research-based readings of these researchers were assigned and discussed. Further, videotapes from their project work, as well as from Nancy Mack's fraction work, were viewed at each session.

The multiplication and division problem types and children's solution strategies (Carpenter, Carey, & Kouba, 1990) were discussed, as were students' understandings of place value (Fennema & Carpenter, 1988; Fuson, 1990). Interviewing techniques were presented (Labinowitcz, 1985) as an assessment tool. The exploration of manipulative materials, their appropriate use, and their roles in developing understanding were also discussed. Other topics included alternative algorithms, children's representations of their thinking processes, and facilitating children's understanding of fractions (Mack, 1990). Further, following each in-service session, the teachers wrote about what they had changed in their classrooms. An outline of the six spring sessions is provided in the Appendix.

The intent of the summer in-service was to provide teachers time to collaborate. The one-week (25 hours) in-service took place before the beginning of school. Planning a mathematics unit reflective of both the *Standards* (NCTM, 1989) and the research was one of the goals of the summer in-service. The objectives of this in-service were:

- to allow teachers time to share ideas on how to use the information from research to better plan for mathematics instruction (short- and long-term).
- to allow teachers to become familiar with professional journals that keep teachers current on more effective mathematics instructional decision making.
- to provide teachers the opportunity to discuss and plan a mathematics unit that reflected recommendations from both the *Standards* and current research.
- to discuss alternative methods of assessment that are currently being employed in the school.

Discussions during the in-service week focused on how to use the research-based information to plan for mathematics instruction. Teachers again read and discussed research-based articles. Videotapes showing children solving addition, subtraction, multiplication, and division problems involving whole number operations and place value concepts were viewed and discussed. Alternative methods of assessment were presented. Teachers at each grade level met and restructured their sequence of mathematics instruction for the following school year. An outline of this session is provided in the Appendix.

At the beginning of each day a mathematics problem was posed to the teachers to develop their own strategies for solving problems. The intent of this task was to promote discussion of problem-solving situations to which teachers could relate. During the problem-solving session, teachers were encouraged first to work individually and then in groups to solve problems used in mathematics classes for elementary teachers at the university. At first, teachers complained about the difficulty of the tasks. However, as the week progressed, complaints subsided, strategies developed, and the time needed to solve a problem lessened. An example of one problem follows:

> Problem Day Four: If 15 people enter a room and each shake hands with everyone else exactly once, how many handshakes will occur? (It is assumed that when two people shake hands only one handshake occurs.)

Following the summer session and prior to the beginning of the school year, Ms. K. held a parent information night, at which time she communicated to the parents the status of the project, addressed any questions they had, and distributed handouts. Information on the rationale for change and the implications for teaching and learning were discussed.

The final intervention session in early fall focused on how using students' thinking creates changes in the learning environment. Grade level needs were discussed, and follow-up classroom visits for observation were scheduled by Dr. L.

Ms. K. played an instrumental role throughout the change process. She became familiar with the contents of the *Standards* document. She disseminated research-based articles to her staff on a regular basis and provided opportunities for her staff to discuss mathematics during both grade level and full faculty meetings. She encouraged ongoing communication about mathematics curriculum, manipulative materials, pacing, and student assessment and achievement. She modified her thinking from classroom evaluation based only on the sequence of the mathematics text to inclusion of more open-ended assessments of the students' understandings.

Belief Survey

A belief survey was administered to the teachers before and after the intervention. Participants were asked to respond to 48 statements regarding the teaching and learning of mathematics. The survey used was adapted from the Cognitively Guided Instruction Project, and responses were scored on a Likert 5-point scale from "strongly agree" to "strongly disagree." The original CGI belief survey was divided into four constructs, involving either teaching (Constructs II and IV), learning (Construct I), or the content of mathematics (Construct III).

Construct I *ranges from the belief that children receive mathematical knowledge from teachers to the belief that children construct their own mathematical knowledge (learning).*

Construct II *ranges from the belief that skills should be taught in isolation to the belief that skills should be taught in relationship to understanding and problem solving (teaching).*

Construct III *ranges from the belief that the structure of mathematics provides the basis for sequencing topics for instruction to the belief that children's natural development of mathematical ideas should provide the basis for sequencing topics for instruction (content).*

Construct IV *ranges from the belief that mathematics instruction should be organized to facilitate the teacher's clear presentation of knowledge to the belief that mathematics instruction should be organized to facilitate children's construction of knowledge (teaching style).* (Fennema, Carpenter, & Peterson, 1989, p. 183)

For each of the four constructs a continuum was developed that indicated to what degree teachers considered students' thinking related to teaching and learning mathematics. One end of the continuum could be classified as less cognitively based, with the student viewed as the receiver of knowledge and the teacher viewed as the provider of knowledge. The other end of the continuum could be classified as more cognitively based, with the students viewed as constructors of their own knowledge and teachers viewed as facilitators developing students' understandings. Fennema, Carpenter, and Peterson (1989) characterized teachers with more cognitively based beliefs as those making decisions about instruction that facilitated children's learning, developed children's belief in their own abilities to understand and do mathematics, and promoted higher cognitive-level skills. The more cognitively based perspective recognizes that, to be understood and learned, new information must be integrated into a previously existing network of knowledge. A high score on the belief survey indicated a cognitively based perspective (Peterson, Fennema, & Carpenter, 1991a).

The Model Mathematics Lesson

Each participant planned and taught two mathematics lessons for the data collection. To provide support, the principal videotaped mathematics lessons both before and after the intervention. The preintervention lesson was taped early in the second semester. The postintervention lesson was taped late in the first semester of the following school year. Teachers were asked to respond to survey questions prior to each videotaping (see video lesson plan form in Appendix). Another group of questions, designed to stimulate reflection on the lesson, was completed by teachers as they viewed and analyzed their own videotaped lessons (see videotape assessment form in Appendix). Questions were designed to determine on what the teacher focused both before and after an instructional session: the content, the manipulatives or materials, the task, or the students' thinking.

RESULTS

After the intervention the data set was analyzed. The questions to be answered by this analysis included: Is there a change in reported beliefs? Considering the outcome of reported beliefs, do instructional practices reflect these beliefs? What did teachers consider a model lesson, both before and after the intervention?

Belief Survey

When all the constructs for the survey were aggregated pre- and post-intervention, the average for the 11 subjects changed from 3.852 to 4.338, a net change of +0.486. A two-tailed t-test on all the constructs and the means for all 11 subjects showed significance at the .05 level. The preintervention average for Construct II was 3.606 and changed +0.847 to a postintervention average of 4.453. A statistical summary is found in Table 9.1. These results reveal that reported beliefs shifted toward a more cognitively based perspective on the learning and teaching of mathematics.

Model Lesson

The pre- and postintervention lessons of each of the participants were examined to provide information on instructional practices. Answers to questions on the prelesson form provided information about teachers' decision making prior to instruction. What teachers considered in planning, as well as what they reflected on following instruction, provided insights into beliefs about teaching and learning. This information was examined to determine if instructional decisions were reflective of teachers' reported beliefs. Constructs I and IV were grouped together because, in practice, beliefs relating to how children learn (Construct I) affect the teaching methods employed (Construct IV). Lessons were labeled "primarily yes" (reflective of the cognitively based perspective) or "primarily no" (not reflective of the cognitively based perspective of Constructs I and IV) based on the following questions (see Table 9.2):

- Are different solutions acceptable to or encouraged by the teacher?
- Are multiple solution strategies to problems recognized and explored?

- Is the teacher considering children's thinking in his or her instructional decision making? How, and to what degree?
- What is the focus of instruction?

Similarly, evidence of Construct II (teaching using problem solving versus teaching isolated skills) was evaluated in the teachers' lessons (see Table 9.1). The following criteria were used:

- Is problem solving used?
- Are mathematical skills being related and taught in the context of problem solving?
- How does the teacher exhibit an expanded view of children's mathematical knowledge and thinking?

Again, each lesson was labeled as "primarily yes" or "primarily no" as a reflection of the evidence whether instruction was cognitively based. Examples to illustrate these changes are discussed in the section "Examples from the Classroom." Construct III was not used because the two lessons did not provide the data to determine the basis for examining sequencing of topics in mathematics.

Classroom Discourse

To better understand how intervention could change instructional practices, classroom discourse was examined in terms of one quantitative measurement, time. Teacher-centered time was compared to teacher–student and student–student interaction time. Teacher-centered time was defined as time when the teacher was giving directions,

TABLE 9.1
Pre-Intervention Means Compared to Post-Intervention Means on the Belief Survey

Teacher	Pre-Intervention	Post-Intervention
1	4.020	4.415
2	3.793	4.665
3	3.705	4.520
4	3.543	4.020
5	4.082	4.188
6	4.020	4.627
7	3.793	3.895
8	3.705	4.185
9	3.543	4.227
10	4.082	4.435
11	4.082	4.540

TABLE 9.2
Classification of Videotaped Lessons as Reflective of Cognitively Based Instruction

CGI Belief Constructs	Pre-Intervention Lesson		Post-Intervention Lesson	
	primarily no	primarily yes	primarily no	primarily yes
I, IV	11	0	1	10
II	10	1	2	9

instructing, explaining, or asking content and knowledge (lower level) questions. Teacher–student and student–student-centered time was characterized by interaction and higher level questions that required application, analysis, synthesis, or explanation of thinking.

To account for the varying length of the lessons, teacher-centered time versus student–teacher and student–student interaction time was expressed in percentages of the total lesson time. Figure 9.1 shows the percentage of teacher-talk time exhibited during the entire lesson.

Preintervention lessons revealed teacher-talk time ranged from 27% to 99% of total lesson time. The average clustered at 92%. Postintervention lessons averaged 22% teacher-talk time, with a range from 6% to 90%. Not only did the type of classroom discourse change, but so did the nature of that discourse. Preintervention lessons were characterized by content and knowledge level questions. Students were expected to respond to teacher questions, but there was little or no opportunity for discussion or interaction, with the exception of one teacher's classroom, where the preintervention lesson began with a problem-solving session. This particular teacher had taken a summer course with Dr. L. prior to the staff development intervention. In contrast, teachers doing the postintervention lessons asked higher-level questions, which required students to explain their thinking, and helped students to make connections.

Self-Reported Changes

Responses to the probe "Something I've changed in my classroom" varied; however, a common theme emerged. That theme reflected the belief that students' thinking and understandings were being considered during instruction. Examples of teachers' responses follow:

- They [students] worked in their cooperative learning groups to solve [problems]. I discovered some very interesting ways of thinking about the problems.
- We stop more often to figure out a problem instead of me figuring for them.
- We do problem solving before I teach the basic fact strategies.

- I start every day with a story problem. The students may use slates/chalk, manipulatives, discussion—any means to derive the answer. [Then] discuss.
- Problem solving now. Other years, I have waited until the beginning of the second semester.
- I continue to work on problem solving. I am using more manipulatives and less paper work.
- Every morning for 15 minutes we are doing oral story problems and discussing how we were thinking when we solved our problems.

Some teacher reflections provided support for a cognitively based perspective of Construct I/IV (learning and teaching):

- When giving an answer for word problems, I would have students tell me how they "figured it out."
- We talked a great deal about thinking strategies while assessing also during class time.

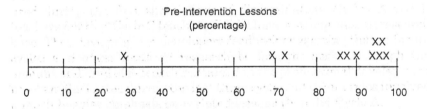

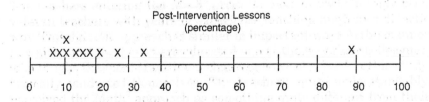

FIG. 9.1. Teacher centered time in videotaped lessons of teachers participating in intervention project.

- [We]. . .spend more time talking about what we are doing.
- [I] allowed individuals to use manipulatives at will.
- I have interviewed a few students as to their levels of learning.
- Students explained the different ways that they came up with the same answers to a specific problem.
- The technique of having students explain "how" they solved a problem has been very enlightening and exciting.
- I have become more aware of individual strategies.
- I listened more carefully to how the students were finding answers.
- I really feel more confident in not teaching directly from the text.
- I'm not as pressured to cover every unnecessary page in the text; have omitted many pages of text that are repetitious.

Teacher Confidence

Following the intervention, teachers were asked to respond to the question, "How comfortable are you with your ability in the area of mathematics?" A 5-point scale, ranging from very comfortable to very uncomfortable, was used. One teacher reported being very comfortable, four reported being pretty comfortable, three reported being comfortable, one reported being a little uncomfortable, and only one felt very uncomfortable. When asked," How comfortable are you with your ability to teach mathematics?" One responded very comfortable, five pretty comfortable, and four comfortable. Eight teachers, including the principal, agreed the project was very valuable, and three reported it was valuable.

Examples from the Classroom

As beliefs and knowledge changed in response to the intervention, teacher decision making and instructional practices also changed. Prior to the intervention, content selection was based on textbook suggestions and was restricted to topics and numbers that the textbook recommended. Implementation of planned lessons was again greatly influenced by the textbook and by previous experiences both as a teacher and as a student. After the intervention, suggestions from the teachers' manual received decreased attention. To illustrate these changes, we discuss three examples.

Example One

A second grade teacher's preintervention lesson focused on an activity that practiced regrouping, in anticipation of doing subtraction with regrouping. After demonstrating that eighteen 1s equals one 10 and eight 1s, she asked "What will we do for subtraction? We'll take away or trade back a 10 for 1s." Pairs of children demonstrated this task with straws. She asked them if they could "do it without telling me?" The focus was on learning the procedure. In the postintervention lesson, children were encouraged to reflect on their own thinking. The teacher asked students to "Tell me how you did it" and exclaimed, "We found three ways to do this problem." Even though the postintervention lesson occurred earlier in the school year than the preintervention lesson, larger numbers were used: 134 + 246, 150 + 266. The preintervention regrouping lesson strictly used numbers less than 20. After intervention, the teacher was obviously not restricted by the content of the textbook; her instructional decisions reflected a belief that second-grade students could handle more difficult concepts with understanding.

Example Two

One third-grade teacher chose to use beans and cups to work with 2 and 3 as divisors. As reported in her prelesson form, selection of the preintervention lesson was influenced by "security—go strictly by the book, [be] nice and safe." This same teacher began her postintervention lesson by posing this problem: "Think of the number 100. Go all the way down to 0 by subtracting the same number. First, think of one number you can subtract 4 times to get to 0." She later asked her students to find all possible combinations of numbers. Reflecting on her lesson after viewing her teaching video, she wrote:

> The lesson didn't go at all how I thought it would. I thought the students would do subtraction but they didn't. *All* the students chose to use repeated addition, which was fine because we began discussing multiplication. We learned that repeated addition is the same as multiplying. The students were able to tell me that if we switched the numbers around, the problem would still be the same. For example, 4 x 5 = 5 x 4. The students were able to relate their knowledge of addition to multiplication. The problem helped the students become enthusiastic about multiplication. It is going to be exciting to explore multiplication. . . so involved in the problem that we ran out of time.

This example illustrates how postintervention instruction was organized to involve children's thinking and to develop children's understanding. The teacher asked the students to tell what they knew about addition and multiplication, as well as how it was related to the problem posed. She used the students' thinking to build on their knowledge.

Example Three

A learning disabilities teacher planned a preintervention lesson for two fourth-grade students that involved addition and subtraction, with the students responsible for choosing the appropriate operation after word problems were read to them. An array of counters, such as Unifix Cubes and "dinosaur" counters were readily available. The objective stated by the teacher was "that they would have to decide what operation to use . . . and I used 'put together,' 'in all,' 'plus,' and 'add' so they could choose the term or terms that work best for them . . . and [the students] were ready for this activity because they had mastered all the separate components and with guidance were ready to put it all together." Sums and differences less than 12 made up this lesson, and the students were asked to represent the numbers in the addition and subtraction situations in standard vertical form.

The postintervention lesson again involved fourth-grade students, and the objective was to organize gathered data to create a graph and then formulate problems from the graph. In planning, this teacher considered questions to be used during discussion, realizing the need for rephrasing them and considering "sample problems that could be solved using the graphs." The reflections following the postintervention lesson were considerably longer and revealed more introspection than occurred after the first lesson, where the reflection consisted of a brief summary of the lesson. In contrast, the teacher focused on what went well or didn't go well, explored the changes that could be made, and included some self-evaluation of her own teaching. She commented that it was important to include problems that emphasized the skills of addition, subtraction, and comparison, "because these are the skills my students need to learn to use," but that "they need more exposure to the types of problems that can be solved using graphs before they compose their own questions." She wrote that she needed to sharpen her questioning techniques as well as "to back off in some situations and let them have more time to find their own solutions and answers." She noted that she was "there with a helping hand, even when it is not required," but also indicated that "I would choose to work together more and walk them through the activity with questions." On one hand, she wanted to give the students the time to work on problems, but she also had difficulty relinquishing the opportunity for more guided practice. As a result of information gained from students during this lesson, she made a decision to change the following week's activity. She decided that as the students gathered real-life data using double-digit numbers (attendance), they would record questions and then use the graph of this information to "find solutions to these questions and problems."

An In-Depth Analysis from the Primary Grades

An in-depth analysis of the data sets provided us with more detailed information on how teachers understand, implement, and adapt research information to their classroom situation in light of their prior beliefs and previous experiences. Four different teachers are discussed in detail to illustrate specific areas of change.

The first two teachers, Ms. D. and Ms. F., were chosen because they were at the same grade level and because their postintervention belief score averages were very close (near 4.5), reflecting similar cognitively based perspectives. Yet, even with apparently similar perspectives, their interpretation and internalization of the belief changes precipitated by the intervention project differed. The pre-intervention lessons were examined to see how these teachers differed prior to the intervention. The data were examined postintervention to determine how and to what extent these similar postintervention perspectives affected instructional planning, classroom discourse, and instructional practices.

Ms. D.   Preintervention lesson. Ms. D. teaches first grade. We classified Ms. D.'s preintervention lesson as teacher-centered and teacher-driven. She began the lesson by announcing to the class that because they had worked with subtraction facts to 11 last week, they would work with subtraction facts to 12. Ms. D. related in her prelesson form that she chose this activity because it was "suggested by [the] book and I thought they would be good strategies for practicing subtraction." She showed an awareness of her students' previous experiences in her planning stage. She had indicated in her prelesson form that the students "already know counting back with 1, 2, and 3; counting on with numbers close together"; that the class had already discussed the idea of part–part–whole; and that she would tap previous discussions of doubles.

Materials for the lesson consisted of a sheet with 12 dots and a peek cover. Ms. D. wrote "12–3" on the board and asked the students to uncover three dots on the left side. "How many are left covered up?" she then asked. The children were told to check whether nine dots were indeed hidden. Ms. D. then asked, "If you don't have 12–3 memorized, what would be the easiest way for you to figure 12–3? Counting back was suggested by a student, and the group, with Ms. D. as leader, counted back, "12-11-10-9." The class moved on to other examples, but many were confused by the peek sheet, including Ms. D. She reflected after viewing her teaching video:

> In all honesty, what I was thinking during this activity was that it was very poor and I would never do it again. In preparing for the lesson, I thought it seemed like a good strategy to try to explore subtraction from 12. However, as you view the tape, it was quite confusing to both me and the students. The students were given the number sentence "12–3 =." They were to expose the 3, try to figure out what was hidden, then uncover and count. The problem, as I see it, is that if 3 were *taken away* from 12, it would be more logical to cover up the 3 to show that it was taken away. But . . . I trudged along.

Ms. D. and the class continued with examples and the classroom discourse was characterized by quick, one-word responses from the children. The lesson concluded with Ms. D. writing "12–7" vertically on the board. Ms. D. said, "Since you're not subtracting 1, 2, or 3, you can't count back. The numbers are not close together, so you can't count forward, so what do you suppose is the easiest way to do 12–7?" There was no wait time for a student response. Ms. D. emphatically said, "Remember it, memorize it. When you hear and see it, your mind says 12–7 = 5." These vignettes illustrate that Ms. D.'s instructional practices reflected a less cognitively based perspective prior to the intervention. Facts were being taught in isolation (Construct II), and Ms. D. hoped to convey her knowledge about facts (Construct I) to her students.

Postintervention lesson. Ms. D.'s postintervention lesson consisted of three word problems, which she chose to provide "exposure to real-life story problems to help make the connection with computation." In planning, she wrote that she had "tried to give some higher level as well as lower level thinking skills to meet the needs of as many students as possible." She exhibited an awareness that her students were at different levels.

The problem types were varied (part–part–whole, whole–unknown; compare, difference unknown; and a two-part problem). Numbers chosen (12 + 11, 32–18, 15 + 40 + 32, 89–87) were challenging, in contrast to the subtraction facts using 12 in the preintervention lesson. Students were encouraged to share their solution strategies with the group as a whole; three children shared different solution strategies for each problem. Multiple solution strategies were expected, and the students responded accordingly.

Students were arranged in groups of four, again in contrast to the "desks in rows" configuration of the earlier lesson. Student–student interaction was encouraged. For example, Ms. D. often gave directions such as, "Before you share with me, I want you to share with the group your solutions."

Ms. D. routinely asked the students to write some type of representation for their solution strategy. These symbolic representations reflected their strategies and thinking, and when a student was unable to do this, Ms. D. questioned and discussed the solution with the student in order to help clarify his or her thinking to the point where representation emerged. The last teacher-generated problem provides an example of this process:

Mike needs 89 stickers to fill his sticker book. He has

15 Halloween stickers

40 Thanksgiving stickers

32 Christmas stickers

Does he have enough to fill his sticker book? If not, how many more does he need?

While one student volunteered her solution of "pictures" and was drawing on the board, another student went up to the hundreds chart, and the following interchange between the student and Ms. D. took place:

Student: I started at 40.

Ms. D.: Okay.

Student: And then I added on 32 more. Instead of counting them all, I went 50, 60, 70, and 71 and 72.

Ms. D.: Okay.

Student: And then I added 15, and that was 82 and then I went 83, 84, 85, 86, 87. And then I knew I didn't have enough, and then I went 88, 89. Then I knew I needed 2 more.

Ms. D.: How would you show that? You did a lot of counting and you did a lot of that in your head and with your fingers. How would you show that? (student writes "40 +") You started with 40, then what did you tell me you did next? (student adds "32 = 72" and on the next line writes "72 + 15 = 87") Okay, you're at 87. Then what did you do because you still had one more thing to figure out? Now you had to tell if he had enough to fill his sticker book (student writes "87 + 2 = 89"). Okay, good job! 40 plus 32 equals 72. That's how you thought about it first. Then 72 plus 15 equals 87. When you were at 87, you knew you had to add on 2 more to get 89. Good job!

A third child volunteered her solution and used a counting on strategy with the hundreds chart. She started with 15 and counted on 40, stopping at 55. Ms. D. asked why she had stopped there. The student explained, "I added on Thanksgiving." Ms. D. prompted, "What did you do next?" The student counted on 32 for Christmas. In this particular case, the student needed a great deal of help in writing symbolic notation, but Ms. D. used the student's thinking to symbolically represent the situation as shown here:

$$\begin{array}{ccc} 15 & 55 & 87 + 2 = 8 \\ \underline{+40} & \underline{+32} & \\ 55 & 87 & \end{array}$$

During the 14-minute preintervention lesson, 99% of the time was characterized as teacher-centered. In contrast, the teacher-centered time in the postintervention lesson was only 7% of the 45-minute lesson. Ms. D. spent much more time listening to students and their solution strategies during the postintervention lesson than during the preintervention lesson.

Ms. F.   Preintervention lesson. Ms. F. also teaches first grade. Her preintervention lesson focused on an activity involving the part–whole concept. Her decision to teach this content was influenced by the textbook. In her prelesson form, she wrote, it was "suggested by Addison-Wesley textbook; I felt this content would be valuable for my students to learn and experience." The children were led through the activity, with one-word or two-word responses by the children. Teacher-centered time comprised approximately 95% of the 20-minute lesson. Ms. F. drew two circles on the overhead projector, placed some counters in one circle and the rest of the counters in the other circle (two and three were typical). The students were asked to tell how many counters were on the entire screen and then how many were in each circle. As Ms. F. wrote in her video lesson assessment, [I] "used numbers less than six due to the fact that these numbers were previously covered." After a few more examples, Ms. F. wrote their answers to the question, "How many?":

$$5\ 3\ 2$$
$$3\ 1\ 2$$
$$2\ 1\ 1$$

The children were directed to do the same activity in small groups. Three students were assigned to be either a writer, a speaker, or a leader. The children were led through the activity as follows: "The leader should take 6 counters. Put some counters in one circle and some in the other circle. The writer should write down the number of counters in each part." The speaker reported what the leader had done with the counters, and Ms. F. summarized and repeated the responses. All the questions and activities were taken from the textbook, and discussion was not encouraged in the cooperative group setting. One question asked for some evaluation: "If you traded papers, would they be the same?" There was a mixed response from the students, so she again focused on the task, noting that "some had put 3 and 3 for 6, and some had put 4 and 2." The last activity, where the students were asked to find as many ways as possible to show six, was also directed: "Write down your numbers on the lines below 6 with 3 and 3," she suggested.

Postintervention lesson. The postintervention lesson, by contrast, we classified as student-centered, with about 90% of the 45-minute problem-solving session devoted to student thinking and sharing. Four different problem types were embedded in the word-problem format, using a previously read book, *Hershel and the Hanukkah Goblins* (Kimmel, 1985). These problems included multiplication, part–part–whole, with whole unknown, and the last two were part–part–whole with part unknown. Due to the absence of apparent action, part–part–whole with part-unknown problems are difficult for students to solve. However, her decision was deliberate as she explained in her lesson plan, "I know my students can figure these types of problems. However, very often they get so 'wrapped up' in the numbers that they fail to hear the question." As she wrote in her prelesson form, she chose numbers "under 100 to ensure success for the majority of my students." These first graders were solving these types of problems two months earlier than the students in the preintervention lesson, who worked with numbers less than or equal to eight.

Children were encouraged to share their solution strategies, and all strategies were accepted. All student answers were written on the board whether they were "right" or "wrong." Students with incorrect solutions were also invited to share their thinking. The expectation that all students would do mathematics was encouraged by such questions and statements as, "Did someone figure this another way?" "Talk with your group and see if they agree." "Explain how you got 30." " How did you know to use . . . ?" "Did anyone get another answer?" These probes helped clarify the students' thinking and were based on responses from them.

In her self-reported changes, Ms. F. indicated that she now does problem solving daily, assessing individuals by listening to their thinking, and encouraging students to solve their own problems, instead of showing them a solution herself. This confirms the more cognitively based perspective that children construct their own knowledge and are not provided knowledge by teachers. The following lesson illustrates this perspective: "As Hershel walked home, he dreamed of all the potato latkas he'd eat during the 8 days of Hanukkah. If he eats two helpings each day of Hanukkah, how many helpings of latkas will he have eaten by the end of Hanukkah?"

After students shared some solutions (such as $2 + 2 + 2 + 2 + 2 + 2 + 2 + 2 = 16$), one student, who correctly solved the problem, wanted to use the numbers 2, 8, and 16 and relate them to each other. Students suggested addition and subtraction, but none of them obtained the desired results. Ms. F. wrote in her reflection regarding this segment:

> I asked [the original] student which he would choose hoping it would be more meaningful. We had *very* briefly talked about multiplication so I thought maybe this particular child would relate multiplication to this problem. I then turned to others in class who may have another suggestion. No solution was found. I will spend morning Oral Math time discussing this further. If no solution is found, it will be a challenge problem to work on during free time or at home. This was not a situation I planned on encountering. Most students (at this point) find or hear the answer and then are satisfied. I have a few students who are becoming more inquisitive.

In accepting various solutions, Ms. F. helped students make connections. For one particular problem, three different solutions were discussed, and Ms. F. carefully related the symbolic notation that she wrote on the board to the student's thinking, and commented on how these were ways to think about the same problem. The problem posed was: "As Hershel was walking, he passed some houses on the right. He passed 6 houses on the left. He looked back and noticed that he passed 17 houses. How many houses were on the right?" Two answers were volunteered, 11 and 23. First, a student who got 23 was called on to explain how she got 23. The student explained that she started at 17 and counted on 6. Ms. F. asked why she did that; the student replied that she had added. Ms. F. queried, "Is that what my story asked you?" When the student replied "No," Ms. F. instructed the student to go back to her notes (each child had a mathematics booklet) and think about it again. The next student shared that he "started at 6, but after I found there was 11, I said 11 + 6 = 17." Ms. F. probed with "Tell me more," and discovered that he was estimating. She wrote "__ + 6 = 17" on the board and asked him, "Does this look right?" He said yes and said that he had first tried 13, but got 19, so he tried 12 and then 11. Ms. F. continued by asking "Did anyone else get 11?" The next student said that she had started at 17 and counted back 6 to get 11. Ms. F. then wrote these representations of their solutions: "17–6 = 11"; "__ + 6 = 17." She encouraged the students to write their solutions in their mathematics booklets, but did not indicate preference or correctness of any one particular representation. The students were encouraged to use the representation that corresponded to their thinking.

Comparison of Ms. D. and Ms. F.   The instructional decisions, practices, and classroom discourse of both first-grade teachers examined in the case studies changed toward a more cognitively based perspective after the intervention project. Both Ms. D. and Ms. F. relied less on textbooks and more on their knowledge of children's thinking in choosing mathematical content and problem types and numbers for word problems. The oral word problems were used from the beginning of the year, with emphasis not on learning facts or computation but on understanding and helping students make connections.

In comparing preintervention lessons with postintervention lessons, both teachers' classroom environments changed. The students sat passively during the preintervention lessons, answering lower level questions with short responses. In the postintervention lessons, in contrast, students were enthusiastic and interested in doing mathematics. Both teachers employed cooperative groups to somewhat different degrees. Ms. F. continually encouraged the children to share strategies and discuss solutions with their partners and seemed to be comfortable with the atmosphere that resulted. Ms. D., on the other hand, provided more structure for the groups and peer interaction. She often instructed the students, "First, work alone. Then share with your group," or after first working alone, she selected students to share with the group, and the rule was, "The only person talking is the one who has a solution." After intervention, both teachers, though, encouraged and listened to students' solution strategies, a major change from their preintervention lessons. Ms. D. wrote in reflection of her postintervention lesson, "I did not expect that all students would be able to do all problems, but by allowing students to share their strategies, I feel the continued exposure (daily) will give other students ways to begin thinking about the problem." The difference in their handling of peer interaction implies that these teachers did adapt the information from the intervention to their beliefs about discipline and management of students. Ms. D. is a bit more hesitant to abdicate all authority, and peer interaction is more controlled in her classroom than in Ms. F.'s classroom.

Both Ms. D. and Ms. F. were careful that symbolic notation matched students' thinking, but varied in the emphasis they gave to that notation. Both teachers asked that students show their solution strategies in mathematics booklets, but Ms. D. gave more emphasis to standard notation, whereas Ms. F.'s emphasis was not as strong. Ms. F. wrote the appropriate notation on the chalkboard after carefully listening to student thinking. Ms. D. asked the students themselves to write it on the board.

Assessment of student thinking appears to be included to various degrees in both classrooms after intervention. Both teachers wrote of assessing while listening to children's solution strategies. In self-reported changes, Ms. F. related that she had taken students aside and assessed them individually using word problems, whereas Ms. D. used individual assessment at the beginning of the school year.

Overall, in these two first-grade classrooms, the focus of instruction changed from activities that were textbook driven to problem solving that was student driven. The classroom discourse changed from teacher-centered "telling" to teacher–student and student–student interaction that promoted sharing and construction of knowledge. Instructional practices were influenced by student thinking and the natural development of mathematical ideas, rather than by the sequencing suggested in the textbook. Minimal or no mathematics courses were taken by these teachers in their college preparation. Ms. D. expressed confidence in her own mathematical ability and noted that she was "pretty comfortable" when asked about her ability to teach mathematics. Ms. F. had no confidence in her own mathematical ability, but after the intervention she noted on the questionnaire she would be comfortable teaching mathematics, but penciled in the phrase "at the first-grade level."

An In-Depth Analysis from the Intermediate Grades

Data from fourth-grade classrooms were also analyzed to examine how content areas beyond the four basic operations affected teachers' understanding and ability to develop students' thinking. Two teachers' data sets were selected for further analysis. Ms. M. and Ms. Q. both now teach in the intermediate grades. Both teachers' belief scale scores reflected change towards more cognitively based beliefs, but Ms. M.'s change in mean on all four constructs (3.705 to 4.185) was quantitatively greater than that of Ms. Q., whose survey score means (pre- and post-) were within one tenth of each other (3.793 to 3.895). Ms. M. was moved from first grade to fourth grade midway through this project.

Ms. M.   Preintervention lesson. The objective for this first-grade lesson was to introduce subtraction facts to 12. In planning, she wrote that "they have had previous instruction in subtraction of facts to 10." She began the lesson by asking the students questions regarding addition: "When we add, what do we do?" After a student responded with "make a higher number," she continued by saying, "Adding means doing what? What do we do with the sets?" The question was asked with a gesture of hands sweeping together in front of herself. The students themselves were then used to demonstrate the idea of subtraction, with 3 children leaving a group of 10 children. Students used chalkboards to record results of the next activity, which involved using Unifix cubes. For example, students were told to "take 8 cubes from your back" (a piece of paper given to them earlier) and "make a train, quickly." They were then told to take away three and asked how many were left. This process continued with four more sets of numbers.

Then students were assigned partners, with one child giving a "problem," and the partner doing the subtraction and writing a corresponding number sentence. After students had practiced for a few minutes, Ms. M. said that the unit they were studying included subtraction from 12 and told the students they could put their cubes together to make a set of 12. As students wrote number sentences, she asked them to write the subtraction in vertical form. As the lesson concluded, Ms. M. said that the following day they would use their adding facts to help with subtraction: "We know 4 plus 4 equals 8, so if we do 8 take away 4, we know that the number we'd have to have here is 4." She provided a few more examples and concluded by saying, "So we can add to subtract." In reflecting on her lesson, Ms. M. remarked that the use of the cubes as manipulatives was to "help them retain the lesson focus." In her reflections, she did not relate the hands-on approach to developing understanding. She further wrote that she did not consider any alternatives during instruction because "my plan was to lead the students to the correct response."

Postintervention lesson. Now teaching fourth grade, Ms. M. wanted to provide "opportunities to explore and measure, to use estimation skills" as her students explored area. She began the lesson by asking students, "What are some things you can tell me about measurement?" As she wrote in her reflections following the lesson, "Students' basic understanding of measurement needed to be 'revived' and brought to their attention; what they already know so they can build on that knowledge." This lesson used real-life experiences. In small groups, students were provided with a variety of tiles, disks, and counters and asked to "prove how many will cover" a piece of paper. Students were first asked to estimate the number, but after the students began covering their paper, they were briefly stopped and asked, "Does anyone want to change [his or her] estimate?" This question allowed students to rethink their estimates, and make new estimates, based on some knowledge. When Ms. M. monitored the groups, she posed questions and made students responsible for their own learning: "How did you get 63?" Or, when a student didn't understand what his group was doing, "What's confusing you, Andrew?" And "Can you help out?" directed to another student in the group.

Assessment was central to the purpose of the lesson: "The activity part of the lesson gave the students the opportunity to estimate and cooperate with others in solving a problem. This was a discovery activity and my purpose was to see how much they already know and what needed to be planned for future activities in measuring area."

Ms. Q. Preintervention lesson. Ms. Q.'s fourth-grade mathematics lesson content was based on the sequence provided by the textbook. In discussing her knowledge of her students, she wrote "My class has done well so far with multiplication. They work well on assignments to get them done." Her assessment was based on what her students could do and, as she reflected on the lesson, she indicated that she was "checking and rechecking a student's thinking" until he finally "did come up with the correct answer." A game was taught and played as a means to "practice concepts." Her interpretation of concepts was revealed when she discussed two students: "Ann and Craig had had difficulty in a previous lesson. They would multiply correctly, but switch numerals (i.e., 8 x 6 = 48, put down the 4, carry the 8). I was probing to see if that concept was clear to them now. It was." The focus was on the multiplication algorithm: "Talk through it step by step. Where do I put the comma?"

As part of guided practice, Ms. Q. asked the students to practice 4-digit by 1-digit multiplication and divided the group into "Ladies" and "Gentlemen," with each group given a problem such as 4703 x 4. One student was then chosen to represent a gender group and put the computation up on the board. Each group was asked to check over the problem: "Look over Craig's problem; see if you agree with it. Start with the gentlemen. Is there any gentleman who feels there's a problem with what is up there?" Ms. Q. verified the answers, "Thirty-two thousand, three hundred and thirty-four and, eighteen thousand, eight hundred and twelve are correct answers." This procedure was duplicated again, and when a "lady" wrote "3,5504" as her answer, Ms. Q. asked the student to "Pick someone to tell you what it is they think you did wrong." The placement of the comma was corrected.

Ms. Q. emphasized directions as students began to learn a game. Examples were done together, and a strategy for "winning" became apparent under her direction: When students finished placing the digits rolled on a die, she asked "Do you see how it's going to make a difference?" The 35-minute lesson ended with "one more check on you before we go to the game," and students were directed to do a computational problem from the textbook. During the lesson, 95% of the time was teacher centered and directed.

Postintervention lesson. A key component of more cognitively based instruction is that instructional decisions are based on what is known about each child's cognition. Ms. Q.'s postintervention lesson was on an entirely different topic, "time," but was also very different in its initial approach to the topic. She began the lesson by asking students to tell her everything they knew about telling time. In her prelesson form, she indicated that a written pretest "showed a lack of understanding" of this topic.

Questions grew out of students' contributions. When a student volunteered hour and minute, Ms. Q. asked, "Can you give me any kind of relationship there?" and continued with "How many hours in a week?" after a student noted that there were 24 hours in a day. When a student suggested "light-year" as a term used in time, Ms. Q. asked volunteers to go to the library to do research. When they returned, the information students had gathered was discussed. Ms. Q. asked students how long a second was. After having students count "one-one-thousand, two-one-thousand . . . ten-one-thousand," the class looked at how far light could travel in ten seconds and Ms. Q. posed this problem: "If the distance around the earth is about 25,000 miles, how many times could light travel around the earth in a second?" As the lesson progressed, a clock face was drawn on the board, and more than one response was encouraged when Ms. Q. indicated times using this clock: "1:15, what's another way of saying that?" All possible responses were solicited, but when a student volunteered, "A quarter after," Ms. Q. required an explanation. She asked students to justify their answers and complimented a student by saying, "An excellent way of figuring this out." She wrote in the post-lesson reflection:

> I was impressed with their knowledge on all levels of time. They really threw me with light-years. . . I changed gears and allowed 'research' to go

on to find out what it meant. As a result of discussion, they are able to tell time in many different ways. . . and they realize there are many different "correct" answers. That was what I was after. I feel they understand the concept much better.

Comparison of Ms. M. and Ms. Q. Ms. Q.'s model postintervention lesson showed a shift away from a procedural emphasis evident in her earlier lesson. She was open to various responses, but also still did not relinquish control of the chalkboard. Ms. Q. directed the lesson and questioning from the front of the room. She viewed herself as a person who should have the answers. When the "light-year" issue came up, she said, "It's been a while since I've done it. I'm showing my ignorance because I cannot pull that out from here (pointing to her head)." Ms. M. appeared to be more comfortable in relinquishing the authoritarian role and turned verification of answers over to the group. Ms. M. clearly indicated that this lesson was an assessment that would have an impact on instructional planning. Ms. Q. used a written assessment to determine the content for this particular lesson. Ms. M., on the other hand, appeared more willing to abandon the textbook. She wrote in her self-reflections:

> I really feel more confident in not teaching directly from the text. I do need the "security" of what to teach. So far I have pretested students out of two chapters, have determined the weak areas that need to be worked on. They have done very little pencil-and-paper math. As a final check on certain skills I have assigned a minimum number of problems from a math page. This blows their mind. Some of them still do the whole page because they can't believe they don't have to. I am now in the process of going through the next chapter trying to determine activities that can be developed to help those who do not yet have the skills.

Ms. Q. indicated that the pretest helped her determine students who would "do enrichment and peer tutor others." For the other students, the textbook still played a major role in determining content and sequence of instruction.

A major shift demonstrated by Ms. Q. was her interest in exploring several solution strategies after the intervention. This was illustrated both by the videotaped lesson and self-reported changes, where she emphasized the "process" and "digging much deeper in my questioning":

> Open discussion on ways to do fraction word problems. Some know, some add, some subtract and some divide—Amazing isn't it? Questioned more as to *how* they arrived at that answer (received some interesting answers in division problems and fraction problems).

The content involved in the intermediate grades did not appear to prevent these teachers from using children's thinking in planning, implementing, and assessing children in mathematics.

DISCUSSION

The major implication is that change reflective both of more cognitively based instruction and of the *Standards* (NCTM, 1989) can be achieved. The spring sessions, followed by the summer in-service and follow-up fall session, provided the knowledge and support to effect a change, not only in beliefs, but in practice. In this particular project, the principal of the school also played an influential role.

By participating in this project, Ms. K. outwardly communicated to her staff that what they were doing was important and that the information they were presented was necessary for her to know as well. Reflecting on her role during the intervention, she reported that she believed effective communication was instrumental to the success of the staff development project. Ms. K. discussed five areas she felt important to her role: (a) encouraging collaboration between the university and her school staff, (b) providing information to parents about the change process, (c) finding funds for materials for her staff, (d) encouraging collaboration among her teachers, and (e) recognizing faculty and student achievements. She believed recognition of successful efforts to be important and wrote articles for both the school newsletter and the town newspaper, which informed the public of her school's progress in mathematics education.

We found change among all the teachers in this project, but degree of change and the manner in which teachers changed varied. However, some common changes in instructional practices were apparent. All teachers modified the amount of time they spent explaining procedures, inquired more about how their students solved problems, and acquired a better appreciation for students' thinking.

None of our data indicated that teachers had difficulty with the content at their grade levels. We believe this is due in part to their years of experience teaching, their mathematics preparation, or both. As teachers explored and developed different teaching strategies, content was not a constraint. Inability to relinquish to their students some of the responsibility for learning proved a constraint for some of the teachers. This problem was particularly evident in Ms. Q.'s classroom.

For educators, changes in beliefs and practices are difficult to effect. As one teacher reflected following a lesson: "I also need to back off in some situations and let them have more time to find their own solutions and answers. I [was] always there with a helping hand, even when it was not required." The intervention project may provide an example of how teacher change develops when teachers are given access to a well-organized body of research and knowledge, are provided with opportunities to "construct" their ideas of effective instruction, and are given administrative and peer support. This type of change will ultimately empower teachers to make instructional decisions that positively change curriculum, students' mathematical dispositions, and school mathematics.

We believe the implications of this project are many. Teachers at Grades K–4 can modify their instructional practices to include a consideration of students' thinking. We are confident that in most classrooms what we observed on the videotapes reflected regular classroom routine. In these classrooms, children provided detailed explanations of their thought processes, reflected in our discussions of the first-grade classrooms. The learning environment we observed on tape, in which student explanations were developed, could not have occurred if problem solving were not done on an ongoing basis.

A limitation of the study is that the focus of the analysis was on whole-number operations, and other mathematics topics were not addressed. Further studies need to consider teacher change in the areas of geometry, fractions, and other K–4 topic areas, in addition to addressing the issue of change over a more extended period of time. Also, it would be interesting to know how, over time, these teachers adjust their theoretical perspectives in relation to the teaching and learning of mathematics. Will teachers make belief changes or merely assimilate the new information to which they have had access?

ACKNOWLEDGMENTS

The research reported in this chapter was funded by a grant from the State of Illinois Board of Higher Education under the Dwight D. Eisenhower Mathematics and Science Education Program. The opinions expressed do not necessarily reflect the views of this program.

The authors contributed equally to the work that produced this chapter.

REFERENCES

Ball, D. L. (1988). The mathematical understandings that prospective teachers bring to teacher education. *Elementary School Journal, 90*, 449–466.

Burns, M. (1985). The role of questioning. *Arithmetic Teacher, 32(6)*, 14–16.

Carpenter, T. P., Carey, D. A., & Kouba, V. (1990). A problem solving approach to the operations. In J. Payne (Ed.), *Mathematics for the young child* (pp. 111–131). Reston, VA: National Council of Teachers of Mathematics.

Carpenter, T. P., & Fennema, E. (1992). Cognitively guided instruction: Building on the knowledge of students and teachers. In W. Secada (Ed.), *Curriculum reform: The case of mathematics in the United States. Special Issue of International Journal of Educational Research* (pp. 457–470). Elmsford, NY: Pergamon.

Carpenter, T. P., Fennema, E., Peterson, P. L., Chiang, C. P., & Loef, M. (1989). Using knowledge of children's mathematics thinking in classroom teaching: An experimental study. *American Education Research Journal, 26* (4), 499–532.

Carpenter, T. P., & Moser, J. M. (1984). The acquisition of addition and subtraction concepts in grades one through three. *Journal for Research in Mathematics Education, 15* (3), 179–202.

Cohen, D. K. (1991). A revolution in one classroom: The case of Mrs. Oublier. *Educational Evaluation and Policy Analysis, 12* (3), 311–329.

Cooney, T. J. (1985). A beginning teacher's view of problem solving. *Journal for Research in Mathematics Education, 16,* 324–336.

Fennema, E., & Carpenter, T. P. (1988). *Cognitively guided instruction: A program implementation guide.* Madison, WI: Wisconsin Center for Education Research, University of Wisconsin-Madison.

Fennema, E., Carpenter, T. P., & Peterson, P. (1989). Teachers' decision making and cognitively guided instruction: A new paradigm for curriculum development. In N. F. Ellerton & M. A. (Ken) Clements (Eds.) *School mathematics: The challenge to change* (pp.174–187). Geelong, Victoria, Australia: Australian University Press.

Fuson, K. (1990). Conceptual structures for multi-unit numbers: Implications for learning and teaching multi-digit addition, subtraction and place value. *Cognition and Instruction, 7 (4),* 343.

Hiebert, J. (1989). The struggle to link written symbols with understandings: an update. *Arithmetic Teacher, 36,(7)* 38–44.

Kimmel, E. ((1985). *Hershel and the hanukkah goblins.* New York, NY: Scholastic.

Labinowicz, E. (1985). *Learning from children.* Menlo Park, CA: Addison-Wesley.

Loef, M. M., Carey, D. A., Carpenter, T. P., & Fennema, E. (1988). Research into practice: Integrating assessment and instruction. *Arithmetic Teacher, 36,* 53–55.

Mack, N. (1990). Learning fractions with understanding: Building on informal knowledge. *Journal for Research in Mathematics Education, 21* (1), 16–32.

National Council of Teachers of Mathematics. (1989). *Curriculum and evaluation standards for school mathematics.* Reston, VA: Author.

National Council of Teachers of Mathematics. (1991). *Professional standards for teaching mathematics.* Reston, VA: Author.

National Research Council. (1989). *Everybody counts: A report to the nation on the future of mathematics education.* Washington, DC: National Academy Press.

Peterson, P. L., Carpenter, T. P., & Fennema, E. (1989). Teachers' knowledge of students' knowledge in mathematics problem solving: Correlational and case analysis. *Journal of Educational Psychology, 81* (4), 558–569.

Peterson, P. L., Fennema, E., & Carpenter, T. P. (1991a). Teachers knowledge of students' mathematics problem-solving knowledge. In J. Brophy (Ed.), *Advances in research on teaching, Vol. 2* (pp. 49–86). Greenwich, CT: JAI.

Peterson, P. L., Fennema, E., & Carpenter, T. P. (1991b). Using children's mathematical knowledge. In B. Means (Ed.), *Teaching advanced skills to educationally disadvantaged students* (pp. 103–128). Menlo Park, CA: SRI International.

Schram, P., & Wilcox, S. K. (1988). Changing preservice teachers' conceptions of mathematics learning. In M.J. Behr, C. B. Lacampagne, & M. M. Wheeler (Eds.), *PME-NA: Proceedings of the tenth annual meeting* (pp. 349–355). DeKalb, IL: Northern University Press.

Skemp, R. R. (1978). Relational understanding and instrumental understanding. *Arithmetic Teacher, 26(3),* 9–15.

Thompson, A. (1984). The relationship of teachers' conceptions of mathematics teaching to instructional practice. *Educational Studies in Mathematics, 15 ,* 105–127.

Thompson, A. (1992). Teachers' beliefs and conceptions: A synthesis of the research. In D. A. Grouws (Ed.), *Handbook of research on mathematics teaching and learning* (pp. 127–146). New York: Macmillian.

APPENDIX

Outline of Spring Sessions Intervention

1. During this session, a belief survey was administered to collect baseline data. Dr. L. led a discussion on recommendations from research on children's thinking in various topic areas, but specifically addition/subtraction, multiplication/division, place value, and fractions (including decimals). A focus was placed on addition/subtraction problem types and solution strategies. Videotape from the CGI project: *The Knowledge Tape.* The teachers were asked to read chapters 1–3 (Fennema & Carpenter, 1988).

2. The teachers were asked to determine how to make better instructional decisions about the types of problems in their mathematics textbooks. Using a variety of problem types and encouraging different solution strategies was discussed. A discussion concerning assessment of students' strategies involving addition/subtraction was the focus of this session. Unifix cubes and their use in developing understanding was discussed. Videotape: *CGI Problem Types / Solution Strategies.* The teachers were asked to read about questioning techniques used in assessment from Burns (1985), Skemp (1978), and Loef, Carey, Carpenter, & Fennema (1988).

3. Dr. L. presented information about multiplication/division problem types and strategies used by children for solving these. The teachers were asked to assess their textbooks involving these problem types and strategies. Small group discussions by grade levels on instructional decisions involving multiplication/division were the focus of this session. Videotape: Problem types related to multiplication and division. A reading by Carpenter, Carey, & Kouba (1980) was assigned.

4. Dr. L. presented information about place value as related to children's understandings. The focus of this seminar was on alternative algorithms for place value and children's representations of their thinking processes. The manipulative base 10 blocks were used for demonstration purposes. Articles by Fuson (1990) and Hiebert (1989) were assigned.

5. Dr. L. presented information on how children think about solving problems involving fractions (Mack,1990) and decimals. The focus of this seminar was on the use of the manipulatives, fraction pieces, and

decimal squares, to facilitate understanding when using students' thinking to make instructional decisions. Videotape: *CGI Multidigit numbers*.

6. The final spring session involved a summary of the research presented and a planning session for teachers for the summer in-service. Videotape: Nancy Mack Interview.

Outline of Summer In-service Intervention: August

The daily format of the session was a one-hour presentation by Dr. L., two hours of small group work (by grade level), and two hours of individual teacher planning time monitored by Dr. L. and Ms. K. The outcome for each teacher was a unit of study and a restructuring of the sequence of instruction for her school year. Videotapes from CGI were selected to be viewed as they related to the teachers' needs. The focus of these tapes was on children's solution strategies.

Day One: Long-range planning.

The teachers collaborated on a year-long plan with their grade level colleagues. The plan reflected their knowledge of students' thinking and used information from readings in order to make instructional decisions about sequencing topics of study.

The teachers refined their plans individually by using additional sources to support their needs: *Arithmetic Teacher* articles, manipulatives, articles provided by Dr. L. as needed.

Assignment: readings from Labinowicz (1985) in preparation for the next topic.

Day Two: Assessment alternatives

The teachers discussed assessment alternatives by grade level, selected a topic, and created an alternative to the assessment to which they currently had access. Assessment measures were shared with the large group. Readings from the *Curriculum and Evaluation Standards* (NCTM, 1989) were used.

Day Three: Short-term planning:

Units of study integrating mathematics with other areas, especially science and language arts were chosen by the teachers to be developed. Teachers at each grade level did not replicate topics. Integration with other topics within the curriculum was encouraged.

Day Four: The Standards revisited

Teachers planned, both in small groups by grade level and individually, tasks that were appropriate for use with their units of study. Examples from the *Professional Standards for Teaching Mathematics* (NCTM, 1991) were used.

Day Five: Planning for the fall

The teachers shared their units of study with their grade level colleagues and discussed their implementation plans for fall. Units were collected and bound by grade level. Using information they received from seminars, the teachers placed orders for the manipulative materials needed for their learning environments. $500 of manipulative materials were ordered for the library.

Video Lesson Plan Form

Name_____   Date_____
Grade_____

You may want to attach another sheet with your responses to these questions.

1. What is the purpose (objective) of today's lesson?
2. What is the content of your lesson today?
3. What influenced your decision to teach this content?
4. What grouping organization will you use and why?
5. Briefly, what activities have you planned?
6. What influenced the choice of activities?
7. What material are you using today and why?
8. Have you considered any alternatives to implement during instruction, should your lesson not proceed as planned?
9. Did you consider anything about what your students know while planning? Please discuss.

Videotape Assessment Form

Name_____   Lesson Topic_____
Grade_____   Date_____

Please complete the Video Lesson Plan and then videotape yourself teaching one mathematics lesson.

AFTER taping please do the following:

1. View the lesson as soon as possible after taping the lesson. (The same day is recommended.) Then select three critical segments on which to focus. A critical segment is defined as a part of the lesson that focuses on the development of concepts.
2. After identifying the critical segments, view the tape again and focus on the following questions:
   a) What were you thinking during this incident and why? For example: Why are you asking those questions? Using that worksheet? Focusing on those numbers?
   b) What were you noticing about the students? For example: What makes you think they can solve that problem? Complete that worksheet? Answer those questions? Why did you call on that student?
   c) During and after instruction, how are you going to use the information you obtained from the student responses you received during the lesson?
   d) Did you consider any alternative activities (actions) during this part of the lesson? Did any student response cause you to act differently than you had planned?

For the lesson in general:

   a) What caused you to make decisions about changing activities?
   b) If drill or skill lessons were involved in this lesson, discuss why (i.e., What was the purpose of their inclusion).

Write a short lesson summary that contains the responses to the above questions.

10

Teachers Creating Change: Examining Evolving Beliefs and Classroom Practice

Megan Loef Franke
University of California, Los Angeles

Elizabeth Fennema
Thomas Carpenter
University of Wisconsin, Madison

Teachers across the country are being asked to transform their mathematics teaching. This transformation entails more than posing different problems, asking different questions, or calling on different students; it demands that teachers make changes in their basic epistemological perspectives, their knowledge of what it means to understand and thus learn mathematics, and their classroom practice (see Cobb, Wood, Yackel, & McNeal, 1993; Schifter & Fosnot, 1993, for elaboration of teaching for understanding). For the past 10 years, we have worked with teachers attempting to transform their mathematics teaching. We have watched, listened, questioned, and reflected on the ways in which the teachers have changed. In this chapter, we outline what we have learned about teachers transforming their mathematics teaching. Specifically, we discuss the patterns of changes in beliefs and classroom practice that we have seen as teachers engaged with knowledge of childrens mathematical thinking. We then discuss the role of practical inquiry in the changes of these teachers.

Acknowledging that over time teachers change in quite different ways, researchers have begun to document change by examining the relationships between teachers' changing thoughts and actions. Researchers agree that changes in beliefs, knowledge, and practice do not occur in isolation from one another (Fennema, Carpenter, Franke, & Carey, 1992; Hunsaker & Johnston, 1992; Schifter & Fosnot, 1993;

Wood, Cobb, & Yackel, 1991). Researchers do, however, take different perspectives on how beliefs, knowledge, and classroom practice are related in the process of change.

Two different perspectives dominate research on teacher change patterns. One perspective is drawn from the work on teacher thinking and decision making (Clark & Peterson, 1986; Pajares, 1992; Putnam, Lampert, & Peterson, 1990; Shulman, 1986; Thompson, 1992). This research is based on the assumption that what an individual thinks influences what that individual does. This implies that if we influence teachers' beliefs and knowledge, we influence their practice. An alternative perspective was put forth by Guskey (1986), who suggested that, as teachers engage in given practices, they will see and hear things that have an impact on their beliefs.

Each of these perspectives seems plausible, and different researchers have found evidence to support each contention. However, many of the current reform efforts ask teachers to make changes that extend beyond the implementation of behaviors that can be modeled or beliefs that are easy to instantiate. Neither of these perspectives fully explains what happens when teachers attempt self-generated, self-sustaining changes in how they teach mathematics.

In this chapter we describe Cognitively Guided Instruction, a project that engaged teachers in changing their mathematical beliefs and classroom practices. We outline the ways we measured teacher change, the patterns of change that occurred over a 4-year period, and a way of thinking about patterns of change that leads to self-generated, self-sustaining change.

BACKGROUND

We are only beginning to understand what teachers take from their learning opportunities and how that influences a teacher's changing beliefs, knowledge, and classroom practice (Grant, Peterson, & Shojgreen-Downer, 1994; Schifter & Fosnot, 1993; Simon & Schifter, 1991; Tharp & Gallimore, 1988; Wood, Cobb, & Yackel, 1991). Case studies are the most prevalent form of teacher change research. Examination across these studies shows little consistency in terms of whether teachers initially change their beliefs, knowledge, or practice, or in how those changes evolve. Although some studies find that Guskey's perspective (that classroom practice changes first) fits with their findings (Grant, Peterson, & Shojgreen-Downer, 1994; Tharp & Gallimore, 1988), other studies appear to question Guskey's perspective. Richardson, Anders, Tidwell, and Lloyd (1991), in examining the relationship between beliefs and classroom practice, found that some teachers' belief changes preceded changes in practice.

Although the data are varied, studies of individual teacher change have laid the groundwork for attempting to understand what groups of teachers learn and how they develop within a given approach to teacher change. To understand teacher change across teachers, it has become necessary to develop ways to capture and systematically identify what teachers learn from their experiences and how that learning evolves over time. Simon and Schifter (1991), in attempting to understand teachers involved in the Summer Math for Teachers project, used the Levels of Use (LoU) instrument developed by Hall and his colleagues (Hall, Loucks, Rutherford, & Newlove, 1975), as well as an adaptation of that instrument to assess instruction based on a constructivist epistemology. Simon and Schifter (1991) collected interview data to be used as the basis for placement of teachers into levels. Use of these levels allowed the authors to learn that the teachers generally changed more in implementation of a particular strategy than in their views about learning, as enacted in instruction (Schifter & Fosnot, 1993).

Tharp and Gallimore (1988) proposed a way of examining teacher change across teachers. Tharp and Gallimore based their understanding of teacher change on the work of Vygotsky. The basis of their perspective is that learning occurs when assisted performance is provided to the learner within the learner's zone of proximal development. Tharp and Gallimore applied these theories of how learning occurs to the learning of teachers. They proposed a sequence of teacher change stages. There are four stages in this sequence that focus on the regulation of behavior. In Tharp and Gallimore's framework, teachers may change either in their thoughts or in their actions at each stage. However, thoughts and action are not explicitly distinguished at each stage. Although the focus in this work is on the evolution of a new cognitive structure for the teacher, depending on the scaffolding provided, teachers may be led to initially change either their practice or their thinking. Interestingly, the "more capable others" determine the path of change for a teacher.

Cobb, Wood, and Yackel (1990; Cobb, Yackel, & Wood, 1992; Wood, Cobb, & Yackel, 1991) proposed a dialectical approach for thinking about how teachers change. They discussed the critical nature of teachers interactions in the classroom environment. "The project teacher, in creating a setting that focused on the mathematical activity of her students, encountered major contradictions with her prior traditional practice. It was during these periods of conflict, followed by reflection and resolution, that opportunities for her to learn occurred" (Wood, Cobb, & Yackel, 1991, p. 610). The focus for Cobb, Wood, and Yackel was on conflict that occurred between the teachers existing beliefs and new classroom practices, the teachers existing beliefs and evolving beliefs, or between the teachers existing practices and the new practices of the project. Cobb and his colleagues reported that the collaboration of the teacher with the research team was crucial for teacher change, in that the teacher and the researchers continually worked on constructing shared meanings of the teacher's role and the children's role in the classroom.

In Cognitively Guided Instruction (CGI) we have struggled, and continue to struggle, with describing the details of teacher change. Our goal has been to understand the nuances that occur in teachers' changing beliefs, knowledge, and practice in ways that will enable us to understand patterns of change. We have tried to look beyond the implementation of a particular set of ideas and understand the principles underlying the specific changes being made. As we examine change, we focus on the relationships between the teachers' thoughts and actions as they attempt to build understanding of (a) their students' thinking, (b) the mathematics, and (c) teaching. We view the teachers as coming to each situation with existing knowledge, beliefs, and practices. These individual conditions drive what the teachers notice—in their classrooms, with their students, in workshops, and in discussions with other teachers—as opportunities for reflection and action in transforming their mathematics teaching.

COGNITIVELY GUIDED INSTRUCTION

Cognitively Guided Instruction is both easy and difficult to describe. It is easy in that we can explicitly put forth the knowledge about children's thinking that we share with teachers, and we can describe in detail the forms through which the knowledge is shared. It is difficult to describe because the power of the knowledge is in how the teachers come to make sense of it, use it, and build on it. So the explicit knowledge we share with teachers is critical, but it is not static, isolated, or narrowing. It is not just that we share with teachers robust knowledge about children's developing thinking in a range of content areas; it is the fact that this knowledge fits together in frameworks that teachers come to make sense of and make their own. The teachers talk about CGI as a philosophy, a way of thinking about the teaching and learning of mathematics, not as a recipe, a prescription, or a limited set of knowledge. Yet, these global terms do not capture the complexity of CGI. Teachers engaged with CGI take the knowledge of children's thinking that is shared and make sense of it in light of their other knowledge, they continually build on the knowledge, they figure out how to make use of it in the context of their on-going practice, and every day they seem to learn more and adjust their existing frameworks. Our goal is to provide teachers with knowledge, derived from research, about the development of children's mathematical thinking and to let the teachers decide how to make use of that knowledge in the context of their own teaching practice. So, although it fails to capture what CGI is about, understanding the knowledge that we share with teachers and how it fits into organized frameworks is critical to understanding CGI.

In Cognitively Guided Instruction, we help teachers understand childrens mathematical thinking by helping them understand the development of children's thinking in well-defined content domains (Carpenter, 1985; Carpenter & Fennema, 1992; Carpenter, Fennema, & Franke, in press; Carpenter, Fennema, Peterson, Chiang, & Loef, 1989; Fennema, Carpenter, Franke, Levi, Jacobs, & Empson, 1996). Constructing models of children's thinking entails focusing on organized, principled knowledge about problems, including what might make one problem more or less difficult than another. This leads to a connection between the problems and the strategies that children use to solve them. The strategies discussed with the teachers are related to one another in principled ways. The strategies build within problems, in terms of mathematical sophistication, and classes of strategies exist across problems. For instance, for the grouping problem, Tessa has six boxes of crayons. Each box contains five crayons. How many crayons does Tessa have? a child can solve the problem by physically representing the six boxes and the five crayons in each box and counting the total number of crayons represented (direct modeling). Or a child may count by 5 (5, 10, 15, 20, 25, 30), keeping track of the six boxes on his or her fingers. This second strategy builds on the first and fits into a broader principled scheme about how strategies develop in terms of mathematical sophistication. The strategies can be discussed in detail in terms of what the strategy would look like for a given problem or more generally in terms of how the strategy would be applied in solving a wide range of problems. For example, the direct modeling strategy can be described specifically in relation to a given problem, as in the case of the first strategy described in the crayon problem, or in terms of how direct modeling is used to solve a variety of problems, including problems involving all four operations, place value, or fractions.

Knowledge of the problem types in each domain allows the teachers to understand the breadth and depth of the domain. Knowing the possible range of strategies for each problem helps teachers understand what makes problems more or less difficult for children. The frameworks of children's mathematical thinking (a) link problem types and strategies, (b) characterize the ways in which problems lend themselves to particular strategies, and (c) focus attention on how strategies can and cannot be generalized across problem types. The principled ideas underlying problems and strategies allow teachers to interpret the mathematical understanding of the children in their own classrooms (Carpenter, Fennema, & Franke, in press). For instance, teachers do not often think about posing a problem like the following:

Keisha had some markers. Her grandmother went shopping and bought Keisha 6 more markers. When Keisha counted all of the markers she now had, she found that she had 14 markers. How many markers did Keisha have before her grandmother gave her the new ones?

Knowing that direct modeling is the least sophisticated strategy a child can use to solve many addition and subtraction problem correctly enables a teacher to see that this particular problem may be difficult because it is not easy to direct model. Children who typically direct model will not know how many counters to put in their initial set and thus may not know how to get started. To direct model, a child would need to begin by putting out some counters (a number of counters the child thinks represents the "some" in the problem), add six to that set, and count to see if there were now 14 counters altogether. If not, the child would need to adjust the initial set and begin the process again. Understanding the relationship between an initial unknown quantity and the direct modeling strategy allows the teacher to think beyond this particular problem and think about what can make problems difficult for children to solve and why. As teachers listen to their students' thinking, they learn more about possible problems to pose, strategies to expect, and relationships that exist between problems and strategies. This new knowledge is connected with their existing knowledge, and the teachers continue to elaborate and build their frameworks. Teachers in this project interacted with knowledge about children's thinking in the domains of addition and subtraction, multiplication and division, place value, fractions, and geometry.

Frameworks

The power of the knowledge of children's thinking comes from the dynamic nature of the frameworks that teachers create. The frameworks are more than lists of problems to pose and their corresponding strategies; the frameworks are evolving structures. They can be thought of as scientific concepts, as defined by Vygotsky (1962), that provide a basis for interpreting, transforming, and reframing the teachers' informal or spontaneous knowledge about the mathematical content and children's mathematical thinking. There is no expectation that the frameworks for each teacher look the same following CGI workshops, or evolve in the same ways; we know that they do not (Loef, 1990). The teachers develop their problem/strategy frameworks based on the development of children's mathematical thinking, and adjust, build, and expand them based on the knowledge they gain as they interact with their students and the mathematics.

These frameworks have proven to be powerful in terms of (a) providing the basis for our interactions with teachers, (b) helping teachers transform their knowledge, beliefs, and classroom practice, and (c) providing a framework to measure teacher change. The power comes both from the focus the framework provides to our decision making and from the match between the changes occurring and the changes being measured. The frameworks of children's mathematical thinking form the basis for our workshops, our interactions with the teachers, and our assessment of the teachers' beliefs, knowledge, and classroom practices. The frameworks also drive our decision making about what questions to ask teachers, what to focus on in the classroom context, and how to characterize change. The frameworks the teachers develop, based on the frameworks of children's thinking, provide the basis for the teachers' thoughts and actions related to the teaching of mathematics. This perspective may be construed by some as narrow; however, we feel power comes from articulating what we have done in engaging with teachers, describing how we have come to understand the teachers (so that others can interpret and understand our work), and from learning all that we can, in as many ways as we can, specifically about how teachers use children's mathematical thinking.

Our focus on frameworks of children's mathematical thinking provides opportunities for teachers to change either in beliefs or in classroom practice. In some cases, teachers' beliefs might be challenged by what they hear about the types of problems that children can solve and the strategies they will use to solve them. In other cases, teachers might pose problems based on the frameworks (with some expectation of the strategies the children might use) without necessarily changing their beliefs about the teaching and learning of mathematics.

Teacher Development

The teachers in the CGI project had the opportunity to participate in a series of workshop sessions focusing on understanding children's mathematical thinking. The underlying goal of each workshop was to help the teachers understand children's mathematical thinking, often through the examination of their own students' thinking. The sessions did not explicitly provide a way to make use of the knowledge of children's mathematical thinking; however, the teachers were given the opportunity to discuss with their colleagues and the CGI staff their own ideas for classroom practice (for a more complete description of the workshops, see Fennema et al., 1996).

The other sources of teacher support included a graduate assistant assigned to each school, a mentor teacher in each school, and teachers in the same grade and school working with CGI. The focus of both the graduate assistant and the mentor teacher was on helping teachers understand children's mathematical thinking in the context of their classrooms. The explicit type of support varied, depending on the mentor and the teacher. Examples of what occurred included observing in the teacher's classroom and discussing with the teacher afterwards what was noticed about the children's thinking, planning lessons together, and assessing children together. Teachers provided this support for each other as well, acting as sounding boards for each other as they thought about how to use their knowledge of children's thinking in their classroom practice. (These support roles are described in detail in Fennema, Carpenter, Franke, Levi, Jacobs, & Empson, 1996.)

UNDERSTANDING AND DOCUMENTING
THE PROCESS OF TEACHER CHANGE

We wanted to document teacher change across teachers engaged in CGI. We were interested in understanding potential patterns of change. To accomplish this, we developed a way of documenting change that could be systematically applied across teachers by different observers and coders. What follows is the description of our documentation of teacher change within CGI. We begin with a description of the areas of change we examined and how we have defined them within CGI. We then discuss how we have used the definitions of the areas to document change over time.

Areas of Teacher Change

The areas of teacher change examined include teachers' beliefs, knowledge, and classroom practice. Our characterizations of beliefs, knowledge, and practice derive from theoretical and research perspectives in the field, along with the theoretical basis of CGI and our observations of CGI teachers over a period of 6 years (Carpenter & Fennema, 1992).

Teacher Beliefs. A major premise of CGI is that the purpose of instruction is to build on children's mathematical thinking in a way that enhances understanding. In thinking about this premise, it becomes clear that to carry out instruction with this goal, certain beliefs about the teaching and learning of mathematics must exist. First, teachers must believe that children come to any situation with some knowledge of mathematics and that acquisition of this knowledge occurs through the interaction of the student with a problem-solving (broadly defined) environment. Thus, students can solve mathematical problems without direct instruction from the teacher. Problem solving is seen as the focus of instruction; skills and understanding are seen as interrelated.

The second belief, which follows from the initial premise, encompasses the teachers' beliefs that what they learn from listening to their students should inform their instructional decision making. Children's thinking, specifically the thinking of children in the teacher's class, should drive instruction.

In order to reliably code teachers' beliefs, we separated stated beliefs from beliefs in practice. When we talk about teachers' beliefs here, we mean beliefs explicitly stated by the teacher, either in the context of teaching or in the interviews. Beliefs in practice are incorporated in the classroom practice category.

Classroom Practice.   Our characterization of classroom practice includes three dimensions revolving around the teacher's creation of the classroom environment: (a) providing opportunities for children to solve mathematical problems in their own ways, (b) listening to children's mathematical thinking, and (c) using children's mathematical thinking in making instructional decisions.

The first dimension documents the extent to which the teacher provided opportunities for students to engage in mathematical thinking. These opportunities refer to situations in which children made use of their existing mathematical knowledge, talked about their thinking, and listened to other students' ideas. For CGI teachers, providing opportunities typically consisted of posing mathematics word problems. The extent to which these opportunities were provided is considered along with how these opportunities were adapted for individual children: Were the same opportunities provided for all children or were opportunities adapted to fit the needs of individuals in the class?

The second dimension follows from the first and involves the extent to which teachers listened to their children's thinking, looking specifically at whether the teacher asked the students for their mathematical thinking and whether the teacher provided the time and opportunity for the child to respond without interference. In CGI classrooms, asking children about their thinking is the first step in listening. Often, teachers want to move the lesson along and tell the child a better strategy, rather than listen actively to their students' thinking.

The third dimension of classroom practice builds on both providing opportunities for solving problems and on listening to children's thinking. This dimension involves the teachers' use of their students mathematical thinking. Evidence of teachers' use of children's mathematical thinking is seen in the decisions teachers made both during classroom instruction and between class sessions. During classroom practice, teachers can make use of children's thinking when interacting with an individual child and making changes in the problem posed or asking questions about the strategy the child used. Across class sessions, teachers can be seen to make decisions about the types of problems to pose next, the number sizes they will use, and the follow-up questions they might ask.

Teacher Knowledge.   In this chapter, we focus on the knowledge of children's thinking about the whole number domains of addition, subtraction, multiplication, division, and place value. We wanted to document, not whether teachers could identify the problem types and strategies within each domain, but rather their ability to make use of the knowledge. In our earlier work we found that teachers, before any introduction to CGI, possessed a great deal of knowledge about differences among problems and the strategies children use to solve them (Carpenter, Fennema, Peterson, & Carey, 1988). However, the teachers did not have a framework for connecting and integrating this knowledge. So, we wanted to document the teachers' knowledge in action. What knowledge of children's thinking did teachers exhibit when teaching or talking about their teaching?

Although useful from a conceptual point of view, examining knowledge in action has some practical limitations. We are only able to draw information from occurrences in the context of teaching or talking about teaching. However, because a teacher does not mention or observably use particular knowledge does not mean that the teacher does not possess it. So rather than looking at knowledge separately—which would be somewhat inconsistent with what we wanted to know—or creating a new category of knowledge in practice, we decided to include knowledge as a part of beliefs and classroom practice. We realized that inferences about a teacher's knowledge of children's thinking could be drawn from observing the problems posed, the strategies elicited, and the connections drawn across strategies as well as from listening to the teachers talking about the problems they posed, the strategies they expected, and the information they acquired about individual children. Thus, for the purposes of this work, teacher knowledge is captured and discussed as a part of the beliefs and classroom practice measures.

LEVELS OF TEACHER CHANGE

In an attempt to systematically characterize and document the process of teacher change, we identified levels that encompass information about a teacher's beliefs, knowledge, and use of children's thinking in classroom practice. The intent of these levels is to provide a mechanism for making decisions across teachers and across coders about teacher change. The levels reported here characterize the development of CGI teachers.

The levels evolved as we attempted to understand the process of teacher change. Initially, we listed teacher actions, teacher–student interaction patterns, and rationales for why teachers did what they did, and attempted to count them. We counted, refined our categories, counted, and refined. However, through this process we ran into difficulties in interpretation due to differences in the context in which the thought or action occurred. So, rather than focus on the number of instances of particular statements or behaviors of teachers, we attempted to explicate emerging patterns. As a group, those involved with the CGI project for several years reflected on what would it mean for teachers' knowledge or beliefs or practice to change within CGI. We reflected on the work of others in the field and focused on what change would look like within the parameters of CGI. We thought about what the teachers and their students had shown us about change in the past. We made hypotheses about which characteristics of change we could accurately capture and thought about how best to capture them. We then tested our hypothesis to see not only if the characteristics could be captured, but also if, taken together, the different characteristics provided a complete picture of ongoing teacher change for a CGI teacher.

Through this process we created our first set of levels, markers of change that included aspects of teacher beliefs, knowledge, and practice. We attempted to code one teacher's observations and interviews at one point in time to see if the levels were explicit enough to characterize a teacher. We discussed our coding and revised the levels. This process continued for over a year. The levels reported here represent our current thoughts on what becoming a CGI teacher entails.

There are four general levels, each level building on the previous one, with the fourth level being partitioned into sublevels. The levels include decision points about teachers' beliefs and about their classroom practice. Our goal is to portray the process of change as continuous so that we have snapshots at different points in time that we can then closely align with a particular level. Each level provides a picture of a teacher's thinking and implementation of CGI; however, not each teacher fits best with any particular level, nor do teachers necessarily progress systematically through each level. Teachers may, for instance, have beliefs consistent with one level on the continuum but practice consistent with the preceding level. Some teachers skip a level or go back a level before moving on.

Level 1

The beliefs and classroom practice of teachers at Level 1 are not consistent with the premises of CGI. A teacher at this level who was asked about his or her children's mathematical thinking would respond by talking about the procedures that the children had been taught to use in solving problems.

Beliefs. A teacher at Level 1 does not believe that the students in his or her classroom can solve problems unless they have been taught how. This translates to the expectation that all children will solve problems in similar ways—the ways in which they have been taught. Level 1 teachers make little use of the knowledge that they have of their own students, but rather look outside of themselves for expert help in deciding what to teach and when to teach it.

Classroom Practice.   A teacher at Level 1 would not provide opportunities for children to solve word problems using their own strategies, or ask the children how they solved problems. Typically teachers at this level show their students procedures they would like them to use when solving a given problem. The teachers question the students to see if they can reproduce the procedure. Reproduction of the procedure becomes almost synonymous with understanding how to solve the problems. Asking students to show their work and providing an opportunity for the children to practice are Level 1 teachers attempts to understand and build children's mathematical thinking. Teachers at this level do not use children's mathematical thinking (except in the case of use and application of a particular procedure) in making instructional decisions.

Level 2

At Level 2, a shift occurs as the teachers begin to view children as bringing mathematical knowledge to learning situations. These teachers begin to see that children can solve problems in a variety of ways, and the teachers feel that each solution has value in relation to the children's developing understanding.

Beliefs.   Teachers begin to believe that children can solve problems without being explicitly taught a strategy. They begin to talk about the value of a variety of solutions and expand the types of problems they use in addressing the domain. However, teachers at this level are still not convinced that they do not have to show children how to solve problems. Level 2 teachers make statements about the conditions under which they would find it necessary to tell a strategy to a child. For example, a Level 2 teacher may say that she will give the children until December to solve problems in their own ways, but then she must show the children how to solve the problem. Or a Level 2 teacher may comment that a given child is not a good math student, so the child must be shown how to solve the problems.

Classroom Practice.   Level 2 teachers provide some opportunities for children to solve problems in their own ways and at times ask the children how they solved the problems. However, they do not do this consistently. Although at times teachers find that it is relevant to elicit the children's thinking, at other times the teachers walk the children through a procedure that they expect each child to use for a given problem. When teachers at Level 2 do elicit, the purpose is to give the children a chance to share, not necessarily to create an opportunity to understand the child's thinking. For example, teachers may interrupt children before they finish sharing their strategies or probe children in a manner inconsistent with what had been said.

Level 3

Teachers at Level 3 generally see that children can solve a variety of problems and recognize that the childrens solutions to those problems differ based on the structure of the problem. The teachers see that part of teaching mathematics is to foster the development of different strategies through posing problems that differ in structure, context, and number choice.

Beliefs. The teacher at Level 3 believes that children can solve problems without having a strategy provided for them. They find very few exceptions to this belief. They believe that different children will attempt to solve a given problem in different ways, and that different problems will elicit different strategies. They believe that it is beneficial for the children to solve problems in their own ways because their own ways make more sense to them, and the teachers want the children to understand what they are doing. Level 3 teachers are beginning to make statements referring to the idea that what they hear from the students should have an impact on what they do in the classroom.

Classroom practice. Level 3 teachers have seen their students respond to problems in a variety of ways and see how the solutions differ, given the problem type posed. The teachers provide a variety of different problems for children to solve and provide an opportunity for the children to discuss their solutions. The teachers listen to the children talk about their thinking. The teachers, in a variety of different classroom contexts, usually pose a problem, ask a child to solve the problem, and then ask if anyone has solved the problem in a different way. This routine continues across class days, yet the teacher does not often adjust the problem choices or the questions posed, given what is heard. Level 3 teachers know enough to listen, they know what questions to ask to solicit children's thinking, and they know when to stop asking questions, but they do not always understand the subtleties or implications of what the child says. Typically, issues other than children's thinking drive the selection of problems and activities (e.g. the teacher wants to do a unit on dinosaurs, and particular problems fit best with that unit).

Level 4

At Level 4, the teachers begin to make use of knowledge they have gained about their students' mathematical thinking. Teachers at Level 4 possess knowledge about children's thinking as well as knowledge about their own students. We divided Level 4 into 2 sublevels, 4A and 4B. These levels are differentiated because we find teachers differ significantly in their knowledge of their students and their ability to put this knowledge into practice.

Level 4A

Teachers at Level 4A believe that children should drive many of their instructional decisions. They feel that children should be allowed the opportunity to build their own mathematical understanding and that the teacher's role is to create an environment in which this can occur. The teachers believe that children's mathematical thinking should determine the evolution of the curriculum and the ways in which the teachers individually interact with the students. Although these beliefs are salient for Level 4A teachers, the teachers are not always consistent.

Beliefs. Teachers at this level not only believe that children can solve problems without explicit instruction, they also believe that what they learn about their children's mathematical thinking can help them make instructional decisions. Teachers at Level 4A feel that it is their responsibility to find out and understand their children's mathematical thinking. They know that understanding their students' thinking and what it means in terms of understanding the mathematics is critical in enabling them to make instructional decisions. However, at times, teachers other beliefs about the affect of the children, the pressures of the next grade or the lack of knowledge about the children's thinking takes precedence and impacts decision making.

Classroom Practice. Teachers at this level use information about children's thinking to consider how children as a group are thinking about mathematics. For instance, the teacher may decide that she or he will pose a particular type of problem because some of the children are having difficulty with it, or because it is the next problem in terms of difficulty. This use of information about children's thinking is also seen in the teachers' interactions with individual children. The teacher might give responses or ask questions that are the same regardless of the knowledge of the student. They might ask a struggling child to show them with the cubes instead of trying to see where that particular child is having trouble and building from there. The key here is that the teacher does not necessarily or consistently base practice on knowledge of children's thinking.

Level 4B

Level 4B teachers consistently talk about individual children. When they talk about individual children, they include a discussion of the child's mathematical thinking. These teachers know how what an individual child knows fits in with how children's mathematical understanding develops. These teachers have developed ways to create opportunities to build on their children's mathematical thinking and ways for the children to build on their own thinking.

Beliefs.   Teachers at Level 4B believe that they can and should use what they learn about their students' mathematical thinking to drive their instruction. They believe that knowing the individual children is of utmost importance. Level 4B teachers interviews and discussions of their classroom are filled with descriptions and discussions of individual children and how what they have heard from an individual child on a given day fits not only with what they know about that child but also with what they know about the development of children's mathematical knowledge.

Classroom practice.   We see teachers at Level 4B make use of what they know about individual children in designing the curriculum and in interacting with individual children. Teachers at Level 4B think about individuals. This does not mean that all of the decisions that a teacher makes in the classroom are based on the mathematical understanding of individual children; rather, these teachers have specific knowledge of their children that they can use when they want to base their decision on children's mathematical thinking, whether it be in the context of an individual interaction, an interaction with the group, or a plan for how to proceed. In interacting with students, a teacher at this level might not always pose a problem or ask a question that looks as if it will clearly build on the child's mathematical understanding (often the teachers pose more open-ended problems, appropriate for a variety of understanding levels), but the teachers at this level do consistently make use of what they know about the individual students throughout the interaction, and thus do not do things considered counter to the child's mathematical understanding.

LONGITUDINAL NATURE OF CHANGE

We used the CGI Levels to examine the change of 21 teachers over a 4-year period of time. We attempted to understand change both within and across teachers. We wanted to see if teachers changed, the degree to which they changed, and how changes in beliefs and practice were related. Specifically, we investigated whether the teachers' beliefs and classroom practices changed at the same time and to the same degree, or if teachers changed their practices first and then changed their beliefs.

Teacher Changes

We found that the teachers changed both beliefs and classroom practice. Ninety percent of the teachers became more cognitively guided and were categorized at a Level 3 or higher (see Fennema et al., 1996). Eighteen of the 21 teachers came to believe more strongly that children would solve problems without being consistently shown procedures for solving them, and that they could enable children to learn mathematics by thinking about what the children knew and choosing problems and answering questions accordingly. Although there was variability in the classes, 18 teachers changed their classroom practices. For each of these teachers, there was an increased emphasis on problem solving, more communication from the children about their mathematical thinking, and evidence that the teacher was more often using her students' thinking when making instructional decisions.

Examining teacher change for the group of teachers, we found that, at the end of the project, 6 teachers had beliefs at Level 3, 11 teachers beliefs were above Level 3, and 4 had beliefs below Level 3. In examining the same pattern for classroom practice, we found that at the end of the project, 12 of the teachers engaged in classroom practices characteristic of Level 3, 7 teachers ended above Level 3, and 2 ended below Level 3.

Change in Relation to Initial Conceptions. A somewhat startling finding related to teachers' changing beliefs and classroom practice was that the teachers' initial beliefs and classroom practice had little direct relationship with when, how much, or in what ways they changed. Teachers beginning the project with beliefs and practice more consistent with CGI did not change more quickly, nor did they make greater changes throughout the study than teachers who started at Level 1 (Fennema et al., 1996). A number of teachers with initial beliefs and practice inconsistent with those of CGI changed across more than one level in beliefs or practice in the first year of the study. Although some of the teachers, who made the less dramatic changes, were teachers who began with beliefs and practice consistent with CGI, the teachers initial beliefs and practice did not seem to influence whether teachers changed beliefs before practice, practice before beliefs, or changed in beliefs and practice concurrently.

Patterns of Change

The patterns of teacher change that emerged in the evolution of beliefs and classroom practice reflected all possible sequences. In examining the relationship between beliefs and practice for the 17 teachers who changed in both beliefs and practice across the four years of the project, we found 6 teachers' beliefs changed before their practices changed, 5 teachers' practice changed before their beliefs, and 6 teachers changed beliefs and practice concurrently. Some teachers were not convinced by readings, videos, and discussions of children's thinking in the workshops, but they were willing to adopt some of the practices discussed in the workshops. These teachers seemed to need to prove to themselves that all children, their students' in particular, could solve problems in a variety of ways not explicitly set forth by the teacher; they did this by trying out the problem types with their own students. These teachers were compelled, then, by what they heard from their students as they solved these problems, especially because what they heard fit with what they expected based on the frameworks of childrens thinking. Other teachers were convinced by the readings, videos, and group discussions that their students were coming to their classrooms with a great deal of mathematical knowledge. These teachers then worked on putting their beliefs into practice. Other teachers seemed to work through issues of practice and beliefs more or less simultaneously.

Closer examination of the patterns elaborates the developing relationship between beliefs and classroom practice. We found that when classroom practice changed before beliefs, the change always occurred in the earlier levels, Level 1 to Level 3 (Although not all changes at the early level involved changing practice first). At these early levels, teachers were able to adapt classroom practices from what they had seen and heard in the workshop. Even though we did not prescribe particular classroom practices, many practices were modeled or described through videotapes of childrens interviews as well as in discussions and activities with teachers. At the early levels, the teachers posed problems drawn from the workshops to their students, and asked their students to describe how they solve problems. These teaching practices can be instantiated without corresponding changes in beliefs. Using the classroom practices drawn from the workshops allowed the teachers to hear their students thinking thus influencing teachers beliefs, much as Guskey (1986) proposed.

However, for teachers to move beyond Level 3 in classroom practice, belief changes are essential. No teacher moved beyond Level 3 in classroom practice without Level 4 beliefs. Level 4 classroom practices involve teachers building on the mathematical thinking of the children in their classrooms. Level 4 teachers must create classroom practices that match the needs of their students and fit with their own views about the teaching and learning of mathematics. At this level, particular practices cannot be prescribed or explicitly modeled; making decisions about classroom practice depends on a strong epistemological base. Therefore, a shift in teachers beliefs must accompany or precede their changes in practice at Level 4.

CASE EXEMPLARS

To further elaborate the findings related to the identified patterns of change, we examined more closely the changes of three teachers, each representing a different pattern of change (for further description see Franke, Fennema, Carpenter, Ansell, & Berhend, in press; Franke, Fennema, Carpenter, & Ansell, 1992).[1]

Changing Practice

Ms. Nathan consistently focused her attention on the details of classroom practice. For Ms. Nathan, practice changed prior to an equivalent change in beliefs. At the beginning of the project, Ms. Nathan was at Level 1 in both beliefs and classroom practice. By the end of the project, Ms. Nathan was at Level 3 in both beliefs and classroom practice and had succeeded in engaging in many classroom practices consistent with the premises of CGI. She posed problems for her children to solve that allowed multiple strategies, and she elicited children's thinking and provided students the opportunity to talk to each other about mathematics.

Initially, Ms. Nathan was skeptical about what CGI and knowledge about children's thinking had to offer to her and her third-grade students. Yet she felt she should try it. She focused on what she could do in the classroom that would be considered doing CGI. When Ms. Nathan created the opportunity to use the problems presented in the workshop with her students, she discovered that both she and her students were learning.

Focusing on details of practice helped her pose problems to elicit the children's thinking which in turn helped her change her beliefs about children's ability to solve problems and solve them in multiple ways. This began a cycle of change for Ms. Nathan. Posing problems and asking for children's responses (without providing them with a strategy), just to find out what they would do, allowed Ms. Nathan to listen to her children, see that they could solve the problems, and build her own knowledge of her children's mathematical thinking:

---

[1] The names of the teachers discussed are pseudonyms.

I'm sort of a practical person by nature, and I guess the things that helped the most were some of the practical things you gave us, the problem types, seeing the kids on the videotapes. I think I am less philosophical at this point in my life. So particularly when you gave us the different multiplication types and division types, and we could use those to integrate with problems—that really worked well. And plus the addition and subtraction types . . . although I found the class that I had this year had pretty well mastered most of those by the time they got here. So I really don't spend that much time, other than using them, integrating all the different processes together.

By the end of the project, Ms. Nathan had come a long way in changing both her classroom practice and her beliefs. She struggled with implementing practices she felt exemplified CGI and then struggled with the implications those practices had for her beliefs. However, Ms. Nathan had difficulty getting to the point of using what she knew about her students to make instructional decisions, an issue that goes beyond implementing particular practices. Ms. Nathan was only beginning to become intrigued with what her students were thinking. She found that her students could solve problems in ways that she would not have expected, but she did not know the details of how the children solved the problems or how these strategies were related to other strategies. A continued focus on practice made it difficult for Ms. Nathan to develop her framework in ways that would help her make instructional decisions built on the mathematical thinking of her students. Even so, by the end of the project, Ms. Nathan engaged in classroom practices that included posing a variety of problems to her students, eliciting the students' thinking, and accepting a variety of solutions.

Changing beliefs

Ms. Carroll started the project at Level 3 in both beliefs and classroom practice. Over the four years of the project, we heard a change in Ms. Carrolls beliefs, but failed to observe a corresponding change in classroom practice. Ms. Carroll knew about CGI prior to engaging in our project, and in her first year she was already implementing the practices most clearly related to CGI. Ms. Carroll talked in an informed way about CGI and the principles underlying it. Her classroom had the signs of a teacher listening to her students' mathematical thinking, which was especially impressive because she was a first-year teacher.

By the end of the first year, Ms. Carroll's beliefs had changed to Level 4A. Her classroom practice remained at Level 3. Ms. Carroll stated that her role was to remove barriers and to understand what the children knew so that she could help them. Her role was "helping kids discover their abilities, and to take off any glass ceilings they've set for themselves[because] if you don't know it's there, you can't use it." When probed about how she did this she said, "When something comes up I'll try to maybe mention the next step without saying this is the next step. But you say, 'Wouldn't it be interesting if we . . .' or 'have you heard about . . .' and bring in these other things."

Ms. Carroll talked about no longer putting conditions on when children should be allowed to use their own strategies, and she believed that she needed to make instructional decisions based on what she heard from the children. She told us, "Children learn at different rates and . . . they have to have a body of knowledge to build on, and when you take this body of knowledge that they're building on, and they understand and keep building themselves, they really get a nice solid foundation with it. The children bring a lot into class already, and you take where they are and just help them move along." However, Ms. Carroll was not able to talk about using her children's thinking to make instructional decisions in any more specific terms than you build on what the children know.

When deciding which problems to pose in a given lesson, Ms. Carroll usually reported that she made her decisions based both on children's affect and on wanting to provide a conducive learning environment. She did not report basing decisions on the children's mathematical thinking. Her goals were "to validate the worth and the effort of the problems that they [children] do. And to again talk about that there is more than one way. . . . When you get them to listen to each other, they are learning new ways." We did not hear Ms. Carroll talk specifically or in much depth about her children's thinking. After searching all of her interviews, the most specific, in-depth examples we could find came from her post observation interview in the spring of Year 3:

> And I was real pleased at, you know, some of the little odds and ends strategies that came up. And the thought of removing the petals. I liked that. That was a nice way to explain. They explained well, I thought. And so that tells me that they are more comfortable. Just keep them on it.

> But it's still not really, because what you do, you listen and you file this away so that the next time these come up, you know, I wanted to tell Jose, "Oh wasn't that a clever way that you did so and so?" And I'm going to tell Max, "I really liked when you were still kept talking about thousands ƒ And so you file away all those things that you can tell kids what a good job they did. And then they know that you understand and then they're more willing to take the risk because they know that it was okay that they tried. And even when people forget what they going to say, I say, "Oh, I'm glad you tried."

> And Keisha. She is, Jose is, and he's come to what the tens concepts. Keisha is not. She's direct one to one. And it's okay for her. And she'll just have to keep working on it. Like, keep going over it. She'll get there.

In these examples, Ms. Carroll commented on strategies of specific children. She talked about the strategies being clever, the children being comfortable and having a nice way to explain their thinking. She never explicitly dealt with the substance of the strategies the students used. Even when she talked about the place-value knowledge of Jose and Keisha, she did it in general terms. The generality of these comments stands in contrast with Ms. Andrew's comments (see next case) about children's thinking.

After engaging in the project, Ms. Carroll was able to articulate her beliefs more clearly, but she had not shifted in her ability to make use of children's mathematical thinking. Nor had Ms. Carroll come to see the value in knowing specifics about her children's mathematical understanding and how that understanding fit into the broader conception of developing mathematical understanding.

Changing beliefs and practice consistently

Ms. Andrew balanced her focus on beliefs and classroom practice, striving to understand the specifics of children's thinking and the principles that tied those specifics together. She began with beliefs and practice very different from those of CGI and still changed dramatically and consistently in both beliefs and classroom practice throughout the four years of the project. Ms. Andrew began the project with beliefs and classroom practice at Level 1. Her beliefs and practice changed more or less simultaneously throughout the four years of the study. By the end of Year 1, Ms. Andrews beliefs and classroom practice were at Level 4A. She remained at Level 4A through Year 2, and by the end of Year 3 she was at Level 4B.

Ms. Andrew reflected at the end of the project on how she had changed:

> Oh, definitely. As I told you before, remember the first time you guys came in to our classroom? I always have to crack up about this . . . when I was at the board telling the children how to carry their 1s and that kind of business. And now it's completely different than that. I mean, you don't just tell the kids how to do it. They, in fact, figure it out on their own. And so it's like a complete reversal, where you're not the center focus of the instruction anymore like you used to be. It's now like they're the center. Their thinking is the center. And that's what it should be. For years the opposite way is the way we taught. And the kids . . . you'd find out . . . they'd go to take these tests or they'd go to do these problems, and if they'd forget which step they were on, why, then, they wouldn't know how to do it. You know, so you weren't really . . . they weren't really solving the problems from what they thought, it was from what you told them to think. And so that is a big change.

Ms. Andrew's ongoing reflection was captured in part by her excitement about what her students could do with mathematics. She found it fun to try to understand the children's strategies and how those strategies related to how other children and she herself might solve the problems:

> I mean, they're doing even more than I ever believed a second grader could do. You know, I often bring my problems home and say, look at this problem. I say to my husband, look at what this kid can do. And I brag about it to my family and my friends whenever I can. And so I think if anything, it's raised my expectations of kids at this level. Even as a teacher. You know, I've learned a lot just from listening to some of these kids. I'm thinking, wow, I never figured it out that way. But you know, I even find myself using some of their ways. I mean, it's a riot . . . and that's what's kind of neat about this, is that you find yourself drawing these analogies and saying, well, what do you think about the way so and so did it?

Ms. Andrew constantly strove to understand her students' mathematical thinking and how the students' thinking related to what she knew about the development of children's mathematical thinking. Ms. Andrew took the knowledge about children's mathematical thinking and made it her own. She never tired of learning about her students' thinking. She did not just focus on global aspects of the children's thinking, she wanted to know specifics. For example, Ms. Andrew described some ways children used knowledge of tens to solve the problem, 124 + 137:

> One child had 100 plus 100 is 200; he said, "I know that. And then I know that 20 and 30 is 50, and then I know that 7 and 4 is 11. I saw a couple of different ways of adding on." Anna said, "Well, I had 250, and 7 more was 257." And then she counted up 4 more. Then I had another child do . . . it was 250 and 11 more. Well, I know there's another 10 in 11. So that was 260 and 1 more.

With the specifics that she learned from her students, Ms. Andrew created her own framework for children's mathematical thinking, which built on what she had learned in the CGI workshops, and organized the specifics into broader principles. The framework that Ms. Andrew created provided her with a coherent, consistent basis for reflection and decision making.

Ms. Andrew's consistent changes in beliefs and classroom practice seem to be related to her ability to reflect back and forth from her classroom practice and what she heard from her students, to her belief systems and her knowledge of the problem types and strategies, to what she expected her children to do and understand.

Summary

Ms. Nathan, Ms. Carroll, and Ms. Andrew all felt strongly that they had changed due to their interactions with CGI. Yet it was also apparent that the changes were different for these three teachers. Ms. Nathan spoke of her practical nature and the need to get in and use some of the problems with the children. Posing problems and listening to students' strategies had allowed Ms. Nathan to begin to hear her students' thinking. She still did not feel comfortable with her implementation of CGI but stated that she felt more comfortable all the time. Ms. Carroll talked eloquently about how CGI had helped her and the impact it had had on her teaching. She believed quite strongly in the principles underlying CGI; however, she had difficulty extending her classroom practice beyond initially instantiated behaviors. Ms. Carroll did not focus on the specifics of how her children thought about the mathematics. She did not hear her children in detailed ways, but she had some notion of what to expect and operated from there. This made it difficult for Ms. Carroll to continue to change her practice. Ms. Andrew talked at great length about the impact CGI had had on her teaching and learning. But what stood out most about Ms. Andrew was the amount of time she spent expressing her excitement about the strategies her children would use to solve problems, how she struggled to understand her children's thinking, and how she wanted continually to learn more.

FOCUSING TEACHERS PRACTICAL INQUIRY

Reflecting on the changes of the CGI teachers, what stands out most is that there was no single pattern of change. The teachers fell almost equally into patterns of belief changes first, classroom practice changes first, or coinciding changes in beliefs and practice. We could not predict from teachers' initial beliefs and classroom practice which pattern they would follow. The powerful finding regarding the relationship between beliefs and classroom practice was that teachers needed changes in beliefs in order to make changes in classroom practice at the higher levels. Changing practice might help teachers initially engage in transforming their mathematics teaching. However, continuing to change practice, without changes in beliefs, may not engage the teachers in self-generated, self-sustaining changes that enable teachers to create opportunities in the classroom that reflect the needs and understanding of their students.

The cases of Ms. Nathan, Ms. Carroll, and Ms. Andrew help us understand why teachers engage in particular patterns of change. We have come to view teachers as being engaged in a form of practical inquiry (see Franke et al., in press). In her 1994 article, Virginia

Richardson talked about teachers engaging in practical inquiry. We have adapted Richardsons conception to include a different view of formal research. Richardson (1994) stated that many teachers still consider that research on teaching does not inform their day-to-day teaching. She pointed out that formal research is "helping us understand the ways in which teachers develop knowledge that they use in solving the immediate needs of their classroom" (p. 8), which may then lead to a form of research that fits with teachers' methods of acquiring and constructing practical knowledge. We view formal research as providing the basis for teachers' practical inquiry. Rather than fostering a way to teach, teacher research attempts to foster a teacher's practical inquiry.

Practical inquiry can be viewed as a teacher questioning and reflecting about his or her practice in a specific focus. The focus of a teacher's practical inquiry determines what a teacher sees as critical, what constitutes an opportunity for reflection, and how a teacher chooses to work on developing opportunities. Teacher change can be seen as driven by the focus of a teacher's practical inquiry. The focus in the case of CGI is children's mathematical thinking. In other cases, it may be on constructivist principles or on understanding the content of the mathematics.

We are beginning to see that teachers who consistently engage in practical inquiry, focused on children's mathematical thinking, are the ones who change beyond Level 3 in beliefs and classroom practice. That these teachers also change their beliefs before, or in conjunction with, changing their practice highlights the importance of teachers reflection on opportunities. Engaging in practical inquiry entails more than changing classroom practice, it entails changing classroom practices in ways that relate to a set of corresponding beliefs.

If we consider the goal to be self-generated, self-sustaining change, teachers' practical inquiry must be focused on how children think about and solve specific mathematical problems. Such focus in teachers inquiry allows them to build frameworks where existing ideas can be connected to daily interactions with children. As a teacher interacts with children, she hears or sees something that a child does and mentally relates that to what she already knows. If what is heard is different from what was expected based on her existing knowledge, it causes the teacher to reflect about why it was different and how it may fit. If the teacher reaches an impasse in her interactions with a child, she reflects on why she has reached that impasse. Is it that she does not know enough about that child's mathematical thinking, about children's mathematical thinking in general, about the mathematical content they are engaging in, or about what question to ask to help the child in his or her thinking? As teachers reflect on these questions, they build frameworks that start from a focus on children's mathematical thinking and extend to relationships with mathematical knowledge, pedagogical knowledge, and so on.

Potentially, what becomes critical for teachers is a focused practical inquiry. The focus allows the teachers to engage inquiry that connects pedagogy, content, and children's thinking. Otherwise what results is scattered inquiry, question asking, and reflection, that do not become connected. Using what is learned about a child's mathematical thinking in the classroom to make instructional decisions requires that content, pedagogy, and children's thinking be interconnected.

CONCLUSIONS

We propose that almost all of the CGI teachers have been engaged in practical inquiry. What differed was the level at which they were involved and the degree to which the teachers were able to focus their inquiry. We are not sure why some teachers were able to engage in practical inquiry focused on children's thinking. We do know that it was not related to the teachers' existing beliefs and classroom practice. In many ways, it was easier to identify what kept teachers from focusing their practical inquiry than it was to see why some teachers were able to focus.

We noticed that some teachers, like Ms. Carroll, decided at some point in the process to implement CGI. Rather than focusing on learning about children's mathematical thinking, which never ends, they focused on implementing their visions of the program. What happens then is that teachers do not see the need to continue focusing their practical inquiry on developing deeper understanding of children's thinking, and they focus on something else. When opportunities for reflection arise that would help a teacher understand her children's mathematical thinking or challenge the teacher's beliefs about teaching and learning mathematics, the situations are not noticed or viewed as opportunities for reflection.

Other teachers have had a difficult time changing the focus of their inquiry from teacher behavior to student behavior. These teachers focus their inquiry on managing the class. This focus enables these teachers to build repertoires of pedagogical skills and knowledge, but these repertoires are isolated and not connected to their knowledge about children's thinking or the content of the mathematics. Focusing on classroom management keeps these teachers from noticing opportunities that potentially would enable them to make connections. Different foci for practical inquiry may lead to different outcomes, particularly in terms of connections between beliefs, knowledge, and classroom practice.

Focusing inquiry on children's mathematical thinking encourages teachers to ask about their own students' thinking. Such focus facilitates teachers' thinking about the relationship between children's thinking and the content, often in terms of the problems they will pose to build on the children's thinking. It also lends itself to reflecting on which pedagogical practices enable them to best engage their students in problem solving and thus understand their thinking. CGI teachers have a framework of children's mathematical thinking that they can build on and make their own. When the teachers notice opportunities for reflection, they can connect their observations and thinking to the frameworks in a way that is not static or unidimensional.

Practical inquiry provides an avenue for understanding teacher change and enables us to begin to understand change both within the context of a particular project and across projects. We can begin to think about the various mathematics reform projects in terms of the focus they provide for practical inquiry and thus the ramifications they have for teacher change.

ACKNOWLEDGMENTS

The research reported in this study was supported in part by the National Science Foundation under Grant Numbers MDR-8955346 and MDR-8550236. The opinions expressed in this chapter are those of the authors and do not necessarily reflect the views of the National Science Foundation.

REFERENCES

Carpenter, T. P. (1985). Learning to add and subtract: An exercise in problem solving. In E. A. Silver (Ed.), *Teaching and learning mathematical problem solving: Multiple research perspectives*. (pp. 17–40). Hillsdale, NJ: Lawrence Erlbaum Associates.

Carpenter, T. P., & Fennema, E. (1992). Cognitively guided instruction: Building on the knowledge of students and teachers. *International Journal of Educational Research, 17*(5), 457–470.

Carpenter, T. P., Fennema, E., & Franke, M. L. (in press). Cognitively Guided Instruction: A knowledge base for reform in primary mathematics instruction. *Elementary School Journal*.

Carpenter, T. P., Fennema, E., Peterson, P. L., & Carey, D. A. (1988). Teachers' pedagogical content knowledge of students' problem solving in elementary arithmetic. *Journal for Research in Mathematics Education, 19*, 385–401.

Carpenter, T. P., Fennema, E., Peterson, P. L., Chiang, C. P., & Loef, M. (1989). Using knowledge of children's mathematics thinking in classroom teaching: An experimental study. *American Educational Research Journal, 26*(4), 499–531.

Clark, C. M., & Peterson, P. L. (1986). Teachers' thought processes. In M. C. Wittrock (Ed.), *Handbook of research on teaching* (pp. 255–296). New York: Macmillan.

Cobb, P., Wood, T., & Yackel E. (1990). Classroom as learning environments for teachers and researchers. In R. Davis, C. Maher, & N. Noddings (Eds.), Constructivist views on the teaching and learning of mathematics. *Journal for Research in Mathematics Education Monograph, 4*, 125–146.

Cobb, P., Wood, T., Yackel, E., & McNeal, B. (1993). Mathematics as procedural instructions and mathematics as meaningful activity: The reality of teaching for understanding. In R. Davis & C. Maher (Eds.), *Schools, mathematics and the world of reality* (pp. 119–134). Needham Heights, MA: Allyn & Bacon.

Cobb, P., Yackel, T., & Wood, T. (1992). Interaction and learning in mathematics classroom situations. *Educational Studies in Mathematics. 23*, 99–122.

Fennema, E., Carpenter, T. P., Franke, M. L., & Carey, D. A. (1992). Learning to use children's mathematical thinking: A case study. In R. Davis & C. Maher (Eds.), *Schools, mathematics and the world of reality* (pp. 93–117). Needham Heights, MA: Allyn & Bacon.

Fennema, E., Carpenter, T. P., Franke, M. L., Levi, L., Jacobs, V., & Empson, S. (1996). A longitudinal study of learning to use children's thinking in mathematics instruction. *Journal for Research in Mathematics Education. 27*(4), 403–434.

Franke, M. L., Fennema, E., Carpenter, T. P., & Ansell, E. (1992, April). *The process of teacher change in Cognitively Guided Instruction.* Paper presented at the annual meeting of the American Education Research Association, San Francisco, CA.

Franke, M. L., Fennema, E., Carpenter, T., Ansell, E., & Behrend, J. (in press). Understanding teachers' self-sustaining change in the context of mathematics instruction: The role of practical inquiry. *Teaching and Teaching Education.*

Grant, S. G., Peterson, P. L. & Shojgreen-Downer, A. (1994, April). *Learning to teach mathematics in the context of systemic reform.* Paper presented at the annual meeting of the American Educational Research Association, New Orleans, LA.

Guskey, T. R. (1986). Staff development and the process of teacher change. *Educational Researcher, 15*(5), 5–12.

Hall, G. E., Loucks, S. F., Rutherford, W. L. ,& Newlove, B. W. (1975). *Levels of use of the innovation: A framework for analyzing innovation adoption.* Austin, TX: The Research and Development Center for Teacher Education.

Hunsaker, L., & Johnston, M. (1992). Teacher under construction: A collaborative case study of teacher change. *American Educational Research Journal, 29*(2), 350–372.

Loef, M. (1990). *Understanding teachers' knowledge about building instruction on children's mathematical thinking: Application of a personal construct approach.* Unpublished doctoral dissertation, University of Wisconsin, Madison.

Pajares, M. F. (1992). Teachers' beliefs and educational research: Cleaning up a messy construct. *Review of Educational Research, 62*, 307–332.

Putnam, R. T., Lampert, M., & Peterson, P. L. (1990). Alternative perspectives on knowing mathematics in elementary schools. In C. B. Cazden (Ed.), *Review of research in education*, Vol. 16 (pp. 57–150). Washington, DC: American Educational Research Association.

Richardson, V. (1994). Conducting research on practice. *Educational Researcher, 23* (5), 5–10.

Richardson, V., Anders, D., Tidwell, D., & Lloyd, C. (1991). The relationship between teachers' beliefs and practices in reading comprehension instruction. *American Educational Research Journal, 28*(3), 559–586.

Schifter, D., & Fosnot, C. T. (1993). *Reconstructing mathematics education: Stories of teachers meeting the challenge of reform.* New York: Teachers College Press.

Shulman, L. S. (1986). Those who understand teach: Knowledge growth in teaching. *Educational Researcher, 57*(1), 1–22.

Simon, M., & Schifter, D. (1991). Towards a constructivist perspective: An intervention study of mathematics teacher development. *Educational Studies in Mathematics, 22*, 309–311.

Tharp, R. G., & Gallimore, R. (1988). *Rousing minds to life.* New York: Cambridge University Press.

Thompson, A. G. (1992). Teachers' beliefs and conceptions: A synthesis of the research. In D. A. Grouws (Ed.), *Handbook of research on mathematics teaching and learning* (pp. 127-146). New York: Macmillan.

Vygotsyky, L. S. (1962). *Thought and language.* Cambridge, MA: MIT Press.

Wood, T., Cobb, P., & Yackel, E. (1991). Change in teaching mathematics: A case study. *American Educational Research Journal, 28*(3), 587–616.

11

Educational Reform and Professional Development

Janet Stocks
Carnegie Mellon University

Janet Schofield
University of Pittsburgh

In the current era of educational reform, a plethora of issues has arisen about how best to achieve change in the classroom. Research on cognition, and particularly constructivist approaches to learning, call for substantive changes in the way learning is conceptualized (Brown, Collins, & Duguid, 1989). Translating this knowledge into practice, whether in developing new pedagogical approaches for the classroom or new approaches to professional development, has proved challenging.

Just as new views of teaching and learning have led to major reform efforts designed to create classroom structures and practices that look quite different from more traditional ones (Blumenfeld, Krajcik, Marx, & Soloway, 1994; Stocks & Schofield, 1994; Wood, Cobb, & Yackel, 1991), so these new views imply the need for new approaches to teacher professional development. The new approaches to teaching and learning suggested by reform thinking are likely to contrast sharply with the more traditional didactic form of professional development (Carpenter, Fennema, Peterson, Chiang, & Loef, 1989; Wood, Cobb & Yackel, 1991). Yet questions arise such as: How will reform thinking inform professional development models? What would a model of professional development based on such ideas look like? How would an approach to professional development based on these ideas work? What factors facilitate or impede such an approach? How can we structure professional development efforts so that they are consistent with the new understanding of teaching and learning and are effective in bringing about major change, yet do not demand so many human and financial resources that they are unlikely ever to be adopted on a wide scale?

283

EDUCATIONAL REFORM PRINCIPLES

Two strands of thought—sometimes woven together, sometimes seen as distinct—form the framework for what we call the reform approach to mathematics learning. The first of these strands has to do with individual cognitive processes and the current focus on how learners actively incorporate information into an existing set of understandings. This strand of thought, often referred to as constructivism, is in the tradition of Piaget (1970, 1980). Emphasis here is put on the scaffolding of knowledge (Wood, Bruner, & Ross, 1976) and the necessity of learners building concepts in a meaningful way. It highlights the fact that learners enter any situation with preexisting knowledge and experiences that they draw on when discovering and assimilating new information. For this new information to be meaningful to learners, instructors must help them build a cognitive framework that can accommodate such information, taking careful account of the initial understandings with which the learners enter the learning situation.

The other emphasis in current work on mathematics education on which we focus in this chapter has to do with the social context of learning. Mathematics education can be viewed as a process of enculturating the learner into the practices of an intellectual community (Cobb, 1994a, 1994b; Driver, Asoko, Leach, Mortimer, & Scott, 1994). This viewpoint argues that communities of practice have been constructed in different disciplines, into which a learner must be initiated in order to take part effectively in the practice of that discipline. For example, referring to science education, Driver et al. (1994) explained:

> The view of scientific knowledge as socially constructed and validated has important implications for science education. It means that learning science involves being initiated into scientific ways of knowing. Scientific entities and ideas, which are constructed, validated, and communicated through the cultural institutions of science, are unlikely to be discovered by individuals through their own empirical enquiry; learning science thus involves being initiated into the ideas and practices of the scientific community and making these ideas and practices meaningful at an individual level. (p. 6)

In this chapter we use the term *reform approaches* to refer to both of these emphases, the individual and the social. As Cobb (1994a) argued, the "analysis of mathematics learning as individual construction and as enculturation are complementary" (p.4).

OPERATIONALIZING REFORM PRINCIPLES

Constructivist perspectives on knowledge development necessitate the development of new models of mathematics teaching and mathematics teacher education. However, constructivism does *not* provide the blueprint for the creation of these models. (Simon, 1994, p. 1)

Many in the education community have become convinced that students are not blank slates, but active constructors of knowledge, and that a teacher's job is to help enculturate students into a community of knowledge, with an awareness of how new information is actively constructed by the individual learner. In response to this, many somewhat different constructivist and other reform-oriented teaching strategies have arisen (Blumenfeld et al., 1994; Prawat & Floden, 1994). However, as Simon (1994) and Cobb (1994a) pointed out, an understanding of constructivism does not translate into a "direct instructional recommendation" (Cobb, 1994a, p.4) for classrooms.

Similarly, an appreciation of the ideas underlying the reform approach to education does not yield a specific blueprint for how we might best structure teacher education and professional development efforts. An understanding of reform principles does, however, clearly imply that traditional didactic approaches that rely on a transmission–reception model of learning in professional development need to be reevaluated. If we accept that learning is an active process, we can hardly expect didactic presentation of uniform information to be an effective way of changing either teachers' understandings of their work, or their practices.

In this chapter, we present a case study of the evolution of a professional development program designed to disseminate an innovative elementary mathematics curriculum called Math^3 (Intuition Invention Interaction), which is based on current theory and research in the area of mathematics learning. Through this case study we explore the difficulties that arise in attempting to use constructivist and other current educational reform principles in the design of a professional development model.

Specifically, developers of Math^3 encountered issues that we believe exist in any attempt to create a constructivist professional development program. These are (a) the importance of teachers seeing the need to change their practice, (b) the tension between formal research and practical inquiry, (c) the importance of teachers feeling a sense of ownership in the innovation, (d) the "constructivist dilemma" of teaching content knowledge while respecting teacher constructions, and (e) the importance of building a community of practice.

MATH[3]

Math[3] began as a one-to-one collaboration between a teacher, Rachel Dalmer,[1] and a researcher, Lauren Resnick. Dalmer was teaching at an urban elementary parochial school with a largely low-income African American population. Over the course of a number of years, Dalmer had become very frustrated, about her inability to teach mathematics as effectively as she wished to. Her students' standardized test scores were consistently low (20th to 30th percentile), and the feedback she received from teachers who taught her students in the upper grades was that the students were not well prepared in the basics.

Dalmer became acquainted with a researcher from the Learning Research and Development Center at the University of Pittsburgh who was doing a computer project in her school and working with some of the children in her class. The researcher saw Dalmer's frustration and need for alternative ideas. The researcher started

> slipping me *Arithmetic Teacher* articles, and I would read them and thank her and ask for some more. You know, "Oh, if you have any more, I'll take some more." So she kept slipping me research. It was a really nice resource. Every week I got research articles slipped to me and I would read them. She'd slip me some more.

During the summer after this first school year of reading research articles, Dalmer spent time at the Learning Research and Development Center reading more research articles, reflecting on her own experience as a classroom teacher and collaborating with Resnick and other researchers on how to apply these ideas to her classroom: "And it was just like coming alive again. I mean, all of a sudden now I was studying and reading, and now I'd never leave [teaching]. You know, now it's what a profession should be." During the next couple of years, Dalmer significantly changed the way she taught math and saw the results in her students' standardized test scores, in their enthusiasm for math, and in their retention of the material (Resnick, Bill, Lesgold, & Leer, 1991). Out of this experience, the Math[3] program was born.

Through study of a wide range of current research on student learning and mathematics education, as well as reflection on her own practice, Dalmer, along with Resnick, developed an elementary mathematics curriculum built around six principles: (a) develop children's trust in their own knowledge; (b) draw children's intuitive knowledge into the classroom; (c) use formal mathematical signs and symbols to record informal classroom discussion; (d) introduce key mathematical operations as quickly as possible; (e) encourage students to find and solve mathematics problems in everyday life; and (f) talk about mathematics, don't just do arithmetic (Resnick, Bill, Lesgold, & Leer, 1991).

[1] All teachers' names are pseudonyms.

These principles were the basis of a curriculum that looked quite different from a traditional elementary mathematics curriculum. Mathematics instruction in Math[3] classrooms involves a great deal of discussion about students' inventive algorithms, with teachers taking the role of facilitators rather than that of leaders of didactic lessons. An ideal daily lesson involves, first, a short (usually 10-item) drill to reinforce concepts already introduced, followed by a "dilemma," which generally revolved around one problem based on a real-life situation (such as dividing a box of candy among several friends so that each would get an equal number of pieces). This dilemma would generally be expanded by working in-depth on one problem, using manipulatives, and exploring the varieties of ways different students reasoned about the problem. This approach to instruction contrasts with the more traditional transmission–reception model, in which a solution strategy is suggested by the teacher and then practiced by the class, using a number of similar problems such as those in consumable workbooks. An ideal Math[3] class period would end with students working in cooperative groups on mathematics "labs"—hands-on activities, which the children usually found enjoyable, that would introduce new mathematical concepts.

Math[3] requires teachers to change their practices in significant ways. They are encouraged to work with cooperative groups in their classrooms, a technique that many teachers had not used prior to their involvement with this program. Teachers must think about mathematics problems in a different way. Rather than simply presenting one method of solving a problem, they must consider the knowledge with which their students enter the classroom and anticipate the possible ways these children might approach any given problem, especially because no traditional algorithms are taught in Math[3] classrooms. They must be ready to adjust their plans every day, on a moment's notice, when they see how their students are interacting with the content of the day's lessons. They must learn to play the part of coexplorer of the material, as opposed to a more traditional didactic style of teaching. In addition to these issues, teachers must organize manipulatives, student notebooks, and other resources on a daily basis. They must have access to copying facilities and be given time to have the papers ready for class each day.

THE PROFESSIONAL DEVELOPMENT MODEL

Because of the significant initial success of the collaboration between Dalmer and Resnick, the program grew to incorporate more teachers. As one of the developers of the professional development model explains, this was a complex transition:

> Moving from the luxury of a one-to-one relationship between a researcher and a teacher to a one-to-many relationship between a teacher-researcher

and many teachers was particularly challenging. We are finding that implementation of the Math[3] program depends on a highly skilled teacher who understands the mathematical content, knows how to interpret children's language and actions, and can proceed flexibly from day to day while still maintaining a highly organized and carefully planned overall program structure. Grounded in the belief that children must construct their own knowledge, Math[3], thus, calls for a substantial revamping of classroom organization and a new way of thinking about mathematics knowledge and ability in children.

Extending the innovations of Math[3] to significant numbers of teachers and schools could not be done through traditional methods of textbook preparation or curriculum dissemination; nor would the traditional "in service" models of professional development (one-shot courses taken by individual teachers or workshops for groups of teachers conducted usually by outsiders and without effective follow-up) address the type and magnitude of change required (Leer, Resnick, & Bill, 1994, p. 2).

Working out a professional development strategy for this new approach to teaching math was a process that was not always smooth, and the developers learned as much as the teachers. The model evolved as developers responded to teacher feedback, new developments in educational research, and their own experiences with the program. Because there was significant change in the professional development model as it evolved, it is impossible to give a simple description of the model, but we can describe key principles of this model at different points in time. Although there was a great deal of change, certain principles were central and important to the project developers throughout as they designed and implemented the program. One of these principles was a heavy reliance on current research in mathematics education to guide practice. Another was the avoidance of didactic pedagogical techniques, both in the elementary classrooms and in the teacher professional development efforts. Rather than taking a didactic approach, the program developers sought to respect the knowledge of the learners as they entered the learning situation and to use discussion and real-life examples as teaching and learning opportunities. A third central principle of the professional development model was to provide a great deal of ongoing support to the teachers as they attempted to implement this new approach to teaching mathematics.

The Math[3] staff was made up of Dalmer, who also maintained responsibility for her classrooms during the first three years of this staff development effort, one other full-time person, a visiting scholar, and a postdoctoral research associate. There were five years, Cycles A–E, of the program (see Table 11.1 for detail of these five years). A total of 301 teachers from 68 schools took part in the program during its 5 years. Most of these teachers were in kindergarten through third-grade class-

TABLE 11.1
The cycles of Math³: Demographics About Math³ Programs, Schools, and Teachers

	CYCLE A *1990-1991*	*CYCLE B* *1991-1992*	*CYCLE C* *1992-1993*	*CYCLE D* *1993-1994*	*CYCLE E* *1994-1995*
Number of Program Teachers					Totals
Catholic school teachers	17	26	32	48	58	181
Public school teachers	0	9	15	32	64	120
Total Number of Teachers	17	35	47	80	122	301
Number of Lead Teachers					
Catholic school lead teachers					14
Public school lead teachers					13
Total Number of Lead Teachers					27
Number of Program Schools					
Catholic schools	7	10	12	12	12	53
Public schools	0	2	2	3	8	15
Total Number of Schools	7	12	14	15	20	68

rooms, but during Cycles C–E a small number of fourth-and fifth-grade teachers participated.

Teachers entering the program participated in a one- or two-week summer seminar session to introduce them to the principles on which the Math³ program was based, as well as to techniques that could be used in their classrooms. Once the school year began, teachers attended monthly Saturday workshops where they continued to discuss current research pertinent to the program and spent time together planning lessons to use in their classrooms. In addition, program staff visited teachers' classrooms to team-teach and to videotape lessons to help teachers reflect on and evaluate their own practices.

STUDYING THE PROFESSIONAL DEVELOPMENT PROGRAM

We conducted a qualitative study of the professional development experiences, designed to disseminate this innovative elementary mathematics curriculum, as part of a larger study of the adoption of the Math³ program (see, e.g., Jamar, 1994; Resnick, Bill, & Lesgold, 1992; Resnick, Bill, Lesgold, & Leer 1991). Neither of the authors of this chapter were involved with the development of the Math³ program or the professional development model used to disseminate it.[2] The study focused largely on social aspects of the change process.

---

[2]Both authors are based at the Learning Research and Development Center of the University of Pittsburgh, where Resnick is codirector and Dalmer is based.

The three major methods of data gathering utilized in the study of Math[3] included interviews, qualitative observations, and the collection of archival material. In-depth, semistructured, open-ended interviews were conducted with approximately 35 teachers participating in the program. Because the professional development model evolved markedly over time, we were careful to include teachers who entered the program during each of the first four years of the program. We also interviewed the program developers, attended professional development workshops, and collected the materials given to the teachers during these experiences. In addition, first-, second-, and third-grade math classes taught by a subgroup of the teachers were observed weekly during a two-year period. During this time we also observed first- and second-grade teachers who were teaching math in a more traditional way.

Field notes from these observations were dictated immediately and later transcribed. Field notes were made as factual and concretely descriptive as possible. Interpretive comments were included, but were clearly distinguished from the descriptive account. Because even the most complete field notes cannot possibly include everything that transpires, the fact that two researchers were involved in the observational activities allowed for discussion of the differences between the two researchers' notes, which helped make both observers aware of their individual biases and preconceptions.

Interview questions were developed after a substantial amount of time had been spent in the field to alert researchers to relevant experiences and questions. Interview questions were both semistructured open-ended and closed-ended. Interviews were tape-recorded and then transcribed.

Data analysis was an ongoing part of this research project. Transcribed field notes and interviews were carefully read, reread, and coded for themes that emerged (Glaser & Strauss, 1967; Miles & Huberman, 1984; Strauss & Corbin, 1990). The results of this analysis helped us adjust the focus of further data gathering.

CONSTRUCTING A CONSTRUCTIVIST APPROACH TO TEACHER PROFESSIONAL DEVELOPMENT

Teachers Seeing the Need to Change

One of the basic principles of constructivist thinking in education is that knowledge needs to be actively constructed rather than passively received (see, e.g., Wood, Cobb, & Yackel, 1991). This implies that for professional development models to be effective, teachers, as well as students, must be active learners and participants. The developers of

Math[3] were well aware of this implication of constructivist theory and took active involvement on the part of teachers as a crucial feature of the professional development experience they created.

Implementing the Math[3] program required very fundamental and complex changes in the way teachers thought about teaching and in their classroom practice, as do many other reform-based approaches to teaching. For teachers to become invested sufficiently in this process of professional development for such change to occur, they must first come to believe that their current practice is in some way problematic, or at least that change would be clearly beneficial (Cobb, Wood, & Yackel, 1990; Simon, 1994). The developers of Math[3] were especially cognizant of the importance of teacher dissatisfaction with current practice as an important precondition for change, because dissatisfaction with the results of current practice was at the core of Dalmer's efforts to change her practice and the development of the Math[3] program itself.

Because the professional development experiences for Math[3] were designed to expose other teachers to the approaches Rachel Dalmer had developed, Dalmer wanted the participants in those experiences to be teachers who volunteered specifically because they wanted to change, as she had wanted to change. This decision came out of her recognition of the importance of self-motivation to change as a factor crucial to active learning.

During the first year of the dissemination of Math[3] (Cycle A), teachers were selected for the program through the Pittsburgh area Catholic schools. Dalmer worked with a mathematics curriculum consultant who recruited teachers into the program, asking the consultant to locate volunteers who were interested in changing their current approaches to teaching math. However, Dalmer later discovered that many of the teachers did not freely choose to become part of the project. Many had been encouraged by their principals to learn new instructional skills. Some of the teachers had volunteered to participate because of the extra money they would receive for taking part in the professional development experience ($1,800),[3] rather than because of any deep desire to change. Many of the teachers were not given adequate information concerning the intensive nature of the program and the long-term commitment to the project. At the time, the teachers were being asked to make a 2-year commitment to the project. This included a 2-week seminar during the first summer, one Saturday meeting per month during the school year, the willingness to be observed by project staff during the teaching of classroom lessons, and detailed documentation of their work in the classroom. This commitment contrasted sharply with most professional development experiences the teachers had been exposed to in the past. Mrs. Jones, a second-grade teacher, explained her first exposure to Math[3]:

> Initially when it was first presented to us, it was just presented as another way to do math and I guess one of the biggest incentives at the time was the monetary incentive that went with it. There was not much . . . other than you had to go to these workshops, you know, one every other month. It sounded like, well, a new method would be nice to learn and I thought it wouldn't be something that would be too burdensome. I thought!

Apparently at least some teachers who enrolled did not do so because they had identified problems in their current practices.

Although Dalmer had hoped teachers in the project would be already highly motivated to change, she did not assume that such preexisting motivation would necessarily be at an optimal level in all participants. As others like Cobb et al. (1990) had done, she and her colleagues searched for ways to include elements in the professional development program that would help teachers question their practices and see the benefits of change. One approach was to show videotapes of Dalmer's classroom so that teachers could see what children could do when complex problems were used and children were given opportunities to construct meaning and invent solutions to these problems. After the first year of the program, videotapes of other teachers were shown to stress that there was more than one way to teach these concepts. The assumption here, of course, was that teachers would value the kind of mathematical learning demonstrated in those tapes, which would help motivate a desire to change.

Dalmer and other program staff visited the classrooms of project teachers to coteach or demonstrate lessons with the teachers' own students as part of the professional development experience. These demonstration lessons often included problems with concepts not normally taught to children at that grade level.[4] This was done for several reasons. Through experience, the Math[3] staff had realized that students can work with skills and concepts much earlier than they are generally given opportunities to do so. It was assumed that demonstration teaching minimized the risk of making the teachers feel inadequate, because the lessons being demonstrated were not lessons that the teachers would have been expected to teach. Teachers were generally quite surprised at what their children were capable of and were excited by it. Through these experiences some teachers who had not been initially highly motivated to change their teaching came to question their former practices and to see possible reasons to change. When such demonstra-

---

[3] Funding for teacher pay came from Contract No. R117G10003 with the National Research Center on Student Learning, Contract No. R168D00191 with the Dwight D. Eisenhower Mathematics and Science Education Program, and contributions from some of the participating schools.

[4] For example, in first and second grade, lessons were taught that included the addition of fractions with like denominators, solving for equivalent fractions, and work with geometry that went beyond what students had been exposed to previously.

tions went well in the teachers' eyes, as they quite often did, they served to provoke meaningful questions that may not have arisen for the teachers before. Specifically, when a teacher's students performed in ways more impressive than the teacher had anticipated they would or could, it was no longer possible for that teacher to attribute the students' typically less-than-impressive performance in her class to deficiencies in the students' own motivation or intelligence. Instead, the issue of the role of the teacher's behavior in contributing to the students' prior relatively lackluster performance became much more salient without any direct comment or criticism having to be made. These experiences may not have been sufficient to motivate major efforts to change in all participants, especially the most initially reluctant or indifferent, but they did seem to be helpful in building and maintaining many teachers' desire to change.

Formal Research and Practical Inquiry

Motivation for change, whether preexisting or stimulated by well-planned professional development experiences, is not enough in and of itself to efficiently and effectively foster adoption of a complex and demanding new approach to teaching. The emphasis on ideas such as scaffolding and enculturation, contained in current reform views of education, suggests the importance of providing an environment that helps individuals move toward new understandings and practices. The notion that individuals construct rather than just incorporate knowledge does not imply that a viable construction can and will emerge without intervention on the part of a teacher. In fact, Wood, Cobb, and Yackel (1991) emphasized the social nature of learning and the importance of opportunities for learning that occur during social interaction with those who may have more expertise than the learner.

In her initial design of the professional development experience for Math[3], Dalmer relied heavily, if implicitly, on the model that had worked for her, expecting that other teachers would react the same way she had to reading and reflecting on research. Thus, the two-week summer professional development experience she first designed centered on giving the teachers articles to read, getting them together to discuss the papers, and talking with them about her own experiences. Teachers did not react very well to this heavy emphasis on research. Many expressed difficulty reading and comprehending these articles, and most did not seem to know how to take the information they learned from reading the research, pull out its implications, and translate it into practice.

Dalmer arranged for groups of children to participate in a "math camp" in order to give teachers hands-on experience relating research to practice. The teachers, however, generally felt unprepared to use the information from research articles to work with these groups of children during the summer session. Whereas Dalmer had two years to absorb this research and integrate it into her practice, these teachers had only a few days. As Ms. Bock put it:

> We were just totally overwhelmed because they were moving so quickly. They gave us two or three days of kind of showing us the video tapes and doing some demonstrations lessons. Then they had us immediately up trying to do that [teach the lessons to the children in the math camp] and that was just too soon. We needed to have more time to talk.

And another teacher, Ms. Reese, expressed the same sentiment:

> I liked working with the children, but what I didn't like is that the children. . . . One day you just had ideas; the next day children were there, whether you were ready for them or not. I think that was a little too fast. To bring in the children right away. I think you needed a good time of discussing and talking before you're faced with the children. I think that was a little too soon.

Another important component of the initial professional development model was teachers' monthly participation during the school year in Saturday workshops where they continued to discuss research and share experiences from their own classrooms. Dalmer learned, however, that her reaction to the research and the excitement of translating relatively abstract concepts into practice was not shared by many of the teachers in the Math[3] professional development program:

> I just thought they'd come in really excited about having all this stuff, and I forgot that, well no, I didn't forget they had lives, because so did I. I had two babies. My kids were babies, you know? But I just liked it. I just, I don't know, something about me got really turned on with the research. And all of a sudden, everything I was doing in the room was making sense, and I was saying, "This is why this isn't working. This is what I'm doing wrong. I never did this. Oh!" And things that I had discovered—to realize that they had already been written about and studied already. Things like counting on, counting all. I already discovered my kids were doing those things, but then I started thinking about ways that I could promote it. I mean, it was just one thing led me to the other, and the more excited I got, and then I started taking notes. And I just assumed everybody was going to have that kind of reaction, and the whole room [of teachers] was like furious with me for bringing them in and wasting their time.

The teachers in the program wanted lessons. They wanted much more specific and detailed information on how to translate the formal research they were reading into something practical they could use in their classrooms. Moving from formal research to practice was too large a leap for them. They wanted some "scaffolding" of these concepts. They felt that practical lessons would help them understand the implications of the theoretical ideas to which they were being exposed. One third-grade teacher, Ms. Cellar, interviewed in her second year of teaching Math[3], said of the summer seminar:

> They had a lot of wasted time in there where there was . . . a lot of research reading and then going over it, which I could do on my own. You know, I want to be taught, I wanted to see more videos of Dalmer teaching the program, and things like that, and how to map the manipulatives, and what you're actually going to be doing in your classroom rather than the research behind it. I'm not crazy about reading research in the first place. . . the summer workshop should train you what to do in your classroom. And really they didn't, it was mainly just research things like that.

Another teacher, Ms. Fox, commenting on reading research in preparation for her summer seminar, said:

> I hate research articles. Just tell me what it is about, summarize it, present it to me and I'll say O.K., but don't ask me to sit there and read. At first they threw a ton of research articles at us. We read them. I was sitting out on my raft in my pool reading and outlining this stuff and the next day I didn't really see a relevance to how it was connected.

The teachers spent time discussing research during the first year of the professional development model and sharing some of the ways Dalmer's practice had changed as a result of reading these materials. But the two-week summer workshop was an extremely short time to read and discuss a wide variety of research papers and to have teachers begin to work toward developing ideas of their own for classroom practice based on the readings, even with Dalmer's experiences and example as a guide. Teachers were expecting a professional development experience to equip them to teach in a particular way. Thus, whereas Dalmer had been able to read the research and develop her approach to teaching based on it over a fairly extended time and in an explicitly exploratory model, the teachers did not have such an extended period of time to explore and reflect on these new concepts. Rather, they entered this professional development experience expecting to be told how to implement an already developed and apparently successful approach to mathematics instruction. But the summer workshop was not run in the didactic manner most teachers expected, based on previous experience with professional development workshops. Nor did it give them a highly structured curriculum with specific pedagogical techniques.

When Dalmer visited the classrooms of these teachers during the school year following the professional development experience, the changes she noted had more to do with things such as the introduction of manipulatives and more classroom talk than with the depth of mathematics instruction she had hoped to see. Although the teachers felt that they were changing their approach to teaching math in significant ways, they were not confident that this approach was better than methods they were more comfortable with.

In an effort to be responsive to teachers' desire for more specific practical help with the implementation of the Math[3] approach in their classrooms, and to help teachers progress toward incorporating the six principles of Math[3] instruction, Dalmer wrote a few model lessons for the teachers during the first year of the professional development effort. After the teachers tried out these first few lessons, they requested more.

In Dalmer's observation of classrooms after the dissemination of these model lessons, she began to see more significant change in actual mathematics instruction. Although this encouraged her, she decided that she would not write a complete curriculum. Much of the research she had read stressed the importance of the active involvement of teachers in this type of complex pedagogical change. Dalmer gave the teachers skeleton lessons and had them jointly work out the details during their monthly Saturday workshops (much the same way that Resnick had worked with Dalmer). Through this process, Dalmer saw her group of teachers develop into a cohesive team. By the end of this first school year, the teachers came to feel that they had developed a much better understanding of how to take the formal research they had read and translate it into usable knowledge—daily lessons for their classrooms.

Indeed, in developing and refining the daily lesson plans in their own classrooms, they came to appreciate formal research in a different way. Rather ironically, given their initial reactions to it, many came to believe, in subsequent years, that the reading of research should be retained as a formal component in future cycles of professional development for Math[3].

In exploring the teachers' reactions to the Cycle A professional development experience, it becomes clear that, as reform approaches to classroom teaching suggest, individuals are much more able and likely to make use of information if they can interpret it within a context that they understand and value. Other programs attempting to bring about complex changes in teacher practice have also found that teachers want practical information first. Only then can they begin more usefully to apply concepts from formal knowledge. For example, Blumenfeld et al. (1994), in their dissemination of an innovative science program, stated that "For much of the first year of our efforts, teachers primarily concentrated on practice—what to do and how to do it—rather than on grappling with the premises underlying project-based instruction" (p. 545).

Richardson's (1994) distinction between "formal research" (conducted by researchers to contribute to a general knowledge base), and "practical inquiry" (conducted by practitioners to improve their practice) is helpful here. Dalmer initially presented the teachers with formal research, believing that they would construct from it a set of practices consistent with the practices she herself had developed during her two years of practical inquiry into approaches to teaching suggested by formal research. Most teachers, however, perhaps partly because of years in an educational system in which learning is assumed to be a rather passive experience, and partly as a result of very real limitations on time and effort, were not able or willing to do that. Teachers were, however, open to a kind of practical inquiry in which they would try out the lessons developed by Dalmer, design lessons themselves with other teachers, and then reflect with a group of their peers on how well these approaches worked and on how they might be improved.

When the second group of teachers came to be trained the next summer (Cycle B), Dalmer modified her approach, starting them with slightly less research (and that research more practitioner oriented) and the use of daily lessons from the very start. These teachers reacted considerably more positively to the program. In Cycles C and D, in the following two years, Dalmer continued to experiment with the amount and kind of research to give to teachers. In Cycle C there was less reliance on the reading and discussion of research than there was in Cycle B. Because teachers from Cycles A, B, and C were now working with one another during the monthly Saturday workshops, they became aware that there had been different professional development models used during the first three years of dissemination. Cycles A and B teachers felt that Cycle C teachers did not have a strong enough research base. They gave program developers feedback suggesting that in future cycles a stronger focus on research be brought back. Although the amount and kind of research contained in the professional development program fluctuated during the last three cycles, all three cycles involved a much heavier emphasis on scripted lessons than did Cycle A.

Ownership

The teachers entering the Math[3] program have overwhelmingly been veteran teachers with years of experience teaching math in a didactic way. This didactic approach is similar in important ways to the manner in which most teachers were educated and to the way their colleagues, who taught the more traditional classrooms we observed in this study, typically conducted themselves. The teachers, quite understandably, perceived the Math[3] approach as something quite different from their normal approach to teaching.

Implementing Math[3] requires a lot, and many layers, of change. Because of concern about their ability to make these complex changes with only a limited amount of preparation time and practice, teachers requested fairly detailed daily lesson plans, as already indicated. Some of these lesson plans were written by project staff and a small group of teachers from Cycles A and B. The result was a significantly scripted set of lesson plans that often included likely student responses (see Fig. 11.1). These lesson plans helped meet teachers' need for practical assistance in knowing how to implement the program, but they raised another problem—that of ownership. In fact, with the advent of the scripted lessons, some teachers started talking of Math[3] as "Ms. Dalmer's program," and the question of the teachers' "ownership" of the approach began to arise.

Teachers who were just entering the Math[3] program were anxious to incorporate all the various aspects of the complex change, and often stuck to the scripted lessons very closely. One teacher, Ms. Bock, who entered the program in Cycle B and was interviewed in her second year in the program, explained:

> I think that the first year, we all thought that we had to be Dalmer. She has a personality unto herself. As the year went on I think we realized that you are who you are and we can't all be Dalmer. I think that was one of the problems with that first year. It took us a while to realize it. You're going to use the language, and you're going to use the techniques, but you're basically who you are and you're not Dalmer. . . . I had more confidence in myself this year. Last year it was like we were reading from a script. Where now, you just read over the problem and you know where you're headed and how to get there.

Teachers found themselves relying on scripted lessons, particularly in their first year of teaching in the program, as a way of dealing with the many layers of change in their practice. This reliance was problematic, though, in that the philosophy of the Math[3] program requires that teachers be flexible and responsive to their students' needs as they arise. Heavy reliance on a scripted lesson compromised this flexibility.

Another element of the professional development model that had an impact on the teachers' feelings of ownership of the program was that Dalmer and other project staff visited teachers' classrooms and videotaped lessons. One of the primary purposes of such activities was to encourage teachers to reflect on their teaching strategies with the aim of transforming their practice. During these visits, Dalmer and other project staff offered feedback to teachers about their implementation of the Math[3] approach, which provided an opportunity for discussion of the teachers' own concerns.

Because Math[3] required so many complex changes, there was virtually always room for improvement in practice. Teachers, who were not accustomed to being observed and critiqued in this way, sometimes took offense at this feedback, feeling they were expected to teach "Ms.

NCTM Standards	Problem

NCTM Standard 1:
Formulate problems from
everyday situations.

You have a box of popsicles. There are 24 popsicles in the box:

6 banana
8 grape
10 cherry

NCTM Standard 2:
Relate pictures and diagrams to
mathematical ideas.

You and your friend can share the popsicles. But you must tell me
how many popsicles you will each get. Tell me which flavors you
will receive and which flavors your friend will receive. Make sure
I know which flavors to give you.

Whole class discussion

After students' work is completed, discuss several students'
solutions. For example, you might want to discuss the following
solution.

NCTM Standard 7:
Relate mathematical language
and symbolism to problem
situations.

$$3 + 3 = 6$$
$$4 + 4 = 8$$
$$5 + 5 = 10$$
$$3 + 4 + 5 = 12$$

If the student uses this solution strategy, the student takes half of
each flavor.

Look for students in the class who put the information above in
the form of a chart. Engage students in a discussion about the
difference and similarity between the two sets of information. Ask
them if they know more about the students from one set than from
the other.

NCTM Standard 2:
Reflect on mathematical ideas
and situations.

	Me	My Friend
banana	3	3
grape	4	4
cherry	5	5

NCTM Standard 3:
Justify their answers.

Some examples of student work are shown below. Think about
how the students solved the problem.

How can you make connections between problems?

For example, can you ask students to think about how the
following two problems can both equal 12? How can $6 + 6$ and
$10 + 2$ both equal 12?

Ask students to explain how they can use the answer to $10 + 2$ to
thik about the solution to the problem $5 + 4 + 3 = 12$.

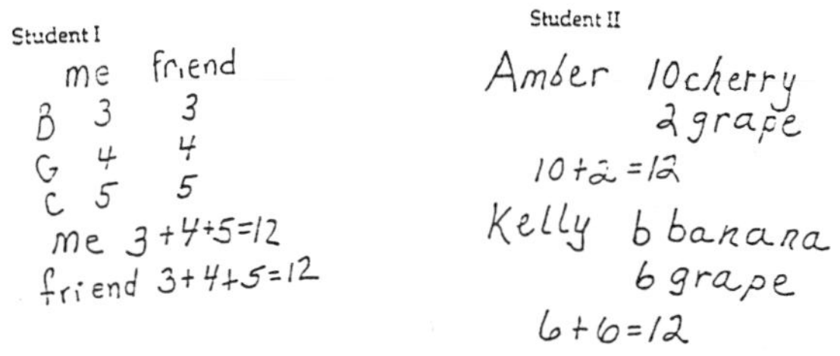

Student I

me   friend
B   3   3
G   4   4
C   5   5
me 3+4+5=12
friend 3+4+5=12

Student II

Amber 10 cherry
        2 grape
10 + 2 = 12

Kelly 6 banana
       6 grape
6 + 6 = 12

FIG. 11.1.   A sample Math³ lesson: Grade 2, day 20.

299

Dalmer's way." The fact that Dalmer and other project staff often went out of their way to mention problems they themselves had faced when attempting to change their own practices did not completely alleviate the sense of being judged. Teachers were especially reluctant to put themselves in a position of being critiqued in front of other teachers. One teacher explained her feelings:

> I think whenever teachers did get up to do some of the things [during the workshops] some of them felt openly criticized. And I don't think it was meant to be that way. But when you're the person up there doing something and someone says, 'I wouldn't have done it that way, I would have done it this way.' I know it's supposed to be for the instruction. But when it comes not [from the other teachers] but from somebody teaching you the program, it sort of is taken as a criticism.

Another factor influencing teachers' sense of ownership in Math^3 was Dalmer's sense of urgency about the need to incorporate all the different elements of this complex new program. She worried that this sense of urgency was not shared by the teachers:

> Our teachers are very laid back. I mean, even in this project. "If I get to it, okay. If I skip drills, if I don't do the labs, it's okay. I do what I can do." And I don't have that sense of . . . It's not okay. I mean, you're not doing what a child needs then. This is very, this is crafted so that everything builds off of something for the future. Okay? And if you don't do all those pieces, they think nothing of it. I mean, I don't understand this at all. And they all, "If I only have forty minutes," I say, "Well I only have forty minutes too." It's just, you make yourself get it in. And it just means being very well prepared. I mean, I go in and I'm ready to roll.

Teachers had a difficult time making all the changes they were expected to make at once. Dalmer and other project staff had a difficult time prioritizing the various elements of the Math^3 approach so that teachers could incorporate some at first and gradually add additional elements when they were comfortable with their mastery of prior changes. Because teachers were faced with making these changes as a package, they tended to pick and choose elements that worked best, or made more sense to them, and left others alone. Teachers, for example, all seemed to incorporate the use of manipulatives into their practice, although even this change was complicated for teachers because it meant managing the distribution and use of the manipulatives, something that was new to almost every teacher in the program. But working with cooperative groups, or having the children do labs (small projects done in groups) daily, were things the teachers tended not to incorporate into their practice, at least not at first.

A feeling of ownership on the part of the teachers was especially important because the commitment the program requires—the time and effort it takes to make teaching math this way work—is more than that required by a more traditional math curriculum. This commitment includes greater teacher time in preparation for a lesson in addition to the actual teaching of the lesson. Ms. Jones, who entered the program in Cycle B and was interviewed in her second year in the program, explained:

> For me, at least, and I think, listening to other teachers, one of the major weaknesses is number one, the length, the amount of time it takes to teach these lessons, the amount of preparation time that it takes, and quite often I feel like I'm not doing an adequate job because I *don't* have time to get all of this together and my math period is supposed to be limited to a forty-five minute period. And I often have to run over in that. Sometimes I'm an hour, more frequently I'm an hour with these lessons or longer and that's just too much time because then the kids really start to get tired with it. And they (the Math[3] professional development staff) say, "Well, you could just stop," you know, "you know your class." But then you miss a lot of the concepts that they're trying to develop there and I feel like, while I'm covering a lot of concepts in one lesson, they're not always getting enough pencil/paper practice for what they need to do, even with the homework and the drills. I can't fit all of that in that way and I know they're trying to get away from that approach but they still need the practice, particularly for basic facts. They still don't really know their basic facts. They know how to find them but they still don't have them locked in their heads like they normally would.[5]

It is unlikely that any complex new approach can be implemented without a transitional period during which the teacher's use of this new approach is not as smooth or skilled as the teacher would like. Even if the teacher understands the new approach and the reasons for it well, actually making it happen in the classroom takes some practice and may occasionally result in unanticipated problems. Yet teachers, especially very experienced teachers, are likely to want, even expect, to feel that they know exactly what they are doing. Experiencing confusion or difficulty can be very demoralizing if the teacher attributes the problem to his or her own deficiencies or does not feel a real commitment to the new approach.

Cobb et al. (1990), in their dissemination of an innovative elementary math curriculum, faced the same dilemma. On one hand, they found that providing daily lesson plans to their teachers was essential because the complexity of the task for teachers, that of changing their practice

---

[5] This quote indicates a concern with time, but it also indicates a concern with the Math[3] approach to teaching and learning math. Many teachers had great difficulty giving up an approach to mathematics teaching that stressed drilling and algorithms.

so dramatically, could be so time consuming that they did not have the energy to pay attention to student needs: "To be sure, we were relatively directive once the teachers began to see their current form of practice as problematic. But this was to make it possible for them to learn in their classrooms rather than to ensure that they taught the way we wanted them to" (Cobb et al., 1990, p. 144). On the other hand, developers came to realize the importance of respecting teacher practical knowledge and the innovations teachers made in the program as they adapted it to their classrooms: "At the outset of the project, we took for granted the goal of attempting to transform the teachers into constructivists who thought just like we did. It was only when working with teachers that we became aware of the gross hypocrisy implicit in this goal" (Cobb et al., 1990, p. 145). This dilemma in constructivist models of professional development is a central one: how to teach something new to a learner while respecting his or her own constructions and novel interpretations.

Teaching Content Knowledge While Respecting Teacher Constructions

A teacher following a constructivist model that leans too heavily on the side of the independent constructions of the individual learner risks not teaching much at all or teaching something quite different from, and possibly not consistent with, what he or she intends to accomplish:

> Pedagogies derived from constructivist theory frequently involve a collection of questionable claims that sanctify the student at the expense of mathematical and scientific ways of knowing. In such accounts, the teacher's role is typically characterized as that of facilitating students' investigations and explorations. Thus, although the teacher might have a variety of responsibilities, these do not necessarily include that of *proactively* supporting students' mathematical development. Romantic views of this type arise at least in part because a maxim about learning, namely that students necessarily construct their mathematical and scientific ways of knowing, is interpreted as a direct instructional recommendation. (Cobb, 1994a, p. 4)

On the other hand, a teacher following a pedagogical model that leans too heavily in the other direction, that of enculturation of the learner, risks being too didactic, or not being sensitive to the different ways people learn and the different understandings with which they enter the learning situation. Prawat and Floden (1994) refered to this as "the constructivist dilemma":

> How does the teacher manage the negotiation process so that both the individual student and the discipline receive their just due? Striking the right balance between honoring the individual student's own effort after meaning while steering the group toward some "intellectually honest"

(i.e., disciplinarily correct) construction of meaning has been described as the "constructivist dilemma." It is one of the most vexing issues faced by social-constructivist teachers. (p. 47)

Dalmer felt the results of this dilemma in her Cycle A professional development attempts. Teachers had difficulty moving from theory to practice. This problem led to the development of a more scripted, less "purely constructivist" (in Dalmer's view) approach in which detailed daily lesson plans were given to the teachers. Daily lesson plans were important, though, because they provided the "scaffolding" teachers needed to be able to translate research into practice. Teachers, over time, seemed not to feel constrained by the scripted lessons. Once they got over the anxiety of the first year and started to incorporate many of the changes into their practice, teachers reported that although they really appreciated having the daily lesson plans available to them, to give them a structure to start with, they also felt the freedom to modify these lessons to meet their own and their children's needs. Mr. Paton, a teacher interviewed in his second year of the Math[3] program, explained:

I like the way the lesson plans are written out. I mean, that's really helpful. Some of the people seem to be afraid to change the words. I have no problem changing words and so that's been really, really helpful. There's enough detail that gives me what to go on, what to do to go on. I'm changing them and using my own speech patterns, so that's really helpful to me.

Teachers are accustomed to being independent professionals with a large degree of autonomy to develop and carry out their classroom practice. Questioning teacher practice enough to motivate them to change and then introducing teachers to substantially different ideas and approaches to teaching must be done carefully and with respect to teachers' identities as competent professionals.

Building a Community of Practice

Collaboration is critical in this work for two reasons. First . . . just as learners in classrooms need to collaborate to develop shared meaning, so teachers need to develop their own socially constructed understanding of their work. Second, collaboration reduces the isolation of teaching. (Blumenfeld et al., 1994, p. 541)

What most teachers in the Math[3] program liked best was the opportunity to meet and talk with other teachers about teaching. Ms. Reese, a teacher from Cycle A interviewed in her third year in the program, said: "I like being with other teachers and talking about things because teaching is a lonely profession. I think the whole business of sharing with other teachers has been very good." And another teacher (Cycle B, interviewed in second year) said: "I love my Saturday sessions. I like the calendars we get and that we can rehash it as a group. You get everyone else's input and you find out that your kids aren't the only ones who are doing this. Or, you get other ideas, which is great."

As teachers attempted to change their practice in complex ways, having others with whom to share their difficulties and triumphs made a big difference. Many times teachers reported feeling bad about the lack of progress they were making in their classrooms, until they came to a Saturday workshop and found out that other teachers were in the same position. For example, one teacher stated that:

> I'm not sure whether it's a fault of the program or my fault, but the feeling I got from the other teachers at the last seminar was I kept my mouth shut because I was truly believing it was me that was backed up and bogged down and was a problem until the other teachers went, "Yeah!" I said, "Well, then it isn't just me."

Dalmer learned to use this feeling of camaraderie among teachers to solve the problems of ownership and of respect for teacher knowledge. She noted that as teachers found problems (and sometimes small mistakes) in some of the early scripted lessons, they took pride in and seemed to enjoy, rewriting these lessons together. Dalmer then began to feel that it was not necessary to make sure the materials were perfect. Working with these lessons encouraged the teachers to think about them carefully and to have a hand in shaping all of the lessons. When designing these lessons, teachers talked among themselves about problems they saw occurring in their own classrooms or aspects of math education they felt were not receiving adequate attention in the program. They then wrote lesson plans to meet these needs. They also shared news of unanticipated triumphs when they discovered that their students could handle material that they had not been exposed to before or when a lesson went unusually well. Working together to design these lessons increased group cohesion and increased a feeling of ownership in the program for the teachers as well as helping them work through issues by discussing with their peers possible solutions to problems that arose.

Even though the monthly workshops meant giving up a free Saturday, which was an issue for most of the teachers, they still remained committed to being there. One teacher expressed a sentiment shared by many others:

> I really like the Saturday workshops and I don't think there would ever be a time that I would miss one of those because the relationship with the group, the teachers at the same grade level going through the things that you go through. When you say, "Oh my gosh! Lesson 32, I had such a

horrible time." And then they say, "You know, I did too." All of a sudden then, I don't feel like, "Oh, it was me! Okay, they did too. Then it has to be something about the way we all presented it, or the way we saw it written, or whatever we did with that." And I think, when you're doing it on your own, you think, "Boy, did I really blow this!" But when you talk to those people and they say, "Oh gosh! It was awful for me too!" I think the grade levels are the best part when you meet with them. You just need it.

Teachers were extremely enthusiastic about the opportunity provided to them to talk with other teachers about their experiences and specifically to discuss both problems and accomplishments in implementing Math^3, and a strong sense of community developed over time. Inherent in the concept of community is a sense of continuity. Because the personal relationships necessary for community take some time to develop, it is hard to imagine a community that exists only for a moment in time. If one views learning as a process that develops over time, with conflict, confusion, and surprise as expected parts of the process (Wood et al., 1991), it stands to reason that to be maximally effective a professional development effort cannot be a one-shot event that is limited to a particular day or set of days. Rather there must be an ongoing community of people who can assist each other as they encounter the difficulties that are an inevitable part of coming to new understandings.

Dalmer was very aware of the importance of such an ongoing support structure, although limitations related to financial constraints made it difficult to provide as much ongoing support as she would have liked. The monthly meetings were an important source of ongoing support. Believing, however, that this might not be sufficient, Dalmer made a point of calling teachers on occasion just to see whether there was anything with which she could help. She also let teachers know that she and the other professional development staff were available by phone, and she encouraged people to contact her when they felt they needed support, in spite of the fact that she and her staff were extraordinarily busy themselves. Teachers also exchanged phone numbers with each other and occasionally called for both practical and emotional support.

Constructing and Negotiating Meaning Through Collaboration

Successful implementation of Math^3 required certain kinds of classroom behaviors on the parts of teachers and students that were at odds with traditional approaches. Many teachers in the Math^3 program, however, functioned in schools where many of their colleagues saw little need for change. One of the most important consequences of building a community of practice was that it created a milieu in which teachers could struggle with redefining the meaning of certain situations in a supportive environment. Perhaps the clearest example of this concerned the issue of what a classroom should look and sound like. Many of the teachers were not comfortable grouping children together and allowing children to talk with one another during math lessons. Their concept of a classroom in which learning was occurring was one in which all children were quietly paying attention to the teacher at the front of the classroom or working quietly at individual tasks. Mr. Paton explained:

> Well, see, I'm very strict. I went through 16 years of Catholic School. You know, you sit in a row and you do this and that. And then I was in a seminary and I just left the seminary when [Dalmer] came to demonstrate this program. I was still into the mold of everybody does the same thing at the same time. And I really wasn't into the manipulatives and the noise and the groups. To me that wasn't learning. But when she did it, I could, you know, sitting back I could see it. And this summer helped too because she had kids in there this summer so I could see that they weren't just chit-chatting and they were actually doing something.

Many of the Math^3 teachers in both public and parochial schools had to contend with school cultures that stressed the importance of quiet, orderly learning. At times principals entered a Math^3 classroom, surprised at the noise and movement, and questioned whether Math^3 was an effective pedagogical approach. Through involvement in a community of practice with other teachers whose views were also changing and who were facing many of the same practical difficulties, however, many of these teachers were successful in redefining for themselves what a good classroom looked like and in changing their practice in substantial ways.

CONCLUSION

Although many in the educational reform community have embraced insights from the current literature and have seen the important implications both for the classroom and for professional development experiences, translating this new and emerging understanding of learning into effective pedagogical techniques is still problematic. As many innovative programs attempt to incorporate constructivist principles, it is important to look closely at both the benefits and the difficulties of incorporating these ideas.

In this chapter we have examined the issues—the importance of teachers seeing the need to change their practice, the tension between formal research and practical inquiry, the importance of teachers feeling a sense of ownership in the innovation, the "constructivist dilemma" of teaching content knowledge while respecting teacher constructions, and the importance of building a community of practice—that arose in the implementation of a professional development model that reflected current views of teaching and learning. This case study allowed us to see both how these issues became problems and how they were dealt with in the evolution of an innovative elementary mathematics program.

Many of the ideas of reform thinking in education have implications for instruction on a number of different levels. Students in classrooms must be recognized as active learners who do not passively incorporate lessons handed to them by their teachers. Teachers, too, must be recognized as active learners who interpret new ideas through their own experiences and make sense of these new ideas only to the extent that they can apply them to what they already "know." Creating professional development opportunities that are effective, especially when incorporating complex new ideas, will remain a challenge—the "constructivist dilemma."

Above all, in working with reform principles in the evolution of pedagogical approaches, it is important for developers to remain flexible and to incorporate teacher feedback. Not only is the approach to professional development changing, but the entire teaching culture is as well. Today's teachers were raised and educated in an era in which didactic approaches to teaching were the norm. The current educational reform movement calls for radical changes in what was considered to be effective teaching and appropriate learning environments. These changes will take time, effort, and a willingness to rethink previously taken-for-granted assumptions about teaching and learning.

ACKNOWLEDGMENTS

The research reported here was funded by Contract No.R117G10003 with the National Research Center on Student Learning. All opinions expressed herein are solely those of the authors and no endorsement of the conclusions by the Office of Educational Research and Improvement (OERI) is implied or intended.

The Authors wish to thank the developers of Math[3] for allowing us to study the progress of their professional development efforts. It is admirable that the developers have allowed us to scrutinize their work in the hope of improving our knowledge base.

REFERENCES

Blumenfeld, P., Krajcik, J. S., Marx, R. W., & Soloway, E. (1994). Lessons learned: How collaboration helped middle grade science teachers learn project-based instruction. *The Elementary School Journal, 94*(5), 539–551.

Brown, J. S., Collins, A., & Duguid, P. (1989). Situated cognition and the culture of learning. *Educational Researcher, 18*(5), 32–42.

Carpenter, T. P., Fennema, E., Peterson, P. L., Chiang, C. P., & Loef, M. (1989). Using knowledge of children's mathematics thinking in classroom teaching: An experimental study. *American Educational Research Journal, 26*(4), 499–531.

Cobb, P. (1994a). Constructivism in mathematics and science education. *Educational Researcher, 23*(7), 4.

Cobb, P. (1994b). Where is the mind? Constructivist and sociocultural perspectives on mathematical development. *Educational Researcher, 23*(7), 13–20.

Cobb, P., Wood, T., & Yackel, E. (1990). Classrooms as learning environments for teachers and researchers. In R. B. Davis, C. A. Maher, & N. Noddings (Eds.), *Constructivist views on teaching and learning mathematics* (pp. 125–146). Reston, VA: National Council of Teachers of Mathematics.

Driver, R., Asoko, H., Leach, J., Mortimer, E., & Scott, P. (1994). Constructing scientific knowledge in the classroom. *Educational Researcher, 23*(7), 5–12.

Glaser, B. G., & Strauss, A. L. (1967). *The discovery of grounded theory: Strategies for qualitative research*. New York: Aldine de Gruyter.

Jamar, I. (1994, April). *The effectiveness of second-generation Math[3] teachers: A first phase of analysis*. Paper presented at the meeting of the American Educational Research Association, New Orleans, LA.

Leer, M., Resnick, R., & Bill, V. (1994, April). *The Math[3] cognitive apprenticeship model of professional development: Building a community of reflective practitioners*. Paper presented at the meeting of the American Educational Research Association, New Orleans, LA.

Miles, M. B., & Huberman, A. M. (1984). *Qualitative data analysis: A sourcebook of new methods*. Beverly Hills, CA: Sage.

Piaget, J. (1970). *Genetic epistemology*. New York: Columbia Press.

Piaget, J. (1980). *Adaptation and intelligence: Organic selection and phenocopy*. Chicago: University of Chicago Press.

Prawat, R. S., & Floden, R. E. (1994). Philosophical perspectives on constructivist views of learning. *Educational Psychology, 29*(1), 37–48.

Resnick, L. B., Bill, V. L., & Lesgold, S. (1992). Developing thinking abilities in arithmetic class. In A. Debetriou, M. Shayer, & A. Efklides (Eds.), *Neo-Piagetian theories of cognitive development: Implications and applications for education* (pp. 210–230). London: Routledge.

Resnick, L. B., Bill, V. L., Lesgold, S., & Leer, M. (1991). Thinking in arithmetic class. In B. Means, C. Chelemer, & M. S. Knapp (Eds.), *Teaching advanced skills to at-risk students: Views from research and practice* (pp. 27–53). San Francisco: Jossey-Bass.

Richardson, V. (1994). Conducting research on practice. *Educational Researcher, 23*(5), 5–10.

Simon, M. A. (1994, April). *The impact of constructivism on mathematics teacher education*. Paper presented at Interdisciplinary Perspectives on Directions for Constructivism in Mathematics and Science Education: A conference in honor of Ernst Von Glaserfeld, Atlanta, GA.

Stocks, J., & Schofield, J. (1994, April). *Math[3] in action: Implementing a "new paradigm" elementary mathematics program*. Paper presented at the meeting of the American Educational Research Association, New Orleans, LA.

Strauss, A., & Corbin, J. (1990). *Basics of qualitative research*. New York: Sage Publications.

Wood, D. J., Bruner J. S., & Ross, G. (1976). The role of tutoring in problem solving. *Journal of Child Psychology and Psychiatry, 17*, 89–100.

Wood, T., Cobb, P., & Yackel, E. (1991). Change in teaching mathematics: A case study. *American Educational Research Journal, 28*(3), 587–616.

12

Project IMPACT: Influencing and Supporting Teacher Change in Predominantly Minority Schools

Patricia F. Campbell
University of Maryland at College Park

Dorothy Y. White
University of Georgia

Project IMPACT (Increasing the Mathematical Power of All Children and Teachers) is a National Science Foundation-funded (NSF) project focused on improving the quality of the content and pedagogy of elementary mathematics in urban schools located in Montgomery County, Maryland, outside Washington, D. C. As a teacher enhancement project, Project IMPACT seeks to support and enhance teachers as they attempt to change their teaching practices in order to increase the mathematics achievement of children. Although all children should benefit from these teaching approaches, the Project is based in predominantly minority schools where there are high numbers of children who have not flourished with traditional teaching practices. As a longitudinal research effort, this project examines the systemic implications of teacher enhancement and the nature of school-based reform.

In this chapter, we (a) characterize the origins and influences that impelled the project design, (b) describe the intervention model, (c) offer evidence of teacher change, and (d) analyze the implications of this project for instructional reform in mathematics education.

ORIGINS AND INFLUENCES

Project IMPACT is a collaborative venture between the University of Maryland at College Park and Montgomery County Public Schools,

Maryland (MCPS). Both of these parties had significant input into the design of the project. In particular, MCPS' struggle to implement new curriculum objectives revealed the need for a more focused and supportive teacher enhancement model, particularly in schools where traditional mathematics instruction was producing limited achievement differentiated by student racial ethnicity. University researchers were interested in demonstrating ways of transforming research on the teaching and learning of elementary mathematics into effective school practice through school-based professional development. Both of these perspectives influenced the design of the project that was to be known as IMPACT.

Local Perspective

In the fall of 1988, MCPS released elementary mathematics curriculum objectives that had an increased emphasis on problem solving and concept development. For example, this curriculum included objectives such as acting out word problems in kindergarten; interpreting simple bar graphs in first grade; explaining the need for a common whole when ordering concrete representations of fractions in second grade; creating word problems from data in third grade; classifying shapes by self-selected criteria and describing the classification scheme in fourth grade; and explaining the difference between fractions and ratios in fifth grade. These new objectives were not limited to a traditional, hierarchical behavioral design. Students were expected to explore, describe, and explain. In many regards, these revised objectives represented a school district's efforts to align its goals with the perspective of the *Curriculum and Evaluation Standards for School Mathematics* of the National Council of Teachers of Mathematics (NCTM, 1989).

Professional development efforts in MCPS had focused on school-based workshops to acquaint teachers with the content of the revised curriculum; sample activity-based lesson plans were provided to characterize the kinds of lessons envisioned for classrooms. Many teachers correctly interpreted this new curriculum as involving more hands-on activities for students; however, typically teachers felt that completion of these manipulative activities was to be directed by the teacher. Further, many teachers presumed that mere engagement in these manipulative tasks would be sufficient to increase students' mathematical understanding. The revised primary curriculum included new assessments that evaluated clusters of related objectives, frequently expecting children to explain using manipulatives. These integrated assessments did lead to some confusion, particularly when children failed to reach the recommended standard. Primary teachers asked, "How do I know which objective to reteach?" Finally, in the upper elementary grades, insufficient funding and time resulted in limited assessment revision. Although the objectives and sample lessons in the upper elementary grades were focusing on concept development and problem solving, many of their assessments still addressed prescribed skill-based routines. Despite these limitations, the vision and courage reflected in MCPS' early efforts to reform elementary mathematics curriculum, instruction, and assessment remain quite laudatory.

Concurrent with the release of the new elementary mathematics curriculum package, MCPS completed a self-study that examined the performance and participation of females and minorities in mathematics (Gross, 1988). One component of this study examined historical data reflecting the performance of students as a rate of progress through MCPS mathematics curriculum objectives over time. This study indicated that by the end of second grade, racial patterns in mathematical achievement favoring White and Asian students were already present; these patterns were not evident at the end of first grade. In addition, the declining pattern of mathematics achievement for Black and Hispanic children became more pronounced over the ensuing academic years. This study revealed that, despite the presence of MCPS School Board priority goals for educating every student in key academic areas, ethnic–racial differential performance was present.

MCPS district administrators were very concerned that existing in-service efforts and administrative directives as implemented by the school system had failed to change and would not address differential mathematics achievement. Their self-study raised questions as to whether a student's *opportunity* to learn mathematics in the classroom was being influenced by prior achievement. Indeed, once a student evidenced declining achievement in mathematics, MCPS data insinuated that it was improbable that the student would ever reverse that descending trend. In the existing instructional pattern, once a student began to lag in mathematics, "even at a very early age, that student could realistically expect to continue to fall further and further behind his or her age-level peers and to simultaneously be denied the mathematics instruction provided to those peers" (Campbell, 1996, p. 455). District leaders recognized that if children were to reach their full potential with respect to participation and performance in mathematics, then it was necessary to address their instructional needs in the primary grades. Change at the classroom level was critical.

Theoretical Basis

A constructivist theory of knowledge is characterized by two basic principles: (a) learners actively construct knowledge through interaction with their surroundings and experiences, and (b) learners interpret these occurrences based on existing knowledge and their rendering of the experienced observations and actions (Noddings, 1990). Although there are philosophical and epistemological distinctions in the resulting implications drawn by constructivist theorists (e.g., von Glasersfeld, 1990), the perspective that knowledge is actively constructed rather than passively received has had critical implications for mathematics education.

As noted by Pirie and Kieren (1992), there was "no 'constructivist teaching model' out there waiting to be implemented" (p. 506). However, researchers were beginning to hypothesize characteristics of instructional approaches that would be compatible with constructivist learning models (e.g., Cobb, 1988). In addition, primary research studies addressing the teaching and learning of addition, subtraction, and place value offered striking exemplars of increased student achievement and teacher change in classrooms that focused on problem solving and mathematical understanding with instructional decisions incorporating teachers' knowledge of children's thinking (Carpenter, Fennema, Peterson, Chiang, & Loef, 1989; Cobb, Wood, & Yackel, 1991; Cobb, Yackel, Wood, Wheatley, & Merkel, 1988).

A simultaneous review of exemplary intervention programs in mathematics and science for women and minorities yielded a characterization of successful programs. Namely, effective approaches included a strong academic component focused on problem solving, understanding, and applications; early, sustained instruction rather than remediation; high expectations with positive, substantive teacher–student interactions; mathematics interaction not only between the teachers and the students, but also among the students; multiyear involvement with the students; teacher enhancement to ensure that teachers were competent in the subject matter and approach; use of a variety of instructional strategies including hands-on manipulative teaching; teachers convinced of the students' ability to learn; integration of the intervention objectives into the educational institutions accessed by the students; university–school cooperation; identification of participants from the entire target population within a locale to maximize peer involvement; parental involvement; and an evaluation component that included careful data collection (Beane, 1985; Clewell, Thorpe, & Anderson, 1987; Lockheed, Thorpe, Brooks-Gunn, Casserly, & McAloon, 1985; Malcom, Aldrich, Hall, Boulware, & Stern, 1984). Each of these components was incorporated into the Project IMPACT model.

An Emerging Prototype

To permit ongoing evaluation and modification of its implementation model, Project IMPACT was initially limited to kindergarten through third grade classrooms, with the kindergarten and first grade commitment occurring in the first year, followed by second and third grade implementation in the next two years respectively. Thus, the Project executed a longitudinal model, both in terms of implementation and evaluation. Because of the emerging success in the primary grades, Project IMPACT was ultimately extended into the fourth and fifth grades.

From the outset, the premise was that decisions within the Project had to revolve around a single criterion: implementation of a policy of expecting and supporting the mathematical understanding of each child. Observation of classrooms prior to the teacher enhancement phase of the project revealed that even use of manipulative materials such as base-10 blocks was being directed by teachers and practiced by children as if the blocks were a three-dimensional symbol system. Yet mathematics instruction that depends on memorization and focuses only on obtaining a particular answer can be forgotten by students because it is not understood (National Research Council, 1989). The teacher enhancement model, therefore, had to address teachers' pedagogical and mathematical content knowledge (Ball, 1991; Peterson, Fennema, & Carpenter, 1991; Putnam, Lampert, & Peterson, 1990; Thompson, 1985), supporting and encouraging instructional change and decision making (Carpenter et al., 1989) away from the prevalent focus on teacher direction and definition followed by student practice. Further, the teacher enhancement model had to directly address equity issues, moving beyond equal opportunity for students to equal treatment and equal outcomes (Fennema & Meyer, 1989).

Research indicates that understanding builds on prior knowledge (Hiebert & Carpenter, 1992). For young children who are just entering formal schooling, prior knowledge is the informal knowledge gained in out-of-school experiences (Carey, Fennema, Carpenter, & Franke, 1995). Project IMPACT's focus in the primary grades, therefore, encouraged teachers to foster children's interpretation of mathematical relationships in problems based on whatever intuitive knowledge or unique experiences the children had outside of school and to build on those experiences with instructional activities that might extend or deepen existing knowledge. This premise also carried over to the upper elementary grades; however, there was an increased concern that children in these grades consider implications for mathematical generalization and utilize appropriate symbolization (Lampert, 1989) and efficient recording schemes. The Project focused on conceptual knowledge and problem solving, using that as a base for developing skills (Cobb, Wood, & Yackel, 1990; NCTM, 1989). Teachers were asked to consider the implications of permitting children to solve problems in their own ways. Teachers were also asked to characterize instructional schemes that might allow all children to benefit from the various solution strategies that were being used in the classroom. In particular, the role of communication and interaction was highlighted as teachers considered the implications of children sharing their strategies with their classmates, explaining how they solved the problem and why they solved the problem in that way (NCTM, 1991). The intent was for teachers to construct instructional approaches whereby they guided the problem-solving process, caused children to examine and validate reasoning, and focused children's attention on the mathematics underlying expressed thinking. The intent was for the children and the teachers to come to see mathematics as "making sense" (NCTM, 1989, 1991; Lappan & Briars, 1995). Based on current research, the Project staff believed that such an approach would make elementary and higher level mathematics more accessible to all students. This approach is a modified constructivist approach to the teaching and learning of mathematics.

School-based Reform

Project IMPACT utilized a school-based model. The assumption behind this model is that the critical unit for change in mathematics teaching and learning is the school (Wideen, 1992). As a result, this project did not seek teachers who would volunteer for professional enhancement nor did it involve a variety of schools across the school district. Rather it addressed the enhancement of all of the mathematics teachers in identified urban elementary schools that served a predominantly minority population of children.

At the initiation of Project IMPACT, a research design that presumed mandatory participation in school-based, mathematics teacher enhancement was atypical. However, principals and mathematics coordinators uniformly noted that traditional mathematics instruction in urban settings seemed impregnable, with prior district-supported half-day and after-school workshops having had no discernible influence. Similarly, prior district efforts to address student achievement in mathematics through in-service efforts for volunteer teachers had not been effective in the urban centers because few of the volunteer teachers were from the urban schools in the district and because classroom implementation following these teacher enhancement efforts had been infrequent or absent. Recognition of the ineffectiveness of the district's prior in-service models was coupled with the knowledge that it is difficult for isolated teachers to effect real instructional change (Fullan with Stiegelbauer, 1991), much less isolated teachers in urban schools coping with constraining social and environmental conditions. Yet district personnel recognized the urgency of addressing the academic needs of high numbers of children who were not flourishing with the existing, traditional teaching practices in the urban schools, children who would need consistency in mathematics instruction in subsequent years of schooling. Therefore, district administrators and IMPACT investigators decided that if this project was to have any effect on the longitudinal mathematical achievement of the children in the district's urban schools, then it would have to facilitate instructional change across the complete mathematics program of those schools, not merely in unique classrooms. Further, Project IMPACT's implementation could not be limited to one strand of the mathematics curriculum; it had to support teachers as they attempted change across the entire spectrum of mathematical topics for which they were accountable.

Ultimately most classroom teachers came to agree with these decisions. To involve each teacher required advance planning. Project IMPACT used grade-specific summer in-service programs to introduce the mechanisms of change. In this way the summer program was viewed as being more relevant to the needs of the teachers. Project IMPACT's experience has been that when teachers knew of the summer program by the preceding February, when teachers knew that this would be the mathematics program of their grade, and when teachers knew that they would have school-based support during implementation, teachers agreed to participate.

The exception to this occurred during the first year of the Project. At one school, the principal did not inform her teachers of their involvement in the project until mid-spring. The lack of teacher participation in the decision-making process at this school subsequently led to dissension and animosity, with a union grievance suit being filed. Nevertheless, when the kindergarten and first-grade teachers at this school learned more about the summer in-service program and the school-based supports available to participating teachers in the upcoming academic year, each one of these teachers decided to participate in the summer teacher enhancement. In the subsequent summers, the other teachers in this building were consistently willing to attend the summer program. Project IMPACT's experience has been that very few teachers will leave a building to escape an in-service program. Indeed, teachers come to view the expected summer in-service with either acceptance or eagerness.

CHARACTERISTICS OF SCHOOLS

School Selection

In 1990, there were 21 predominantly minority elementary schools in MCPS. Schools were ranked on the following criteria: percentage of minority students enrolled; percentage of families receiving free or reduced-fee breakfast, lunch, or both; percentage of low scores on the Grade 3 statewide assessment (California Achievement Test in 1989); and percentage of students categorized as below grade level on the school system's mathematics curriculum assessment on leaving Grade 3. Third grade achievement was used as a measure of academic tradition because the project was initially funded only for kindergarten through third-grade implementation.

The principals of the six highest ranking schools in these categories were invited to join the Project. Schools had to commit to Project IMPACT prior to identification of treatment or comparable-site status. Once cooperating schools were identified, the schools were paired, and the assignment of project status was determined by three coin tosses, conducted in the presence of the school principals or their designees. Designation of treatment or comparable-site status was the choice of the winning schools. Both treatment and comparable-site schools had to permit classroom observations in the fall and spring and student assessment in the winter and spring.

Of the six schools initially identified, two schools decided against participation. One principal wanted a guarantee of treatment status. The other principal declined because she did not have unanimous faculty approval. The next two schools on the ranking agreed to the terms of the Project. Following the coin toss, two of the principals requested treatment status; one principal requested that his school be a comparable site.

Three of the six identified schools were primary schools, enrolling children through Grade three; the other three schools were elementary schools. In 1993, MCPS funded the Project's summer in-service program for those primary grade teachers in the comparable-site schools who wished to participate. At the same time, NSF provided funding to continue the Project into the fourth and fifth grades. At that time, two additional schools became involved in Project IMPACT; these were fourth through sixth grade schools that enrolled the children who had matriculated from one of the three original primary schools.

Student Demographic Characteristics

The eight Project IMPACT schools enrolled children representing differing demographic patterns. Three of the predominantly minority schools enrolled both African American children and White children. Two schools enrolled many children of Hispanic heritage from Central and northern South America, as well as many Black children who were either African American or immigrants from Africa, Haiti, or the Caribbean. These schools also enrolled some children from Vietnam or Korea. The remaining three schools enrolled many children from Africa, Haiti, the Caribbean, Central America, Cambodia, Vietnam, and the nations of Southwest Asia and the Middle East. These children were recent refugees from the political and domestic turmoil in their native lands. Over the course of the Project there were substantial variations in the student racial/ethnic distributions due to a high student mobility rate (averaging 66% during 1990–93). Across the cooperating schools, the student population was about 9% Asian, 26% White, 30% Hispanic, and 35% Black.

In each of the five implementation years, approximately 500 children formed a grade-level cohort across the cooperating schools. Across the schools, approximately 60% of the children received free or reduced-fee breakfast, lunch, or both meals, and 25% of the children were enrolled in English classes for speakers of other languages.

Teacher Demographic Characteristics

Project IMPACT's school-based model required the participation of every mathematics teacher in the treatment schools during a grade-level summer in-service program. This did occur. The faculty at the original kindergarten through third grade treatment sites reflected greater racial diversity than at the comparable-site schools, although both sets of schools were populated with a predominantly female, white faculty. Approximately one third of the fourth and fifth grade teachers were African American; one sixth of the upper grade teachers were male. Over half of the targeted teachers in the schools participating in Project IMPACT had less than five years of teaching experience. This is not an unusual phenomenon in urban schools.

An expectation in Project IMPACT was that, after completing the summer enhancement, the kindergarten through fourth grade teachers would stay at their identified schools for two years to permit long-term implementation and concurrent classroom observation and student achievement data collection. In reality, over a 2-year period, the personal needs of individuals and the reality of teacher–system contractual agreements interfered with this restriction. The following characteristics have each caused at least one Project IMPACT-enhanced teacher to leave a treatment school during 1990–1995: Relocation to other states, retirement, in-system reassignments to nonclassroom positions, leaving the profession, illness and long-term leave, death, emotional breakdown, transfer to other schools because of personnel conflicts within their own school, transfer to other schools because of commuting time, and transfer to other schools because other sites are perceived as offering fewer adversities and greater teacher appreciation.

Of the 73 kindergarten through fourth grade teachers who completed one of the summer teacher enhancement sessions by 1993, 26 teachers (35.6%) were no longer teaching in an IMPACT treatment classroom at the end of the 1994–1995 academic year. Two of these teachers (2.7%) were reassigned as mathematics specialists to maintain the IMPACT model at two sites following the funding of the project. Of the 24 teachers who left the IMPACT treatment sites by the end of the 1994–1995 academic year, 13 are still teaching in MCPS. Thus, 54% of enhanced teachers who were no longer in an IMPACT classroom one year after implementation left through voluntary lateral transfer procedures within MCPS. In every case, these teachers moved to MCPS schools that have less racial-ethnic diversity and a higher economic base in their surrounding communities.

THE TEACHER ENHANCEMENT MODEL

The Project IMPACT teacher enhancement model involved (a) a summer in-service program for all teachers of mathematics, (b) an on-site mathematics specialist in each school, (c) manipulative materials for each classroom, and (d) teacher planning and instructional problem solving during a common grade-level planning time each week. This model provided teachers with an introduction to the rationale for and characteristics of instructional reform in mathematics during the summer, separate from the demands of academic year teaching. For their effort, teachers were paid a financial stipend and received three graduate credits. Many of the elementary teachers in the Project schools required supplemental income during the summer; in addition, in order to maintain certification, many teachers needed continuing professional development. It was anticipated that a remunerated summer in-service program would encourage attendance and that full-time attendance would bolster commitment and reflection. Because existing instructional-support materials in the classrooms were not in sufficient quantity to permit implementation of active, hands-on learning, manipulative materials were funded. To support implementation in the reality of public schooling and to encourage collegial interaction, each school was assigned a mathematics specialist and school-based, grade-level planning was instituted. The following sections describe each of these components of the teacher enhancement model in more detail.

Summer In-service Program

The summer program was grade related, involving all of the kindergarten and first-grade teachers in the participating schools during the first summer and teachers of subsequent grade levels participating by grade in the following summers. The summer programs for the kindergarten through third grade teachers lasted for 22 days. To limit costs, the summer sessions for the fourth and fifth grade teachers were only 16 days long. Each summer in-service addressed (a) adult-level mathematics content; (b) teaching mathematics for understanding, including questioning, use of manipulative materials, and integration of mathematical topics; (c) research on children's learning of those mathematics topics that were deemed critical to the grade-level focus, as well as research addressing a constructivist theory of learning; and (d) teaching mathematics in culturally diverse classrooms. The summer in-service program accessed a summer school program for children, providing teachers with an opportunity to begin instructional change with a small group of children without all the demands associated with academic year instruction. The in-service program also included time to plan for the coming academic year.

The assumption that learners construct rather than absorb or receive knowledge (Noddings, 1990) was a tenet of both the curricular content of the summer teacher enhancement and the instructional model implemented by Project staff during the summer in-service program. Project staff members recognized that only individual teachers could decide what, if any, changes to make in their instructional approach, and that those decisions would be influenced by individual teacher knowledge. Thus, the degree and definition of any instructional change in classrooms would be the result of beliefs and knowledge regarding mathematics and mathematics instruction as constructed by individual teachers (Fennema et al., 1996; Schifter & Fosnot, 1993). Just as children could not be expected to understand and learn mathematics without involvement and individual cognitive constructions, neither could teachers be expected to understand and implement a reformed perspective of mathematics instruction without involvement and individual cognitive constructions. Thus, the summer in-service program was designed to involve teachers in both mathematical and pedagogical problem solving, supporting conceptual understanding of both mathematics content and mathematics education research.

Mathematics Education Research. A number of sessions examined mathematics education research addressing a constructivist interpretation of knowledge and children's learning of mathematical topics that were critical to a given grade level. This component was based on prior NSF-funded teacher enhancement efforts that had demonstrated significant instructional change with enhanced decision making when teachers had increased knowledge of their students' emerging mathematical understandings (Carpenter et al., 1989; Cobb, Wood, & Yackel, 1990).

Project-developed videotapes of children's problem solving and of classroom instruction provided a catalyst for discussion addressing children's construction of mathematical knowledge. In particular, the classroom videotapes provided an opportunity for teachers to consider how "constructivist teaching" might take place. These tapes also permitted discussion of the teacher's role as a facilitator of learning, the crucial nature of teacher questioning, and the meaning of students' responses. Similarly, the problem-solving videotapes offered a context in which to discuss research on children's learning of mathematical topics as teachers struggled with characterizing how the understandings of a particular child might be interpreted, given that child's videotaped solution strategies and explanations.

For example, both the second and third grade summer programs examined research on children's emerging understanding of place value. The work of Leslie Steffe and colleagues was highlighted (Steffe, Cobb, & von Glasersfeld, 1988) as teachers considered what it meant for children's understanding of a unit to become more sophisticated, developing from cardinal counting with a unit of 1 until eventual construction of a fluidity between units of 10s and 1s. Videotaped problem-solving segments such as the following were shown, and the teachers were asked to characterize the children's understandings in light of place-value research.

The problem 25 + 37 = ___ (horizontal presentation) is placed before the child. No manipulative materials are available.

Teacher: I have a, an addition problem here, and I would like you to work this problem for me.... Figure out the answer to this problem for me.

[Child starts to make slash marks below the problem.]

Teacher: If you want to talk while you're doing it, that would be okay.

[Child has now made a row of 10 slash marks. She then recounts quietly.]

Teacher: I cannot hear you.

Chanthou: 10, [Child starts making a second row of slash marks, with the first ten of these marks aligned with the row above.] 11, 12, 13, 14, 15, 16, 17, 18, 19, 20, 21, 22, 23, 24, 25.... [Child looks again at the problem. Starts to count on from 37, pointing to the slash marks in turn.] 37, 38, 39,... , 40, 41, 42, 43, 44, 45, 46, 47, 48, 49,... , 50, 51, 52, 53, 54, 55, 56, 57, 58, 59,... , 60, 61, 62. [Writes 62.]

Teacher: Why don't you explain what you did?. . .

Chanthou: Uh... but this is an easy way. I don't want to do it that way [moves hand rapidly over the slash marks].

Teacher: Okay. So you've got another way?

Chanthou: Yeah.

Teacher: Okay. Go ahead.

Chanthou: You have to count the 3 with the 2 [referring to the tens digits in the problem], so it's 3, 4, 5. It's 5. Right?

Teacher: Uh huh.

Chanthou: And after that you counts the ones. So it's 7, 8, 9, 10, 11, 12. It's 12. So, uh, you count, uh... [recounts 7, 8, 9, 10, 11, 12]... 12. [Writes 12 below the slash marks...Points to the problem.] So it's 9, right? [Writes 9 below and off to the side of the written 12.] So, uh, so you count 9....

Teacher: What's 9?

Chanthou: Wait a minute. [Crosses out the 12.] Well,..., um, you, um, this is.... 7 plus 2 is 9, right?

Teacher: Okay. Why do you add 7 plus 2?

Chanthou: Um... and... this isn't right.... Oh, yeah. It's 62 [emphatically].

Teacher: Okay. And... do that way and... show me why you get the answer 62. What you were talking about doing when... with adding tens and ones.

Chanthou: Well, I would get this instead [pointing to the slash marks].... It's hard enough.

Teacher: So you don't want to show me the other way?

Chanthou: It's hard to explain.

The problem 64–49 = ___ (horizontal presentation) is placed before another child. No manipulative materials are available.

Teacher: Now here's a subtraction problem. Would you write the answer to this problem for me?

[Writes 13.]

Teacher: How did you know that? Tell me your thinking.

Colin: I started with 64 and took away 40 to make it... to make it 24. And then I took away 10 so it would be 14. And added.... I took away 40 to make it 24. Then I took away.... [Crosses out the 13 that was written.] Not 13.... It's 15. [Writes 15.] Because... you take away 40 from 64 to make it 24.... And then... you take away... 10.... And it'll be 14. And since you're only supposed to take away 9, you add 1. So it would be 15.

Teachers also discussed the implications of children's existing mathematical knowledge for future instruction. The approach was to review a child's problem solving on videotape or to discuss a videotaped segment of instruction that included children's explanations of a mathematical concept. Then the teachers were asked to consider what approaches they might use if these children were in their classes, given their accountability for curricular goals and the need to maintain a standard of generalizable mathematics. The intent was to engage the teachers in a discussion of mathematical focus, instructional approaches, and curricular emphases, raising discussion questions in an effort to focus the teachers' attention on children's learning.

These and other sessions examined how instruction may foster or discourage student construction, expression, motivation, and interaction. Teachers were challenged to defend proposed instructional decisions in terms of their possible influence on the understanding, growth, and esteem of each student. For example, the question of how to respond to students' mathematically incorrect responses was a primary issue in every summer in-service program. Early in the summer program each year, a number of teachers would suggest that the teacher should correct the errant student, gently noting that the child was in error and telling the child how to solve the problem correctly. Teachers were challenged to defend that perspective if they were simultaneously attempting to have children work together to solve problems in ways that were meaningful to the children and to have the children defend the validity of their reasoning within the socially constructed mathematics culture of their classroom. Teachers were challenged to consider how "setting a child straight" supported or inhibited a child's future efforts to independently figure out a solution or to persist in the face of challenge. Instructional moves distinct from "telling the child what to do to fix the mistake" were discussed. The intent was to enhance the basis from which teachers would be making decisions in their classrooms.

Adult Mathematics Content.   Pedagogical approach and curricular integration were also addressed indirectly during adult-level mathematics content sessions. Project IMPACT instructors used these periods as a means of modeling the constructivist approaches being suggested for the in-service teachers' classrooms. The intent was to address the mathematical knowledge of the teachers, while having the teachers experience what it meant to learn mathematics in this fashion (Even & Lappan, 1994). The adult-level mathematics sessions illustrated how a teacher could relate skills to understanding and problem solving and could utilize manipulative materials and questioning to foster thinking. At the same time, the in-service teachers were in a setting that stimulated cooperative interaction and discussion of mathematical reasoning.

Some adult-level problems were selected because they did not trigger an algorithmic solution and there was more than one way to solve them. A problem of this type was the Locker Problem (House, 1980). These problems were used in each of the summer in-service programs, regardless of the grade-level focus for that summer. Other problems served to address mathematical concepts that were relevant to the grade-level focus for that summer, although these were still adult-level problems. These problems changed every year or two over the five summer in-service programs. For example, the summer sessions for the fourth- and fifth-grade teachers included a problem that examined maximizing area for a fixed perimeter because area and perimeter were components of the upper elementary mathematics curriculum. Sessions involving these content-focused problems were typically followed by related pedagogical sessions in which the teachers were challenged to define or examine problems or tasks appropriate for their students that addressed the same content. When a student-level problem was provided, the teachers were asked to anticipate how a student might solve the problem and to craft questions highlighting the critical mathematics inherent in the problem. The intent was to forge a connection between the teachers' understanding of mathematical content and the teachers' pedagogical content knowledge.

Equity and Diversity.   Influences that define classroom equity were discussed, with particular consideration given to the implications of teachers' questioning, expectations, use of praise versus encouragement, and grouping practices. Project staff led discussions addressing the ramification of consistent use of homogeneous student groups on student achievement in mathematics (e.g., Oakes, 1985, 1990). Subsequently, the alternative of "culturally relevant" teaching (Ladson-Billings, 1990, 1992) was offered, particularly the potential of situating problem solving in culturally rich contexts, the implication of asking children to explain their reasoning and rationale both in terms of their mathematical conceptualizations and their cultural perspective, and the possible opportunities for using mathematics to examine questions important to the children. This aspect of the summer in-service addressed the notion that a culture existed in every classroom. The question was how to catalyze a classroom culture where children's efforts were valued and where children had the confidence to work and to persist at problem solving because they knew they had the power to make sense of mathematics.

Summer School.   In order for teachers to experience and to refine their as-yet-being-constructed instructional approach with children, the summer in-service program accessed a summer school. The teachers taught summer school children during 10 mornings of the primary teachers' summer in-service program and during 5 mornings of the summer enhancement for the fourth- and fifth-grade teachers. During these mornings, the teachers taught mathematics, discussed their teaching in small debriefing groups facilitated by one of the IMPACT staff members, and planned for the next day's instruction. The IMPACT teachers worked with children who were either entering or exiting the grade-level focus identified for that summer.

Materials and Activities.   During the first summer session, Project IMPACT did not offer teachers "ready-to-use" activities for classroom use, primarily because there was insufficient time to prepare or locate such activities. Instead, commercial materials were made available to the teachers, and time was spent considering standards for selecting materials and activities, as well as reflecting on how to utilize an idea or activity presented in a commercial lesson as a context for a constructivist investigation with young children.

During the second summer in-service, the Project did provide numerous "ready-to-use" activities. This was a mistake. During implementation in 1991–1992, some of the specialists indicated that there were teachers who seemed to rely on these sample activities without fully addressing their mathematical potential. These teachers communicated the intent of the tasks, fostered the children's completion of the activities, and had some children share their strategies. At the same time, however, there seemed to be inadequate discussion of the mathematics underlying the tasks. Although this may have been simply a natural aspect of the process of instructional change, the Project staff felt that it may have also been due to the teachers' inadequate understanding of the activities. Indeed, there is always a danger that teachers might view an enhancement project as simply a "bunch of activities" that they are to carry out with their students.

Therefore, during the subsequent summer in-services, Project staff members attempted to involve the teachers in more activity creation, examination, and modification, with attention to the underlying mathematics. Three approaches were utilized. One scheme was to provide time for examination and discussion of commercial materials that addressed appropriate mathematical topics. Another approach was to present a task as a vehicle for pedagogical review. For example, a problem or activity might serve as an illustration of how children could be engaged in re-examining a mathematical construct. In another setting, the teachers would first be given a task appropriate for children; then the teachers would be asked to write questions that might ascertain what the children's mathematical understandings were, regarding that task. A third approach was to present an adult-level mathematics session, and then to challenge the teachers to create a task appropriate for their students that would focus on that same mathematical topic. In this way at the end of the summer program, the teachers not only had a collection of appropriate problems and activities and knowledge of commercial materials, but also had the confidence that, with their team and with their specialist, they could make decisions and determine needed tasks.

Mathematics Specialists

An important component of Project IMPACT's teacher enhancement model was the assignment of a mathematics specialist to each school. The specialists in Project IMPACT worked daily with the teachers in their schools, helping them examine alternatives and address the challenges that accompany professional change. In many ways, the IMPACT specialists served the role of "helping teacher" or "advising teacher," as characterized in the teacher development literature (Loucks-Horsley et al., 1987). During the summer, specialists served as instructors, observed the instruction of participants in the summer school program, conducted debriefing sessions, assisted with summer school planning, and provided general guidance. At the end of the summer in-service, each specialist met with the newly enhanced teachers from her building to plan a scope and sequence for the academic year, to identify and pace the MCPS mathematics content objectives for the month of September, and to plan for the first week of school.

Specialists supported teachers' efforts to attempt reform in the reality of the urban classroom (Shaw & Jakubowski, 1991). When asked to characterize their role, IMPACT specialists indicated that they aided teachers in

> Making connections between mathematical topics and between mathematics and other disciplines; planning appropriate mathematical activities and lessons; creating "non-contrived" problems that were meaningful to the culture of the classroom and addressed critical mathematical objectives; developing questioning and wait time; responding to incorrect answers and fostering involvement and growth among all children; supporting reflection regarding instruction and student needs; learning how to share with colleagues and how to support colleagues; and communicating with parents and the principal. (Campbell, 1996, p.461–462)

The specialists did provide demonstration teaching in classrooms after coplanning with the classroom teacher. This primarily occurred in the first semester after the summer enhancement and was always supposed to be followed with a debriefing and planning for subsequent instruction. Specialists occasionally covered a classroom in order to permit a teacher's observation of a colleague. The specialists also observed instruction and conducted subsequent debriefing–planning sessions with individual teachers, led the weekly grade-level planning meetings, managed manipulative materials, helped to design and make instructional materials that were not purchased, and generally made themselves available to help teachers find answers to questions that might otherwise interfere with continued efforts to implement the advocated instructional approach.

Grade-level Planning Meetings

A collegial relationship between teachers has been identified as a critical aspect of successful schools (Little, 1990) and of schools that have evidenced change (Fullan with Stiegelbauer, 1991). For many teachers, the instructional reforms being raised in Project IMPACT represented a major pedagogical shift, particularly if their prior instructional approach had been to present problems, to show students how to solve the problems, and then to evaluate their effectiveness by determining whether the students obtained the correct answers and successfully mimicked the procedure that was being taught. The problems that teachers face when attempting to implement a constructivist perspective in their instruction are very different from the problems faced when using the traditional approach of direct instruction (Simon, 1995; Stein, Silver, & Smith, in press). Romberg and Pitman (1994) noted that it is important for teachers to feel that they are part of a supported venture as opposed to an isolate, and that they are "in a position to participate actively in reform efforts rather than ... to react passively to new issues and developments" (pp. 49–50). To ease tension and to define and encourage alternative efforts, it was critical that the IMPACT teachers have a mechanism for meeting and supporting each other throughout their implementation efforts. For this reason, Project IMPACT required cooperating schools to organize their weekly schedule to permit hour-long grade-level planning meetings during one school day each week.

During the first three years of the project, this occurred as envisioned. Generally, the children of a given grade would simultaneously have either library, art, music, or physical education just before lunch on one day, with all children of that grade attending another one of these classes following the lunchtime recess on that same day. This released all teachers of that grade for approximately 1 hour 45 minutes, sufficient for both mathematics planning and lunch. However, as the Project expanded into the upper grades with more classrooms per grade in some schools, scheduling became more difficult. Therefore, some sites utilized extended half-day grade-level planning meetings every two weeks or once a month, rather than weekly hour-long meetings. One school eventually abandoned planning meetings during school hours and scheduled such planning after school. Every school team, however, managed to schedule some form of grade-level planning meetings with their mathematics specialist on a regular basis.

Many teachers find it very difficult to look at children's work or to listen to children's explanations and understand the intent or the mathematical implication of what they have just seen or heard. Teachers must learn how to interpret children's responses to gain the information that is needed to develop or modify future instruction and to define questioning strategies to foster or challenge the understanding that is being revealed by individual children. All of this is necessary to teach and to plan effectively. Planning based on observed student performance also demands that teachers take a research perspective with respect to their children's learning of mathematics. As teachers evaluate the understanding of their students, they must reflect on how to advance the student to a new or more mature understanding of the mathematical content or how to encourage the use or development of more efficient strategies that coincide with the student's current mathematical conceptualizations. One of the important functions of the mathematics specialist and the weekly grade-level planning meetings was to support and foster the construction of these competencies in teachers.

Instructional Resources

Each treatment school was issued classroom sets of manipulative materials by the project. During kindergarten and first grade implementation, the manipulative materials were identified in advance by the project staff (e.g., 1000 Unifix cubes per classroom, 5 buckets of pattern blocks per classroom, 25 geoboards for every two classrooms). In subsequent years, the teachers participating in Project IMPACT offered suggestions regarding selection of the classroom manipulative materials, in consultation with their mathematics specialist. The teachers knew that all classrooms had to be similarly equipped because of the research nature of the Project. In addition, each school's grade-level team was given modest funding to purchase commercial professional materials to support instruction. These resources had to be selected by each grade-level team in cooperation with their mathematics specialist, and no duplicate copies were funded in any one school in order to encourage the team to share resources. Typical resources included the series *Used numbers: Real data in the classroom* (e.g., Russell & Corwin, 1989) and the *TOPS Communication Card Decks* (Greenes, Schulman, & Spungin, 1993). Each cooperating teacher was also provided a professional reference text (e.g., Baroody, 1987) and copies of selected readings; these resources varied with the grade-level focus of the in-service program.

EVIDENCE AND NATURE OF TEACHER CHANGE

The potential of any teacher enhancement effort is ultimately evidenced in the participants' classrooms. Project IMPACT sought to evaluate the effectiveness of its efforts by examining quantitative data reflecting student achievement and by collecting both quantitative and qualitative data regarding teacher change. Because student achievement is not the focus of this chapter, the following section refers only to the teacher change data. Information addressing student achievement is available elsewhere (Campbell, Rowan, & Cheng, 1995).

Project IMPACT collected both quantitative and qualitative data in order to yield a more complete definition of the nature and degree of teacher change across IMPACT classrooms. Surveys of teacher beliefs and confidence were administered to characterize the rationale that might be guiding teachers' actions, yielding data for quantitative examination. Classroom observations provided information regarding the teachers' actual conduct; this qualitative data allowed a characterization of the nature of instruction across the IMPACT classrooms. Each of these perspectives are presented in turn in the following sections.

Teacher Beliefs and Confidence

Teachers are constantly making decisions in the classroom. Those decisions will be influenced by teachers' knowledge and beliefs (Clark & Peterson, 1986; Peterson, Fennema, Carpenter, & Loef, 1989). Two surveys were constructed to examine the teachers' rationale and perspectives. One survey characterized teachers' beliefs about mathematics, mathematical pedagogy, and equity; the second survey estimated teachers' confidence for implementing instructional reform. The Project IMPACT Mathematics Beliefs Scales were developed as a modification of the Mathematics Beliefs Scales developed by Elizabeth Fennema, Thomas Carpenter and Penelope Peterson for the NSF-funded project Cognitively Guided Instruction (CGI; Peterson et al., 1989). The IMPACT beliefs scales contain the four CGI constructs that addressed assumptions of research on children's learning of mathematics, as well as one construct addressing the nature of mathematics and one construct addressing equity. The Project IMPACT Mathematical Practice Survey addressed two constructs. It was labeled "Practice" rather than "Confidence" in order to minimize conflicting reactions on the part of the respondents. It was felt that teachers might bias their responses rather than admitting a lack of confidence. One set of practice items provided an estimate of the teachers' confidence in their ability to interact with mathematics; the second construct contained items addressing teachers' confidence for teaching mathematics in a method parallel to the tenets discussed in the in-service program.

Each construct was evaluated through eight items in the associated inventory; four of the items were statements agreeing with one extreme of a continuum of beliefs and four of the items were statements that indicated disagreement with that same extreme. The items for a subscale were scattered throughout an inventory. Teachers completed the questionnaire using a 5-point Likert scale for each of the 16 confidence-practice items and the 48 belief items.

Belief Scale One considered how children learn mathematics. Items on this scale ranged from the belief that children construct their own knowledge to the belief that children receive knowledge. Scale Two addressed the relationship between mathematical skills and mathematical understanding and problem solving. The continuum on this scale went from the belief that skills should be taught in relationship to understanding and problem solving to the belief that skills should be taught separately. Scale Three addressed the basis for sequencing topics in mathematics instruction. These items ranged from the perspective that what is known about the development of children's mathematical ideas should provide the basis for sequencing topics for mathematics instruction to the belief that formal mathematics should provide the basis for sequencing instruction. Scale Four addressed how mathematics should be taught. The continuum on this scale went from the belief that instruction should support children's construction of knowledge to the belief that teachers should present information. These four scales were identical to those used in CGI (Peterson et al., 1989). Scale Five was concerned with the nature of mathematics. This scale had items that characterized mathematics as a process-oriented, dynamic subject as well as items that presented mathematics as a rule-oriented, static subject. Scale Six considered characteristics of equity in mathematics education. The continuum on this scale went from the belief that equity occurs when all students are encouraged and prepared to take advantage of challenging mathematical instruction regardless of past achievement to the belief that equity occurs when all students are provided with instruction that meets their assessed needs and existing skills.

Scale One of the Project IMPACT Mathematical Practice Survey asked teachers to evaluate how they felt about accessing opportunities to apply existing mathematical knowledge or to learn more mathematics. Items on this scale ranged from expressions of confidence and anticipation to statements of inadequacy and anxiety. Scale Two was concerned with confidence about implementing approaches that are felt to facilitate children's construction of knowledge. The continuum on this scale went from expressions of confidence about teaching this way to statements that indicated the need to direct all instruction.

The beliefs scales and confidence survey were completed by teachers at the beginning of their grade-level summer in-service program, at the conclusion of their summer in-service program, and during the spring of their first implementation year. The beliefs scales were always administered immediately after the confidence–practice questionnaire.

Beliefs. The Project IMPACT Mathematics Beliefs Scales were administered to 101 teachers from 1990–1995. Prior to the summer in-service, the mean and standard deviation of the primary teachers' responses to the Beliefs Scales was 2.285 (.341), whereas the fourth- and fifth-grade teachers' mean and standard deviation were 2.275 (.403). Lower scores on the 5-point Likert scale indicate beliefs more compatible with a focus on teaching for understanding by fostering children's construction of mathematical concepts. Prior to the summer teacher enhancements, there were no significant differences between the primary and upper grade teachers' beliefs as indicated by either total scores or subscale scores on this measure.

At the conclusion of the summer in-service, the beliefs of the teachers were again assessed. These data were then analyzed using analysis of variance techniques, examining whether there was a significant difference in the change in beliefs scores between the primary and the upper grade teachers. This analysis revealed a significant difference in the change in beliefs scores due to grade ($F(1,98) = 8.6236$, $p = .0041$). Although the beliefs of each group of teachers changed in a direction indicating more emphasis on student understanding, this change was more pronounced among the primary teachers. This significant difference was the result of a stronger change in the primary teachers' beliefs on three of the six subscales. The primary teachers assumed a more constructivist perspective regarding how children learn mathematics and how mathematics should be taught than did the upper grade teachers. Further, the primary teachers' perspectives of equity in mathematics education favored supporting every child's access to challenging mathematics, whereas the upper grade teachers were more likely to base instructional decisions on an evaluation of children's existing skills and assessed needs. There was no difference between upper and lower grade teachers' change in beliefs regarding (a) the relationship between skill and understanding or problem-solving instruction, (b) the way mathematics instruction should be sequenced, or (c) the nature of mathematics. Within each of these constructs, the primary and upper grade teachers made comparable shifts toward a more reform-based perspective.

It is not surprising that the IMPACT teachers evidenced a significant change in their beliefs at the conclusion of the in-service. They had just spent 16 to 22 days being enhanced and supported. Thus, it may be that these immediate posttest scores reflect a Pollyanna effect. To evaluate this, the beliefs of the teachers were reevaluated at the conclusion of the academic year. In the spring following one year of implementation, the Beliefs Scales were administered again.

There was no significant difference in the change in beliefs between the primary and upper grade teachers between the end of the summer in-service and the conclusion of the subsequent academic year. Both sets of teachers made a slight shift away from beliefs reflecting a reform perspective as the reality of classroom practice became evident; however, this shift was not significant in either grade level.

Confidence. The same 101 teachers completed the Project IMPACT Mathematics Practice Survey. Prior to the summer in-service, the mean and standard deviation of the primary teachers' responses to the confidence survey was 2.399 (.475), whereas the fourth- and fifth-grade teachers' mean and standard deviation were 2.202 (.525). That is, there was a difference between the primary and upper grade teachers' confidence prior to Project involvement, with that difference lying in the upper grade teachers' greater confidence for interacting with mathematics.

At the conclusion of the summer in-service, the teachers' espoused confidence toward practice was again assessed. Analysis of variance techniques were used to examine whether there was a significant difference in the change in confidence between the primary and the upper grade teachers. This analysis revealed a significant difference in the change in confidence scores due to grade ($F(1,98) = 9.3313, p = .0029$). Although the confidence level of each group of teachers changed in a direction indicating more willingness to interact with mathematics and to implement instructional approaches supporting reform, this change was more pronounced among the primary teachers. This significant difference was the result of a stronger change in the primary teachers' confidence level as compared to the upper grade teachers on both of the subscales.

To evaluate whether a Pollyanna effect was present in the confidence data, the practice survey was readministered in the spring following one year of implementation. There was no significant difference between the primary and upper grade teachers' change in total confidence scores between the end of the summer in-service and the conclusion of the subsequent academic year. Both sets of teachers made a strong shift evidencing more confidence for interacting with mathematics over the course of the academic year (Scale One). As the reality of classroom practice became evident, primary teachers became slightly more confident about their ability to implement a reform perspective, whereas the upper grade teachers became slightly less confident (Scale Two). These grade-level distinctions for Scale Two were not statistically significant.

Instructional Practice

Classroom instruction was observed in order to characterize the growth and changes evidenced in the teachers. Although analysis of this data is not complete, it is possible to characterize a somewhat fragmented interpretation of the instructional change evidenced in classrooms. These data represent observations of 93 teachers from 1990–1995; the special education teachers and resource teachers who participated in the summer programs are not reflected in these data. This characterization has three assumptions. If a teacher was still in the classroom of an IMPACT school after two years of implementation, the status of instruction at the end of those two years is characterized. Thus, for these teachers, the growth evidenced by the end of the second year of observation and implementation was critical, not their growth at the end of the first year of implementation. If a teacher left an IMPACT school prior to two years of implementation, the evaluation of her instructional change was fixed at the level evidenced when she was last observed at an IMPACT site. For one kindergarten teacher and one fourth-grade teacher, this was at the conclusion of only one semester of implementation. For 12 primary teachers, 4 fourth-grade teachers, and all 21 fifth-grade teachers, this was at the conclusion of 1 year of implementation. Therefore, the characterizations that follow present a distribution skewed towards less change for the upper grade teachers, as none of the fifth-grade teachers had had 2 years of supported implementation. Finally, each of the following frequency estimates are truly only educated predictions, subject to further analysis and interpretation of the classroom observation data.

All of the teachers in the urban schools accessed by the Project IMPACT teacher enhancement did not become model "*Standards-based*" teachers. About 10% of the primary teachers (5 out of 52) and 17% of the upper grade teachers (7 out of 41) made no real change in their instruction. Another 17% of the primary teachers (9 out of 52) and 24% of the upper grade teachers (10 out of 41) moved considerably beyond routinized practice and direct instruction. These teachers made continued attempts to implement new instructional approaches, focusing primarily on their own behavior. Use of manipulative materials was common in these classrooms, but the use of the materials was frequently demonstrated and interpreted by the teachers. These teachers used small-group activities. Students were generally asked to explain how they solved a problem, but students' explanations were not pursued. These teachers frequently asked if anyone solved a problem in another way, but they were unsure as to how to use incorrect responses as an instructional probe. The different strategies suggested by children were accepted, but these teachers generally did not know how to relate responses. Teacher talk still dominated in these classrooms, but the teachers were trying to provide more wait time after their questions.

About 19% of the primary teachers (10 out of 52) and 37% of the upper-grade teachers (15 out of 41) evidenced instructional changes consistent with a constructivist perspective. These teachers thought about what their class understood, seeking the input of their specialist or other teachers, although they would sometimes presume that the responses of a few children were evidence of the understanding of the entire class. The questioning of these teachers when manipulative materials were in use indicated that they were keeping a mathematical focus. These teachers used small-group problem solving and monitored the involvement of each child, but generally permitted volunteers to speak for a group's solution strategy. Children in these classrooms often shared alternative strategies, and these teachers might briefly summarize the differing methods. In these classrooms, it was not uncommon to hear a teacher probing the reasoning behind a child's response. These teachers responded to student questioning by turning the question over to the class or by asking a sequence of leading questions to cause the child to frame a self-response. There was more student talk in these classrooms. Some of these teachers periodically used a system to ensure each child's verbal sharing during a class period. Wait time was obvious.

In about 54% of the primary classrooms (28 out of 52) and 22% of the upper grade classrooms (9 out of 41), instruction was supportive of children's construction of knowledge and attentive to the nature of the mathematical ideas being constructed. These teachers made links between mathematical topics, and asked questions frequently to focus the children's attention toward mathematical generalizations or abstractions. These teachers considered whether it was time to support a child's move to a more symbolic or abstract representation or strategy, focusing on the understandings inferred from individual children's responses or submitted work. Group identification was frequently redefined in these classrooms as the teacher reflected on the mathematics being addressed and students' needs or strengths. These teachers often used questioning to highlight mathematical reasoning and connections or to focus children's attention on a mathematical relationship. Questions were also asked as a means of addressing the similarities or differences between offered strategies. When students responded incorrectly, these teachers tried to ask questions that might cause the children to reexamine their procedure or reasoning. These classrooms were characterized by an atmosphere of trust and patience.

Teacher Change

Another way to consider the instructional shifts evident in IMPACT classrooms is through examination of narratives of classroom interaction. All enhanced teachers were observed teaching two consecutive lessons in the fall and two consecutive lessons in the spring during their first two years of implementation. A few teachers were also observed in the spring immediately prior to their involvement with the Project. The following segments are selected from the limited cadre of teachers who were observed both prior to and during Project participation. These segments were chosen to exemplify three different types of changes evidenced across the IMPACT sites. Although these are specific episodes, they typify the distinctions apparent in classrooms over time.

Change in Pedagogical Focus.   Prior to the enhancement, much instruction had the following flavor. Teachers would demonstrate a procedure, present a definition, or tell students how to manipulate some mathematical materials. Then one or two specific examples would be presented as a means of clarifying that procedure, definition, or manipulation. These examples might be accompanied by questioning wherein some children were asked to state what action in the procedure should come next or what rule should be applied. Subsequently the children would be given exercises to reiterate some aspect of the definition or to facilitate practice of the procedure or manipulation. These practice opportunities would be guided by the teacher if necessary. Finally, the children would be given homework or classroom exercises that provided additional practice in using the definition or in applying the procedure or manipulation. Thus the focus of these lessons was on stimulating recall or routinization; the rationale underlying the procedure, skill, or definition was not paramount in either the teacher's explanations or in the responses expected of the children.

In the following exemplar, a third grade teacher was addressing her whole class, using a felt board and cutouts to define sets and to represent a fraction of that set. This exchange took place in late April, prior to this teacher's registration in an IMPACT summer in-service program. As this segment begins, a child had just placed 20 cutout figures of chicks and ducks on the feltboard easel. The expression "2/5 of 20" was written on the blackboard. The children were seated on a rug near the easel; they had no access to individual manipulatives.

Teacher: Okay. We've got 20 there, and we want to figure out what two-fifths of 20 is going to be. What do we need to do?... We want to figure out what two-fifths of 20 is going to be. What do we need to do?... Can we leave them in twentieths? What did we do when we wanted to figure out what a third of 15 was? [Preceding problems were to find one third of 15 and then to find two thirds of 15.] When we wanted to figure out what a third of 15 was, how many groups did we divide 15 into? How many groups did we make? Marcel? When we talked about a third of 15, how many groups did we divide them up into? [no response] Were you here? Okay, we divided them up into three groups and then talked about what a third is. Now we're talking about two fifths of 20 [indicates the expression on the blackboard]. How many groups do we need to divide the 20 into?

Marcel: Two.

Teacher: You're looking at the numerator. Look at the denominator.

Marcel: Five.

Teacher: Five groups. Who can come up and help divide these up into five groups? Into five equal groups. Rachel?... Think about your five friends, Rachel, that you want to give them to. [Rachel begins to distribute the felt cut-outs into subsets.] Take a look at what Rachel is doing and see if you would do them the same way.... Okay, I see one, two, three, four friends. [Rachel is distributing the cutouts into four subsets.] What about your fifth friend? [Rachel creates a fifth set.] There you go. You be sure not to leave any of your friends out when you're passing them out.... I'm glad you guys are paying so close attention, because in about three minutes you guys are going to be doing this on your own.

Tia: On a felt board?

Teacher: I don't have enough felt boards for everybody to use felt boards, but you'll have some... different things to move around. Does she have a remainder? Thank you, Rachel. Okay, everybody.... And they've been sitting for a long time.... Stick with me for just about two more minutes. Okay. Rachel divided these up.... Rachel divided these up among her five friends. How many did each friend get? There's 1, 2, 3, 4, 5 friends [pointing to the five sets]. How many did each friend get?

Maureen: Four.

Teacher: Okay, each friend got four. Now, we're talking about two fifths of 20. Who can tell us first what one fifth of 20 would be? Here we have.... This is one friend, two friends, three friends, four friends, five friends [pointing to the five sets]. What's one fifth of 20? Shauna? One fifth of 20... we're talking about sets. How many would one fifth of 20 be? Here's a fifth, a fifth, a fifth [pointing to the sets]. Remember, we've got them divided among her five friends.

Shauna: One fifth.

Teacher: What would one fifth be? How many is one fifth? Can you show me? Can you come up and show me where one fifth would be?

Shauna: Here [pointing to one set].

Teacher: Okay. This is one fifth, here.

Shauna: Uh huh.

Teacher: Two fifths, three fifths, four fifths, five fifths [pointing to the sets]. Okay, remember she divided them up among her five friends. So how much is one fifth?

Shauna: Four.

Teacher: One fifth is four. Great. How much would two fifths be, then? How much would two fifths be, Tarina? Come up and show us.... Okay. Now, Shauna told us that one fifth was four. How much would two fifths be?... There's the one fifth. [Points to one set.]... This is one fifth. [Points to one set.] How much would two fifths be? Can you count them up with me? Here's a fifth [points to one set] that Shauna just talked about. This is two fifths, three fifths, four fifths, and five fifths. [Points to the sets in turn.]... One fifth, two fifths. So how many would two fifths be? This is two fifths. [Points to the two sets.] How many are in two fifths?

Tarina: Eight.

Teacher: Eight are in two fifths. Great. Thank you, Tarina.... Was that a silent cheer you were giving yourself? All right.... It's kind of confusing and it takes a lot of practice. What we want to do now.... Boy, we're still not going to get to our papers today. We have 10 minutes, and during the next 10 minutes you're going to get a chance to do some of these problems individually and [the instructional assistant] and I will come around and help you.

The purpose of this exemplar is not to critique this instruction but to offer it as a contrast to this same teacher's instruction in June, two years later. At the time the following segment was observed, the teacher had participated in Project IMPACT for one summer session and for two academic years. She was teaching a second/third grade combination class of children; that evening she and the other third grade teachers in the school were taking their children for an overnight camping trip. Five word problems addressing the camping trip had been posted. The children had spent time at their desks solving as many problems as they could complete, with large sheets of construction paper available to display their work. One problem was the following: On the campout we ate chocolate bars as a late night snack. Michael, Monique, Julian, Kate, Desiree, Gregory, Jacquanna, and Antoine each ate 1/3 of a chocolate bar. How many chocolate bars did they eat in all? As this segment begins, the teacher had asked a second child to share her solution strategy for this problem. One child had already shared a correct strategy yielding the response of 2 2/3 chocolate bars.

> Tawanna: First I drew.... [Child waits as some children are not paying attention.] First I drew 8 people because, um, there was 8 people in that [points to the posted problem]. And then I drew... 8 thirds. And... and I colored in one third because it's one third. [Beneath each of 8 stick figures, there is a ◕ . Stick figures are each labeled with a child's name from the problem. To the right of these drawings is the numeral, "4."] And two halves make one whole so that's one, and anoth-, another two halves make another whole so that's two, and these two halves make a whole, and these two halves make a whole. [Points sequentially to pairs of representations of thirds as she says "two halves" until all 8 thirds have been "added."]... Marcel.

> Marcel: Why... ? Why... ? Why, you have 4 right, 4 right here? [referring to the numeral "4"]... There's 1, 2, 3 [noting three representations of thirds]. See... so that's, ... that's a whole [uses hand to span three of the representations of the thirds] and that's a whole [uses hand to span three of the representations of the thirds] and that's left overs [points to the two remaining representations of thirds], right?... I don't get it. [Marcel has come to the front of the classroom and pointed to Tawanna's drawing.]

> Teacher: So, Marcel, are you saying you think that three people together would be one candy bar?

> Marcel: No.

> Teacher: Show me what you were just doing with your hands again that you said, "That's a whole."

Marcel: That's one candy [uses hand to span three of the representations of the thirds]. That's one candy bar [uses hand to span the next three representations of the thirds] and half of a candy bar.

Tawanna: Eight... eight is an even number so... so these, these two halves make a whole and these two halves make a whole and these two halves make a whole and these two halves make a whole [sequentially points to pairs of representations of thirds].

Teacher: Tawanna, I am a little bit confused because at first you said you were making thirds. But now when you're counting them up, you're counting them as halves. Can you talk a little bit more about that?

Tawanna: Um....Um....Because I remembered that somebody said that if there's two halves or if there's two halves and then it makes a whole. And if you have a box [rectangle] and it has a little triangle in it and another triangle, then that makes a whole, a whole. So you call that a whole. You count all the triangles.

Teacher: So you are saying that, that you know that two halves make a whole? How many, how many, um, thirds make a whole?

Marcel: Two halves make a whole.

Tawanna: Um.... Two.

Teacher: Two, two thirds make a whole? Marcel, you seem like you had an idea about that cause you, when you said, "That's a candy bar and that's a candy bar and those are left over." What were you saying would be a candy bar?

Marcel: These three and these three and left overs [sequentially points to two sets of three representations of thirds and the last pair].

Teacher: Why were you saying that three people would be one, one candy bar?

Marcel: Because.... Let me see.... Um.... Ah... ah.... It does. I thought only two halves, of a whole will make, uh, a whole.

Tawanna: But you said that three, three halves make a whole and if you draw these two parts [points to two of the drawings] that will make a whole circle. And if you have three halves [points to three of the drawings].... This will make a whole [points to two of the drawings] and this will be a half. It won't be a whole. Has to be two, two parts like this one and you draw that one. That will make a whole circle [points to two of the drawings].

Teacher: Marcel, are you talking about halves or are you talking about thirds when you were counting?

Marcel: I was.... Let me see [rereads the problem to himself]. One third. Okay.

Tawanna: Marta. [Calling on another student to contribute.]

Marta: How come you called them, how come you called them halves when you cut them into three pieces?

Tawanna: Marce-, Marcel said that three, three, three halves make a whole. But I say that two halves make a whole and if there are three halves [points to three of the drawings], these two will make a whole [referring to two of the three drawings] and this won't, this won't be a whole [referring to the remaining single drawing]. This will just be a half.... Susan?

Susan: I disagree with you cause, um. Whenever like, whenever you have a circle and they cut it into like three halves and it will equal a whole because.... [Susan's explanation wanders as she struggles with examples of differing numbers of pieces composing a whole.] If you put two together in the bottom.... See, if you pretend that this one was cut out, right [points to one of the thirds]? Then, if you put it together [points to another one of the thirds in the same drawing] and then it won't be a whole because there's a piece missing right there [points to the last third in that drawing]. So it won't be a whole. [Susan has joined Marcel and Tawanna in the front of the classroom.]

Marcel: Susan is giving me an idea. Why didn't?... I think.

Teacher: [Interrupting Marcel.] Jorge, did you have something to add? [Jorge comes to the front of the classroom and questions Tawanna regarding which pieces she decided to shade in her drawing. Tawanna explains how the numerator and denominator give information regarding the pieces and how many to shade. Jorge says he knows that. He is questioning which pieces.]

Teacher: Lots of different ideas about this one. [Marcel suggests which shaded pieces make a whole.]

Jorge: I think that these three will make a whole, these three will make a whole, and here you don't, these two don't make a whole [sequentially pointing to three of the drawings and then to the last two drawings].

Teacher: I wonder how many.... Since we're talking about thirds in the problem, how many thirds make a whole? Tawanna, you have been saying that two halves make a whole. How many thirds... would make one whole?

Jorge: Three.

Teacher: Is that why you were saying, Marcel, that three people together would be one candy bar?

Marcel: Yep.

Teacher: That that would be because you say that three thirds would make a whole? [Marcel says it's three. Then Marcel questions Tawanna's spelling at the bottom of the displayed picture. The teacher asks Marcel, Jorge, and Susan to sit down.]

Teacher: It looks like this is one that we need to do a little bit more thinking on. It gets a little bit confusing when we're talking about fractions. But I, ah, appreciate those of you who shared your ideas and your thinking on what, what would make a whole, how many thirds would make whole, and how many halves would make a whole. Maybe we could go back and look at this problem again or even tonight we might actually be able to act this problem out with real chocolate bars.

This second exchange shows a shift in the teacher's pedagogical focus to an expectation that the children were responsible for explaining their solution strategies and that the teacher was responsible for interpreting and questioning the children's understandings. Prior to this exchange, the correct answer had already been voiced. The issue was not simply for some child to voice the intended answer to a mathematics problem. The teacher was seeking clarification as a means of indicating the strength of a child's perception, as a means of inferring the reasoning behind a child's response (for both correct and incorrect responses), and as a means for raising a process or interpretation for consideration by the entire class. This teacher knew that Tawanna still had an incorrect response. With the information the teacher garnered from this discussion and the prior discussion of this problem, she decided that this mathematical concept needed further study by some children in her class, but not at that moment. The children knew that this mathematical topic was something they would continue to consider, perhaps that very night. Contrast this to the first exchange. In that "discussion," the teacher did not expect her children to explain their solutions, nor did she attempt to infer their understanding. Indeed, she led them to find the solutions. The resulting solutions then may or may not have made sense to the children; it really was not important as long as the correct solution was offered.

Change in Mathematical Emphasis.   Many of the teachers in the participating schools had manipulative materials in their classrooms. They also had varying expertise in terms of locating or creating hands-on activities to provide a setting for highlighting mathematical relationships or for situating mathematical representations. The following exchange took place in a third-grade classroom in May, before Project involvement. The children had individual plastic bags containing differing quantities of types of finger foods; every bag contained 12 separate pieces of food. The children had verified that there were 12 items in their bags. This exchange took place during whole-class instruction.

Teacher: What fractional part of your bag is pretzels? Everybody's won't be the same. What fractional part of your bag is pretzels?... Janice?

Janice: Four twelfths.

Teacher: Yours is four twelfths. [Writes 4/12 on the board.] April?

April: Six twelfths.

Teacher: Yours is six twelfths. [Writes 6/12 on the board.] Rudy?

Rudy: Um, three fourths.

Teacher: Three fourths. [Writes 3/4 on the board.]

Rudy: I mean one fourth.

Teacher: One fourth?

Rudy: [Nods his head affirmatively.]

Teacher: Okay. One fourth. [Changes 3/4 to 1/4 on the board.] So Rudy grouped his into four parts. Julio?

Julio: Four twelfths.

Teacher: Four twelfths. Just like this one [indicating a prior written response]. Mikal?

Mikal: Six sixths.

Teacher: Six sixths. Six sixths. That means that all, your whole bag is pretzels. Is that right?

Mikal: No. I have six pretzels.

Teacher: You have six pretzels. Okay. So six out of how many in all, Mikal? How many parts in your bag in all?

Mikal: Sixteen.

Teacher: Six are pretzels. That's the top number.

Mikal: Six out of twelve.

Teacher: Good. So, six twelfths is pretzels.

This activity is compelling for primary children, as it is natural for children to count to determine quantity. The distinct distributions of components within a fixed quantity are of interest to the children, particularly given the context of finger foods. Thus, there is motivation for applying a different way of describing the content of a bag; in this task, fractions provide an accurate descriptive mechanism not provided by whole numbers. However, throughout the exchange, the teacher did not ask the children to explain their responses, she led an errant child to the correct response, and she did not avail herself of an opportunity to examine fractional equivalence (when Rudy responded "one fourth").

Contrast this with the following exchange. This segment occurred in this same teacher's classroom during the following January, after one summer and one semester of Project involvement. At this point her focus included linkages between mathematical concepts as she asked a child to explain how his distinct measuring technique was inferred from his understanding of a property of rectangles. Once again, the teacher was confronted with an incorrect response, but her reaction now was to focus on the mathematics of measuring and geometry as opposed to a computation error. Indeed, her children knew that they, and not the teacher, were responsible for checking their computations. The children were being asked to use connecting links to measure the perimeter of desks in the classroom. Two boys measured the perimeter of the teacher's desk. She asked them to share their strategy with the class.

Teacher: How did you do the measuring? People keep saying, "I measured, I measured, I took it and what's it?" And how did you actually do the measuring? Timothy?

Timothy: Um, me and Todd, um, put the rings, um,...um, around one side. Which was 23 for the short part.

Teacher: So you put 23 links for the short part.

Timothy: And added 23 to 23 because it would be the same as the other side.

Teacher: So this side's the same as this side? [Points to the long and short sides of the desk.]

Timothy: No, the other side.

Teacher: You mean the opposite side over here? This side is the same as this over here? [Points to the two short sides of the desk.]

Timothy: Uh huh.

Teacher: Oh, so you didn't need to measure both sides because you knew it was the same. How did you know it was exactly the same?

Timothy: Because it wouldn't be a rectangle if it was... different.

Teacher: Oh, so you knew that this [points to the top of the desk] is a rectangle. You looked to see that the top was, of my desk, was a rectangle. You measured one side because you knew that the opposite sides were the same length?

Timothy: Uh hum. And the other one was, um, side, was 44. And I added 44 to 44.

Teacher: So you measured the short side and added the two short sides together.

Timothy: I got 20, 46 for the short sides and I got 88 for the other sides.

Teacher: And then you added the two longer sides together. Okay. So you have 88 and... ?

Timothy: 26. I mean 46.

Teacher: And 46.

Timothy: Which was 154.

Teacher: So then, how did you get 154?

Timothy: I added the 88 and 46 together.

Teacher: And why did you add 88 and 46 together?

Timothy: Because it would be around the top of the desk.

Teacher: So you added all the sides together, to get 154. And that, that, that's how many links went across, around the top, of my desk, without measuring all around. So that's one way of doing the measuring. Really good thinking. [Two other children share their measuring of desks.]

Todd: Um, well, I have something to say about the, um, the desk.

Teacher: Okay.

Todd: Um, I got a different, um, answer than my partner. I just realized it. I added, um, 54 [misreads 46] plus 88, and then I got 134.

Teacher: Thank you for checking, Todd. And you checked on your own by doing it again. Good. I think I am not so concerned about the number of links, actually. I was interested in how you did it.

Change in Classroom Organization.   Perhaps the most visible evidence of change in mathematics instruction across the IMPACT classrooms concerned student involvement, grouping practices, student expectations, and questioning. For example, one third-grade teacher was observed four times prior to the IMPACT enhancement. On three of these occasions, she had separated her class into small groups of four or five children for mathematics instruction. She gave each group a task or worksheet to complete; different groups could be completing unique tasks. She intended to make her way around to the groups. Unfortunately, she typically would only get to one or two groups, as her time allotment for mathematics instruction averaged only 21 minutes.

In the following exchange, three boys (Damien, Stewart, and Dat) and two girls (Carmen and Alana) formed a group. Each child was given a unique number of coins totaling less than one dollar. Their task was to determine how much change they would get from one dollar if they spent their coins. Damien erred counting his collection of money (counting 16 cents as 61 cents), but was able to correct his error after being asked to recount by the teacher. She then told Damien to figure out how much change he would get back if he bought a candy bar for 61 cents. Stewart correctly counted his money, but then stopped. The teacher told him that the 16 cents he counted was what an eraser would cost; he was to figure out how much change he would get back from one dollar. Dat correctly counted his money, but he erred when symbolically subtracting the cost from $1.00. The teacher told him to correct his subtraction by adding. The three boys were then given $2 in change, told unique values between one and two dollars, and again asked to figure out their change from two dollars. At this point the teacher turned to the girls who had counted their money, but who had not computed change from one dollar. Carmen said she did not know what problem she was supposed to solve. The teacher told her to figure out the change from one dollar. The teacher then turned to Alana, who counted 15 cents, and began to subtract $1.00 - .15, for Alana. The teacher described the traditional algorithm as she proceeded; Alana was then given a problem to figure change from $2. In the midst of this, the boys began amusing themselves as they seemed to have completed their second problem. Carmen, meanwhile, was asking for help.

> Teacher: All right, Damien, Stewart, Dat. I would like for the three of you to go back to your seat and finish your morning work. Because you understand this one.
>
> Dat: I don't understand. I don't understand.
>
> Teacher: No, go back to your seats.
>
> Stewart: I want something harder.
>
> Teacher: You need to finish your writing.
>
> Stewart: I've finished my writing.
>
> Teacher: No, I want you to go finish.... Dat,... unless you would like to do it during lunchtime and recess, then that's it.

The teacher then turned her attention to Carmen, who could not recall how to subtract with regrouping. The teacher told her to just use her coins and began to direct her progress. Meanwhile, Alana still could not subtract with regrouping so she was unable to determine the change from $2; the teacher led her through that regrouping. Although Carmen eventually found her change from one dollar by counting up coins, the teacher then asked her to repeat the problem using the traditional algorithm. Unfortunately, Carmen could not subtract with regrouping symbolically, so the teacher led her through the algorithm. The time available for mathematics then ended, and the children left the room for another activity.

Throughout this lesson, the other children in the classroom had no teacher interaction at all as they worked at their desks on the "morning activity" involving writing. Although the teacher and her principal felt that small-group instruction provided children with the most intensive sessions for instructional contact, they failed to consider how short the duration or infrequent the sampling of that instruction might be. When children in this class could not recall or understand, this teacher either led them through the procedure or denied their lack of understanding as evidenced by their correct procedure. Questioning was relegated to a factual domain.

Consider this teacher during the second semester of her first year of attempting instructional change, meeting regularly with her specialist and her grade-level team. Her observed mathematics lessons at that point averaged one hour and 11 minutes in length. Her dominant mode of instruction had shifted to a discussion of the mathematical topic by the whole class, clarification of the expectation of the activity or problem-solving task with the whole class, separation of the class into cooperative pairs or triples, monitoring of the groups with teacher questioning, and finally sharing of group work with the whole class. Thus the teacher changed her classroom organization to involve more students in mathematical work, to use grouping as a means of encouraging student collaboration, teacher observation, and student evaluation rather than as a means of delivering primary instruction, to use questioning to raise issues for discussion and to clarify student reasoning or approach, and to demand that every child participate in the mathematical activity.

For example, in the following segment, the teacher presented the children with a chart depicting four differing objects with price tags in the first column and these three headings across the next three columns: "Pay with $1.00 "; "Pay with $5.00"; and "Buy 3. How much will it be if you buy 3?" The children discussed the meaning of this chart in a whole class setting. The cells in the first two columns were to be filled in with the change resulting if either $1.00 or $5.00 was offered for payment. The entries in the last column were to reflect the cost of three items. Eleven of the 19 children in the class contributed to this discussion. Then the children were paired and sent off to select chart paper, meter sticks, pencils, glue, and pictured items with price tags. They were to create their own chart and fill in each cell with either the computed change, an "X" to signal that the item costs more than the available sum of money, or the cost of three identical items. The teacher had a meaningful exchange with each of the nine groups as she monitored instruction. Then six children offered an explanation of one problem from their chart during the concluding whole-class discussion.

More important than the stylistic and organizational change, this teacher provided more focus on the mathematics. Children's solution strategies during this lesson included estimating to the nearest 10, counting up to $1.00, and traditional subtraction. All approaches were valued, and all approaches were held accountable for explanation. For example, the following segment typifies an exchange during the teacher's group monitoring of two children, Myra and George.

Teacher: Oh, now you have to find out how much change you get back if it costs 48 cents and you pay with a dollar....

George: I know how much you get back. You get back 52.

Teacher: How did you get... for which one? You're doing this one? [Points to the item costing 48 cents. The teacher is surprised because the child displayed no written work.]

George: Yeah.

Teacher: How did you know if you buy a thing that costs 48 cents, how do you know you get 52 cents back?

George: Because if,... if you have.... Okay, if you have 48 cents, you have, you count by 2's. Get up to 40, 50.

Teacher: All right, wait a second. Slow down, okay? All right, Myra, are you listening? Cause I think it's important for you to hear this too.

George: You add, you add the 50. You add the 50. Uhm, if you add 50 extra and you add 2 because, um.... If that was 50 right there [points to the price of 48 cents], you would have 50 [cents in change]. So that's why. Because it's the forty-..., 2 more up.

Teacher: Wait a. Wait a second. So you added. You're adding 2 cents to 48.

George: No.

Teacher: No.... You're adding 50 to 48?

George: Yeah. No. Not.... I know what.

Teacher: All right think about it for a second....

George: I think that if I had to get up to 50, and it's 48, I would add 2 cents. And so that's two 50's.

Teacher: Okay. Myra, did you hear what he just said? Did you hear what he just said?

Myra: No.

Teacher: All right. Well, George, explain it again slowly to Myra. Turn and look at her and explain it to her. And I'm gonna listen again, but you explain it.

IMPLICATIONS

School-based Change

At its inception, Project IMPACT's focus on the school as the unit of change, with the involvement of all mathematics teachers in selected elementary schools, was unique for an NSF project. Further, although its focus on predominantly minority urban schools was not singular (e.g., Silver, Smith, & Nelson, 1995), it was not the typical setting for mathematics education research projects. Over the last 5 years, shifts in funding have triggered more systemic reform efforts across varying school settings. Nevertheless, the field of mathematics education is only now beginning to identify the issues associated with mathematics reform efforts and the factors that support or limit instructional change across school settings.

Project IMPACT is an effort to link teacher development with educational change addressing innovation in both curriculum and instructional practice. When reflecting on the implications of IMPACT for other reform efforts, it is useful to consider the framework of teacher development posed by Fullan and Hargreaves (1992). In particular, these researchers proposed that the values, goals, and perspectives of individual teachers must be acknowledged by the teacher development effort, and then these individual paradigms must be confronted and reexamined within a context of joint learning. Fullan and Hargreaves termed this addressing "the teacher's purpose" and "the teacher as person." In many ways, Project IMPACT did this. The summer in-service program each year began with the Project director's recognition, in the form of a statement to the participants, that the intention of the summer program was to address instructional change—change in their teaching. But she immediately followed that pronouncement with the acknowledgment that everyone present—every classroom teacher, every staff member, and she—had much to learn and that together, that summer and during the next year or so, they would all learn from each other. Throughout the summer in-service and the following academic years through grade-level planning and teacher–specialist interactions, teachers' views and opinions were sought, their assumptions and knowledge were confronted, prior experiences were respected yet examined (experiences of both teacher participants and Project staff), and an effort was made to foster a community of learners. In addition, although IMPACT spanned the grades, professional interaction in IMPACT was typically grade-level focused so that curricular challenges and accountability as well as the social context for teaching and learning, could be considered. Finally although much teacher change was fostered through the project's on-site support mechanisms, there was eventual recognition of the need to support the continued renewal and growth of the specialists, and for the specialists and the Project staff at the university to examine and consider the challenges being faced by specialists and teachers in distinct schools. Fullan and Hargreaves (1992) termed these aspects recognition of the context and the culture of teaching.

The teacher development framework proposed by Fullan and Hargreaves does not presume school-based involvement, although such a design is clearly amenable to their framework. Nevertheless, it is easier to change within a support milieu; achievement is more likely when people share ideas, successes, and failures, joining together to pursue a common goal relevant to their needs (Fullan with Stiegelbauer, 1991). There is ready evidence that voluntary professional development efforts have not changed urban instructional practice; indeed, it may seem as if the present status in urban systems is to promote a "pedagogy of poverty," which will frustrate reform (Haberman, 1991). Perhaps the context and challenge of urban teaching makes voluntary teacher change even more isolating. This is not to say that teachers in urban centers will never volunteer for such programs. It is simply recognition that volunteer urban teachers may not only face isolation in their schools as they attempt change, they may also face constraints, in the context and culture of their teaching, that are distinct from those of the other volunteer teachers in their cadre who teach in other communities. If those constraints are not addressed, then the urban volunteers may also feel isolation within their professional development cadre. These dual isolating experiences will, at the least, hinder instructional change. At the worst, it may lead the urban volunteer teacher to decide that the instructional reform being envisioned just "won't work with my kids." It may be that in urban centers, the profession has no ethical choice other than the involvement of every mathematics teacher and attention to the concerns of the school community.

In Project IMPACT, urban teachers were not isolated. Indeed the longitudinal nature of Project IMPACT, coupled with district-level support, yielded an unspoken promise to teachers that they would not be left alone in their efforts to attempt instructional change and to implement curricular reform, in their efforts to develop mathematical content knowledge and pedagogical content knowledge, and in their efforts to communicate with administrative authority. The result was that many teachers came to trust and to view the Project as their personal opportunity for growth, as opposed to this year's educational fad. It must be recognized that all teachers did not embrace the Project, nor did all teachers change their instructional practice. There were teachers who viewed the Project with the attitude that "this too will pass." Although some of these teachers were associated with schools having supportive and knowledgeable principals, these teachers were more prevalent in schools with principals who either felt no choice but to reluctantly accept the Project or who did not understand the Project's constructivist approach.

Project IMPACT's experience has been that initial reluctance on the part of teachers does not necessarily imply resistance. Indeed, reluctant teachers may be incredibly reflective or unsure or committed. Although initially unyielding and "physically present" teachers provide provocation within a school-based effort, inclusion of all teachers in the summer in-service program allows even inflexible teachers some crucial beginnings for eventual change. Project IMPACT's experience has been that some teachers evidence little growth or understanding until the second year of implementation. There is no pattern associating this with the teachers' initial eagerness or reluctance. Indeed, if any pattern seems evident, it is this. Teachers who are ultimately committed to the learning and understanding of their students will work incredibly hard to understand mathematical content and pedagogy, making every effort to effectively apply these understandings within their instructional decisions. Within IMPACT, the role of the mathematics specialist in this transformation was critical. Teachers need a means to advocate change, to nurture performance, to advance thinking, to increase mathematical understanding, to salute attempts, and to provoke further development (Campbell, 1996). In Project IMPACT, that role was assumed by the on-site specialist.

Mathematical Expertise

The mathematics reform envisioned in the *Curriculum and Evaluation Standards for School Mathematics* (NCTM, 1989) presumes both mathematical content knowledge and pedagogical content knowledge on the part of teachers. The implication is that lack of either is detrimental. The importance of pedagogical content knowledge is often cited in teacher education literature. However, research on teaching has afforded less attention to studying the implications of mathematical content knowledge, noting that, "except in the most basic sense that teachers cannot teach what they do not know, teachers' *subject-matter knowledge* does not directly determine the nature or quality of their instruction" (Brophy, 1991, p. 350). Nonetheless, this same literature on teaching recognizes that when teachers' subject-matter knowledge and pedagogical content knowledge

> is more explicit, better connected, and more integrated, they [teachers] will tend to teach the subject more dynamically, represent it in more varied ways, and encourage and respond more fully to student comments and questions. Where their knowledge is limited, they will tend to depend on the text for content, deemphasize interactive discourse in favor of seatwork assignments, and in general, portray the subject as a collection of static factual knowledge. (Brophy, 1991, p. 352)

The perspective in Project IMPACT was that the mathematical content knowledge of teachers would be critical and should be enhanced, simultaneously addressing teachers' pedagogical content knowledge and teachers' beliefs or viewpoints (see also Fennema & Franke, 1992).

At the primary level, less mathematical expertise may be essential, although even primary teachers can be challenged and confused by the mathematics questions raised in their classrooms. Generally, primary teachers know if the strategy offered by a young child is mathematically valid, in the sense that each step is correct, and generalizable, in the sense that it always yields correct answers. However, primary teachers may have no idea why a child's strategy "works." This lack of understanding will ultimately limit that primary teacher's ability to raise interesting and challenging questions about the strategy or to raise mathematical connections. In IMPACT, these occurrences in the primary grades were generally infrequent, but they did transpire. The lack of mathematical expertise among upper grade teachers can be even more debilitating. Children can offer solution strategies in the upper elementary grades that require sophisticated mathematical knowledge to determine whether the proffered strategy is logically valid, much less mathematically generalizable. Unique strategies offered by students can leave teachers unsure of how to respond and cause them to feel threatened or inadequate. Insufficient mathematical knowledge can hinder teachers' understanding of their students' thinking. In IMPACT, the specialist often served the role of mathematical mentor for the upper grade teachers, working together to comprehend the mathematical meaning of a child's strategy as well as the implications of that strategy in terms of that child's understanding and that child's future instruction. These specialist–teacher interactions frequently addressed the meaning of mathematical content. It may be that for the upper grade teachers, the place of mathematical content knowledge in the teacher enhancement model is more important than originally presumed by the Project staff. Without the presence of the specialist, issues regarding mathematical content could have been frustrating for some of the teachers. Indeed, there were occasions when the specialists called on Project staff at the university to clarify mathematical content for them and their teachers.

If there was any distinction evident between IMPACT's experience with primary and upper grade teachers in mathematics classrooms, it was this: Upper-grade teachers are very conscious of the influence of prior mathematical knowledge (although they often mean mathematical recall) on children's potential for future learning. Too often they view this knowledge not as an indicator of strength that can be accessed, but as evidence of deficiency. This perspective is probably encouraged by the volume and abstraction of the mathematical topics for which they are accountable. It may also be related to the teachers' own understanding of and beliefs about mathematics, which may have more emphasis on procedural routines as opposed to conceptual meaning. If a teacher's perspective is more focused on mathematical procedures, then upper grade mathematics can be seen as being more dependent on and more concerned with procedures than is primary mathematics simply because there are more procedures to learn. All teachers initially question whether students will ever be able to learn mathematics or to solve problems if the teachers do not meet their perceived responsibility of telling the students what to do. But this perspective can be overwhelming in the upper elementary grades. As a result, upper grade teachers can lose their focus on student understanding and be swayed to simply introduce and present curricular objectives.

The Challenge

There is really very little that is known about instructional change, much less instructional change in urban settings. Instruction will never be well defined because it is the result of the interplay between individual teachers, their students, and the culture of the classroom that they create together. In Project IMPACT, we admit this to teachers. But we also admit that the current status of mathematics education is not adequate and that children, particularly urban children, are being limited by traditional practice. Project IMPACT made a commitment to work together with teachers and MCPS to accomplish more.

Project IMPACT was not designed to compare or contrast differing approaches to reform, yet some features of its enhancement model were probably critical. First, the Project's process for advancing mathematics education reform was to address teacher knowledge and professional development. This emphasis was essential. Too often, particularly in urban centers, teachers are instructed to implement the latest instructional or curricular directive with little recognition of the teachers' need to understand the rationale for the change, with no respect for the teachers' prior experience or current challenges, and with minimal attention to enhancing the teachers' knowledge, particularly the way it will influence decision making in the classroom. Instead, urban centers frequently offer "This is what you do; let me walk you through this" workshops as a pretense of professional development. Project IMPACT's intent was to enhance the base from which teachers would make decisions and to support teachers in their efforts to change, permitting teachers to decide what aspects of reform they would initially address, but presuming that reform would be attempted.

Second, the Project's involvement of every mathematics teacher in the school was critical. The Project's school-based, grade-level design not only addressed the real challenge of teacher isolation, but it also permitted recognition and examination of the teachers' knowledge and beliefs in the context of their urban experience. The potential of transforming teachers from a school into a professional community of learners has been documented previously (Stein, Silver, & Smith, in press), noting that teachers benefit from shared resources and from psychological and sociological support, as well as from increased knowledge when they work together. However, it may be that the challenges and constraints of urban education make school-based design not simply a preference, but a requirement. Indeed, even further commitment is optimal. Those schools where the Project not only encompassed every mathematics teacher but also eventually engaged their principal became an environment where professional risk taking was valued and where instructional change was expected. In those settings, teachers and principals worked together to define their mathematics program, to expand their instructional expertise, to engage students in a common perspective of mathematical work, and to articulate their approach and rationale to parents. Perhaps the message is that schoolwide commitment is the ideal.

Finally, mathematics education reform addresses the intellectual and pedagogical culture of elementary schools. The Project sought to engage teachers in the sustained construction of their mathematical and pedagogical knowledge, challenging the teachers to experience and understand mathematics differently, to interpret and clarify the mathematical goals of their grade-level curriculum, and to examine and define their own mathematics teaching from the perspective of fostering their students' knowledge and thinking. But the Project did not determine the mathematics program of any school; that was the responsibility of the teachers, and presumably the administration, at each school. However, because of the Project's district-level support and sustained presence on site in the person of the specialist, the Project's commitment to champion and challenge schools and teachers in their efforts to articulate their mathematics programs and to struggle for change was clear.

Project IMPACT demonstrates the potential of school-based professional development for elementary mathematics reform. It has done so in the reality of public schools that do not have a tradition of strong mathematics achievement. If the potential and problems associated with reform are to be understood, if the implications of reform for urban centers are to be recognized, and if the vision of mathematical power for all students is to be realized, then reform cannot only be situated in idealized settings. The challenge for all mathematics educators is to expand and maintain the commitment, not just to reform in selected classrooms, but to educational change across schools, including urban schools.

ACKNOWLEDGMENTS

The research reported in this material was supported by the National Science Foundation under Grant Numbers MDR 8954652 and ESI 9454187. The opinions, conclusions, or recommendations expressed in these materials are those of the authors and do not necessarily reflect the views of the National Science Foundation.

REFERENCES

Ball, D. L. (1991). Research on teaching mathematics: Making subject-matter knowledge part of the equation. In J. Brophy (Ed.), *Advances in research on teaching: Vol. 2. Teachers' knowledge of subject matter as it relates to their teaching practice* (pp. 1–48). Greenwich, CT: JAI Press.

Baroody, A. J. (1987). *Children's mathematical thinking: A developmental framework for preschool, primary, and special education teachers*. New York: Teachers College Press.

Beane, D. B. (1985). *Mathematics and science: Critical filters for the future of minority students*. Washington, DC: The American University, The Mid-Atlantic Center for Race Equity.

Brophy, J. J. (1991). Conclusion. In J. Brophy (Ed.), *Advances in research on teaching: Vol. 2. Teachers' knowledge of subject matter as it relates to their teaching practice* (pp. 349–364). Greenwich, CT: JAI Press.

Campbell, P. F. (1996). Empowering children and teachers in the elementary mathematics classrooms of urban schools. *Urban Education, 30,* 449–475

Campbell, P. F., Rowan, T. E., & Cheng, Y. (1995, April). *Project IMPACT: Mathematics achievement in predominately minority elementary classrooms attempting reform*. Paper presented at the annual meeting of the American Educational Research Association, San Francisco, CA.

Carey, D. A., Fennema, E., Carpenter, T. P., & Franke, M. L. (1995). Equity and mathematics education. In W. G. Secada, E. Fennema, & L. B. Adajian (Eds.), *New directions for equity in mathematics education* (pp. 93–125). New York: Cambridge University Press.

Carpenter, T. P., Fennema, E., Peterson, P. L., Chiang, C. P., & Loef, M. (1989). Using knowledge of children's mathematics thinking in classroom teaching: An experimental study. *American Educational Research Journal, 26,* 499–531.

Clark, C. M., & Peterson, P. L. (1986). Teachers' thought processes. In M. C. Wittrock (Ed.), *Handbook of research on teaching* (3rd. ed., pp. 255–296). New York: Macmillan.

Clewell, B. C., Thorpe, M. E., & Anderson, B. T. (1987, May). *Intervention programs in math, science, and computer science for minority and female students in grades four through eight*. Princeton, NJ: Educational Testing Service.

Cobb, P. (1988). The tension between theories of learning and instruction in mathematics education. *Educational Psychologist, 23,* 87–103.

Cobb, P., Wood, T., & Yackel, E. (1990). Classrooms and learning environments for teachers and researchers. In R. B. Davis, C. A. Maher, & N. Noddings (Eds.), *Constructivist views on the teaching and learning of mathematics (Journal for Research in Mathematics Education Monograph No. 4,* pp. 125–146). Reston, VA: National Council of Teachers of Mathematics.

Cobb, P., Wood, T., & Yackel, E. (1991). A constructivist approach to second grade mathematics. In E. von Glasersfeld (Ed.), *Radical constructivism in mathematics education* (pp. 157–176). Dordrecht, The Netherlands: Kluwer Academic Publishers.

Cobb, P., Yackel, E., Wood, T., Wheatley, G., & Merkel, G. (1988). Creating a problem-solving atmosphere. *Arithmetic Teacher, 36*(1), 46–47.

Even, R., & Lappan, G. (1994). Constructing meaningful understanding of mathematics content. In D. B. Aichele & A. F. Coxford (Eds.), *Professional development for teachers of mathematics 1994 Yearbook* (pp. 128–143). Reston, VA: National Council of Teachers of Mathematics.

Fennema, E., Carpenter, T. P., Franke, M. L., Levi, L., Jacobs, V. R., & Empson, S. B. (1996). A longitudinal study of learning to use children's thinking in mathematics instruction. *Journal for Research in Mathematics Education, 27,* 403–434.

Fennema, E., & Franke, M. L. (1992). Teachers' knowledge and its impact. In D. A. Grouws (Ed.), *Handbook of research on mathematics teaching and learning* (pp. 147–164). New York: Macmillan.

Fennema, E., & Meyer, M. R. (1989). Gender, equity and mathematics. In W. G. Secada (Ed.), *Equity in education* (pp. 146–157). Bristol, PA: Falmer.

Fullan, M., & Hargreaves, A. (1992). Teacher development and educational change. In M. Fullan & A. Hargreaves (Eds.), *Teacher development and educational change* (pp. 1–9). Bristol, PA: Falmer.

Fullan, M. with Stiegelbauer, S. (1991). *The new meaning of educational change.* New York: Teachers College Press.

Greenes, C., Schulman, L., & Spungin, R. (1993). *Techniques of problem solving communication deck.* Palo Alto, CA: Dale Seymour.

Gross, S. (1988). *Participation and performance of women and minorities in mathematics. Volume I: Findings by gender and racial/ethnic group* (Final Report of the National Science Foundation Grant No. MDR-8470384; available from the Department of Educational Accountability, Montgomery County Public Schools, 850 Hungerford Drive, Rockville, MD 20850)

Haberman, M. (1991). The pedagogy of poverty versus good teaching. *Phi Delta Kappan, 73,* 290–294.

Hiebert, J., & Carpenter, T. P. (1992). Learning and teaching with understanding. In D. A. Grouws (Ed.), *Handbook of research on mathematics teaching and learning* (pp. 65–97). New York: Macmillan.

House, P. A. (1980). Making a problem of junior high school mathematics. *Arithmetic Teacher, 28*(2), 20–23.

Ladson-Billings, G. (1990). Like lightning in a bottle: Attempting to capture the pedagogical excellence of successful teachers of black students. *Qualitative Studies in Education, 3,* 335–344.

Ladson-Billings, G. (1992). Culturally relevant teaching: The key to making multicultural education work. In C. A. Grant (Ed.), *Research and multicultural education: From the margins to the mainstream* (pp. 106–121). Bristol, PA: Falmer.

Lampert, M. (1989). Choosing and using mathematical tools in classroom discourse. In J. Brophy (Ed.), *Advances in research on teaching, Vol. 1* (pp. 223–264). Greenwich, CT: JAI Press.

Lappan, G., & Briars, D. (1995). How should mathematics be taught? In I. Carl (Ed.), *Seventy-five years of progress: Prospects for school mathematics* (pp. 131–156). Reston, VA: National Council of Teachers of Mathematics.

Little, J. W. (1990). Teachers as colleagues. In A. Lieberman (Ed.), *Schools as collaborative cultures: Creating the future now* (pp. 165–193). New York: Falmer.

Lockheed, M. E., Thorpe, M., Brooks-Gunn, J., Casserly, P., & McAloon, A. (1985, May). *Sex and ethnic differences in middle school mathematics, science and computer science: What do we know?* Princeton, NJ: Educational Testing Service.

Loucks-Horsley, S., Harding, C. K., Arbuckle, M. A., Murray, L. B., Dubea, C., & Williams, M. K. (1987). *Continuing to learn: A guidebook for teacher development.* Andover, MA:

The Regional Laboratory for Educational Improvement of the Northeast and Islands and The National Staff Development Council.

Malcom, S. M., Aldrich, M., Hall, P. Q., Boulware, P., & Stern, V. (1984, December). *Equity and excellence: Compatible goals* (AAAS Publication 84–14). Washington, DC: American Association for the Advancement of Science.

National Council of Teachers of Mathematics. (1989). *Curriculum and evaluation standards for school mathematics*. Reston, VA: Author.

National Council of Teachers of Mathematics. (1991). *Professional standards for teaching mathematics*. Reston, VA: Author.

National Research Council. (1989). *Everybody counts: A report to the nation on the future of mathematics education*. Washington, DC: National Academy of Sciences

Noddings, N. (1990). Constructivism in mathematics education. In R. B. Davis, C. A. Maher, & N. Noddings (Eds.), *Constructivist views on the teaching and learning of mathematics (Journal for Research in Mathematics Education Monograph No. 4*, pp. 7–18). Reston, VA: National Council of Teachers of Mathematics.

Oakes, J. (1985). *Keeping track: How schools structure inequality*. New Haven, CT: Yale University Press.

Oakes, J. (1990). *Multiplying inequalities: The effect of race, social class, and tracking on opportunities to learn mathematics and science*. Santa Monica, CA: Rand Corporation.

Peterson, P. L., Fennema, E., & Carpenter, T. P. (1991). Teachers' knowledge of students' mathematics problem-solving knowledge. In J. Brophy (Ed.), *Advances in research on teaching: Vol. 2. Teachers' knowledge of subject matter as it relates to their teaching practice* (pp. 49–86). Greenwich, CT: JAI Press.

Peterson, P. L., Fennema, E., Carpenter, T. P., & Loef, M. (1989). Teachers' pedagogical content beliefs in mathematics. *Cognition and Instruction, 6*, 1–40.

Pirie, S., & Kieren, T. (1992). Creating constructivist environments and constructing creative mathematics. *Educational Studies in Mathematics, 23*, 505–528.

Putnam, R. T., Lampert, M., & Peterson, P. L. (1990). Alternative perspectives on knowing mathematics in elementary schools. In C. B. Cazden (Ed.), *Review of research in education (Vol. 16*, pp. 57–150). Washington, DC: American Educational Research Association.

Romberg, T. A., & Pitman, A. (1994). A strategy for social change. In N. L. Webb & T. A. Romberg (Eds.), *Reforming mathematics education in America's cities: The Urban Mathematics Collaborative Project* (pp. 48–66). New York: Teachers College Press.

Russell, S. J., & Corwin, R. B. (1989). *Statistics: The shape of data*. Palo Alto, CA: Dale Seymour.

Schifter, D., & Fosnot, C. T. (1993). *Reconstructing mathematics education: Stories of teachers meeting the challenge of reform*. New York: Teachers College Press.

Shaw, K. L., & Jakubowski, E. H. (1991). Teachers changing in changing times. *Focus on learning problems in mathematics, 13*(4), 13–20.

Silver, E. A., Smith, M. S., & Nelson, B. S. (1995). The QUASAR Project: Equity concerns meet mathematics education reform in the middle school. In W. G. Secada, E. Fennema, & L. B. Adajian (Eds.), *New directions for equity in mathematics education* (pp. 9–56). New York: Cambridge University Press.

Simon, M. (1995). Reconstructing mathematics pedagogy. *Journal for Research in Mathematics Education, 26*, 114–145.

Steffe, L. P., Cobb, P., & von Glasersfeld, E. (1988). *Construction of arithmetical meanings and strategies*. New York: Springer-Verlag.

Stein, M. K., Silver, E. A., & Smith, M. S. (in press). Mathematics reform and teacher development: A community of practice perspective. In J. Greeno & S. Goldman (Eds.), *Thinking practices: A symposium on mathematics and science learning*. Hillsdale, NJ: Lawrence Erlbaum Associates.

Thompson, A. G. (1985). Teachers' conceptions of mathematics and the teaching of problem solving. In E. A. Silver (Ed.), *Teaching and learning mathematical problem solving: Multiple research perspectives* (pp. 281–294). Hillsdale, NJ: Lawrence Erlbaum Associates.

von Glasersfeld, E. (1990). An exposition of constructivism: Why some like it radical. In R. B. Davis, C. A. Maher, & N. Noddings (Eds.), *Constructivist views on the teaching and learning of mathematics* (*Journal for Research in Mathematics Education Monograph No. 4*, pp. 19–29). Reston, VA: National Council of Teachers of Mathematics.

Wideen, M. F. (1992). School-based teacher development. In M. Fullan & A. Hargreaves (Eds.), *Teacher development and educational change* (pp. 123–155). Bristol, PA: Falmer.

13

Mathematics in Context: Impact on Teachers

Thomas A. Romberg
University of Wisconsin–Madison

The purpose of this chapter is to synthesize findings from studies that focus on how teachers have coped with the transition from traditional forms of instruction in mathematics classrooms to a reform approach. The research was carried out in relationship to the reform vision for school mathematics described in three documents prepared by the National Council of Teachers of Mathematics (NCTM): *Curriculum and Evaluation Standards for School Mathematics* (1989), *Professional Standards for Teaching Mathematics* (1991), and *Assessment Standards for School Mathematics* (1995). These documents argue that all aspects of school mathematics—content, teaching, and assessment—need to change, and that those changes must be reflected in the work of students and teachers in classrooms.

To investigate how teachers respond to such changes, the studies summarized in this chapter have been conducted in schools whose staffs have collectively agreed to work toward reform and have been using prepublication versions of instructional units of the *Mathematics in Context (MiC)* middle school curriculum (National Center for Research in Mathematical Sciences Education & Freudenthal Institute, in press–a) being developed under the auspices of the National Science Foundation. This curriculum has been designed to reflect NCTM *Standards* and includes 40 instructional units, 10 for each grade (Grades 5–8). Following a blueprint prepared by the staff and an advisory committee of the National Center for Research in Mathematical Sciences Education (NCRMSE) at the University of Wisconsin–Madison, the units were designed by the staff of the Freudenthal Institute at the University of Utrecht, The Netherlands, and adapted for American schools by NCRMSE staff.

Underlying this curriculum is the belief that mathematics is fallible, changing, and, like any other body of knowledge, the product of human inventiveness (Ernest, 1991). To this end, teachers are expected to provide students opportunities to develop these beliefs by engaging in a variety of problem situations in a classroom environment that rewards alternative solution strategies, encourages appropriate mathematical modeling, invites reflective thinking, and allows genuine sharing of information. Learning mathematics in this curriculum is seen as a constructive problem-solving process carried out in the social environment of the classroom. It is based on contemporary psychological models, which portray learners as active constructors of knowledge. Instruction in these units is based on the belief that activities should motivate students to struggle constantly to understand what they are doing and to reinvent important mathematics. Thus, all mathematics learning is seen as problem-solving activity carried out with others.

MiC APPROACH TO INSTRUCTION

The emerging theory of instruction on which *Mathematics in Context* is based has been labeled "Realistic Mathematics Education"(RME; de Lange, 1987; Freudenthal, 1987). This approach to mathematics instruction begins with a concern about students acquiring a critical attitude toward the role of mathematics in contemporary society. Aware that the user of mathematics is involved in a complex set of activities that goes far beyond the use of specific techniques often taught in specific mathematics courses, the RME approach starts with the assumption that students should begin their investigations with contextual, real-world problems. The initial instructional activity should be experientially real to students, so that they engage in personally meaningful mathematical work (Gravemeijer, 1991). Next, students are expected to identify information needed to answer the questions by working through a number of activities that encourage them to search for, and use, that information. Finally, students work to build a coherent case to answer the questions originally raised. This sequence of activities assumes that each activity is justifiable in terms of potential end points in a learning sequence.

Cobb (1994), in his analysis of the RME approach to instruction, stated that

> this implies that students' initially informal mathematical activity should constitute a basis from which they can abstract and construct increasingly sophisticated mathematical conceptions. At the same time, the starting point situations should continue to function as paradigm cases that involve rich imagery and thus anchor students' increasingly abstract

mathematical activity.... Instructional sequences should involve activities in which students create and elaborate symbolic models of their informal mathematical activity. This modeling activity might involve making drawings, diagrams, or tables, or it could involve developing informal notations or using conventional mathematical notations. (pp. 23–24)

With appropriate guidance from teachers, a student's informal models can evolve into models for increasingly abstract mathematical reasoning (Gravemeijer, 1991). The development of ways of symbolizing problem situations and the transition from informal to formal semiotics are important aspects of these instructional assumptions.

This theoretical perspective was followed as the 40 instructional *Mathematics in Context* units were developed. During the past 5 years, much information has been gathered in classrooms for formative purposes (to improve the units); concurrently, in-depth case studies have been carried out by staff members on how students and teachers cope with the transition from traditional forms of instruction to this reform approach. This chapter focuses on information derived from studies that examined the impact on teachers as a consequence of teaching units from *Mathematics in Context* in their classrooms.[1]

THE CASE STUDIES

To prepare the following summary about teachers in transition, I used comments from nine separate case studies and combined them with formative information gathered as the units for *Mathematics in Context* were being pilot- and field-tested in classrooms. One case study was carried out in a traditional school, and eight concerned the teaching of *Mathematics in Context*. Each case study provides rich descriptions of the experiences of teachers and students in specific mathematics classrooms. Each tells a slightly different story, but taken together they suggest common themes about the teacher's role in the reformed classroom and the difficulties in making the transition from traditional to reformed instruction. As Sarason (1971) in his examination of the culture of schools argued, "any attempt to introduce a change into the school involves [challenging] some existing regularity, behavioral or programmatic" (p. 3). In each case where units from *Mathematics in Context* were being taught, the traditional school culture and the common instructional routines for mathematics classes were being challenged.

---

[1] These are not the only studies carried out in this program of research. They are, however, the completed studies where evidence was gathered with respect to teachers and how they were coping with teaching mathematics from a reform perspective.

This chapter is not the place for a lengthy description of each study. However, a brief overview of each study follows, and the rationale for its inclusion in this chapter is given. We should also point out that the struggles teachers were having, and the changes observed, were in every case influenced by the very positive responses to the *Mathematics in Context* units by their students and by the support of project personnel.

The first study (Weller, 1991) is not about teachers involved in reform, nor about using *Mathematics in Context*; rather it is a recent description of the teaching of mathematics in a traditional middle-class American school. Weller's characterizations of some traditional teaching practices in mathematics classrooms are used here to highlight the difficulties teachers have as they attempt to change both what and how they are teaching mathematics. In his case study, Weller situated the teaching of core subjects, such as mathematics, in the culture and instructional traditions of a typical suburban junior high school and then gave portrayals of two different Grade 8 mathematics classes: one, a general mathematics class and the other, an algebra class.

The next six studies examine the teaching and learning of mathematics when one or more *Mathematics in Context* units were used by teachers in their mathematics classrooms. It should be noted that these studies were carried out in field-test classrooms, where the primary focus was to gather formative information on the use of the instructional units in classrooms for clarification and possible revision. de Lange, Burrill, Romberg, and van Reeuwijk (1993) reported the initial trial of a prepilot statistics unit based on the RME approach to mathematics, *Data Visualization* (de Lange & Verhage, 1989), in seven algebra classes in a middle-class suburban high school in 1989. It was this study that led to the decision to develop the complete middle-school curriculum and led to the name *Mathematics in Context*. The sections written by Burrill, the department chair, convey the voice of teachers as they taught the unit. All of the teachers in this study, who were fully qualified and experienced in the classroom, had surprises and difficulties with the unit. Nevertheless, the study made "it obvious that constructive change toward the vision implied in the *Standards* will take effort and support, but that it is possible" (p. 167).

In his study, D. Clarke (1993) examined the reactions of two sixth-grade teachers (working in roughly equivalent teaching situations in a middle-class urban school) to expected changes in their roles as a consequence of teaching pilot versions of MiC units. B. Clarke (1995), in another study conducted in a small town, rural middle school, followed two seventh-grade teachers as they taught units from *Mathematics in Context* designed to introduce students to notions of trigonometry through "realistic" contexts. The challenges these teachers experienced often involved the unexpected nature of student responses to problems.

Spence (1996) observed two eighth-grade teachers in a middle-class small town school as they taught units from the algebra strand of *Mathematics in Context*. The focus was on how the teachers' traditional knowledge of algebra and their beliefs about the domain influenced what they did in their classrooms. One teacher had a strong traditional background in mathematics and the other, a weak mathematics background. Although Shew (1995) focused on the impact of *Mathematics in Context* on students in an urban fringe school rather than on their teachers, some of the information Shew gathered reflects what the teacher of these students emphasized and the struggles the teacher encountered when teaching mathematics in her classroom.

Shafer (1996) and van den Heuvel-Panhuizen (1995) shifted the focus from instruction to assessment as an integral aspect of the reform movement. van den Heuvel-Panhuizen included several interviews with teachers from a variety of schools about how to assess student understanding of percentage. In particular, when teachers wrote problems, they tended to stress short tasks and computational skills connected to preceding instructional activities. Shafer examined in depth the daily assessment practices of a middle school teacher in a middle-class urban school committed to the reform movement, who had participated in the pilot testing and field testing of *Mathematics in Context*. In particular, Shafer examined the struggle this teacher had in collecting, summarizing, and reporting evidence about student growth in algebra.

The final study (Hutchinson, 1996) used four potential teachers in a small state university serving a rural area to support the analysis of the transitions teachers face in classrooms. Her study involves the reactions of these preservice students to this approach to mathematics as they worked through selected activities from *Mathematics in Context*. The four preservice teachers were selected to represent the four crossed cells involving strong versus weak mathematics background and belief in reform instruction versus belief in traditional instruction.

TEACHERS COPING WITH INSTRUCTIONAL TRADITIONS

The challenges to traditional instructional practices being faced by the teachers in these studies was first described by Burrill (quoted in de Lange et al., 1993) when the mathematics staff of Whitnall High School agreed to prepilot *Data Visualization*, a unit on descriptive statistics:

> The Mathematics Department, whose members have a long history of working together to develop curriculum and teaching activities, readily agreed to use the booklet in each algebra class. In the initial meeting with the observer, although there was concern on the part of those who were

new to the idea, there was still no real anticipation of the radical changes we would be called upon to make in our classrooms. We knew about the NCTM *Curriculum and Evaluation Standards*. We were prepared for something new but not something so different. As we worked through the project, however, the *Standards* came to life. We began to recognize that we not only needed new ways of teaching but a new way of thinking about what mathematics we should teach. (p. 154)

All of the teachers who participated in the eight studies where *Mathematics in Context* units were used (with the exception of the Hutchinson [1996] study with preservice teachers) were experienced, fully certified, confident in their ability to teach, and committed to reform. Thus, no claim is made that they are typical teachers such as those in Weller's (1991) study. Teaching a new unit to these teachers sounded relatively easy. They believed they would "gain a few new ideas that we could use in our classes once the project was over" (de Lange et al., 1993, p. 153). Instead, as they taught the units, the traditions commonly held about teaching mathematics in American classrooms were being challenged. Such challenges to traditions, as Shafer (1996) found, were still being encountered by an "exceptional teacher... who had been involved in both pilot- and field-testing of the curriculum" (p. 6) in his third year with the program. The implication is that, because experienced teachers were taught mathematics traditionally, and in turn taught mathematics from that perspective, changing their practices would be very difficult even if they were committed to reform.

To summarize the impact on teachers as a consequence of teaching units from *Mathematics in Context*, I have chosen to focus on five aspects of the materials that are different from traditional practices in school mathematics: the change in redefinition of instructional practice, authority, and expectations; mathematical content; teacher's knowledge of mathematics; assessment of progress toward performance standards; and the challenge to conventions of community-valued authority.

The Redefinition of Instructional Practice, Authority, and Expectations

Although there was considerable variation in the reactions of teachers to their use of the *Mathematics in Context* units in their classrooms, the initial challenges they all faced were about the shift in the daily pattern of instruction. In Weller's (1991) study of traditional mathematics classrooms, he found a common daily pattern of instruction in both classes: "It was evident that a repeating pattern of instruction occurred which consisted of three distinctive segments: a review, presentation, and study/assistance period. This 'rhythm of instruction' was not unplanned or coincidental" (p. 128). All of the teachers found that teaching a *Mathematics in Context* unit constituted a departure from this traditional daily pattern. Burrill reflected (quoted in de Lange et al., 1993) on this challenge:

> The surprise came when we tried to teach the first lesson. There was little to "teach"; rather, the students had to read the map, read the keys, read the questions, determine what they were being asked to do, decide which piece of information from the map could be used to help them do this, and finally, decide what mathematics skills they needed, if any, in answering the question. There was no way the teacher could set the stage by demonstrating two examples (one of each kind), or by assigning five "seat work" problems and then turning students loose on their homework with a model firmly (for the moment) in place. (p. 154)

The changes in the pattern of instruction forced some teachers to reconsider how they interacted with their students. Three aspects became apparent in these studies. First, authority in the traditional classroom resides with the teacher or, as Weller (1991) argued, with the textbook author. Weller found that, "The expert knowledge of the teacher was deliberately subjugated to that of the textbook. As a result of that process, the teacher was able to camouflage his role as authoritarian, thus eliminating student challenges of authority" (p. 133). For example, one teacher "introduced the lesson on the metric system as follows: 'When I teach this section, I have to review this system because I have no reason to ever use it. You have to learn it because maybe some day you'll use it rather than me. Besides, this is the chapter which comes next and that's what they want you to learn'" (p. 124). Furthermore, when this teacher "presented new material and assigned homework, [he frequently used] the third person 'they'.... [and stated] 'I don't consider myself the source of knowledge, the center of knowledge'" (p. 126–127). This use of the term *they* as the authority for what, how, and why something is done echoes what Provenzo, McCloskey, Kottkamp, and Cohn (1989) found: "The use of 'they' by the teacher allows her to express her feelings concerning the forces that are influencing and shaping her day-to-day work, without having to specify their actual source and origin" (p. 563).

In the field testing of *Mathematics in Context*, teachers could not fall back on the use of the term *they* in the same manner. This may have been because the student booklets contained tasks for students to read and make sense of under the guidance of the teacher. This approach to instructional authority changed the work environment for both teachers and students from well-rehearsed routines to a variety of nonroutine activities.

For most teachers in these studies, the adjustments in what they and their students were expected regularly to do was unsettling. In an earlier paper (Romberg, 1992), I noted that classrooms are work environments for both teachers and students: "In traditional classrooms, the work of the teacher is to 'transmit' knowledge, and the job of the student is to receive it, regurgitating it on demand" (p. 764). In a *Mathematics in Context* classroom, this was not the case. For example, when reflecting on the work of the two teachers in her study, B. Clarke (1995) noted that the teachers struggled with how much to tell the students:

> Both too little and too much structure seemed to limit the students' thinking. For example, with the initial presentation of problems there was a need to clarify, but at the same time not to present complete explanations. The challenge was to present a problem in such a way that the students could make a start, while not limiting their thinking by over explanation. (p. 159)

She also noted that "the teachers encouraged conjecturing and inventing as students solved problems. This led to critical incidents for the teachers as they tried to understand the students' methods of solution on the spur of the moment. Insightful student responses led to more critical incidents than any other type" (p. 156). In particular, she found that for these teachers, "the reality of changing authority is difficult. There were a number of times when the students were able to provide the clarification of a difficulty. This was powerful, though potentially threatening to the authority of the teacher"(pp. 157–158). In fact, in most classes teachers occasionally had to admit they did not know how to approach a problem and thus had to work on the tasks with the students as equals.

D. Clarke (1993) found that as a consequence of teaching a *Mathematics in Context* unit, teachers began to change their instructional habits: "The interplay between beliefs and practice seemed evident in this study... ([e.g.,] the use of non-routine problems as the starting-point and focus of instruction, without the provision of procedures for their solution), reflection upon classroom events appeared to prompt a small change in beliefs about particular teaching strategies, which then led to further small changes in practice, and so on" (p. 219).

Second, in traditional classrooms, the way a small number of adults (teachers and others) are able to organize and control a large number of students is seen as a management problem. Management is a particular problem when, as Weller (1991) found, students "do not necessarily participate willingly in the pursuit of the goals established by the community and the school system" (p. 202). In this sense the traditional teacher is primarily a manager of resources and personnel, and his or her task is to get students to complete pages or do sets of exercises. One common management approach has been to reduce the intellectual struggle for students. For example, B. Clarke (1995) found that for one teacher in her study, the conflict between her view of student comfort and struggle was disturbing:

> The emotional well being of the students was very important to this teacher, and she worked very hard at making the classroom environment comfortable and successful. . . . Students were not generally encouraged to struggle and it is this very struggle, the grappling with mathematical ideas, that reform documents encourage. This represented a contradiction between the practices this teacher believed allowed students to be comfortable and successful and the intended purpose of the unit. (p. 160–161)

She also found that both teachers in her study struggled with the changes in behavior in their students as they worked in groups: "Student involvement and engagement was often high and at times discussion occurred that was not directed through the teacher. In these situations the teacher was not the controller in the traditional sense, and student enthusiasm sometimes led to boisterous interactions, which although task oriented, nevertheless challenged traditional classroom norms" (p. 157). The shift in how to manage students in such situations was not easily resolved. For example, Spence (1996) found that, when confronted with situations where he was unsure of how to proceed in an activity, one teacher's relations with his students came to dominate lessons, and learning mathematics became secondary.

Third, one significant outcome for teachers in these studies was a changed view of the students and their capabilities as a consequence of working *Mathematics in Context* activities. In fact, all the teachers were surprised by the work their students were able to do. As one field-test teacher commented, "what we're finding in some of our work, too, is that the kids get things that we thought might be hard for them" (Romberg & Shafer, 1995, p. 8). Burrill (quoted in de Lange et al., 1993) wrote that "The students were excited about ideas—they were thinking and interpreting problems that were real and not contrived. No one said 'When will I ever need this?'" (p. 158). One field-test summary found that "most teachers were amazed that students could communicate and were excited about talking and doing math. They were able to make connections to the world around them and to other areas of study in school" (Romberg & Shafer, 1995, p. 16). A consequence of this was summarized by Burrill (quoted in de Lange et al., 1993), "About a week or so into the booklet, one teacher suddenly exclaimed, 'we are not teaching statistics; students are learning how to use statistics to solve problems!'" (p. 155).

The impact of having students "do mathematics" in this manner had two consequences. First, as Burrill found, "Students who had been labeled as 'poor in math' found they could succeed, and some who considered themselves 'good in math' decided 'this isn't math'" (p. 160). van den Huevel-Panhuizen (1995) found similar results when teachers administered open assessment tasks:

One teacher even discovered something new about the students' understanding by means of the test: "Some of my quieter students displayed a greater understanding than I had given them credit for, some displayed a sense of humor." This same teacher went on to make the following comment about the assessment for the unit: "I feel it offers more than most objective sorts of tests. It allows students to explain their thinking—a very valuable piece of information. (p. 71)

It should be understood, however, that not all students reacted favorably to studying mathematics in this new problem-solving manner. As one field-test teacher commented,

> I do have to say that probably each classroom has a couple of students that still have reservations. They are good mathematicians, but they are book learners and they say, why don't we just do the book? Just give us 20 problems... We still have a couple per room that would be very content to go back to that, but I think the learning is much richer using this method. I think we have greater student growth. (Romberg & Shafer, 1995, p. 10)

This perspective, held by some students, is a concern voiced by many field-test teachers, often in sympathy. The danger, of course, is the tendency to augment reform instruction with traditional practices, and then to modify and change activities so that they resemble past lessons. For example, B. Clarke (1995) found that, "there was also a tendency on the part of one of the teachers, having taught the lesson once, to vary the presentation in subsequent lessons, with increasing levels of structure, as a response to feelings of personal discomfort" (p. 159).

In summary, the work of teachers and students in a *Mathematics in Context* classroom is complex and often confusing to both teachers and students. The difficulties teachers face when attempting to teach mathematics in this manner are real and not well understood. For these teachers the difficulties in shifting from familiar instructional practice, authority, and expectations to a reform approach was not easily accomplished.

Mathematical Content

The typical mathematical content in American middle schools has focused on quantities expressed as whole numbers, common fractions, and decimal fractions, and on operations with those numbers. In fact, much of the content in traditional middle school textbooks, as Flanders (1987) described it, was a repetition and review of previously covered material, and very little new mathematical content was included in texts for grades 4 through 8. In contrast, the content in *Mathematics in Context* includes much new content. As described in *Welcome to—"Mathematics in Context"* (National Center for Research in Mathematical Sciences Education & Freudenthal Institute, in press-b), the content included in the units has been organized around four strands:

> *Numbers* (whole numbers, common fractions, ratio, decimal fractions, percents, integers), *algebra* (creation of expressions, tables, graphs, and formulas from patterns and functions), *geometry* (measurement, spatial visualization, synthetic geometry, coordinate and transformational geometry), and *statistics and probability* (data visualization, chance, distribution and variability, and quantification of expectations). (p. 7)

Some of this content is typical of traditional programs, and certainly much is common in the newer programs developed in response to the current reform initiatives. However, there are four features that caused teachers problems as they used *Mathematics in Context* units.

First, in many of the units, ideas typically taught in the high-school curriculum are introduced to middle-school students in an informal manner. The coverage of mathematical topics at an earlier grade than had been common in traditional programs was a concern voiced by many teachers in two ways: surprise (e.g., when students were introduced to integers in grade 5 or expected to write equations in grade 6), and concern (e.g., when will traditional topics be covered?). For example, in the geometry unit that uses glide ratios (in activities involving similar triangles) as an introduction of the tangent ratio, B. Clarke (1995) found that "tasks within the unit and students' attempts at these led to the introduction of a variety of mathematical content areas, some of which were unfamiliar to the teachers" (p. 157). When this occurred, teachers were unsure how to proceed. Furthermore, even if the teachers themselves were familiar with the mathematics, they were often unsure how to proceed because they had never taught it to students. The latter is important because it focuses on the teachers' understanding of the learning process of their students. D. Clarke (1993) found that teachers floundered when "they lacked knowledge of most students' learning of the content of the unit and the means by which such knowledge could be obtained" (p. 222).

Second, even if it was common middle-school content, the placement of topics in *Mathematics in Context* often is different. For example, when a mathematical topic in the materials had not traditionally been taught at that grade (e.g., percentage at grade 5), van den Heuvel-Panhuizen (1995) found that teachers were not sure how to proceed. As one teacher stated: "I do not usually teach percentage. It has not been a part of our (core) math curriculum. I have only used percentage in relation to pie or circle graphs and in interpreting test scores" (p. 67).

Third, many teachers voiced concern over "coverage." The importance of order of "coverage" in traditional classrooms was characterized by Weller (1991): "A goal of mathematics teachers was to cover a prescribed amount of material preparing students to enter the next level of mathematics study. The overall pace of instruction required the [teachers] to teach the textbook, cover-to-cover, as the mathematics curriculum required. The sequential order of concept presentation was determined by the textbook editor and thus embraced by the department" (p. 128). Teaching new or different content clearly challenged this ingrained notion of the order of coverage. Their concern over when or whether to teach traditional topics was voiced by many teachers as the materials were being tested. The teacher in Shew's (1995) study

> had to deal with a conflict between her own personal perception of mathematics and her perception of what mathematics should be for her students. When I asked Ms. Smith what she believed mathematics should be for fifth-grade students, she responded in the following manner.
>
> As far as fifth grade is concerned, um, I'm wrestling with fifth-graders right now because I see them coming up with a very narrow view of math and I'm trying to expand it but yet keep that security blanket in there of the things that they are used to and what parents are used to and, um, you can't turn the apple cart upside down altogether so it's a balance.
>
> [This teacher's] view of what mathematics should be [was] influenced by her beliefs about student and parent expectations and her belief that students should not be put into a situation that would make them too uncomfortable.

As a consequence of this concern, the teacher in Shew's study admitted that she augmented the *Mathematics in Context* units by teaching computational procedures following specific steps from another text.

Fourth, although each unit in *Mathematics in Context* emphasizes specific topics within a particular mathematical strand, most units involve ideas from several strands and emphasize both the interconnectedness of those ideas and the variety of possible procedures to solve problems. This proved challenging to teachers because it was so different from their past practices. In traditional instruction Weller (1991) described that in the traditional class each lesson was on one concept or procedure and "emphasis was placed upon ascertaining the one correct answer, a focus quite apparent to most students. [The teacher] provided a step-by-step explanation of her thinking processes as the exercises were computed. Students who had skipped steps but who arrived at the same answer as the teacher were immediately corrected" (p. 130–131). The consequences of more open lessons emphasizing interconnected ideas and a variety of strategies was commented on by many of the teachers in these studies. For example, Burrill (quoted in de Lange et al., 1993) wrote that

> we had to listen to students, examine their work, and try to learn what they were thinking as they solved a problem. What was valid in that

process and what needed to be altered? As teachers, we had to learn how to probe for understanding and explanations; to listen to what students had to say, and figure out when they said what they did. Student work became more important than ever—numerical answers as such had little value. Communication became an integral part of the classroom dynamics. Before the project, we directed our attention to what part of an algorithm students had misused. Now, we had to try to follow a variety of uncharted and often unexpected directions in student work.... Our role was shifting from that of one who directs the thought processes of the students to one who reacts and guides their reasoning; it was not easy to resist telling students what to do or showing them how, but instead to ask them leading questions. (p. 156)

In summary, the mathematical content included in the *Mathematics in Context* units proved to be challenging to most teachers. In contrast to the traditional curriculum, this program includes important mathematics introduced to students in both an informal manner and at earlier grade levels. All teachers found this challenging, particularly if their own knowledge of mathematics was weak.

Teachers' Knowledge of Mathematics

The middle school teachers field testing *Mathematics in Context*, and described in these studies, varied in their knowledge of mathematics. Many were elementary certified with little formal course work beyond the traditional high-school algebra and geometry courses taken many years ago. Some had undergraduate degrees in mathematics, but had completed those degrees several years before. However, none had ever really done mathematics in the manner approached in these materials. This lack of background knowledge of the mathematics in the units was a serious problem recognized by the teachers. In particular, when developing connections within a context, as B. Clarke (1995) found, "the teachers had personally studied mathematics as isolated areas of content with reasonable success, but when it came to integrating mathematics to solve problems within the context of a 'realistic' unit, they had difficulty. This led to situations where their mathematical understanding was challenged" (p. 157). This is not a problem that can be easily solved. As Lampert (1988) noted, "How can a teacher who lacks a 'network of big ideas and the relationship among those ideas and between ideas, facts, and procedures' develop these things?" (pp. 163–164). Spence (1996) found it to be a particular problem in the teaching of algebra:

> [One teacher] had a rather narrow knowledge of algebra, which reflected his education. He knew one kind of algebra, structural school algebra, which was predominantly the algebra of symbol maniuplation. Although

> [the other teacher] also knew algebra as manipulating numbers and symbols in equations, the salient feature of algebra for him was its abstractness in contrast to arithmetic. This is why he believed that basic number skills must be mastered in order to learn algebra. Concrete must come before abstract....Although both of these teachers saw algebra in a similar way, there was a difference in their knowledge of algebra content...[the second teacher's] knowledge of even traditional elementary algebra was limited....[In fact, he] was unsure of notation and lacked an in-depth and connected understanding of some important basic algebra concepts, such as variable and the structure of the linear equation. (pp. 225–226)

Although there is no question that lack of mathematical background is a serious handicap when attempting to teach such reform materials, this is not the whole story. Hutchinson (1996), when contrasting four preservice teachers, found that their having taken several mathematics classes was not sufficient background for teaching these materials:

> Kate entered the mathematics education class after successfully completing higher-level mathematics courses, both in high school and at the university. She strongly voiced beliefs that were in alignment with the reform documents. During the duration of this study, the beliefs that she stated were being challenged by the content of the unit.... This conflict produced frustration for her; therefore, it became easier and more efficient for her to revert to her traditional practices of equations and procedures. (p. 181)

On the other hand Cindy, a preservice teacher with a very weak mathematics background, "appeared to be constructing a new network of knowledge in the domain of ratio and proportion. Her goal, as she stated numerous times, was to understand mathematics and have it make sense to her.... She appeared to put her previous knowledge of equations in 'storage' as she learned new methods for problem solving that gave meaning to the situations" (p. 183). In fact, from the data gathered in her study, Hutchinson concluded that

> previous knowledge and beliefs about mathematics have a big impact on the learning that takes place in pre-service education classes. When preservice teachers were placed in a situation that challenged their previous knowledge and beliefs, it was apparent that two of them reverted to their previous knowledge as their "crutch.... [For one student with a strong background] the challenges became an opportunity to learn new methods and techniques. [Similarly,] Cindy appeared to abandon her previous experiences as a source of knowledge; she used techniques and strategies that made sense to her. Her focus was on understanding the problem situation, rather than focusing on a procedure and trying to fit the problem to that procedure. (p. 184–185)

The problem with many preservice teachers, even those who had taken a number of mathematics classes, is, as Ball (1993) found, that "the thinness of preservice teachers' knowledge did not allow the preservice teachers the ability to unpack the conceptual underpinnings of the procedures" (p. 188). In these studies, this "thinness of knowledge" about mathematics was a problem for most teachers, regardless of their background. For example, Hutchinson (1996) found that

> when a ratio and proportion problem included a comparison of more than two quantities, Kate had difficulties in finding a solution. Even though Kate had a strong background in mathematics, she became frustrated when activities challenged that knowledge and appeared to revert to traditional methods as the "one right way." Her previous learning in the domain did not appear to be conceptually developed to allow for new challenges to that knowledge. (p. 182)

Of course, thinness of knowledge was not the only problem encountered when teaching a *Mathematics in Context* unit. Although the mathematical background of these teachers was important, the studies suggest that their vision of mathematics as a discipline was also important. For example, Hutchinson (1996) found that

> it appeared that the preservice teachers whose ideas about mathematics and teaching were more in line with the ideas envisioned in the reform documents were more willing to try new strategies and techniques. In this study, the two preservice teachers who valued speed and accuracy were less willing to take risks trying new methods. Traditional procedural methods, rather than reasoning and looking for alternative strategies, were their default mechanisms when placed in a challenging situation. (p. 190)

Spence (1996) also argued that for the two teachers teaching algebra, "They were blocked by lack of knowledge of what constitutes learning and understanding in this mathematical domain. Furthermore, and more seriously, lack of knowledge blocked [one teacher] from recognizing incorrect mathematics" (p. 239).

Information from these studies make it clear that if a reform curriculum like *Mathematics in Context* is to be successfully implemented in middle schools, the weak mathematical background and out-of-date beliefs about mathematics that many of the current teachers have must be challenged and systematically addressed.

Assessing Progress Toward Performance Standards

One particular concern voiced by many teachers as a consequence of teaching a *Mathematics in Context* unit was the fact they "needed ways of finding out what students had learned" (D. Clarke, 1993, p. 222). In the past, information from student homework, occasional quizzes, and chapter tests was sufficient to monitor student progress. However, as the teachers in B. Clarke's (1995) study quickly realized:

> Students' correct solutions also represented different levels of sophistication. Teachers were faced with valuing all genuine attempts at problems, while seeking to move students towards increasingly mathematically elegant methods.... Although incorrect solutions are a common occurrence in a traditional classroom, the importance placed on the value of student thinking and the de-emphasis in the one appropriate solution placed extra demands on the teachers in this study, as they struggled to both understand and build on student thinking. (pp. 156–157)

Similarly, D. Clarke (1993) found that "Teachers in this study were confident that the students they perceived as being particularly able produced excellent work, and that this led to the teachers being affirmed in their beliefs that these kinds of materials were appropriate and useful. However, both teachers agreed that they lacked sufficient information on the learning outcomes of other students in their classes" (p. 218–219). Burrill (quoted in de Lange et al., 1993) voiced a common frustration of teachers: "The possibility that several points of view and, consequently, several answers were reasonable is difficult to accept, especially when you have spent an average of 15 years rewarding thought processes that were identical to yours. Sometimes it was very hard to recognize that new ways of looking at a problem were as good as, or better, than ours" (p. 155). The lack of familiarity with the specific mathematics in a unit and the potential connections to other content was often reflected in the assessment tasks teachers created. For example, van den Heuvel-Panhuizen (1995) found that "[t]he teacher-made problems made clear that [they] had a preference for computational problems and problems which are firmly connected with the contexts and the tasks that are used in that teaching" (p. 70). Similar comments related to assessments were made by many of the field-test teachers when interviewed by the staff as part of the review process (Romberg & Shafer, 1995).

The importance of a new perspective about the role of assessments was voiced by one of the field-test teachers: "I would say that you cannot teach this [*Mathematics in Context*] without assessing daily how they're doing for you. You can't move on. It builds so that you absolutely would be lost, I think. We did a lot of on-the-spot assessing" (D. Clarke, 1993, p. 8). Shafer (1996) in her study of the assessment practices of a teacher experienced with *Mathematics in Context* found that

> [the teacher] recognized that students reasoned mathematically at many levels, and he accepted that mastery wasn't necessarily the primary goal of instruction. He also felt, that when students struggled with solving the

problems during group work, that struggle was an indication of their progress toward understanding the mathematics. [Nevertheless,] the information [he] gathered about his students during group work... focused on monitoring the progress of the class as a whole in understanding the mathematical content of the lesson.... His assessment practice...was not focused on tracking growth in knowledge for individual students, although it seemed to have potential for tracking growth for individual students. (p. 8–10)

She noted that "Tracking a student's growth in knowledge in a mathematical domain requires a different perspective in the assessment process from that of monitoring the progress of the class as a whole" (p. 20).

In summary, although teachers using *Mathematics in Context* units were aware that they were observing and hearing their students reason and think mathematically, they needed assessment procedures that allowed them to document and report progress in new ways.

Challenging Conventions of Community-Valued Authority

The teaching of mathematics in schools does not happen in a vacuum. It happens in communities that have a vested interest in having their students study mathematics. Several social conventions, such as beliefs about what mathematics should be taught to all students, ability grouping as an efficient way of providing for individual differences, the validity and utility of standardized testing, and the utility of conventional grading practices, were being challenged in the field-test sites.

The teaching of mathematics to all students has long been considered important for economic reasons. As Weller (1991) commented: "The traditional core classes are viewed by these students as important for several reasons, one of which is the emphasis their parents place upon these disciplines. A parent stated, 'You can't get a job or get into college by taking art and music.' This sentiment reflects a utilitarian or instrumental view of schooling" (p. 117). This economic rationale has not been challenged by the reform efforts. In fact, it can be argued that the NCTM curriculum standards still reflect this utilitarian view because they were developed in response to *A Nation at Risk* (National Commission on Excellence in Education, 1983). The claims in that document are that America's schools are failing to prepare today's students for tomorrow's workplace. Concern, however, was voiced at all sites as to whether the actual changes in content and instruction, encompassed in *Mathematics in Context*, would satisfy these utilitarian concerns. For example, algebra in Mathematic in Context is approached intuitively. Although the teachers in general liked this approach, changing teaching of mathematics is difficult because of community traditions concerning its role as a social filter. In particular, many parents were concerned about whether their child's study of mathematics via *Mathematics in Context* would adequately prepare him or her for the traditional high-school algebra course. In some communities, being admitted to such a course in grade 8 was an important social signal that their son or daughter was considerably above average in mathematics (i.e., truly college material).

In a closely related manner, ability grouping in mathematics has traditionally been seen to be desirable. Weller (1991) commented that "effective mathematics instruction through grouping was seen to enhance students' chances for obtaining lucrative careers. By identifying student ability, the district could more efficiently sort students into appropriate levels of subject matter" (p. 121). Typically, placement in different courses has been determined by standardized test scores, parental recommendation, and/or counselor placement. Furthermore, as Weller pointed out, "An unintended outcome of differentiated curriculum was the disenfranchisement of the so-called 'average' students" (p. 200). This was true because considerably less direction and help was given to these "unspecial" students than to either the "talented" or "challenged" students.

Teaching students from the reform approach in *Mathematics in Context* challenged the manner in which placements were decided because it was no longer easy to identify who was "talented" and who needed considerable help. As one field-test teacher put it, "This is when we first found out that this math is really successful, because at-risk learners or LD students were doing really well.... We thought it was a good tool for opening up communication between the students" (Romberg & Shafer, 1995, p. 10).

Given such concerns about appropriate grouping of students for instruction, teachers in these sites raised questions about their district's use of standardized tests. In most situations, teachers seemed to pay little attention to or value the results of such testing. This is counter to the community's traditional beliefs, as Weller (1991) pointed out:

> Standardized tests are used by the... school district as a primary means of quantifying student ability in a particular subject matter; consequentially, students and their parents appear to internalize those beliefs regarding their perceived talents and limitations as reified in the level of student placement in the subject matter. The subject matter evaluated by standardized tests takes on a value in and of itself among the community members. (p. 116)

Only in one setting did a teacher report modifying instruction in response to the pressure for her students to do well on the district's standardized test. Shew (1995) commented that the teacher in her study felt constrained by factors inherent in the school situation, particularly standardized tests. Thus she needed "to pay attention to those computational type things out of context" (p. 11). My guess is that this teacher was not alone in her concerns; she was just more open about this with the developers than were the other teachers.

Even if the use of standardized testing was not a voiced concern, grading and reporting grades to administrators and parents was. As Weller (1991) stated, "Obtaining high grades was important to the students, as well. [The teacher] continually told her students that they needed to get grades higher than a C if they expected to attend college" (p. 135). From the project field notes, it became apparent that "one of the major concerns expressed by teachers is how to translate what they are learning about students into grades. They worry about subjective judgments, how to reconcile observations, group work, and project results into expectations for grades" (Romberg & Shafer, 1995, p. 1). As one of the teachers commented, "It was not as clear-cut and easy to grade [as] objective-type tests I have used before. I had to make more judgments on what kind of growth in understanding took place" (van den Heuvel-Panhuizen, 1995, p. 72).

In summary, the traditional concerns of parents, administrators, teachers, and even students about the utility of mathematics, ability grouping, validity of standardized test scores, and teacher grading of students were challenged when teachers taught units from *Mathematics in Context*. The teachers involved in these studies gradually became aware of these challenges, but were unsure how to react. However, only the immediacy of assigning grades was consistently seen as problematic by every teacher.

NONROUTINE TEACHING
IN MATHEMATICS CLASSROOMS

An initial way to characterize the shift in teaching practices faced by the teachers in these studies involves a shift from a "mechanistic" perspective about teaching to an "organic" perspective, which sees mathematics teaching as nonroutine. Weller's (1991) description of the traditional teaching of mathematics reflected the findings of studies about teaching (e.g., Jackson, 1986; Rowan, Raudenbush, & Cheong, 1993; Stodolsky, 1988). These authors found that teachers of mathematics saw their subject as more codified and routine in form than did teachers of English or social studies. Such features are common for a mechanistic form of organizational management considered appropriate for routine work (Perrow, 1967).

This mechanical, but coherent, form of classroom management evolved during the past century in public schools in this country and was designed to transmit a large quantity of information to students via an organized schedule of courses. This system grew out of the machine-age thinking of the industrial revolution. The intellectual content of this age rested on reductionism, analysis, and cause-and-effect explanations (Ackoff, 1974). The machine age was preoccupied with taking things apart. The argument was that if you had something that needed to be explained, or a problem to solve, you broke it into its components via analysis so that they could be studied to determine cause-and-effect relationships. In this sense, the world was conceived of as a machine operating in accordance with unchanging laws. It is this world view that is being challenged by the reform movement in school mathematics.

For schools, machine-age thinking led to information being segmented into subjects, courses, topics, and eventually down to its smallest parts—behavioral objectives. The objectives were related via hierarchies and mechanized via textbooks, worksheets, and tests. Over the last century the consequences of this machine-age thinking have influenced the curriculum, teachers, instruction, technology, and environment to such an extent that their features are considered by many as sacrosanct traditions. Those traditions are now being challenged in the classrooms studied in the research discussed here.

Scheffler (1975) denounced this mechanistic metaphor:

> It is no wonder that this [mechanical] conception isolates mathematics from other subjects, since what is here described is not so much a form of thinking as a substitute for thinking. The process of calculation or computation only involves the deployment of a set routine with no room for ingenuity or flair, no place for guess work or surprise, no chance for discovery, no need for the human being, in fact. (p. 184)

This mechanical metaphor needs to be changed. Knowledge in any field is organized into several related domains. The emphasis of knowledge rests not with the parts of which things are made, but with the whole of which they are part. And second, this conception of knowledge does not rest on a deterministic base of fundamental parts from which everything else is created. Instead, it rests on the signs, symbols, terms, and rules for use—the language that humans invent to communicate with each other. From this perspective, Greeno (1991) proposed a different metaphor. Students develop mathematical understanding when a domain is

> thought of as an environment, with resources at various places in the domain. In this metaphor, knowing is knowing your way around in the environment and knowing how to use its resources. This includes knowing what resources are available in the environment as well as being able to find and use those resources for understanding and reasoning. Knowing includes interactions with the environment in its own terms—exploring the territory, appreciating its scenery, and understanding how its various

components interact. Knowing the domain also includes knowing what resources are in the environment that can be used to support your individual and social activities and the ability to recognize, find, and use those resources productively. Learning the domain, in this view, is analogous to learning to live in an environment: learning your way around, learning what resources are available, and learning how to use those resources in conducting your activities productively and enjoyably. (p. 175)

As described earlier, *Mathematics in Context* reflects this perspective. This approach to mathematics teaching "represents, on the whole, a substantial departure from teachers' prior experience, established beliefs, and present practice. Indeed, they hold out an image of conditions of learning for children that their teachers have themselves rarely experienced" (Little, 1993, p. 130). Such departures from traditional practices were evident in every classroom in these studies. Clearly, these departures are nonroutine forms of teaching new to mathematics teachers, and this should lead to new organizational relationships. In particular, teachers should no longer be isolated from each other: They need to collaborate and share ideas with each other. As Rowan, Raudenbush, and Cheong (1993) argued, "nonroutine forms of teaching lead to organic management because of the independent initiative of teachers who, in response to the challenges of nonroutine work, seek out and participate in organizational processes that help them cope more effectively with nonroutine work" (p. 485). D. Clarke (1993) found in his study that when teachers had shared planning time they "claimed that the support they received from each other, the opportunity to work together in planning and 'debriefing' each day, and the opportunity to have a 'sounding board' present (whether another teacher, a project staff member, or a researcher) all appeared to be facilitative of professional growth" (p. 224). Furthermore, the implications of teaching mathematics from this nonroutine perspective carry over to the professional development of teachers. As Little (1993) pointed out, "The dominant training model of teachers' professional development—a model focused primarily on expanding an individual repertoire of well-defined and skillful classroom practice—is not adequate to the ambitious visions of teaching and schooling embedded in present reform initiatives" (p. 129).

It is premature to claim that from this research program we now are able to create a theory about the nonroutine teaching and learning of mathematics in classrooms. Nevertheless, as Carpenter and Lehrer (1994) have proposed, "some forms of mental activity from which mathematical understanding emerges are (1) constructing relationships, (2) extending and applying mathematical knowledge, (3) reflecting about mathematical experiences, (4) communicating what one knows, and (5) making mathematical knowledge one's own" (pp. 3–4). Each of these mental activities can be fostered in mathematics classrooms. However, the development of understanding by students and teachers takes time. Learning with understanding occurs when learning becomes the focus of instruction, when students are given time to develop conceptual relationships and learn to use their constructed knowledge, and when students are encouraged to reflect about their thinking and articulate their ideas.

As Chevellard (1988) pointed out, currently there is a gap between what is taught and what is learned. He argued that this gap is created when we treat a pupil only as a "student" (someone who studies) and not as a "learner" (someone who learns). For teachers, the transition from working with students to working with learners is difficult, as these studies note. The approaches taken by the teachers in these case studies, as they used *Mathematics in Context* in their classrooms, are steps to closing that gap.

REFERENCES

Ackoff, R. (1974). The systems revolution. *Long Range Planning, 7*(6), 2–20.

Ball, D. (1993). Halves, pieces and twoths. In T. C. Carpenter, E. Fennema, & T. A. Romberg (Eds.), *Rational numbers: Integration of research* (pp. 157–197). Hillsdale, NJ: Lawrence Erlbaum Associates.

Carpenter, T., & Lehrer, R. (1994). *Teaching and learning mathematics with understanding.* Unpublished manuscript, National Center for Research in Mathematical Sciences Education, Madison, WI.

Chevellard, Y. (1988). The student–learner gap. In A. Vermandel (Ed.), *Proceedings of the third international conference on the theory of mathematics education* (pp. 1–6). Antwerp, Belgium: Universitaire Instelling.

Clarke, B. (1995). *Expecting the unexpected: Critical incidents in the mathematics classroom.* Unpublished doctoral dissertation, University of Wisconsin–Madison.

Clarke, D. (1993). *Influences on the changing role of the mathematics teacher.* Unpublished doctoral dissertation, University of Wisconsin–Madison.

Cobb, P. (1994). *Theories of mathematical learning and constructivism: A personal view.* Paper presented at the Symposium on Trends and Perspectives in Mathematics Education, Institute for Mathematics, University of Klagenfurt, Austria.

de Lange, J. (1987). *Mathematics, insight, and meaning.* Utrecht, The Netherlands: Vakroep Ondersoek Wiskundeonderwijs en Onderwijscomputercentrum, Rijksuniversiteit.

de Lange, J., Burrill, G., Romberg, T., & van Reeuwijk, M. (1993). *Learning and testing mathematics in context.* Pleasantville, NY: Wings for Learning.

de Lange, J., & Verhage, H. (1989). *Data visualization.* Utrecht, The Netherlands: Vakroep Ondersoek Wiskundeonderwijs en Onderwijscomputercentrum, Rijksuniversiteit.

Ernest, P. (1991). *The philosophy of mathematics education.* Hampshire, England: Falmer.

Flanders, J. (1987). How much of the content in mathematics textbooks is new? *Arithmetic Teacher, 31*(1), 18–23.

Freudenthal, H. (1987). Mathematics starting and staying in reality. In I. Wirszup & R. Street (Eds.), *Proceedings of the USCMP conference on mathematics education on development in school mathematics education around the world.* Reston, VA: National Council of Teachers of Mathematics.

Gravemeijer, K. (1991). *Developing realistic mathematics education.* Utrecht, The Netherlands: Utrecht CD-β.

Greeno, J. (1991). Number sense as situated knowing in a conceptual domain. *Journal for Research in Mathematics Education, 22* (3), 170–218.

Hutchinson, E. (1996). *Preservice teacher's knowledge: A contrast of beliefs and knowledge of ratio and proportion.* Unpublished doctoral dissertation, University of Wisconsin–Madison.

Jackson, P. W. (1986). *The practice of teaching.* New York: Teachers College Press.

Lampert, M. (1988). The teacher's role in reinventing the meaning of mathematical knowing in the classroom. In M. J. Behr, C. B. Lacampagne, & M. M. Wheeler (Eds.), *Proceedings of the tenth conference of the North American chapter of the International Group for the Psychology of Mathematics Education* (pp. 433–480). DeKalb, IL: Psychology of Mathematics Education.

Little, J. (1993). Teachers' professional development in a climate of educational reform. *Educational Evaluation and Policy Analysis, 15*(2), 129–151.

National Center for Research in Mathematical Sciences Education & Freudenthal Institute. (in press-a). *Mathematics in Context.* Chicago: Encyclopaedia Britannica Educational Corporation.

National Center for Research in Mathematical Sciences Education & Freudenthal Institute. (in press-b). *Welcome to—Mathematics in Context.* Chicago: Encyclopaedia Britannica Educational Corporation.

National Commission on Excellence in Education. (1983). *A nation at risk: The imperative for educational reform.* Washington, DC: U.S. Government Printing Office.

National Council of Teachers of Mathematics. (1989). *Curriculum and evaluation standards for school mathematics.* Reston, VA: Author.

National Council of Teachers of Mathematics. (1991). *Professional standards for teaching mathematics.* Reston, VA: Author.

National Council of Teachers of Mathematics. (1995). *Assessment standards for school mathematics.* Reston, VA: Author.

Perrow, C. (1967). A framework for the comparative analysis of organizations. *American Sociological Review, 79,* 686–704.

Provenzo, E. F., McCloskey, G. N., Kottkamp,R. B., & Cohn M. M. (1989). Metaphors and meaning in the language of teachers. *Teachers College Record, 90,* (4), 1551–73.

Romberg, T. (1992). Problematic features of the school mathematics curriculum. I. P. W. Jackson (Ed.), *Handbook of research on curriculum* (pp. 749–774). New York, NY: Macmillan.

Romberg, T., & Shafer, M. (1995). *Results of assessment.* Unpublished manuscript, National Center for Research in Mathematical Sciences Education, University of Wisconsin–Madison.

Rowan, B., Raudenbush, S. W., & Cheong, Y. F. (1993). Teaching as a nonroutine task: Implications for the management of schools. *Educational Administration Quarterly, 29* (4), 479–500.

Sarason, S. B. (1971). *The culture of the school and the problem of change.* Boston: Allyn & Bacon.

Shafer, M. (1996, April). *Assessing growth in a mathematical domain over time.* Paper presented at the annual meeting of the American Educational Research Association, New York.

Scheffler, I. (1975). Basic mathematical skills: Some philosophical and practical remarks. In *National Institute of Education conference on basic mathematical skills and learning* (Vol. 1). Euclid, OH: National Institute of Education.

Shew, J. (1995, April) *Students in conflict with reform.* Paper presented at the annual meeting of the American Educational Research Association, San Francisco.

Spence, M. (1996). *Psychologizing algebra: Case studies of knowing in the moment.* Doctoral dissertation in preparation, University of Wisconsin–Madison.

Stodolsky, S. (1988). *The subject matters: Classroom activity in math and social studies.* Chicago: University of Chicago Press.

van den Heuvel-Panhuizen, M. (1995, April) *Developing assessment problems on percentage.* Paper presented at the annual meeting of the American Educational Research Association, San Francisco, CA.

Weller, M. (1991). *Marketing the curriculum: Core versus non-core subjects in one junior high school.* Unpublished doctoral dissertation, University of Wisconsin–Madison.

14

Mathematics Case Discussions: Nothing Is Sacred

Carne Barnett
WestEd, San Francisco

Sharon Friedman
Hayward Unified School District

Richardson's 1990 analysis of the research literature on teacher change and learning to teach reveals some important elements to consider regarding changes in teacher thinking and practice. She argued that to promote significant and worthwhile change, "teachers themselves must be involved in making judgments about what change is worthwhile and significant" (p. 14). Furthermore, she suggested that to inform these judgments, teachers should engage in conversations that bring together not only their own experiences, but also the practices and ways of thinking outside their individual experiences. This combination of teacher empowerment and reflection on classroom experience, as well as alternative practices and ways of thinking, is at the crux of Richardson's theory of teacher change. Her ideas are at the heart of a professional development project at WestEd in San Francisco called *Mathematics Case Methods*.

The case approach, long used in professions such as business, law, and medicine, has recently gained momentum in the education profession (Colbert, Desberg, & Trimble, 1996; Merseth, 1991; Shulman, J., 1992; Shulman, L., 1986; Wasserman, 1993). In each profession, cases serve different purposes and have different forms. The purpose of the *Mathematics Case Methods Project* is to build the capacity of teachers to make informed strategic decisions that draw on and anticipate student thinking. This is accomplished by building teachers' pedagogical content knowledge (Cobb, Yackel, & Wood, 1991; Shulman, L., 1986) and critical analysis abilities, which in turn leads to a sense of empowerment and changes in beliefs.

Cases in the *Mathematics Case Methods Project* are accounts of classroom experiences written by teachers. Each narrative describes an instructional sequence in which the teacher is surprised or perplexed by students' responses or by the results of an assessment task. All cases include descriptions or samples of student work or dialogue. In a case discussion, participants read the case, generate questions and issues raised by the case, and then discuss the case, guided by a facilitator. Facilitators are teachers with case discussion experience who have chosen to take on leadership roles and have subsequently been prepared to facilitate case discussions. Groups convene regularly over a period of time, discussing a different case at each meeting.

Although research on the use of cases in education lags behind the interest in the approach, excellent literature reviews are available in Merseth's chapter in the *Handbook of Research on Teacher Education* (1995) and in Sykes and Bird's chapter in the *Review of Research in Education* (1992). Research on the processes and outcomes of the *Mathematics Case Methods Project* (Barnett, 1991; Barnett & Ramirez, 1996; Barnett & Tyson, 1993a, 1993b, 1994; Gordon & Heller, 1995; Gordon & Tyson, 1995; Heller, 1995; Tyson, Barnett, & Gordon, 1995) demonstrates that it provides a powerful stimulus for teacher change. Among the changes documented by our research team are changes in teachers' beliefs about how children learn and how mathematics should be taught, as well as improvements in teachers' mathematical content knowledge. More recent studies trace the influence of case discussions on teaching practice and document the increasing complexity of teachers' pedagogical content knowledge. Research on student cognition and beliefs has proven to be a challenge, and clear results are unavailable at this time.

The authors of this chapter are Carne Barnett, the director of the *Mathematics Case Methods Project*, and Sharon Friedman, a fourth grade teacher and teacher-leader in Hayward Unified School District. Over the past six years, Friedman has become involved in every role currently available for teachers in the *Mathematics Case Methods Project* including case writer, case discussion participant, case discussion facilitator, coconductor of facilitator seminars, and researcher. This chapter is divided into three sections, each beginning with Friedman's reflections about her experiences followed by commentary by Barnett, who reflects on Friedman's narrative as well as on her own process in refining the mathematics case discussion approach. We hope this will convey both the content and essence of the *Mathematics Case Methods Project*.

In the first section, "Thinking about Student Thinking," Friedman relates an experience, illustrating how a deepening pedagogical content knowledge affects her thinking, and then showing how these changes affect her beliefs and practice. Barnett then discusses how cases have evolved to influence teachers' knowledge, beliefs, and practice. This section also contains excerpts from an actual case. Section two, "Criss-crossing Issues," describes the theoretical underpinnings of case design and sequencing that promote flexible thinking and multiple interconnections among ideas. Section three, "Facilitation and the Case Discussion Process," describes the evolution of this approach and gives a detailed description of the project's case discussion process. Throughout the sections we will refer to the themes of empowerment and critical analysis.

THINKING ABOUT STUDENT THINKING

Friedman's Reflections

When I first participated in a math case discussion, I thought that I would be examining instructional practice. I thought that I would share what I do in the classroom and hear about alternatives, which would lead to better informed decisions for my mathematics program. I was right, except for my understanding of what it meant to "examine" instructional practice. I quickly learned that the "examination" entailed more than merely acquainting myself with various instructional methods. Through the discussions, we looked deeply into the way instructional practice influenced and responded to student thinking. Any teaching practice, it seemed, had a consequence in terms of its effect on student thinking. Some curricula even led to confusion. We delved into the thoughts and misconceptions that students carry with them to our math classes, derived from past instruction, experience, and intuition. Good instructional practice, I was to discover, is an interaction between what the teacher says and the experiences he or she provides, and what the students do with it. Good practice is not, as teachers are often led to believe, a preset formula that does what it is supposed to do because the curriculum writers say so. I learned the importance of focusing the impact of my words and actions on children, of framing instruction that could anticipate student thinking as much as possible, and of responding effectively to the results. In planning, I learned to consider an interaction rather than simply a teaching method that does not take student thinking into account.

My reflection process can be illustrated by tracking my quest to find good materials for teaching fraction concepts. As a new teacher, I planned to utilize fraction kits. A fraction kit is a manipulative used by children to compare fractional parts with a whole and different fractional parts with each other. Typically, a kit consists of premade plastic pieces. It may contain, for instance, a red circular piece (the "whole"), two green halves, three yellow thirds, four blue fourths, and so on. Because the sizes of the fractional pieces are calibrated to the same whole, teachers can ask students to determine, "How many thirds cover the whole?" and "How many fourths cover the half?"

An alternate type of fraction kit requires the students to create the pieces from "wholes." They receive several same-sized strips of different colored paper, one of which is designated "the whole." Students fold another strip in half and cut along the fold. The two resulting pieces are labeled "one-half." They fold another strip twice, creating fourths, and go on to create eighths and sixteenths. It is this homemade, paper variety that I used with my fifth-grade class.

After many ostensibly successful activities in which students seemed adept at comparing pieces to each other and to the whole, I was frustrated to find that once I removed the context of the fraction kit pieces, students could not answer written questions like, "$\frac{3}{4} = \frac{?}{8}$." I was baffled because the connections between our activities and the written questions seemed obvious to me. As a new teacher, I shrugged and figured that I would find a better approach next time around.

About a year later, I participated in a case discussion from which the following is an excerpt:

Six-Tenths or Four-Fifths of a Dollar?

"Place your 'whole' on the desktop," I said. "Show me $\frac{1}{4}$ of a whole by placing $\frac{1}{4}$ on top of it." The students responded by placing a "one-fourth" piece on the square representing 1 whole.

By the end of the lesson, they could successfully name and use the fraction kit to show unit fractions like $\frac{1}{2}$ or $\frac{1}{8}$ and nonunit fractions like $\frac{3}{4}$ or $\frac{5}{16}$.

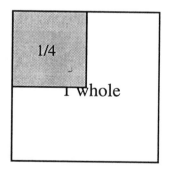
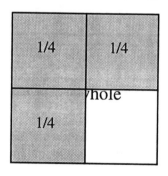

The next lesson focused on equivalent fractions. I asked the students to figure out the answer to questions like how many eighths would be equal to $\frac{1}{4}$ or how many sixteenths would equal $\frac{3}{8}$. They used their fraction-kit pieces to determine the answers. By the end of this lesson, students were very familiar with the relationship among the fraction pieces and could solve simple equivalency problems without using the pieces. I was then ready to have students learn how to compare fractions that have different denominators and numerators. Prior to beginning, I asked them to write about fraction equivalency in their journals so I could assess their understanding of previous lessons and know what information I needed to cover. I asked them to answer this question:

Which would you rather have: $\frac{6}{10}$ of a dollar or $\frac{4}{5}$ of a dollar? Explain your reasons for choosing your answer. After reflecting, the students picked up their pencils and wrote.

Cindy's journal read: "If I had $\frac{6}{10}$, I would have 2 more than $\frac{4}{5}$. I would choose $\frac{6}{10}$ so I could have more money."

Chris wrote: "$\frac{4}{5} = \frac{8}{10}$. $\frac{8}{10}$ is greater than $\frac{6}{10}$. Of course, I'd take $\frac{4}{5}$ of a dollar. Wouldn't you?" He included an illustration:

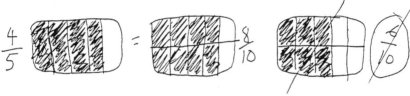

Esmarelda wrote: "No sé. $\frac{6}{10}$ es mas grande."

Nikki drew a picture to accompany her answer: "I want $\frac{6}{10}$. It is bigger."

Only 4 of the 30 students wrote $\frac{4}{5}$. Their journals gave me some hints about how they were thinking about fractions, but I was not sure how to use this information to plan our future work. Since the students were familiar with the fraction kit, I wonder if they would have answered differently if the question had been, "Would you rather have $\frac{3}{4}$ or $\frac{5}{8}$ of a chocolate bar?" [Barnett, Goldenstein, & Jackson, 1994a, pp.46-47]

Someone in the discussion group of this case questioned the use of fraction kits, suggesting that perhaps, when students are answering typical fraction kit questions, they are merely performing a counting task and not actually making part–whole and part–part comparisons. At the time, I did not realize how profound this comment was. The kits are widely used in many classrooms and are standard in many curricula. They are considered, so to speak, a "formula for success" in teaching fractions. I looked on the challenge raised in the discussion as a slight drawback.

Later that year, our school staff participated in an in-service for a math program that was to be available in all classrooms as well as for parents. To give us a sampling of what the program had to offer, the leader had us go through the process of creating the same fraction kit I had made with my students. My fellow teachers were excited by this "take" on fraction kits, which required us, and hence our students, to keep dividing a "whole" and "see" the relationships between the strips and the pieces. People saw the fact that students were creating the kit themselves as preferable to using the premade variety. I would have been excited too, if the activity had not triggered the memory of the lessons I had taught using this very same type of manipulative. The students most certainly did not see part–whole and part–part relationships after the many activities recommended for use with the pieces. The fraction kit challenge that arose in the case discussion began to make more sense to me as a possible reason why the kits had not led to any depth of understanding about fractions. While my colleagues rushed to complete their "sample" kits, I dropped out of the activity, deciding that for the time being I had no intention of using this fraction kit, or any other, with my class.

This experience caused me to ponder which manipulatives might be more effective at leading children to see the relationships essential to the understanding of fractions. I now wanted to avoid any materials that would tempt children to count pieces and to forget about the pertinent "whole." The State of California had recently published a "replacement unit," which I decided to try out. In this unit, children are introduced to fractions through an area model resembling a geoboard configuration. The students look at square arrays of dots and spend several days exploring ways to divide the shape in half. The teacher pushes each child to "prove" that the division on his or her paper is indeed half. The children end up subdividing the whole square into small squares and comparing the areas of the pieces (which, incidentally, may divert students' attention away from comparing and toward counting) or cutting the halves out and superimposing them to see if they make an exact "match." Children go through a similar sequence for fourths, eighths, and sixteenths, and then for thirds, sixths, and twelfths.

I was thrilled with the results. The students initially struggled with demarcating halves, revealing the superficial nature of their knowledge of even this most common and basic fraction. The curriculum was challenging, yet moved them along at their own pace while deepening their understanding greatly.

Because set models were not prominent in the replacement unit, I began to worry about students' abilities to transfer what they had learned on the area model. Looking over standardized test sample questions, I also grew concerned over students' abilities to answer questions with denominators such as 10, 9, and so on, that were not in the unit. I desperately wanted a curriculum that would equip students to answer comfortably and confidently any fraction question considered appropriate for their grade level. I became wary of the replacement unit because it seemed to limit student experience and understanding to one kind of model and context.

Moving to fourth grade, I set out to try yet another method, one recommended to me by a fellow case discussant. In this method, students are given a working definition for a fraction, and every lesson goes back to the basic definition. Whenever a fraction is discussed, they must:

1. Identify what the "whole" or "1" is.
2. Describe or indicate the number of "equal" parts into which the whole has been divided.
3. Describe or emphasize the number of those equal parts being considered.

The applicability of this definition to a wide variety of fraction situations appealed to me. It worked for sets of objects, linear objects, geometric shapes, and even solids. I used it consistently throughout my unit of instruction and even incorporated it into the fraction replacement unit from the previous year. I encouraged students to defend their labels of $\frac{1}{2}$, $\frac{1}{4}$, and $\frac{1}{8}$ on their squares by verbalizing (i.e., "It is $\frac{1}{4}$ because there are 4 equal pieces in the whole square and I have shaded 1 of the 4 pieces"). The more I listened to my students and reviewed their work, the more advantages I saw to this approach. That is why the shock of the California Learning Assessment System (CLAS) sample math question hit me with such force.

The question asked the students to divide a square so that it would show a half, a fourth, and an eighth. It was immediately clear to me that with all the depth of understanding my students had shown, they were completely unprepared for this type of question, perhaps even less so than if I had taught them fractions in a more traditional way. They had become so accustomed to talking about the equal number of parts into which the whole was divided that they could not visualize a whole containing a half, a fourth, and an eighth simultaneously. In a lesson I taught the day before administering the sample CLAS question, I tried to show them how different fractions could be combined in the same whole. They protested that I was breaking my own rule, a rule which I had been holding them to.

Throughout this lengthy process, I found myself focused more and more on student thinking. The true gauge of the value of any fraction teaching method was what it led students to say and do. Just as important as actually trying out new and different curriculum was doing so with a critical eye. Implementing reform methods could leave me, and my students, in the same "stuck" place as the old methods if I did not anticipate student responses and prepare accordingly.

I have now thought much about teaching and learning fractions and find it ironic that knowing more leaves me feeling less resolved than when I first began. However, having become more adept at analyzing the methods I use, I am able to compensate for curriculum pitfalls. My instructional practice is more refined. I owe this sense of expertise to case discussions.

Barnett's Commentary

The case discussion approach in the *Mathematics Case Methods Project* encourages critical analysis of ideas and issues with respect to their impact on student thinking. Participants generate many alternatives, which are always assessed for both strengths and weaknesses. No perspective, idea, material, or strategy—not even a fraction kit—is sacred in a case discussion. As many professional developers know, fraction kits are especially seductive to teachers because they actively involve students in creating the pieces themselves, playing games with the pieces, and finding fraction equivalencies with ease. However, as Friedman notes, their success is deceiving. Students can solve equivalencies using the fraction kit pieces, but they can do so merely by counting how many "red pieces" fit on a "blue piece." Friedman has become accustomed to considering what students are thinking as they do an activity. She has also developed a deeper understanding of the common misunderstandings that students acquire, and is always on the lookout for how those misunderstandings might arise. As she says, she has become increasingly aware of her interactions with students, rather than simply relying on a teaching method that does not take student thinking into account.

Although teachers have the autonomy to make decisions for themselves in their classrooms, they often do not feel empowered to question "higher" authorities for fear that they may not have the knowledge, confidence, or awareness to assess the validity of these claims. For example, in Friedman's narrative it appears that most of the teachers in the fraction kit workshop uncritically accepted the use of the fraction kit as a valid way to teach fraction concepts. Friedman, on the other hand, dropped out because she questioned the value of the fraction kit as it was being used in these activities. Subsequently, she tested new approaches and curriculum materials, each time with an eye toward the impact they had on student thinking. The case discussion experiences were magnified and extended through her own experiences in the classroom.

Some professional development programs have been very successful in using research on learning theory and student thinking as the base for teacher development. Although our case materials provide references to relevant research articles, there was concern that research readings, if required, could reinforce some teachers' beliefs that researchers are sacred authorities. The teachers in the project strongly objected to having required readings for this reason and preferred to decide for themselves whether and when to read these materials. We respected their concern and left research readings as an option rather than as a requirement. So what happens if teachers choose not to read research? How are their long-held beliefs and practices challenged? How do they gain new knowledge about student learning?

Our studies show that even without an emphasis on analyzing research readings, teachers' thinking can change dramatically. We have learned that teachers involved in case discussions move toward a more student-centered approach, learn to adapt and choose materials and methods that reveal student thinking, and anticipate and assume rationality in students' misunderstandings. Moreover, it appears that without being explicitly exposed to these ideas in research literature, teachers naturally move toward a constructivist view of learning and develop a complex knowledge of students' thinking processes and underlying mathematical concepts.

Case discussions provide four pivotal experiences that help move teachers beyond their own perceptions and beliefs. First, teachers discuss cases of teaching practice that are written by other classroom teachers. These cases often contain methods, materials, or ways of teaching that individual discussants have not encountered. Also, the discussion gives teachers opportunities to share and generate alternative approaches in collaboration with their peers.

Second, the case discussions themselves model a way of teaching that many teachers have not themselves experienced. The facilitator of a case discussion does not act as an expert or explainer, but more as a guide and mutual inquirer, beckoning discussants to build on each other's ideas, encouraging them to make connections among issues, and challenging them to justify their views. The role modeled by the facilitator and the experience of being a participant feed into the teachers' developing view of teaching and learning. This role is more fully portrayed both in the facilitator's guide for the casebook (Barnett, Goldenstein, & Jackson, 1994b), which accompanies the casebook developed by the project, and in the project's seminar on learning to lead case discussions.

Third, because the issues in case discussions are seldom totally resolved, teachers are left with a powerful urge to continue the inquiry. They become motivated to test their theories in their own classrooms and to talk to their colleagues about what happened and what to try next. The discussions provide common ground and language for their ongoing discussions. The power of the two-hour case discussion is multiplied many times over as the inquiry and conversations are integrated into daily classroom life.

Finally, I speculate that one of the most valuable external experiences case discussions provide is the opportunity to see classroom experiences through the eyes of students. Because the case discussions provide time for deep reflection about students' thinking, teachers begin to filter their decisions and ideas through the students' perspective. They learn how to detect the misunderstandings of students who seem to understand. They begin to appreciate and uncover the multitude of idiosyncrasies and subtleties that are present in students' thinking. With each new discovery, teachers begin to notice other things that weren't discernible before. The learning experience snowballs, and teachers become more knowledgeable about and capable of assessing student thinking. Not surprisingly, their discoveries strongly resemble the findings of professional researchers on student thinking, even though teachers' discoveries may be articulated in practitioner's terms.

Friedman was primed by her experience in case discussions to notice that students could accomplish the fraction-kit tasks without necessarily understanding part–whole or part–part relationships. She may have been one of few teachers who had an eye critical enough to detect this flaw in the task as it was presented. Her ability to consider the task from the student's view allowed her to mentally test out materials that she considered using. Because she feels empowered as a teacher, she may choose to adapt the fraction kit in some way, or she may invent new experiences for her students to avoid pitfalls such as the one concerning the statewide assessment question.

I am not suggesting that teachers avoid examining and using research findings or attending workshops to learn about new activities and materials for students. I believe that the more experiences teachers have, the more enriched their teaching will become. Instead, I am offering speculation as to how other experiences may be equally as powerful as the study of research. Again, it is the combination of empowerment and reflection on a variety of experiences that brings about significant and worthwhile change. I would, however, argue that reflection about specific student thinking in the context of classroom situations is perhaps the most potent experience a teacher can have.

CRISSCROSSING ISSUES

Friedman's Reflections

As I think back on the experience related earlier, I realize that it followed the same course as a series of in-depth case discussions. It is typical to participate in a discussion holding onto a core belief about learning or practice (in this case, about fraction kits). The use of fraction kits was challenged in one discussion about teaching fraction equivalence, but this did not lead me to reconsider their use. In a later discussion, the concern that a manipulative might cause children to perform rote counting rather than make meaningful connections arose in the context of using base-10 blocks to teach decimals. I saw it yet again in a discussion about using money to teach decimals. Seeing the counting issue crisscross and resurface in a variety of contexts underscored its importance and caused me to examine it more closely. I eventually rejected fraction kits, perhaps to be embraced at a later time. In my classroom, as in a case discussion, I tried out alternatives and analyzed the results. My new practices released my students from the potential dangers of rote counting, but got them into other binds. As long as the constant consideration is student thinking, the changes I make in my practice are improvements, and are headed in the right direction.

Barnett's Commentary

Richardson (1990) emphasized the importance of "practical knowledge that allows a teacher to quickly judge a situation or context and take action on the basis of knowledge gained from similar situations in the past" (p. 13). Friedman's reflections illustrate how she connects an idea or issue spotted in one case to similar ideas or issues in other cases. Such ideas or issues become intertwined with her thinking about her own teaching experiences. Friedman described how each time the same idea or issue is recognized, it becomes more salient and is examined more closely. Close scrutiny, enhanced by increasingly detailed knowledge, led Friedman to question practices and assumptions that were previously unquestioned.

This brings us to the theoretical framework that underlies the content and method of the *Mathematics Case Methods Project*. Spiro and his colleagues (Spiro, 1993; Spiro, Coulson, Feltovich, & Anderson, 1988; Spiro, Feltovich, Coulson, & Anderson, 1989; Spiro, Vispoel, Schmitz, Samarapungavan, & Boerger, 1987) put forth a theory for a case-based curriculum that is effective in helping people acquire advanced knowledge in complex, context-dependent, and ill-structured domains. Most of us would agree that teaching is a domain that clearly fits these criteria. Drawing from themes in other prevailing psychological theories such as situated cognition, constructivism, and cognitive complexity, Spiro et al. (1988) argued for a case-based curriculum that "treats the domain as a landscape that is explored by criss-crossing it in many directions" (p. 6). Each case presents opportunities to reexamine a variety of ideas from different vantage points and in new contexts, thus offering the possibility of establishing multiple connections among cases or experiences that on the surface may seem dissimilar.

Earlier research papers described this theoretical framework in more detail (Barnett, 1991); however, one aspect of the framework should be examined more closely here. In the early design of the *Mathematics Case Methods Project*, I consciously chose to confine the curriculum content of the cases to rational numbers so that the territory in this domain could be thoroughly explored. The drawback, of course, is that unless some of the learning acquired in one territory transfers to other territories, what teachers learn could end up being limited to the teaching of rational numbers.

Friedman's reflection offers insight into why case discussions of rational numbers might influence her teaching of other mathematical topics, as well as her teaching in general. She said, "As long as the constant consideration is student thinking, the changes I make in my practice are improvements and are headed in the right direction." This is a significant statement. Schön (1983) and other researchers (Carpenter & Fennema, 1992; Clarke & Peter, 1993; Richert, 1991; Schifter, 1993; Scott-Nelson, 1993) pointed out that practical knowledge is enhanced most productively if one reflects on both the experience and the results of that experience. The key may be in helping teachers learn to reflect, not just on their experiences, but more on the *results* of their experiences. Case discussions reorient teachers from reflecting on what they did and how it went in general, to attending to the specific results of that experience—student thinking. Friedman noted in a personal conversation that once you view your teaching through the eyes of students, it affects the way you think about teaching everything.

FACILITATION AND THE CASE
DISCUSSION PROCESS

Friedman's Reflections

As a case discussion facilitator, the most dramatic shift occurred as I tried to understand my role. From the start, I appreciated that the case discussion model was completely unlike the "top-down" staff development model, where an expert addresses a group of teachers and offers suggestions and guidance on how to improve our practice. Seeing that distinction was far easier than incorporating it into my demeanor. I kept trying to control the discussion, feeling the need to lead participants in certain directions. I was disappointed to hear shallow discussions in which the discussants did not raise the difficult issues or show interest in issues I nudged them to consider. I would leave discussions feeling frustrated, thinking participants were being uncooperative or that I had let them down.

Through leadership training and debriefing sessions with fellow facilitators, my view changed dramatically. Colleagues reminded me to trust the process and to remember that it takes time for the knowledge and skills of the group to develop. They urged me to utilize the reflection guide, a case discussion tool that asks each discussant to rate the discussion in terms of balance of participation and depth. To communicate the shared nature of the responsibility for the discussion, the facilitator collects the papers and shares the results with the group, asking, "Where do we need to focus our attention?" I realized that the process invites the group to evaluate itself, not me, the facilitator. I let the participants see that the bulk of the responsibility is on the group rather than on the facilitator. This shifting of responsibility causes the discussion to open up and have more meaning for the participants. Trying to overdirect the group toward my agenda sets people up to look toward me for answers. It creates passivity and tension, which lowers the degree of trust and impedes the level of discussion. The most satisfying discussions emerge when the participants pose their own questions and monitor their own responses. The facilitator's voice is equal in weight to that of the participants. A properly balanced relationship among those present should feel symbiotic: from me, to them, back to me; from one participant to another. Each discussion is influenced and shaped by the previous ones. The group eventually becomes the initiating force, the prime movers, the facilitators in the discussion. In a sense, the designated facilitator can melt away. With the change in the group comes a change in the quality and depth of discussions. As I learned to deflect responsibility away from myself and onto the group, I gained faith in the case discussion process.

Barnett's Commentary

Richardson (1990) warned us that professional development that attends only to autonomy and reflection suggests a laissez-faire approach to practice (p. 13). Friedman's dilemma is, in a sense, a struggle with how one fosters autonomy among a community of learners without allowing the discussion to become a laissez-faire conversation. She had to determine how to influence the content of case discussions without undermining the authority of the group.

As a novice facilitator of case discussions, I remember feeling powerless when teachers swung, during the course of their early discussions, from thinking that manipulatives were magic, to thinking that manipulatives were entirely worthless. Eventually, their knowledge became more refined as they learned to look at the benefits and drawbacks of various manipulatives in relation to how they are used in different contexts. Teachers began to develop an understanding of how the use of manipulatives is confounded by language issues. They worried about how working with manipulatives can sometimes be just as "rote" and abstract as working with symbols. They continue to struggle with these and other concerns, and the struggle is truly theirs.

As Friedman pointed out, she had to learn to trust the process. As a facilitator, I also had to learn to depend on case discussion participants to modify their own opinions and ideas as their pedagogical content knowledge grew. However, it was not a laissez-faire approach. I learned ways to evoke deeper analysis of student thinking, to elicit alternative points of view by playing devil's advocate, and to press for justifications and consequences of various ideas. I learned to pull ideas from the group and ways to reflect them back for further analysis. I continue to grapple with the balance between taking an active role in the discussion process, sharing authority with the group, and maintaining my neutrality toward the ideas brought up.

Why is neutrality important? As alluded to earlier, a neutral facilitator is less likely to be seen as the authority figure in the group and is, thus, not as likely to be viewed as a "dispenser" of knowledge. Also, if the facilitator or the cases themselves endorse a particular point of view, interpretation, or theory about teaching and learning, participants are less likely to bring out alternatives for critical analysis. "Teachers who agree with the theory will feel validated, and teachers who disagree may either reject the ideas quietly or may openly resist the ideas" (Barnett & Ramirez, 1996). Because a variety of ideas and views are open to critical discussion, teachers can make better decisions about what they will embrace, based on their knowledge, expertise, and confidence. What is more, they will have a solid rationale for their instructional decisions and a deeper understanding of the benefits of and drawbacks to the choices they make.

The format we now use to conduct a case discussion has evolved with the input of teachers involved in the discussions. A short description and rationale for each phase of a case discussion follows.

Case Discussion Format

Inclusion Activity. Building trust within the group is critical to its success. A short activity (5 to 10 minutes) helps put everyone at ease and helps teachers get to know one another on a more personal level. The inclusion activity may be omitted as the group matures. This activity is usually a question that draws out participants' personalities and humor. For example, we might ask participants to describe what they do that not very many people know about, or to tell an interesting story about their names or nicknames.

Problem. Before the discussion starts, participants are asked to work individually on a mathematical problem for about five minutes. This problem is either drawn directly from the case or is related to the mathematics of the case in some way. Participants are asked to pay attention to their thinking process as they solve the problem. Solving the problem becomes part of the discussion process and quickly transports participants into students' thinking.

Facts. Participants read the case before coming to the discussion. After working on the problem, they are asked to quickly reread the case and highlight important facts. This process helps "level the playing field" by giving teachers an opportunity to note important factual information that they might have missed when they read the case. A fact may be as mundane as the "The students are in the fourth grade," or "Joann used subtraction to solve the problem." Teachers call out the facts quickly while the facilitator or cofacilitator jots them on chart paper. The facts are a reasonably nonthreatening way to get teachers talking and relaxed.

Issues. Participants are then asked to work in pairs to identify issues from the case in question form. An example of an issue might be, "Would it have been less confusing for the students to use another model instead of the array?" After about 10 minutes, the facilitator records a question from each pair of teachers on chart paper and then makes the rounds again until all of the issues are posted.

At first, teachers find it hard to generate the issues, partly because they have difficulty framing issues as questions and partly because they may not notice very many issues in the case. With experience, they become more skilled and less intimidated by this task. Cases that have relatively obscure issues are reserved until teachers have had considerable experience.

Our early case prototypes had questions inserted at the end of each case to orient the discussion. At one point during the field-test phase, I decided to remove the questions and ask participants to write their own issues. They wrote statements. These statements, often slanted toward a particular viewpoint, seemed to stifle the discussion rather than open it. I then asked participants to frame the issues in question form. For example, an issue in the form of a question might be, "Should the students use a pizza instead of beans for the model?" This was a much more successful approach.

Although writing down the issues is a time-consuming process (20 to 30 minutes), it appears to be a critical part of understanding the case in a deep way. As the immediate issues are posted, they stimulate thinking about other issues and draw teachers into the case. Teachers strongly value the process of generating the issues themselves and report that uncovering the issues is an important aspect of their learning. In fact, I hypothesize that recognizing the issues in the case discussions helps teachers see the same issues in other cases as well as in their own teaching.

Discussion.   After all of the issues are posted in the front of the room, they are read aloud by the facilitator or silently by the participants. Then the facilitator asks which issue they would like to use to begin the discussion. Anyone in the group can make a suggestion, and the discussion begins. Discussion of that issue leads to discussion of another, and that discussion in turn relates to another issue. The ideas form a web that is not linear or hierarchical. The facilitator and members of the group are all responsible for returning to issues that have not been discussed. Because many of the issues overlap, no attempt is made to order or group them. In fact, grouping the ideas can devalue their specific meaning.

During the discussion, the facilitator writes phrases and draws on the chart as a way of recording the discussion. Participants are also asked to illustrate their thinking by drawing or writing their ideas on the chart or by demonstrating their thinking with materials such as play money, base-10 blocks, or pattern blocks. These techniques are used to slow the discussion and to make it more concrete and specific with regard to student thinking.

Closing Inclusion Experience.   We have learned to view each case as part of an ongoing conversation in which ideas are always open for further revision and refinement. We also realize that teaching decisions are always a matter of trade-offs and that our goal in case discussions is to help teachers become increasingly informed and strategic decision makers. This may explain why it is so difficult to find ways to close a discussion. We have tried writing in journals, writing according to a prompt, and asking each person to state an issue or question that still remains for them, as well as several other approaches. Everything seems to have its drawbacks. Many teachers are too exhausted after a long day in the classroom to write. Others report that their ideas are so unsettled that they feel uncomfortable writing about them. When we try verbal closures, the discussion usually restarts and continues into the parking lot. Teachers in most groups prefer just to end the discussion without any formal closure or with a brief inclusion experience that signals the end of the discussion.

Process Check.   We have learned the value of having the group reflect on the process by using a guide that asks them to rate and give comments on different aspects of the discussion. The facilitator collects the written reflections and reports back to the group. If problems are reported, such as someone dominating the discussion or feeling attacked, the group discusses how that problem should be addressed.

Friedman noted how this process check puts responsibility for a quality discussion back onto the group instead of onto the facilitator.

Going through all seven components of the format takes about 2 hours for one case, and the ideal number of participants is probably between 7 and 15. Teachers find that holding case discussions monthly over the period of at least one school year is crucial, and most have preferred to be involved for several years. The discussions need to be ongoing for several reasons. First, participants require a few sessions merely to familiarize themselves with the format and to become accustomed to their role in the process. It takes considerable time for teachers to make sense of a staff development approach that has no "expert" in charge and that places the responsibility on them for generating high-level critical thinking and novel ideas. Also, teachers need to spend time with their students between discussions to notice case discussion issues that are mirrored in their classrooms and to experiment with ideas and questions that have been evoked by the discussions. Finally, teachers need to participate in enough discussions to be able to see the crisscrossing of issues among cases. Although learning can occur from one case, the learning is compounded many times over when several cases are discussed.

The development of teachers who continue their involvement in the *Mathematics Case Methods Project* is impressive. Teachers with all levels of mathematics backgrounds, confidence, and experience have valued this approach. The purpose of this chapter is not to tout case discussions as *the* way to support professional growth, but to articulate why we believe it has been successful. We hope that other groups might take these findings into consideration when designing programs for professional growth.

FRIEDMAN: EPILOGUE

It is late spring, and I am teaching fractions again. I have decided to use the fraction replacement unit that focuses on the geometric model, but to vary the configuration of the model so that it does not always resemble the geoboard and so that the dot array is not always symmetrical. Each day I refer to the "fraction definition" from the unit shown to me by my colleague, but I warn the students that when we become more familiar with fractions, I will alter the definition slightly. My case discussion facilitation experience has inspired me to try involving the students more in guiding their own learning. At the end of fraction lessons, I ask the students what they think of the questions and activities we have done. In an effort to convey that we are partners in learning, I try to respond to their comments by sharing the "teacher thinking" behind the tasks. I am hoping that this will cause the students to take more responsibility for what they do during the lessons and to view me more as a facilitator than as a person supremely in charge. In turn, learning should become more self-directed and meaningful for them.

My current approach to teaching fractions will not, I am certain, be the ultimate solution. I am simply trying to avoid rough spots I have previously encountered by making some adjustments. On further reflection, I will likely make additional revisions. I do not expect to discover a fool-proof method.

The culture of case discussions invites close scrutiny of ideas and practice, even of those held most sacred by the teaching profession. Now that I have internalized this culture, I am aware that implementing any instructional decision has benefits, drawbacks, and trade-offs.

REFERENCES

Barnett, C. (1991). Building a case-based curriculum to enhance the pedagogical content knowledge of mathematics teachers. *Journal of Teacher Education, 42*, 263–272.

Barnett, C., Goldenstein, D., & Jackson, B. (Eds.). (1994a). *Mathematics teaching cases; Fractions, decimals, ratios, & percents: Hard to teach and hard to learn?* Portsmouth, NH: Heinemann.

Barnett, C., Goldenstein, D., & Jackson, B. (Eds.). (1994b). *Mathematics teaching cases; Fractions, decimals, ratios, & percents: Hard to teach and hard to learn? Facilitator's discussion guide.* Portsmouth, NH: Heinemann.

Barnett, C., & Ramirez, A. (1996). Fostering critical analysis and reflection through mathematics case discussions. In J. Colbert, P. Desberg, & K. Trimble (Eds.), *The case for education: Contemporary approaches for using case methods* (pp. 1–13). Needham Heights, MA: Allyn & Bacon.

Barnett, C., & Tyson, P. (1993a, April). *Case methods and teacher change: Shifting authority to build autonomy.* Paper presented at the annual meeting of the American Educational Research Association, Atlanta, GA.

Barnett, C., & Tyson, P. (1993b, April). *Mathematics teaching cases as a catalyst for informed strategic inquiry.* Paper presented at the annual meeting of the American Educational Research Association, Atlanta, GA.

Barnett, C., & Tyson, P. (1994, April). *Facilitating mathematics case discussions while preserving shared authority.* Paper presented at the annual meeting of the American Educational Research Association, New Orleans, LA.

Carpenter, T. P., & Fennema, E. (1992). Cognitively Guided Instruction: Building on the knowledge of students and teachers. In W. Secada (Ed.), *Curriculum reform: The case of mathematics in the United States.* Special Issue of *International Journal of Educational Research* (pp. 457–470). Elmsford, NY: Pergamon.

Clarke, D., & Peter, A. (1993). *Modelling teacher professional growth* (Occasional Paper 2). Victoria, Australia: Australian Catholic University, Mathematics Teaching and Learning Centre.

Cobb, P., Yackel, E., & Wood, T. (1991). Curriculum and teacher development: Psychological and anthropological perspectives. In E. Fennema, T. Carpenter, & S. J. Lamon (Eds.), *Integrating research on teaching and learning mathematics.* Albany: State University of New York Press.

Colbert, J., Desberg, P., & Trimble, K. (Eds.). (1996). *The case for education: Contemporary approaches for using case methods.* Needham Heights, MA: Allyn & Bacon.

Gordon, A., & Heller, J. (1995, April). *Traversing the web: Pedagogical reasoning among new and continuing case methods participants.* Paper presented at the annual meeting of the American Educational Research Association, San Francisco, CA.

Gordon, A., & Tyson, P. (1995, April). *Assessing the impact of Math Case Methods on teacher practices.* Paper presented at the annual meeting of the American Educational Research Association, San Francisco, CA.

Heller, J. (1995, April). *Entering a hall of mirrors: On building tools to assess the impact of case-based methods of teacher development.* Paper presented at the annual meeting of the American Educational Research Association, San Francisco, CA.

Merseth, K. (1991). *The case for cases in teacher education.* Washington, DC: American Association of Higher Education and the American Association of Colleges for Teacher Education.

Merseth, K. (1995). Cases and case methods in teacher education. In J. Sikula (Ed.), *Handbook of research on teacher education.* New York: MacMillan.

Richardson, V. (1990). Significant and worthwhile change in teaching practice. *Educational Researcher, 19,* 10–18.

Richert, A. E. (1991). Case methods and teacher education: Using cases to teach teacher reflection. In B. R. Tabachnich & K. Zeichner (Eds.), *Issues and practices in inquiry-oriented teacher education.* New York: Falmer.

Schifter, D. (1993, April). *Voicing the new pedagogy: Teachers write about learning and teaching mathematics.* Paper presented at the 71st annual meeting of the National Council of Teachers of Mathematics, Seattle, WA.

Schön, D. A. (1983). *The reflective practitioner.* New York: Basic Books.

Scott-Nelson, B. (1993, April). *Implications of current research on teacher change in mathematics for the professional development of mathematics teachers.* Paper presented at the annual meeting of the National Council of Teachers of Mathematics, Seattle, WA.

Shulman, J. (1992). *Case methods in teacher education.* New York: Teachers College Press.

Shulman, L. (1986). Those who understand: Knowledge growth in teaching. *Educational Researcher, 15*(2), 4–14.

Spiro, R. J. (1993, April). *Theoretical issues in situation-sensitive construction of understanding.* Paper presented at the annual meeting of the American Educational Research Association, Atlanta, GA.

Spiro, R. J., Coulson, R. L., Feltovich, P. J., & Anderson, D. K. (1988). Cognitive flexibility theory: Advanced knowledge acquisition in ill-structured domains. In *Tenth annual conference of the Cognitive Science Society* (pp. 375–383). Hillsdale, NJ: Lawrence Erlbaum Associates.

Spiro, R. J., Feltovich, P. J., Coulson, R. L., & Anderson, D. K. (1989). Multiple analogies for complex concepts: Antidotes for analogy-induced misconception in advanced knowledge acquisition. In S. Vosniadou & A. Ortony (Eds.), *Similarity and analogical reasoning* (pp. 489–531). New York: Cambridge University Press.

Spiro, R. J., Vispoel, W., Schmitz, J., Samarapungavan, A., & Boerger, A. (1987). Knowledge acquisition for application: Cognitive flexibility and transfer in complex content domains. In B. C. Britton (Ed.), *Executive control processes* (pp. 177–199). Hillsdale, NJ: Lawrence Erlbaum Associates.

Sykes, G., & Bird, T. (1992). Teacher education and the case idea. In G. Grant (Ed.), *Review of research in education* (Vol. 18, pp. 457–521). Washington, DC: American Educational Research Association.

Tyson, P., Barnett, C., & Gordon, A. (1995, April). *From teacher to students and back again: Evaluating math case teacher professional development based on student thinking and interactions.* Paper presented at the annual meeting of the American Educational Research Association, San Francisco, CA.

Wasserman, S. (1993). *Growing teachers: Learning about teaching from studying cases.* New York: Teachers College Press.

V

SUMMARY AND SYNTHESIS

Learning About Teacher Change in the Context of Mathematics Education Reform: Where Are We Going?

Barbara Scott Nelson
Education Development Center, Inc.

WHAT ARE WE LEARNING
ABOUT TEACHER CHANGE?

The chapters in this book, undertaken from a number of different theoretical positions and using a variety of methodological tools, have provided a rich set of insights that help us understand the process of change for teachers. Sketched here are several issues with which teachers grapple in the process of change that emerged quite regularly in the research studies and reports of intervention projects described in those chapters. What follows is by no means exhaustive, but is meant to be suggestive of issues that are reported with frequency.

Several background comments are in order as we contemplate these issues. First, it is not clear that we *know* that these "working ideas" (Ball, 1996) are essential elements of teacher change toward instruction based on new ideas about learning and mathematics. Issues discussed here have emerged from many kinds of evidence, and some have been more thoroughly investigated than others. The degree of support these working ideas have from research projects, such as those described in this volume, lend them credence, although it would be well to maintain a stance of inquiry toward them, continuing the search for the conditions under which they seem to work, and those under which they do not.

Second, there are many overlaps among the issues raised here—these are not discrete items, but are interconnected aspects of the complex activity of teaching. For example, what a teacher hears when she or he listens to students' mathematical thinking is affected by the nature of his or her own mathematical knowledge, and, as the latter changes and deepens, so does the former. A stance of inquiry toward students' mathematical thinking may come to permeate one's orientation toward teaching and also make possible quite different kinds of relationships with colleagues, relationships based on joint inquiry into students' learning rather than on giving advice or sharing teaching techniques.

Finally, the order of the issues here does not imply the order in which they are encountered by teachers. In fact, it is likely that teachers encounter and re-encounter these issues, in slightly different forms, as they move through the landscape of change.

Attending to Students' Thought and Work

It has often been reported, in this volume (Barnett & Friedman, chap. 14; Campbell & White, chap. 12; Franke, Carpenter & Fennema, chap. 10; Goldsmith & Schifter, chap. 2) and elsewhere (Goldsmith & Sassi, 1996; Schifter & Fosnot, 1993; Wood, Cobb, & Yackel, 1991), that it is highly motivating for teachers to hear students explain their mathematical thinking, or to see the written work of students that includes explanations for the mathematical moves made. Because classrooms have often been oriented toward identifying the correct answer to a problem and not toward asking children to explain their reasons for the work that they have done, many teachers are not familiar with the complexity and subtlety of students mathematical thinking. When they see it for the first time—in videotapes of clinical interviews or of discourse-based classrooms, in student portfolios and journals—many teachers are astounded at both what students know and what they don't know. Many teachers say that they had not realized that children were able to use such complex mathematical ideas at very young ages, long before they had been explicitly taught. Others are surprised that the students in their classroom hold such a range of mathematical ideas. Teachers also notice, often with some chagrin, that students who may produce correct answers on mathematics homework and tests often cannot explain why the answer is correct—their conceptual understanding may be quite undeveloped. For many teachers, these glimpses of student mathematical thinking are the spur to investigate it further in their classrooms (Campbell & White, chap. 12, Franke et al., chap. 10, Goldsmith & Schifter, chap. 2, Lubinski & Jaberg, chap. 9, this volume).

Over time, as teachers' experience in listening to students' mathematical thinking increases and their own mathematical knowledge becomes deeper, teachers may find recognizable patterns and deeper mathematical significance in their students' mathematical thinking. Investigating how their students are thinking about the mathematics of the elementary curriculum eventually can become the core of their teaching and can drive instruction (Barnett & Friedman, chap. 14, this volume; Franke et al., chap. 10, this volume; Schifter, 1995).

Dissatisfaction and Uncertainty

Closely linked to new perceptions of students' mathematical thinking is teachers' growing sense that the way they have previously been teaching does not meet their goals (Franke et al., chap. 10, Goldsmith & Schifter, chap. 2, Stocks & Schofield, chap. 11, this volume). They begin to see that, although they may have had mathematical understanding as a goal for their students, they had not appreciated that simply being able to produce the correct answers to given mathematical problems did not ensure mathematical understanding. They also begin to see that students can do advanced mathematics much earlier than they had previously thought possible.

As a new practice emerges, teachers gradually come to view their new teaching as better and more satisfying, and they feel that it produces better outcomes. However, they also begin to realize that they will never "arrive" at a new, finished state. Rather, the quest to understand children's mathematical thinking leaves them forever in an exploratory or experimental stance toward their own teaching. There is always the question: What can I do that will help this child's thinking move forward?

Relearning Mathematics

As Goldsmith and Schifter, Cooney and Shealy, Campbell and White, and Stocks and Schofield suggest in this volume, and as a number of other researchers have reported (Ball, 1991; McDiarmid & Wilson, 1991; Russell et al., 1995; Schifter, 1993), many teachers function in their classrooms with a largely algorithmic view of mathematics, rather than a conceptual view of mathematics that is flexible and fluid. Such mathematics knowledge is not sufficiently deep or flexible to support mathematics instruction that is intended to help students construct a deep understanding of their own. Therefore, a key element in many intervention programs is providing teachers with the opportunity to reconstruct, for themselves, the conceptual mathematics that underlies the elementary mathematics curriculum.

Further, when teachers see that mathematics is *built* by people doing mathematics, feel what it is like to persevere in puzzling out a hard problem, and have the satisfaction of being really solid in their understanding, they often want these experiences for their students. (Cooney & Shealy [chap. 4, this volume] caution that this might not be possible for all teachers, depending on their stance toward authority.) In addition to motivating their own efforts to change their instructional practice, the deepening of teachers' understanding of mathematics and their coming to new appreciations of the nature of mathematical knowledge also make new instructional options available to them (Barnett & Friedman, chap. 14, this volume; Schifter, 1995; Schifter & Bastable, 1996). Some teachers go on to become mathematics learners in their classrooms during the ensuing years (Russell et al, 1995).

Iterative Change in Belief and Practice

It has been clear for a number of years that, for many teachers, the project of transforming their teaching entails changes in their beliefs about the nature of knowledge and learning itself, changes in their knowledge of mathematics and of the process by which children's mathematical knowledge develops, and changes in their own instructional practice. As noted by Franke, Fennema, and Carpenter in this volume (chap. 10), a body of research suggests that such changes in beliefs, knowledge and practice do not occur in isolation, but the relationship among these changes is not yet clear. Some researchers imply that change in belief precedes change in practice (Cooney & Shealy, chap. 4, this volume; Shulman, 1986; Thompson, 1992), some, the reverse (Guskey, 1986). Others (Goldsmith & Schifter, chap. 2, this volume) hold that changes in belief, knowledge, and practice are iterative: new beliefs about the nature of learning, the nature of mathematics, or the ways children develop mathematical thinking provide teachers lenses through which to see new significance in the thinking and discourse of children in their classrooms. With new insight, teachers explore new instructional techniques, and often encounter surprises that further challenge their beliefs about students' knowledge and skills.

Romberg (chap. 13, this volume) shows how using a new curriculum in the classroom can create disjunctions between the teacher's former knowledge and practice that need resolution. Franke and her colleagues (chap. 10, this volume) found that to some degree the question of which comes first, change in belief or change in practice, is a matter of personal style. Some teachers needed to prove new ideas to themselves in their classrooms; others were convinced by readings, videos, and discussions. Still others seemed to work through issues of practice and belief simultaneously. Reinforcing Franke and her colleagues' observation about differences in personal style among teachers, Cooney and Shealy (chap. 4, this volume) argue that the changes in the beliefs in question require teachers to move toward a position in which authority is not externally fixed but is centered in themselves and rests on evidence and argument. They argue that some teachers, by virtue of their own beliefs about the nature of authority, may make the journey toward reformed teaching only with great difficulty and, it is implied, with help in restructuring the nature of those beliefs.

However, Franke and her colleagues note that only at early stages would change in practice occur before change in belief—at that point it was possible for teachers to enact new behaviors without changing their beliefs. At later stages, when instructional practices cannot be prescribed or explicitly modeled, change in beliefs was an integral part of the process. Goldsmith and Schifter (chap. 2, this volume) argue that it is the dynamic between changing practice and changing belief that results in substantial reorganizations of teaching: "Without changes in instructional strategies, decisions, and techniques, teachers will be unable to 'walk the walk and talk the talk.' And teachers' new ideas, beliefs, and understandings are, themselves, developed further as teachers try to enact them in their classrooms, reflecting on the pedagogical and content issues that they raise." (p. 27)

However, the process of working out new beliefs and practices in the real world of teaching can be confusing, and often teachers can envision more for their classrooms than they can actually create. One teacher in the midst of change described herself as " in progress":

> While reading [this portfolio] please keep in mind that I am 'a teacher (not a work) in progress.' This portfolio has forced—yes forced—me to reflect upon the inklings and nagging thoughts that have begun to assault me since the start of this journey. I am confident that one day I will reflect upon this early time and see its stage as necessary for change. Right now I feel piecemeal. I think, I experiment, and I read patiently. I feel hodge-podge. . . . I hope to pull myself together and translate this mayhem into teaching that most prepares and excites my students to the world of mathematics—a world which since high school, has excited and challenged me. (Hammerman, 1995, p.53)

Teaching as Inquiry

Teaching that facilitates students' construction of mathematical knowledge is largely a process of inquiry—of exploring the nature of children's mathematical understanding (Duckworth, 1991; Richards, 1991; Schifter & Fosnot, 1993). Teachers attend carefully to students' oral and written expressions of mathematical ideas; use these to develop conjectures about students' understanding; offer questions, counterexamples, or activities meant to check the depth, breadth, or robustness of students' ideas; and help students clarify and extend their understanding. Franke and her colleagues (chap. 10, this volume) report that it is as teachers develop the practice of practical inquiry focused on understanding children's mathematical thinking that they move to a self-sustaining level of change in their beliefs about learning and teaching, and in their practice. When they observe inconsistencies in children's mathematical thinking or hear a child say something they do not understand, these teachers view this as an opportunity for reflection and the generation of new options for instruction. Barnett and Friedman report the power of cases to prompt inquiry among teachers about mathematics and children's thinking, and the lack of resolution at the end of the case discussion to motivate teachers' inquiry into children's mathematical thinking when in their classrooms. Adopting a stance of inquiry toward the development of children's mathematical thinking and the dilemmas of teaching appears to be what propels teachers into an ongoing process of reflection and learning in their practice. Such inquiry is, for teachers, a pathway with no end—and a continual source of professional growth (Schifter, 1996c).

Participation in a Supportive Community

There are indications from many studies of teacher change and reports from intervention projects, some in this volume, that being part of a *community* of teachers who are exploring new modes of teaching mathematics is an important element of teacher change. The support community may be the group of teachers in an intervention project (Stocks & Schofield, chap. 11, this volume), the group of teachers who comprise the mathematics faculty of the school (Secada & Adajian, chap. 8, Stein & Brown, chap. 7, this volume), or an entire elementary school, including teachers and principal (Campbell & White, chap. 12, Lubinski & Jaberg, chap. 9, this volume).

There is, of course, simple comfort and support in talking with sympathetic colleagues while struggling with new mathematical ideas, or trying to figure out what a student means when he or she says something puzzling, or worrying about whether the questions being asked really give students the opportunity to think harder about a mathematical idea. But working with a group of teachers also provides a wider range of ideas for consideration than is available to individual, isolated teachers. In their work together, teachers craft new community norms for discourse about teaching and build a collegial professional culture whose very existence provides support for the work of re-forming one's teaching. Including the principal in the group provides teachers with organizational support for professional risk-taking and instructional change.

As part of the reconceptualization of teaching itself, some scholars argue that taking part in a strong professional community (Secada & Adajian, chap. 8, this volume), teacher communities of inquiry (Hammerman, 1995), and professional relationships characterized by critical colleagueship (Lord, 1994) is essential to teaching, reconceived. In this view, part of the work of teaching is to continually question, critique, and explore ways to interpret the meaning of what happens in the classroom and to develop the next instructional step. This is best done with colleagues who share the enterprise. Such communities of inquiry and critical colleagueship become places where teachers can voice their doubts and uncertainties, can work through dilemmas of practice, and can contribute to the broader discourse about the nature of teaching.

Stein and Brown, who take a sociocultural view of teachers' learning, would go still further and argue that the community of practice in which teachers are engaged is primary in an analysis of teacher change—that as teachers become more central members of communities in which transformed teaching and the collegial, critical analysis of practice are the norms, they increasingly engage in the transformed practices of teaching themselves. Jones proposes that the several contexts of teaching, be they classroom norms, district, state, and federal policies, an adopted curriculum, or the norms of the mathematics community itself, are interactively constructed and, thereby, reinterpreted by teachers and others in the course of their work.

Issues of Gender, Racial, and Ethnic Sensitivity

Examining the process of teacher change in the context of mathematics education reform intersects with a host of other social issues—increasing the comfort of girls in mathematics classrooms, increasing the comfort of female teachers in mathematics classrooms, helping teachers re-form their instruction so that it provides congenial opportunities for students from a number of racial and ethnic groups, and making such mathematics instruction available for students with a variety of learning styles and capacities. Campbell (chap. 5, this volume) traces gains made to include girls in mathematics, but points out that the work still to be done will require much deeper change on the part of many teachers. Elsewhere, Ball (1995) noted the effect on two women teachers (one African American, one Caucasian) of their own childhood experiences in mathematics classrooms. Damarin (1995) suggested that the primary question is, "How do women experience mathematics?" and argued that the academic disciplines, including mathematics at school and university levels, have not sufficiently acknowledged and valued women's thinking, but have tacitly (and sometimes not-so-tacitly) sent women messages that mathematics was not for them. Women, including women teachers, she argued, might be more confident knowers of mathematics if the social messages were not negative, if there were more opportunity for them to build an intuitive grasp of mathematical ideas, and if the value of their knowledge were continually supported, not undermined.

The issues involved in changing one's teaching so that it *essentially*, not tangentially, provides mathematics instruction that functions well for children of diverse cultures are described by Davidson and Kramer (in press), who argue that we need to change the lens we use to look at every aspect of our classrooms, changing what we take for granted, what we see as "normal." Ladson-Billings (1994) argued for culturally relevant teaching, in which the teacher validates and supports the cultures that students bring to the classroom. Silver, Smith, and Nelson (1995) analyzed the experiences of teachers in inner-city schools who changed their teaching and noted some special challenges that they faced—for example, negotiating mathematical discourse in bilingual (or multilingual) classrooms, finding instructional materials that demonstrated how mathematics has been developed and used in other cultures, and so on. Carey, Fennema, Carpenter, and Franke (1995) reported on the implementation of the Cognitively Guided Instruction project in an urban environment. It was demonstrated that teaching based on knowledge of how understanding of basic arithmetic ideas develops in children in general, and close observation of the mathematical understanding of the children in a teacher's own classroom, is effective in urban classrooms. In this volume, Campbell and White, Secada and Adajian, and Stein and Brown report that in providing professional development in urban and predominantly African American schools, where teacher isolation is typical, the development of a strong, sustaining, professional community among teachers is essential.

The most striking observation in this regard is both the scarcity of a literature that examines how teachers' transformation of their teaching in response to new ideas about learning and mathematics links to developing a teaching practice that provides well for sensitive classrooms that respond to many diverse students, and the separateness of "mainstream" studies of teacher change from the existing research on diversity.

WHERE DO WE GO NEXT?

Since 1989, we have come a long way in our efforts to understand teacher change in the context of mathematics education reform. Theoretical tools from a number of related fields have been brought to bear on the problem, new conceptualizations of teaching have been built, and a substantial number of intervention and research projects have provided a range of new experiences for teachers, and rich learning opportunities for researchers. The working ideas about teacher change discussed in the previous section can give shape and guidance to the provision of teacher education at preservice and in-service levels. These working ideas make it clear that the contours of programs to support teacher change are dramatically different from programs of an earlier era and are informed by some of the same views about learning that inform how we design instruction for children in classrooms.

However, there is still a long way to go. We have not yet achieved a coherent theory of teacher change, though there are promising movements in this direction. And there are a large number of practical issues yet to be addressed.

In the introductory chapter to this book, I called attention to a number of theoretical frameworks that recently have been brought to bear on the task of understanding the process of teacher change. The several psychological positions represented in this book (cognitive science, developmental psychology, ego psychology) may be consistent, one with another, because they focus on subtly different aspects of psychological process. The Cognitively Guided Instruction project, with its cognitive science underpinnings (Franke et al., chap. 10, this volume), and those programs influenced by it (Campbell & White, chap. 12, Lubinski & Jaberg, chap. 9) emphasize the *content* of teachers' knowledge about children's mathematical knowledge, its structure, and the way teachers connect that knowledge to what they see in their classrooms. The Piagetian roots of papers by Goldsmith and Schifter, and by Simon call our attention to the nature and order of the shifts between different structurings of teachers' knowledge and the *mechanisms* by which teachers' concepts about mathematics, learning, and teaching become transformed. The work of Cooney and Shealy, with its roots in ego psychology, focuses on the teacher's sense of the locus of authority as an element of his or her sense of self, the way the *psychological structure* of beliefs, such as those about authority, inform teachers' views of mathematical knowledge and teaching.

However, the relations between these psychological theories of teacher change have not been clearly addressed by the scholars themselves, and there are enough differences in the basic intellectual positions from which they have been derived that compatibility cannot be assumed. For instance, the root metaphor underlying the cognitive science perspective is mechanical (Gardner, 1985), whereas the basic metaphor underlying the developmental perspective is organic (Duckworth, 1987). Such metaphors have subtle but far-reaching consequences within each perspective. For example, within the cognitive science perspective there is a tendency to look at misconceptions on the part of students as incorrect ideas that should be overcome, avoided, or eliminated (Hammer, 1995), whereas a developmentalist would tend to see incorrect ideas as temporarily limited perspectives to be grown through. Instructional moves informed by one perspective might look quite different from instructional moves informed by the other. A useful intellectual project for the future would be to work out the links and relationships between the ways of viewing teacher change drawn from these subtly different psychological perspectives.

In this volume we also see two different ways to approach the social aspect of classroom life and teacher change. In proposing the emergent view of social action in classrooms, which Simon (chap. 3, in this volume) adopts, Cobb, Wood, & Yackel (1990) brought symbolic interactionism, in which people interactively construct the meaning of social knowledge, into the field of mathematics education, and aligned it with psychological constructivism to provide the view that classroom norms emerge from joint construction by individuals: as students and teachers construct new mathematical ideas together, they are simultaneously constructing the norms and practices of the classroom as a mathematics-doing community. These emergent community norms and practices, in turn, both enable and constrain further construction. This view provides a theory of social and community phenomena consistent with psychological constructivism (Cobb & Yackel, in press). The position Jones (chap. 6, this volume) takes, that teachers interactively construct context, thereby interpreting it locally, is also consistent with psychological constructivism.

The sociocultural position, which Stein and Brown adopt, gives primacy to the social unit and locates learning in the enculturation of individuals into culturally organized groups, or "communities of practice" (Lave & Wenger, 1991; Newman, Griffin, & Cole, 1989; Rogoff, 1990). Although there are variations in the sociocultural perspective with regard to the importance of a cognizing individual—for example, Lave and Wenger (1991) took the position that learning *is* participation in communities of practice, whereas Newman and his colleagues (1989) viewed learning as internalization by an individual *from* social interaction—from both perspectives the social and cultural world is primary and given, not interactively emergent as Cobb (1994) proposed.

Cobb (1994) took on the project of bridging this chasm, and he and Yackel (in press) further argue that the issue is not which of these accounts "gets things right," but in which situations one type of analysis or the other is more helpful. They note that psychological constructivism is useful for analyzing the qualitative differences in individual's mathematical thinking and the mechanisms of change from an individual perspective; the emergent perspective is useful for analyzing the development of jointly understood roles and norms of mathematical reasoning in the classroom, produced as individuals interactively construct their mathematics knowledge; and the sociocultural perspective is useful for understanding how established cultural meanings in the larger society become enacted in the classroom. Cobb and Yackel recommend that researchers work toward the elaboration of these complementarities by grounding the theoretical discussion in the particulars of their research. They illustrate how this might be done in a description of the evolution of their own work from psychological theory to symbolic interactionism and its encounter with large-scale social and cultural phenomena that might be well analyzed from a sociocultural perspective (Cobb & Yackel, in press).

Another way to explore what each of these theoretical perspectives on teacher change provides would be to focus on and coordinate psychological, interactively emergent, and sociocultural interpretations of teachers' change in the groups and communities in which they work through this change. This could be done by analyzing from emergent and sociocultural perspectives the professional development programs from which we already have psychological data about teacher change, or by studying both the psychological and sociological characteristics of teacher groups of various kinds—study groups or inquiry groups (Hammerman, 1995); action- or teacher- research groups (Cochran-Smith & Lytle, 1996; Watt & Watt, 1991); teacher networks (Lieberman, 1996), and academic departments (Grossman, 1996; McLaughlin & Talbert, 1993). By and large, we have either psychological studies of teachers in such situations, without complementary analyses of the group as an emergent community or a community of practice, or studies of the group without accompanying psychological analyses. A few paired studies might shed considerable light on the relationship between what we learn about teacher change from looking through psychological, emergent, and sociocultural lenses.

In addition to these theoretical tasks, there are a number of questions still to be addressed in coming to understand teacher change in the context of mathematics education reform. First, there are still a number of questions about teacher change on an individual level.

Although we are beginning to have a sense of the issues that most teachers need to grapple with, we are still unresolved about whether teachers pass developmentally through a series of qualitatively different stages as they do this. Are there, rather, a finite number of pathways that teachers traverse as they move from one issue to another and back to the first but this time from a slightly different perspective, as Goldsmith and Schifter suggest? If so, what might these pathways look like? Cooney and Shealy suggest that teachers' positions about the authority claims of knowledge predispose them to certain paths and that some issues will be predictably hard for them to deal with. Are there other characteristics of teachers' beliefs or states of knowledge early on in the process that would tend to lead them on one pathway through the terrain rather than another? Are there features of teachers' personalities—generosity of spirit, patience, courage, curiosity—that serve them well in transforming their teaching, and if so, how can we nurture the development of such features?

Further, we have a more fine-grained picture of what is involved for teachers in the first months and years of their journey into transformed practice than we do of later periods. We need descriptions and analyses of teacher practice and change over much longer periods of time—up to a decade and more. It has been proposed that transforming one's teaching so that it becomes fundamentally a process of inquiring into mathematics and into students' mathematical thinking is a process with no end (Franke, et al., chap. 10, this volume; Schifter, 1996c), in which teachers continue to grow and change as their ideas deepen and as the children in their classrooms bring up ideas the teachers themselves had not previously considered.

Franke and her colleagues proposed that inquiry focused directly on children's mathematical thinking is the most effective for initially promoting change in a teacher' s practice. Does this remain true over long portions of a teaching career? What other objects of inquiry might take center stage at different points along the way? Are teachers' threads of interest sustained over very long spans of time? What do the evolutions in their thought and practice around those threads look like over many years? Is such inquiry and learning continuous, or are there fallow periods in which no obvious learning or change is occurring?

We also need to know a great deal more about the interplay between teachers' views of the nature of mathematics, their actual knowledge of fundamental mathematical ideas, and their ability to apprehend and analyze the mathematical ideas that their students are struggling with. What is the relation between what teachers learn from deepening their own mathematics knowledge and what they learn from learning about the development of children' s mathematical knowledge? As teachers deepen their knowledge in one domain of mathematics, say, fractions, does that relate to knowledge in other mathematical domains that they may be teaching, such as geometry? Do they develop habits of mind, or a view of the fundamental nature of mathematical knowledge, from their work in one mathematical domain that carries over into new topics?

In addition to this set of questions about individual teachers' development, and others like them, there is still work to be done on reconceptualizing the nature of teaching itself. As teachers move through this landscape, taking on new roles and practices, they help us flesh out what teaching, reconceived, might be. And as teachers begin to share their experiences, they create images through which yet more teachers can grasp a sense of what teaching could be (Schifter, 1996 a, 1996 b). Davenport and Sassi (1995) suggested that for teachers at early stages in the change process, the availability of images of classroom discourse are highly valued. Goldsmith and Schifter (chap. 2, this volume) propose that such images might function as cultural mediators in the development of a new view of teaching. What are other such cultural mediators?

One of the features of reconceptualized teaching that is just beginning to receive attention is the view that teachers are not practicing their craft in isolation in their classrooms, but are functioning in professional communities of support and sympathetic critique within the school and extending beyond it. Several chapters in this volume report that teachers are beginning to learn how to help each other transform their practice. Barnett and Friedman show us teachers, like Friedman herself, who have become the facilitators of case discussions for other teachers; Stocks and Schofield portray Vickie, the teacher whose initial change in practice sparked the development of a multitiered program for other teachers. Stein and Brown and Secada and Adajian talk of whole faculties working together to achieve a transformed mathematics program, and Campbell and White describe the mathematics supervisor as an essential partner in the change process. Elsewhere, Hammerman (1995) analyzed the process by which teachers become members of Inquiry Groups, in which dilemmas of teaching practice are collaboratively examined, and Lord (1994) analyzed how " critical colleagueship" among teachers in a school and beyond can move the profession forward.

The development of professional peer relations is new for many teachers and, like so many elements of this reform movement, is at once exhilarating and risky for them. How do teachers learn to participate in such communities? How are new norms for discourse developed? What aspects of this new way of being with each other are hard? Easy? How can such groups both be authentic communities for and of teachers and yet retain links to others who can bring knowledge resources—about mathematics or children's mathematical thinking, for example—to the group so that it can continue to move forward?

If we are truly to provide a mathematics education for all students, we need to examine how teaching that is gender-sensitive and nurturing of a multitude of cultural backgrounds can be developed. What is it that teachers who teach such students easily and well do? What is it that teachers need to take into consideration as they transform their practice in multicultural environments? We have some beginning studies, but many more are needed.

Finally, how can we deal with the problem of scale in teacher change? Even if we had the time and the resources to reach all teachers, one at a time, the effort would be inadequate. It would not be enough to change every classroom in a school, in turn. What is at issue is a new intellectual culture for schools, a culture that legitimates and supports curiosity and challenge as the engines of learning. Not only will it be necessary for teachers to reinvent mathematics instruction from within a new conceptual frame, it also will be necessary for teachers and administrators together to reinvent school culture from within that new conceptual frame. It will also be necessary for parents and the larger public to develop an understanding of the reform movement' s hopes for their children so that they can knowledgeably provide support. Early work with administrators—elementary principals, district level mathematics coordinators, and associate superintendents of curriculum and instruction—indicates that they, too, bring with them well-formed ideas about the nature of mathematics, teaching, and learning, ideas that influence how they interpret the intent of the mathematics education reform movement and what actions they believe will be effective in forwarding it in their districts (Nelson, 1995). Work with administrators may need to provide opportunities for them, too, to confront the appropriateness of those ideas in an era of reform. Studies of parents' views of performance assessments, in contrast to their views about standardized tests (Shepard & Bliem, 1995), show that the majority of parents interviewed preferred that both standardized tests and performance assessments be used at the district level, but that performance assessments be used to guide classroom instruction. Performance assessments were approved of because they "made children think" (p. 28). When parents had the opportunity to examine performance assessment, they saw that the material was challenging and worth learning. Parents more generally may need opportunities to look at the specifics of childrens' mathematical work in reformed classrooms in order to develop a knowledgeable view of its value.

Research on teacher change in the context of mathematics education reform has been rich and productive in the past several years, and a strong program of work lies ahead. However, it may now be appropriate to consider embedding that work in larger cultural and contextual webs, such as gender and ethnic sensitivity, the development of new, school-wide intellectual cultures, and the links between teachers, schools, and parents.

ACKNOWLEDGMENTS

The preparation of this conclusion was supported in part by a grant from the DeWitt Wallace–Reader' s Digest Fund. I wish to thank Elizabeth Fennema, Lynn Goldsmith, David Hammer, and Deborah Schifter for their comments on earlier versions.

REFERENCES

Ball, D. L. (1991). Research on teaching mathematics: Making subject matter knowledge part of the equation. In J. Brophy. (Ed.). *Advances in research on teaching: A research annual.* (pp. 1–44).Greenwich, CT. JAI Press.
Ball, D. L. (1995). Connecting to mathematics as part of learning to teach. In Schifter, D. (Ed.). *What's happening in math class: Reconstructing professional identities* (Vol 2., pp.1–4). New York: Teachers College Press.
Ball, D. L. (1996). Teacher learning and the mathematics reforms: What we think we know and what we need to learn. *Phi Delta Kappan.* 77(7), 500–508.
Carey, D. A., Fennema, E., Carpenter, T. P., & Franke, M. L. (1995). Equity and mathematics education. In W. G. Secada, E. Fennema, & L. B. Adajian, (Eds.), *New directions for equity in mathematics education.* (pp. 93–125). Cambridge, England: Cambridge University Press.

Cobb, P. (1994). Where is the mind? Constructivist and sociociultural perspectives on mathematical development. *Educational Researcher, 23* (7), 13–20.

Cobb, P., & Yackel, E. (in press). Constructivist, emergent, and sociocultural perspectives in the context of developmental research. *Journal of Educational Psychology.*

Cobb, P., Wood, T., & Yackel, E. (1990). Classrooms as learning environments for teachers and researchers. In R. Davis, C. Maher, & N. Noddings, (Eds.), *Constructivist views on the teaching and learning of mathematics. Journal for Research in Mathematics Education, Monograph no 4,* pp. 125–146. Reston, VA: National Council for Teachers of Mathematics.

Cochran-Smith, M., & Lytle, S, L. (1996). Communities for teacher research: Fringe or forefront? In M. W. McLaughlin & I. Oberman (Eds.), *Teacher learning: New policies, new practices.* (pp. 92–112). New York: Teachers College Press.

Damarin, S. K. (1995). Gender and mathematics from a feminist standpoint. In W. G. Secada, E. Fennema, & L. B. Adajian (Eds.), *New directions for equity in mathematics education.* (pp. 242–257). Cambridge, England: Cambridge University Press.

Davenport, L. R., & Sassi, A. (1995). Transforming mathematics teaching in Grades K–8: How narrative straucrures in resource materials help support teacher change. In B. S. Nelson (Ed.), *Inquiry and the development of teaching: Issues in the transformation of mathematics teaching.* (pp. 37–46). Newton, MA: Center for the Development of Teaching, Education Development Center.

Davidson, E., & Kramer, L. (in press). Integrating with integrity: Curriculum, instruction and culture in the mathematics classroom. In J. Trentacosta (Ed.), *Multicultural and gender equity in the mathematics classroom: The gift of diversty. 1997 NCTM Yearbook.* Reston, VA: National Council of Teachers of Mathematics.

Duckworth, E. R. (1987). *"The having of wonderful ideas" and other essays on teaching and learning.* New York: Teachers College Press.

Duckworth, E. R. (1991, April). *Teaching and research in one: Extended clinical interviewing.* Addrress to the annual meeting of the American Educational Research Association, Chicago, Il.

Gardner, H. (1985). *The mind's new science.* New York: Basic Books.

Goldsmith, L. T., & Sassi, A. (1996, April). *Teachers in transition: Describing the terrain for developing mathematics teaching.* Paper presented at the annual meeting of the American Educational Research Association, New York, NY.

Grossman, P. (1996). Of regularities and reform: Navigating the subject-specific territory of high schools. In M. W. McLaughlin & I. Oberman (Eds.), *Teacher Learning: New policies, new practices.* (pp. 39–47). New York: Teachers College Press.

Guskey, T. R. (1986). Staff development and the process of teacher change. *Educational Researcher, 15,* (5), 5–12.

Hammer, D. (1995). *Misconceptions or P-prims: How might alternative perspectives of cognitive structure influence instructional perceptions and intentions?* Newton, MA: Center for the Development of Teaching, Education Development Center.

Hammerman, J. K. (1995). Teacher inquiry groups: Collaborative explorations of changing practice. In B. S. Nelson (Ed.), *Inquiry and the development of teaching: Issues in the transformation of mathematics teaching.* (pp. 47–55). Newton, MA: Center for the Development of Teaching, Education Development Center.

Ladson-Billings, G. (1994). *The dreamkeepers: Successful teachers of African-American children.* San Francisco: Jossey-Bass.

Lave, J. & Wenger, E. (1991). *Situated learning: Legitimate peripheral participation.* Cambridge, England: Cambridge University Press.

Lieberman, A. (1996). Networks for educational change: Powerful and problematic. In M. W. McLaughlin & I. Oberman (Eds.), *Teacher Learning: New policies, new practices.* (pp. 63–72). New York: Teachers College Press.

Lord, B. (1994). Teachers' professional development: Critical colleagueship and the role of professional communities. In N. Cobb (Ed.), *The future of education: Perspectives on national standards in America* (pp. 175–204). New York: College Entrance Examination Board.

McDiarmid, G.W., & Wilson, S. M. (1991). An exploration of the subject matter knowledge of alternate route teachers: Can we assume they know their subject? *Journal of Teacher Education, 42* (2), 93–103.

McLaughlin, M. W., & Talbert, J. E. (1993). *Contexts that matter for teaching and learning: Strategic opportunities for meeting the nation's educational goals.* Stanford: Center for Research on the Context of Secondary School Teaching.

Nelson, B. S. (1995). *Lenses on learning: How administrators' ideas about mathematics, learning and teaching influence their approaches to action in an era of reform.* Manuscript in preparation.

Newman, D., Griffin, P., & Cole, M. (1989). *The construction zone: Working for cognitive change in school.* Cambridge: Cambridge University Press.

Richards, J. (1991). Mathematical discussions. In E. von Glasersfeld (ed). *Radical constructivism in mathematics education.* (pp. 13–51). The Netherlands: Kluwer.

Rogoff, B. (1990). *Apprenticeship in thinking: Cognitive development in social context.* Oxford, England: Oxford University Press.

Russell, S.J., Schifter, D., Bastable, V., Yaffee, L., Lester, J.B., & Cohen, S. (1995). Learning mathematics while teaching. In B. S. Nelson (Ed.), *Inquiry and the development of teaching: Issues in the transformation of mathematics teaching.* (pp. 9–16). Newton, MA: Center for the Development of Teaching, Education Development Center.

Schifter, D. (1993). Mathematics process as mathematics content: A course for teachers. *Journal of Mathematical Behavior. 12,* 271–283.

Schifter, D. (1995). Teachers' changing conceptions of the nature of mathematics: Enactment in the classroom. In B. S. Nelson (Ed.), *Inquiry and the development of teaching: Issues in the transformation of mathematiacs teaching.* (pp. 17–25). Newton, MA: Center for the Development of Teaching, Education Development Center.

Schifter, D. & Bastable, V. (1996). *From the teachers' seminar to the classroom: The relationship between doing and teaching mathematics, an example from fractions.* Manuscript in preparation.

Schifter, D. (Ed.) (1996a). *What's happening in math class: Envisioning new practices through teacher narratives.* (Vol. 1.) New York: Teachers College Press.

Schifter, D. (Ed.) (1996b). *What's happening in math class: Reconstructing professional identities.* (Vol. 2.) New York: Teachers College Press.

Schifter, D. (1996c). A constructivist perspective on teaching and learning mathematics. *Phi Delta Kappan, 77* (7) 492–499.

Schifter, D., & Fosnot, C.T. (1993). *Reinventing mathematics education: Stories of teachers meeting the challenge of reform.* New York: Teachers College Press.

Shepard, L., & Bliem, C. L. (1995). Parents' thinking about standardized tests and performance assessments. *Educational Researcher, 24*(8), 25–32.

Shulman, L.S. (1986). Those who understand: Knowledge growth in teaching. *Educational Researcher, 57*(2), 4–14.

Silver, E., Smith, M., & Nelson, B. S. (1995). The QUASAR project: Equity concerns meet mathematics education reform in the middle school. In W. G. Secada, E. Fennema, & L. B. Adajian (Eds.), *New directions for equity in mathematics education.* (pp. 9–56). Cambridge, England: Cambridge University Press.

Thompson, A.G. (1992). Teachers' beliefs and conceptions: A synthesis of the research. In D. A. Grouws (Ed.), *Handbook of research on mathematics teaching and learning.* (pp 127–146). New York: Macmillan.

Watt, M. L., & Watt, D. L. (1991). *Teacher research, action research: The Logo action research collaborative.* Newton, MA: Center for Learning, Teaching & Technology, Education Development Center.

Wood,T., Cobb, P., & Yackel, E. (1991). Change in teaching mathematics: A case study. *American Educaional Research Journal, 28* (3) 587–616.

Author Index

Subject Index